INTEGRATED AND HOLISTIC PERSPECTIVES ON LEARNING, INSTRUCTION AND TECHNOLOGY

INTEGRATED AND HOLISTIC PERSPECTIVES ON LEARNING, INSTRUCTION AND TECHNOLOGY

Understanding Complexity

Edited by

J. Michael Spector

and

Theresa M. Anderson

Syracuse University, New York, U.S.A.

KLUWER ACADEMIC PUBLISHERS

DORDRECHT / BOSTON / LONDON

A C.I.P. Catalogue record for this book is available from the Library of Congress.

ISBN 0-7923-6705-7

Published by Kluwer Academic Publishers,
P.O. Box 17, 3300 AA Dordrecht, The Netherlands.

Sold and distributed in North, Central and South America
by Kluwer Academic Publishers,
101 Philip Drive, Norwell, MA 02061, U.S.A.

In all other countries, sold and distributed
by Kluwer Academic Publishers,
P.O. Box 322, 3300 AH Dordrecht, The Netherlands.

Printed on acid-free paper

Printed in the Netherlands.

DEDICATION

With regard to holism, I dedicate this work to Ebru, named for an ancient Turkish art involving abstract colored patterns that initially appear random but evoke meaningful images. With regard to integration, I dedicate this work to the loving memory of my parents who taught me respect and tolerance. With regard to learning and instruction, I dedicate this work to my children, who have taught me that I know less than I am inclined to believe. And, with regard to technology, I dedicate this work to Walt Davis who said that when stuck trying to resolve a complex software problem one should make a single random change and observe what happens.

J. Michael Spector

I dedicate this work to my husband and son whose support and sense of humor help me to achieve my goals

Theresa M. Anderson

TABLE OF CONTENTS

Preface ix

Introduction xi

About the Authors xxiii

PART I: INSTRUCTIONAL FOUNDATIONS FOR LIFE-LONG LEARNING AND UNDERSTANDING COMPLEX DOMAINS

1. **Environments for Lifelong Learning: Ergonomics, Architecture and Educational Design** 1
   Peter Goodyear

2. **Knowledge Management for School-Based Educators** 19
   James M. Marshall and Allison Rossett

3. **Reflections on Developing a Web-based *Teaching with Technology* Course** 35
   Wilhelmina C. Savenye

4. **Static and Dynamic Environments: The Ambiguity of the Problem** 61
   Catherine B. Dunnagan and Dean L. Christensen

5. **Building Theory into Practice in Learning and Instruction** 79
   J. Michael Spector

6. **Leveraging Technology in the Service of Life-Long Learning** 91
   Ellen D. Wagner

PART 2: INTEGRATING TECHNOLOGY AND KNOWLEDGE CONSTRUCTION IN RICH LEARNING ENVIRONMENTS

7. **Integrating Constructivism and Learning Technologies**   103
    David H. Jonassen, Julian Hernandez-Serrano and Ikseon Choi

8. **Mental Models & Instructional Planning**   129
    Norbert M. Seel, Sabine Al-Diban and Patrick Blumschein

9. **Reality, Models and Complex Teaching-Learning Environments** 159
    Frank Achtenhagen

10. **Building versus Using Simulations**   175
    Stephen Alessi

11. **Research Based Principles for Multimedia Presentation**   197
    Ok-choon Park and Michael P. Etgen

12. **Epistemology, Psychology of Learning and Instructional Design** 213
    Sanne Dijkstra

    Conclusion   233
    Theresa M. Anderson

    Bibliography   243

    Index   263

PREFACE

This volume is the result of two seminars held in 1999. The first was held in the Netherlands in March on the topic of epistemology, psychology and instruction. This conference was organized by Professor Sanne Dijkstra and co-sponsored by the University of Twente and the European Association for Research Learning and Instruction (EARLI) Instructional Design Special Interest Group. This meeting involved several invited speakers and discussants (Frank Achtenhagen, Sanne Dijkstra, Ton de Jong, David Merrill, Joseph Scandura, Norbert Seel, Michael Spector, and Jeroen van Merriënboer) and invited participants. The presentations at this meeting addressed a number of themes that fit together surprisingly well. The discussions that were generated led the group to the conclusion that a follow-on meeting was desirable. Sanne Dijkstra suggested that the University of Bergen might consider hosting such a meeting. Professor Spector agreed to accept responsibility for a follow-on meeting in Bergen in October. The sponsors of the second meeting were the University of Bergen's Educational Information Science & Technology Research Program (EIST) and the International Consortium for Courseware Engineering (ICCE).

The theme for the second meeting was based on themes that emerged in the first, including interests in: (1) more complex learning goals; (2) using technology (e.g., interactive and dynamic models and simulations) to develop systemic understanding in complex situations; (3) addressing issues pertaining to the integration of technology into learning and working cultures; and, (4) connecting relevant theories and philosophical perspectives with learning and instructional developments. This collection of themes provided the name for the second meeting and for this volume: "Integrated and Holistic Perspectives on Learning, Instruction and Technology: Improving Understanding in Complex Domains." The second meeting was fashioned after the first with both European and North American researchers invited to present, although twice as many were invited and the conference was twice as long. To preserve continuity of the discussion, some of the same speakers were invited, but new speakers were also invited to contribute. The papers collected in this volume represent revisions and extensions to the work presented at the Bergen conference in October 1999.

The original plan for the book was to have two parts, each representing a day of conference papers. The conference called for presentations aimed at solutions that reflected holistic perspectives and effective integration of learning and technology in complex domains on the first day, and presentations aimed at more global considerations (life-long learning environments, integrating theory and practice, knowledge management and performance technologies, etc.) on the second day. As it happened, many presentations crossed these artificial boundaries. As the papers evolved, it became apparent that the original plan required some modification. As a consequence, we have restructured the papers into slightly different sets and present those more concerned with issues pertaining to life-long learning and the integration of theory and practice in Part One. Part Two is more concerned with the integration of technology into learning and instructional solutions, with Dijkstra's chapter serving as a capstone and a loop back to the theoretical and philosophical perspectives that motivated the conference.

We have occasionally inserted editorial notes to help readers make connections to related ideas found elsewhere. We have used square brackets to indicate such notes. [This note is not found elsewhere in this volume.] The contributors reviewed edited versions and are responsible for their individual chapters. We may have allowed some minor typographical errors to slip in and accept responsibility for those. We owe individual authors many thanks for their patience and diligence in making this volume a reality. We also thank Kluwer's external reviewers for their many helpful recommendations.

By way of special acknowledgement, it should be noted that the Structural Learning, Instructional Systems, and Intelligent Tutors Special Interest Group of the American Educational Research Association (AERA) led by Joseph Scandura has been sponsoring similar meetings for this international research community for the last ten years. These meetings have provided the researchers represented in this volume and elsewhere with an ongoing forum for a sustained dialogue about the nature of learning and instruction. In an important sense, this research community owes much to these and similar discussions. As with so many human endeavors, it is meaningful discourse that moves us forward or at least keeps us moving intellectually.

In short, we owe many thanks to individuals such as Sanne Dijkstra and Joseph Scandura who have served this research community with such dedication for so many years, keeping our research dialogue alive and well. We also wish to express our gratitude to several other individuals who have contributed in significant ways to this volume. Christiane Roll, Publishing Editor for the Humanities Unit at Kluwer Academic Publishing, has been most helpful and patient throughout the lengthy editing process. Jayasri Suresh has graciously provided the index for this volume. It was our belief that an index of terms would prove quite useful to readers since we have exerted considerable effort to make this collection of papers a coherent and integrated body of work, much in keeping with our themes and motivation.

J. Michael Spector
Theresa M. Anderson
Syracuse, New York

J. MICHAEL SPECTOR

INTRODUCTION

Keywords: complexity, design, holism, instruction, integration, learning, systems, technology

Abstract. The instructional design community is beginning to focus on issues related to the integration of technology into learning environments, especially those which are concerned not with discrete and disconnected instructional units but with curricula which involve high level understanding of problems and situations involving complex and dynamic systems. This work focuses on how technology might best be integrated into learning environments which aim at holistic and systemic understanding of complex problems. [From the announcement for the conference held at the University of Bergen in 1-2 October 1999.]

BACKGROUND & RATIONALE

This book is about designing instruction. The issues covered are primarily concerned with what might be called the big issues with regard to instructional design. Which learning perspectives and approaches are appropriate for different instructional purposes? How can we efficiently integrate new technologies in effective learning and instruction? How can we design instruction to promote understanding of complex and challenging subject matter?

These big issues naturally lead to many other concerns. How is learning changing in schools and universities and in business, government and industry? What challenges are introduced by a commitment to life-long learning? What changes are occurring on account of technology? What are the implications of these changes for instructional design? Each of these questions in turn can spawn many more particular questions concerning issues that range across such areas as the following: competency based learning, constructivism, dynamic learning environments, epistemology, knowledge management, instructional models, psychology, simulations, theoretical frameworks, and, of course, web-based learning.

The twelve chapters of this book represent an attempt to address key concerns in these areas. The themes that thread throughout these chapters are reflected in the title and subtitle of this volume. We are concerned with learning and technology and their implications for the design of instruction. We are concerned with facilitating learning in complex domains. We are especially concerned with systemic and holistic approaches rather than with fragmented and isolated solutions to particular problems. However, we do recognize the need to build on the many various bits and pieces that have been constructed, implemented, and evaluated over the years. Those bits and pieces are commonly called learning environments, and the larger enterprise is generally referred to as instructional design. These twelve chapters represent a dynamic discourse, going back and forth, from big issues to the bits and pieces, and then back to the larger concerns. One primary aim of this book is to promote that dynamic discourse among academics and professional practitioners.

The various authors included in this volume represent a variety of disciplines and have diverse perspectives. Nevertheless, there is a common concern that in order to make significant advances in promoting understanding in complex domains it is necessary to adopt a holistic perspective that effectively integrates the learning situation, the many dynamic and interrelated aspects of the subject matter, learners, teachers and technology.

Figure 1. Complexities of instructional design.

Figure 1 represents many of the various dimensions of complexity associated with instructional design. The interactions among these items are dynamic and ongoing but often vague and uncertain. This is partly a result of the fact that learning is not a simple concept. Consider the difficulty of defining objects such as tables and trees. Once a tentative definition is accepted it may still be difficult to apply since items that people would like to call tables or trees might violate the accepted definition. The boundaries between bushes and trees or between benches and tables is not always clear, for example. We can at least point to tables and trees. We can make tables and establish manufacturing standards. We can identify healthy and unhealthy trees and engineer procedures for producing new and stronger variants.

Things are much more complex with regard to learning. Learning involves ongoing activities and processes rather than discrete objects and events. We are inclined to speak of both individual and organizational learning. We generally believe that many animal species are capable of learning. With regard to human learning, we believe that it is possible to design materials and programs which facilitate and promote learning, and, further, that we can evaluate the effectiveness of those materials and programs. Let us accept these assumptions uncritically.

What, then, can be said about the nature of learning? In all of the cases and situations just cited, learning seems to involve changes in abilities, attitudes, behaviors, conceptual frameworks, knowledge, mental models or skills. These changes tend to persist over time and through other changes that the individual or organization may undergo, although it sometimes happens that what has been learned fades or is displaced by new learning. Learning, then, is fundamentally about change. Supporting learning (designing instruction) is, therefore, about the facilitation of change. What instructional designers should recognize is that learners, learning situations, technologies, and learning goals have all changed over the years, and such changes are likely to continue. In one sense, an instructional model will always be provisional.

That the design of instruction is about the facilitation of learning is widely accepted (see, for example, Gagné, 1985, 1995; Morecroft & Sterman, 1994; Reigeluth, 1983, 1999; Richey & Fields, 2000; Scandura, 1995; Tennyson, 1995; Tennyson & Morrison, 2000). That learning involves some kind of change is also widely accepted (see, for example, Lave, 1988; Resnick, 1989; Salomon, 1993; Sternberg, 1986). What is not widely accepted is how to go about this enterprise (designing effective instruction), especially in light of new perspectives on learning and powerful technologies to support learning.

One possible explanation for the variety and diversity of instructional solutions involves challenges associated with a desire to facilitate deeper understanding of complex issues (e.g., modeling environmental situations; managing scarce resources; simulating large scale economies or epidemics; understanding social systems; etc.). It is seldom clear how one develops intuitive understanding in such domains, and less clear how to promote such understanding (Dreyfus & Dreyfus, 1986; Ericsson & Smith, 1991).

Another explanation involves the challenge of embracing life-long learning. There is, of course, much discussion about life-long learning, especially in Europe and North America. Special agencies and programs have appeared to support interest in life-long learning. A similar development has occurred with regard to distance learning and distributed education, often in direct relationship to support for and sponsorship of life-long learning programs and activities.

In a sense, educational researchers and instructional technologists have mastered simpler issues. We generally know how to design effective instruction that teaches geography to children or that trains technicians how to operate a piece of equipment. Such learning tasks are pervasive and the need to develop supporting materials will continue to exist. However, those doing research or wishing to explore new frontiers have taken on more complex tasks. In addition, those seeking to establish professional reputations and publish their work are similarly inclined to explore new territory. Moreover, there are always those who believe that we can do better, even in support of simpler learning tasks, and that we ought to be building a coherent and unified body of academic and professional knowledge (Schott & Driscoll, 1997). Whence the concern for the kinds of issues we address in this volume.

I will next make a few remarks about terminology so as to clarify the key themes. Then, I will provide a quick overview of the various chapters. At that point, the reader should be well situated to work through the chapters that might appear of particular interest or relevance. [The Conclusion contains additional organizational perspectives to assist the reader in relating the material presented in the various chapters.]

CRITICAL TERMINOLOGY

We have carefully chosen the words used in the title and subtitle and each of the seven keywords deserves some elaboration. The following sections are intended as guideposts for the reader and reflect what the contributors generally understood by these terms. As noted in the Preface, these chapters are an outgrowth of meetings held in North America (at sessions sponsored by the Structural Learning & Intelligent Systems Special Interest Group of the American Educational Research Association, AERA) and in Europe (at sessions sponsored by the Instructional Design Special Interest Group of the European Association for Research on Learning and Instruction, EARLI). While these specific chapters are a direct outcome of the meeting held at the University of Bergen, Norway, the work presented here represents the ongoing dialogue of these researchers and our research community.

Integration

The notion of integrating technology into a learning situation is familiar albeit a bit ill-defined. One way to indicate the direction of our thinking is to compare the notions of 'multimedia' and 'multiple media'. Teachers and trainers often use multiple media to deliver instructional materials (textbooks, presentation notes, diagrams, and so on. The notion of multimedia is intended to convey the idea that the various media are integrated in a coherent framework of some kind. A simple integrating framework today might be a web site that allows users to link to texts in the form of portable document format (PDF) files, to send questions to and get answers from tutors via email, to engage other learners in asynchronous discussion groups, to interact with simulation environments, and so on. Readers will see examples of such integrated frameworks in chapters 2, 3, 6, 7, 8 and 10. The sense of integration that we wish to encourage goes beyond the notion of having a common and integrated framework for technology-based items, however. We also wish to promote the notion of integrating theory and practice (see chapters 1, 4, 5, 7, 11 and 12). Additionally, an integrated perspective implies that the learner's situation (i.e., setting, motivation, culture, prerequisite knowledge, etc.) and the learning goals (i.e., type of subject, desired outcomes, institutional considerations and constraints, etc.) should be reflected in the instructional design and harmonized and balanced insofar as possible (Spector, 1995). Chapters 1 and 7 argue for such an integrated view directly and quite strongly.

Holism

The notion of holism and integration are related. The idea of holism can be best illustrated by the concept of an enterprise introduced by Gagné and Merrill (1990). An enterprise is an integrated and purposeful human activity. Gagné and Merrill argued that the proper and most typical target of a unit of instruction is an enterprise. This is in contrast to earlier ideas that a unit of instruction should be aimed at a smaller and less integrated bit of information, such as a fact or a rule or a procedure (an idea found in the earlier works of both Gagné and Merrill). We extend the notion to still larger units of instruction that might be called systems. A system is a collection of interrelated components with some generally recognized boundaries. Components, relationships and boundaries often change over time; such systems are called dynamic (Forrester, 1961). A recurring problem in a wide variety of human endeavors concerns misunderstanding such systems (Dörner, 1996; Forrester, 1971). Since such problems are pervasive and because we have new technologies that provide unique opportunities to represent and experiment with synthetic realities (e.g., virtual worlds), many instructional designers are now addressing how best to support learning in and about large, dynamic and complex systems. Chapters 8, 9 and 10 are especially concerned with addressing holistic learning goals. A complementary notion of holism involves holistic views of learners (as emphasized by advocates of life-long learning) and of learning situations (involving collaborations in a variety of contexts) (Spector, 1998). This notion of a holistic perspective is most evident in chapters 1, 6 and 7.

Learning

I have provided a rough definition of learning as a change in abilities, attitudes, behaviors, conceptual frameworks, knowledge, mental models or skills. The unit of analysis might be an individual, a group of individuals or an organization, all of which are addressed in various chapters of this book. In keeping with previous remarks about integration and holistic perspectives, the learning perspective that threads through this volume is especially concerned to provide a unified and consistent account of learning that reflects current beliefs about learners and instructional design (see Schott & Driscoll, 1997, for example). A variety of metaphors and perspectives can be found in these chapters. As Sfard (1998) argues, it is perhaps best to adopt an inclusive rather than an exclusive attitude with regard to alternative conceptions of learning. Current perspectives on learning are summarized in chapters 1, 7 and 12, which are especially concerned with the notions of "learnplaces", learning ergonomics, socially-situated learning, constructivist designs, and natural epistemology - all of which reflect a view of "learning in the large". While the underlying definition of learning may have remained unchanged, we are certainly addressing new learning concerns.

Instruction

The remarks just made with regard to learning apply equally well to instruction. The underlying definition is largely as it has been - instruction implies support for learning. However, instructional design practice (Tennyson, 1995) has evolved into what might better be called instructional design praxis (the activities and enterprises engaged in by the various persons involved in planning, implementing, evaluating and managing the facilitation of learning, educational programs, instructional systems and performance environments). The ways and means of supporting learning effectively have grown considerably more complex with new technologies. This is one of the core themes echoed in nearly every chapter of this book.

Technology

The word 'technology' is derived from the Greek word 'techne' which refers to a discipline for making things that would today be considered an art or a craft. Technology generally refers to the methods and tools that people use to manipulate their surroundings. In this sense, technology includes much more than equipment - hardware and software. Many professional disciplines emphasize the notion of a collection of methods usually derived from a theoretical foundation that can be systematically applied to achieve predictable results or consistent outcomes. The prevailing view of instructional technology is that it is an art of craft (in that sense of technology), that it is derived from foundations in learning theory, and, when practiced with appropriate rigor, instructional technology results in desired learning outcomes. The rigor and discipline of instructional design are not embedded in any particular instructional model, however. Rather, the rigor and discipline are founded on notions such as evaluating learning outcomes (see chapter 3), on linking instructional design practice to empirically based learning principles (see chapter 11), on linking instructional planning to epistemology and learning (see chapters 8, 9 and 10), and so on. In short, the use of the term 'technology' in this book is concerned with methods as well as with hardware and software. This book is especially concerned with technology-intensive learning situations since they present particular challenges and opportunities for designers (see chapters 2, 3, 6, 7, 8, 9 and 10). Finally, the reader will find a number of chapters focused on a particular technology - namely, simulation-based learning environments - that seems especially promising with regard to promoting understanding in complex domains (see especially chapters 8, 9 and 10).

Understanding

Consistent with the theme of addressing "learning in the large", there is a particular focus in most of these chapters with understanding as the primary learning outcome as opposed to narrower or more discrete learning goals such as mastering a specific skill. The comparison in chapter 6 between a competency-based approach (focused on specific knowledge gaps and desired skills) and a knowledge-management approach (aimed at more global institutional concerns but also quite flexible with regard to instructional purposes) puts this contrast in clear focus. Chapters 1, 7 and 12 argue strongly that the ultimate goal of learning is understanding. Support for this argument can be found in nearly every chapter. Since the emphasis in learning research appears to have shifted from mastery of discrete bits and pieces to deep understanding of complex domains, several chapters specifically target the design of instruction for understanding complex systems (see especially chapters 8, 9 and 10).

Complexity

The concerns of the various contributors with regard to supporting learning in and about complex domains were a motivation for the Bergen meeting and have resulted in this volume. It is only fair to make a few comments about the nature of complexity. The notion of complexity has a number of dimensions, as do the other concepts just reviewed. One dimension of complexity concerns the number of components involved. As the number of components in a system increases (or as the number of factors and variables increases), it is usually the case that understanding the system becomes more difficult. If understanding is operationalized as the ability to accurately predict the behavior of a system in a variety of circumstances, then it is usually the case that we are less able to accurately predict what will happen when more and more components, factors, or variables are taken into account. We might call this kind of complexity computational complexity, and we do have some sense of how to design instruction to deal with it.

Other sources of complexity are much more worrisome to instructional designers: non-linear relationships among various components, delayed effects and influence, fuzziness of variables, uncertainty with regard to critical components, and so on (Forrester, 1961). There are many examples of systems that are complex in this sense - some are also computationally complex and some are not. We know from empirical research that human decision makers do not do well when confronted with such complexity (Dörner, 1996; Merry, 1995). Typically, humans focus on local effects and fail to see the larger system; people are prone to look only at shorter term relationships and correlations and overlook longer term shifts in the relationships of key components (Dörner, 1996). How can instructional technology help improve understanding in complex domains? Practice with timely and informative feedback is critical for learning (Gagné, 1985). How do we apply such an instructional design principle in a meaningful way to promote understanding of a complex environmental problem or the spread of an epidemic? Building and using simulations can prove useful (see chapter 10). Providing rich experimental environments that provide learners with opportunities to collaborate with others and try out a variety of solutions is certainly a promising approach (Spector, 1996; Spector & Davidsen, 1997). That we do not yet know well how to design effective instruction for complex domains is a recurring background theme in this volume.

ORGANIZATION OF THE BOOK

This book is organized into two parts. Part I, "Instructional Foundations for Life-Long Learning and Understanding Complex Domains" deals with what I have called "learning in the large" (those issues particularly focused on life-long learning and the integration of theory and praxis). The kickoff chapter by Goodyear is concerned with the design of learning places that support life-long learners. Goodyear notes that these learners are typically less compliant than traditional students. To satisfy the many and varied requirements of adult learners, Goodyear argues for user-centered technologies and practices.

Marshall and Rossett present a summary of knowledge management as it is emerging in business and work settings. They then ask whether knowledge management has a place in school settings and argue that it does, citing both the many possibilities and the potential pitfalls.

Savenye describes the design, implementation, evaluation and re-design of a web-based university course. Her formative evaluation reflected the desire of learners for more autonomy, consistent with Goodyear's suggestions. Moreover, she shows nicely how the environment changed in response to learner interests and requirements, building a bridge between theory and praxis (an issue treated again in chapter 5).

Dunnagan and Christensen insert a sobering note into a discussion that thus far has been quite upbeat with regard to the possibilities for technology to support learning in and about complex domains. They point out that it is very easy to mistakenly apply an instructional model that was appropriate for simpler static situations to learning situations that really require a more dynamic instructional model. Further complicating the temptation to use simpler models inappropriately is the fact that adult learners in non-academic settings (life-long learners) have entirely different expectations than do typical traditional learners. Their argument foreshadows issues taken up in detail in Part II.

Spector argues that translating theory into practice is a tired and possibly worn out mantra. While applying theory to practice certainly sounds reasonable, it is quite difficult to evaluate when and how well this occurs. He suggests that a more scientific attitude towards instructional design will be needed to insure that progress in this area continues and can be sustained.

Part I ends with an illustration by Wagner of how new technologies can be used to support life-long learning. She compares competency-based (which is fundamentally learner-centered) and knowledge-based approaches, and argues that an approach that has integrated competency-based methods is more likely to be appropriate for and effective with adult learners who, as Goodyear argues, often demand more autonomy.

Part II, "Integrating Technology and Knowledge Construction in Rich Learning Environments" deals with more specific issues pertaining to the effective integration of technology in support of understanding complex systems. The initial chapter in this part by Jonassen, Hernandez-Serrano and Choi presents a comprehensive review of recent developments in learning and instruction. They argue that a new paradigm has emerged. This brave new world is based on a socially-situated learning perspective that emphasizes the role of the learner in constructing mental models. Much of their discussion recalls Goodyear's remarks about adult learners being less compliant and more autonomous. As the discussion unfolds, it becomes clear that the world of instructional design has become enormously more complicated than previously conceived.

The chapter by Seel, Al-Diban and Blumschein makes the same point with regard to designing instruction to facilitate adult learning in a particular complex domain (macro-economics and financial planning). They present a review of cognitive apprenticeship and situated learning as foundations upon which to build. They then report on how those perspectives influenced the design of a learning environment and learning outcomes using measures that were tailored to the complexity of the subject matter. Their empirical research shows that one relevant consideration with strong implications for design is the existence or non-existence of appropriate learner pre-conceptions (about the subject domain or a domain of similar complexity).

Achtenhagen examines the interactions between mental models and simulated environments in a setting involving adult learners following a particular, state-mandated vocational curriculum. Achtenhagen notes that employers were concerned that learners develop deep understanding with regard to real-world systems and that they do well in training. Such a setting is quite distant from a selection model found in some school settings and has much in common with the competency approach advocated by Wagner. Achtenhagen cites many of the same pitfalls alluded to by Dunnagan and Christensen in Part I and demonstrates how a virtual learning environment can be designed to improve adult understanding in a complex domain.

The chapter by Alessi examines tradeoffs and benefits associated with having learners build simulations as opposed to use them (as was the case in Achtenhagen's environment). The process of building a simulation appears to be the more constructivist approach, and, perhaps, the more attractive alternative. Alessi argues that each approach has a place and appropriate range of application. When the learning goal is primarily procedural, using a simulation is likely to be both effective and efficient. When the goal involves declarative knowledge and deep understanding of a complex domain, then the process of building simulations is likely to be more effective. Alessi includes a design model for simulation-based learning environments.

Park and Etgen examine principles for multimedia presentation in terms of different theories of cognition. Their study highlights the fact that our knowledge of learning is incomplete with much basic research remaining to be done. This is one reason for the failure to build stronger bridges between theory and practice discussed by Spector. It is also a reason to be more modest in our claims with regard to instructional design. If instructional design is founded on learning theory and that theoretical foundation is itself incomplete and uncertain, then we ought to hold our instructional design principles and maxims with appropriate degrees of uncertainty. Moreover, we ought to welcome the empirical scrutiny presented by Park and Etgen.

The final chapter in Part II by Dijkstra presents a thoughtful capstone to this volume. He proceeds from a foundation in naturalistic epistemology to an examination of relevant trends in learning theory, similar to those already cited by other contributors. Dijkstra pushes the discussion forward by addressing the psychology of problem solving. He distinguishes categorization, interpretation and design problems, with design problems being the most complex. Each type of problem has an appropriate set of instructional methods and effective techniques for promoting learning. Dijkstra is also careful to distinguish reality from representations of reality and notices that most designers want to support experiential learning but often do so with synthetic realities (representations of realities). Dijkstra echoes many of the themes discussed in other chapters, including the difference between manipulating and constructing artifacts and the need to develop both competence and understanding.

CONCLUDING REMARKS

This volume contains a rich set of arguments, discussions, illustrations and insights into the design of instruction in support of complex subject matter. The contributors examine challenges introduced by a desire to support life-long learning. The appropriate integration of technology is important for progress. A holistic perspective of learners, situations and goals is encouraged throughout. Exploration and experimentation are promoted as means for advancing instructional design knowledge. Finally, many examples of rich learning environments and instructional design models are presented. The reader can view these chapters as a review of the profession itself or as instructional scaffolding for advanced practitioners (see the concluding chapter).

The practice of instructional design is coming of age. Perhaps we have reached adolescence, a period of great growth, filled with both confidence and uncertainty. The world will surely change. Understanding the complexities of these changes will be of increasing significance for our continued well being. We simply must come to understand and deal with complexity better than we now do. The aim of this volume is to make a small contribution towards that grand goal.

REFERENCES

Dörner, D. (1996) (Translated by Rita and Robert Kimber). *The logic of failure: Why things go wrong and what we can do to make them right*. New York: Holt.

Dreyfus, H. L., & Dreyfus, S. E. (1986). *Mind over machine: The power of human intuition and expertise in the era of the computer*. New York: Free Press.

Ericsson, K. A., & Smith, J. (Eds.) (1991). *Toward a general theory of expertise: Prospects and limits.* New York: Cambridge University Press.

Forrester, J. W. (1961). *Industrial Dynamics.* Cambridge, MA: MIT Press.

Forrester, J. W. (1971, January). *Counterintuitive behavior of social systems.* Cambridge, MA: *Technology Review*, Massachusetts Institute of Technology Alumni Association.

Gagné, R. M. (1985). *The conditions of learning (4th ed.).* New York: Holt, Rinehart, and Winston.

Gagné, R. M. (1995). Learning processes and instruction. *Training Research Journal, 1*, 17-28.

Gagné, R. M., & Merrill, M. D. (1990). Integrative goals for instructional design. *Educational Technology Research and Development, 38*(1), 23-30.

Lave, J. (1988). *Cognition in Practice: Mind, mathematics, and culture in everyday life.* Cambridge, UK: Cambridge University Press.

Merry, U. (1995). *Coping with uncertainty: Insights from new sciences of chaos, self-organization, and complexity.* New York: Praeger.

Morecroft, J. D. W., & Sterman, J. D. (Eds.) (1994). *Modeling for learning organizations.* Portland: Productivity Press.

Reigeluth, C. M. (Ed.) (1983). *Instructional design theories and models: An overview of their current status.* Hillsdale, NJ: Erlbaum.

Reigeluth, C. M. (Ed.) (1999). *Instructional design theories and models: A new paradigm of instructional theory*, Vol II. Mahwah, NJ: Erlbaum.

Resnick, L. B. (Ed.) (1989). *Knowing, learning, and instruction.* Hillsdale, NJ: Lawrence Erlbaum.

Richey, R. C., & Fields, D. F. (Eds.) (2000). *Instructional design competencies: The standards (3rd Ed.).* Syracuse, NY: ERIC Clearinghouse on Information and Technology & The International Board of Standards for Training, Performance & Instruction.

Salomon, G. (Ed.) (1993). *Distributed cognitions: Psychological and educational considerations.* New York: Cambridge University Press.

Scandura, J. M. (1995). Theoretical foundations of instruction: Past, present, and future. *Journal of Structural Learning, 12*(3), 231-243.

Schott, F., & Driscoll, M. (1997). On the architectonics of instructional theory. In R. D. Tennyson, F. Schott, N. Seel, & S. Dijkstra (Eds.), *Instructional Design: International Perspectives. Volume 1: Theory, Research, and Models* (pp. 135-173). Mahwah, NJ: Erlbaum.

Sfard, A. (1998). On two metaphors for learning and the dangers of choosing just one. *Educational Researcher, 27*(2), 4-12.

Spector, J. M. (1995). Integrating and humanizing the process of automating instructional design. In R. D. Tennyson & A. Barron (Eds.), *Automating instructional design: Computer-based development and delivery tools* (pp. 523-546). Brussels, Belgium: Springer-Verlag.

Spector, J. M. (1996). Creativity and constructivity in learning environments. *Educational Media International, 33*(2), 55-59.

Spector, J. M. & Davidsen, P. I. (1997). Creating engaging courseware using system dynamics. *Computers in Human Behavior*, 13(2), 127-155.

Spector, J. M. (1998). The future of instructional theory: A synthesis of European & American perspectives. *Journal of Structural Learning, 13*(2), 115-128.

Sternberg, R. J. (1986). *Intelligence applied: Understanding and increasing your intellectual skills.* San Diego, CA: Harcourt Brace Jovanovich.

Tennyson, R. D. (1995). Four generations of instructional system development. *Journal of Structural Learning, 12,* 149-164.

Tennyson, R .D., & Morrison, G. R. (2000). *Instructional development: Foundations, Process, and Methodology.* Columbus, OH: Merrill/Prentice-Hall.

ABOUT THE AUTHORS

Achtenhagen, Frank	Fax: +49 551 394 417
Faculty of Business & Economy Studies	Email:
George-August University	fachten@wwpu00.wipaed.wiso.uni-
37073 Göttingen, Germany	goettingen.de

Frank Achtenhagen is a Professor of Business and Economy Studies and Management Training Director at Georg-August University, Dean of the Faculty of Business and Economy Studies, in addition to holding other distinguished positions such as the President of the German Enquete Commission for Research on Vocational Education. He has more than 300 publications and has earned both national and international awards.

Al-Diban, Sabine	Fax: +1 351 463 7242
	Email: Sabine.Al-
	Diban@mailbox.tu-dresden.de

Sabine Al-Diban is a psychologist and project collaborator at the German Research Society (DFG) at the Department of Education at the Albert-Ludwigs-University Freiburg and assistant lecturer at the Institute of School Education and School Research Department of Educational Science at Dresden University of Technology. Her areas of expertise include educational diagnosis of mental models and evaluation of educational software.

Alessi, Stephen	Tel: +1 319 335 5568
370 Lindquist Center	Fax: +1 319 335 6145
The University of Iowa	Email: steve-alessi@uiowa.edu
Iowa City, Iowa 52242 USA	

Stephen Alessi is an Associate Professor of Instructional Design and Technology at the University of Iowa. His teaching and research emphasize the application of cognitive learning theory to the design of educational software, especially the design of instructional simulations. He is co-author, with Stanley Trollip, of *Computer-based Instruction: Methods and Development*, and is currently writing about educational simulation theory and design.

Anderson, Theresa M.	Email: tma048@aol.com
330 Huntington Hall (SOE-IDD&E)	
Syracuse University	
Syracuse, New York 13244 USA	

Theresa Anderson is a PhD student in Instructional Design, Development and Evaluation at Syracuse University. Her MBA is in Personnel and Industrial Relations from Syracuse University, and she is a graduate of GE's Human Resource Executive Development Program. Prior positions include VP for Drake Beam Morin, Employee Relations and Human Resources Manager at GE, and Director of Human Resources at PriceWaterhouseCoopers.

| **Blumschein, Patrick**
Albert-Ludwigs-University of Freiburg
Seminar für Philosophie und
Erziehungswissenschaft
79085 Freiburg Germany | Fax: +49 761 203 2458
Email: plumbum@ezw.uni-
freiburg.de |

Patrick Blumschein is currently working on a Doctoral Thesis in the field of Instructional Design and is employed at the Seminar of Philosophy and Education Sciences at Albert-Ludwigs-University Freiburg. He graduated with an MA in Sociology, Education Sciences and History from the University of Freiburg in 1997. His research interests are in the areas of new learning theories and evaluation of educational software.

| **Choi, Ikseon**
314 Keller Building
The Pennsylvania State University
University Park, PA 16802-2602 USA | Tel: +1 814 865 0473
Fax: +1 814 865 0128
Email: ixc2@psu.edu |

Ikseon Choi is an instructional systems doctoral candidate at Pennsylvania State University. His area of concentration is naturalistic processes of learning, decision-making, and problem solving. His main interests are building constructivist learning environments, designing cognitive tools and performance support systems for learning and cognitive task analysis.

| **Christensen Dean L.**
CYBER Learning Corporation
1177 Rose Lane
St. Paul, MN 55112 USA | Tel: +1 651 628 0460
Fax: +1 651 628 0461
Email: Chris101@mn.mediaone.net
http://people.mn.mediaone.net/cyberlearning/ |

Dean L. Christiansen, a Senior Fulbright Research Scholar at the University of Bergen and Interim President of the International Consortium for Courseware Engineering, is VP at CYBER Learning Corporation. His prime interests are combining system dynamics theories and advanced learning environments. Prior to CYBER Learning, Dean worked as a senior researcher at Control Data Corporation's PLATO initiative in computer-based training.

| **Dijkstra, Sanne**
Faculty of Educational Science and
Technology, University of Twente
PO Box 217
7500 AE Enschede The Netherlands | Phone: +31 53 489 3563
Fax: +31 53 489 2849
Email: dijkstra@edte.utwente.nl |

Sanne Dijkstra is Professor of Instructional Technology in the Faculty of Educational Science and Technology at the University of Twente and Chair of the Graduate School of Teacher Education. His interests include industrial & educational psychology. His published research is about the effectiveness and efficiency of instructional design models. He has a strong interest in the acquisition of knowledge and skills using problem solving approaches.

| Dunnagan, Catherine B.
CYBER Learning Corporation
1177 Rose Lane
St. Paul, MN 55112 USA | Tel: +1 651 628 0460
Fax: +1 651 628 0461
Email:
Dunna002@mn.mediaone.net
http://people.mn.mediaone.net/cyberlearning/ |

Catherine B. Dunnagan is the founding President of CYBER Learning Corporation. Formerly, she worked for Control Data Corporation on the PLATO initiative that developed and delivered over 10,000 hours of computer instruction. She was instrumental in the establishment of the International Consortium for Courseware Engineering. Her area of interest is the effective use of technology for instructional development.

| Etgen, Michael P.
Senior Technical Staff Member
AT&T Labs
Red Bank, New Jersey USA | Tel: +1 732 530 8000 |

Michael P. Etgen is a Senior Technical Staff Member for AT&T Labs' User Experience Engineering group. Prior to joining AT&T, he was a research assistant at the Catholic University of America and a research Fellow at the Army Research Institute. He received a Ph.D. in experimental psychology from the Catholic University of America in 1998.

| Jonassen, David H.
School of Information Science &
Learning Technology, Townsend Hall
The University of Missouri
Columbia, MO 65211 | Tel: +1 573 882 4546
Fax: +1 573 884 4944
Email: Jonassen@missouri.edu
http://www.coe.missouri.edu/~sislt/ |

David H. Jonassen is Distinguished Professor of Learning Technologies at the University of Missouri. He has taught previously at Pennsylvania State University, University of Colorado, University of North Carolina at Greensboro and Temple University. He is the author/editor of more than twenty books on instructional design, learning technologies, and educational psychology. The focusing theme of his research is knowledge representation.

| Goodyear, Peter
Centre for Studies in Advanced
Learning Technology (CSALT)
Lancaster University
Lancaster LA1 4YL, England | Tel: +44 1524 594 373
Fax: +44 1524 592 914
Email: P.Goodyear@lancaster.ac.uk
CSALT: http://csalt.lancs.ac.uk/csalt/ |

Peter Goodyear is Professor of Educational Research, Centre for Studies in Advanced Learning Technology (CSALT) Lancaster University, England, and teaches in the MSc program in Advanced Learning Technology and conducts research in educational technology. Since 1993, he has been editor of *Instructional Science*. His interests include collaborative and team-based learning, computer-mediated learning, and methodological issues in research.

| **Hernández-Serrano, Julián** Agricultural Sciences and Industries Pennsylvania State University University Park, PA 16802-2602 USA | Tel: +1 814 867 4972 Fax: +1 814 863 0109 Email: jxh323@psu.edu |

Julián Hernández-Serrano is an Instructional Systems doctoral candidate at Pennsylvania State University. His area of concentration is decision-making and problem-solving in ill-structured domains. His main interests are building constructivist learning environments that support ill-structured problem solving, exploring methods for systematically implementing Constructivist learning components, and incorporating emerging technologies in learning.

| **Marshall, James M.** San Diego State University 5500 Campanile Dr. San Diego, CA 92182 USA | Email: Jmmarshall@aol.com |

James M. Marshall has been the Director of Research and Evaluation for The Lightspan Partnership, Inc., a provider of youth educational software and Internet services. Before joining Lightspan, he was a Senior Consultant with Andersen Consulting specializing in multimedia and technology-based training. He teaches instructional design and multimedia development at San Diego State University where he is completing his doctoral studies.

| **Park, Ok-choon** OERI/At-Risk Room 610 US Department of Education 555 New Jersey Ave. NW Washington, DC 20208-5521 USA | Tel: +1 202 208 3951 Fax: +1 202 219 2030 Email: ok-choon_park@ed.go |

Ok-choon Park is a Senior Researcher at the Office of Educational Research and Improvement (OERI), U.S. Department of Education. Before joining OERI in 1997, he was a Senior Research Psychologist at the U.S. Army Research Institute. His other experiences include having been an Assistant Professor at the State University of New York at Albany and educational researcher at Control Data Corporation.

| **Rossett, Allison** San Diego State University 5500 Campanile Dr. San Diego, CA 92182 USA | Phone + 1 619 299 1998 Email: arossett@mail.sdsu.edu http://edweb.sdsu.edu/EdWeb_Folder/P eople/ARossett/Arossett.html |

Allison Rossett is Professor of Educational Technology at San Diego State University and a consultant in performance and training systems. She has authored numerous articles on training and technologies and three award-winning books including *First Things Fast: A Handbook for Performance Analysis,* winner of the 1999 ISPI Instructional Communications Award of Excellence.

Savenye, Wilhelmina C.	Tel: +1 480 965 4963
Division of Psychology in Education	Email: savenye@asu.edu
PO Box 870611	
Arizona State University	
Tempe, AZ 85287-0611 USA	

Wilhelmina C. Savenye is Associate Professor of Educational Technology at Arizona State University. Her interests include web-based learning, instructional design, and evaluation of interactive learning technologies. She has authored numerous publications, presented over 70 international conference papers, and serves as a reviewer for educational technology journals.

Seel, Norbert M.	Fax: +49 761 203 2458
Albert-Ludwigs-University of Freiburg	Email: seel@ezw.uni-freiburg.de
Seminar für Philosophie und	
Erziehungswissenschaft	
79085 Freiburg Germany	

Norbert M. Seel is Head of the Seminar of Philosophie and Education Sciences at the Albert-Ludwigs-University of Freiburg and former Dean of the Faculty of Educational Sciences at the University of Dresden and Professor in Tübingen and Saarbrücken. His interests include mental model research, instructional design decision-making, and multimedia-based learning. He has authored/edited more than 16 books and 90 articles, including *Psychology of Learning*.

Spector, J. Michael	Tel: +1 315 443 3703
330 Huntington Hall (SOE-IDD&E)	Fax: +1 315 443 9218
Syracuse University	Email: Spector@syr.edu
Syracuse, New York 13244 USA	http://soeweb.syr.edu/faculty/Spector/

Michael Spector is Professor and Chair of Instructional Design, Development and Evaluation at Syracuse University and Professor of Information Science and Director of Educational Information Science and Technology Research at the University of Bergen (on leave). He is a founding member and President of the International Consortium for Courseware Engineering, a member of the International Board of Standards for Training, Performance and Instruction.

Wagner, Ellen D.,	Phone: +1 415 626 7343 ext. 113
Chief Learning Officer	Fax: +1 415 626 7345
Informania, Inc.	Email: edwagner@informania.com
444 De Haro Street, Suite 128	Webpage: www.informania.com
San Francisco, CA 94107 USA	

Ellen D. Wagner directs learning design, development, implementation and evaluation at Informania. She was formerly Professor and Chair of Educational Technology at the University of Northern Colorado, Director of the Western Institute for Distance Education and a Visiting Scholar at the Western Interstate Commission for Higher Education. She has published more than 70 book chapters, articles, and monographs.

PETER GOODYEAR

Chapter 1

ENVIRONMENTS FOR LIFELONG LEARNING

Ergonomics, architecture and educational design

Keywords: autonomous learners, compliant learners, instructional design, lifelong learning, reflective task design, virtual learning environments

Abstract. This chapter provides an overview of the emerging responsibility of educational technologists to move beyond the design of instructional tasks to the requirement to become architects and creators of virtual learning environments reflective of real world activities. It describes three issues contributing to this shift, including: lifelong learning strategies and the need to remove barriers in content and structure for learning to occur; increased learner autonomy and the movement away from the notion of a compliant learner; and, the ability of current technology to merge the real and the virtual world. The chapter concludes with a discussion of the requirements of the virtual learning environment and the SHARP distributed learning environment of Lancaster University.

INTRODUCTION

The field of educational technology, and particularly of instructional design, now has a good history of creating innovative technology-based learning resources through the application of principled development methods. These methods have evolved over half a century or more, if we look to the roots of instructional design in the wartime work of people like Robert Gagné. In the last decade, the core practices of educational technology have been facing some severe criticism, particularly from those writing under a neo-constructivist banner (e.g., Duffy & Jonassen, 1992; Wilson, 1996). These criticisms primarily reflect epistemological and pedagogical doubts. Some neo-constructivists proclaim an epistemological relativism that refuses to give a privileged status to any one way of 'knowing' the world. Some assert that 'knowledge transfer is impossible': pedagogy needs to support the individual *construction* of meaning.

The point of departure for my chapter is somewhat different. I want to argue that educational technology is facing a new kind of challenge, or, more positively, a new area of opportunity. I am using the label 'lifelong learning'

1

J.M. Spector and T.M. Anderson (eds.),
Integrated and Holistic Perspectives on Learning, Instruction and Technology, 1–18.
© 2000 *Kluwer Academic Publishers. Printed in the Netherlands.*

as a shorthand for this area. 'Lifelong learning', on one reading, must embrace all areas of learning – kindergarten; formal education in the school years; further and higher education; informal learning in the community, home or workplace; training courses in industry; non-vocational adult education courses in colleges and universities, and so on. The all-embracing character of the term may seem, at first glance, unhelpful. But it does emphasise the need for a *holistic* perspective on learning and for what might be called 'joined-up education' – approaches to education which identify and systematically remove damaging discontinuities between different phases and settings for learning.

Against this background, I want to focus on one main theme: design implications of learner autonomy or learner-managed learning. If we want to develop new practices within educational technology that are compatible with a valuing of autonomous lifelong learning, then we need to recognise that an image of the *compliant* learner has had a strong influence on the mainstreams of educational technology. How should we approach the design of learning environments that are consistent with the needs of autonomous lifelong learners – learners who may, and perhaps should, reject our offerings if they do not meet their needs?

A second theme in this chapter recognises another important shift in design imagery. I have been teaching on Lancaster University's postgraduate 'Advanced Learning Technology' programme since 1989. Our initial curriculum assumed that most of the people we were training would be designing courseware for 'end-learners' who would be occupying relatively low-level, routine jobs in industry or commerce. We can no longer make this assumption. Educational technologists and instructional designers design for all kinds of adult learners in all kinds of organisations, including university students but also company managers, sales staff, doctors, power station workers, pilots and technicians. In addition, our early 'design image' was a clear and simple one: our students would be designing CBT courseware. That image is no longer clear. Some of our students still design courseware, but the range of their work activities is much greater. If there is a central image, it is of the design and management of a learning environment, rather than of a single stand-alone learning product. With the rapid growth of the WWW and the Internet, since 1994, and especially since we have begun to glimpse what user experiences will be made possible by the convergence of Internet multimedia and virtual reality techniques in the near future, the design image has begun to fix around networked ('on-line' or 'virtual') learning environments, configured for use by communities of learners. Some of these communal virtual environments are taking on familiar shapes: virtual universities with campus 'buildings' housing on-line learner-support services like libraries and cafés, for example. It is too early to know what to make of this trend. In 20 years time, this may look like a familiar, understandable but aberrant path, analogous with seeing and designing early versions of the car as a horseless carriage. Or, as some have argued, rendering cyberspace navigable and legible through capitalising on people's ability to 'read' architecture in the material world may be the best – or the only – way to move forward. Whichever reading may prove to be correct, the problem facing us at present is manifesting itself quite clearly. How should we approach the design of virtual learning environments configured to the needs of communities of autonomous lifelong learners?

I want to argue that it is timely to look outside our familiar world of instructional theory and see what people are doing in areas like software engineering and architecture. In making this argument, I want to explore three interconnected sets of issues.

The first of these I refer to as 'the decline of the compliant learner'. By this I mean that it is becoming increasingly difficult to imagine that we can design learning technology systems around an assumption that they will be used by learners in the ways we prescribe. This is an important issue, to which I return in the next section, but which actually underpins my whole argument.

The second set of issues concerns a shift from the creation of 'tasks-in-objects' to 'environments-for-activities'. I claim that a core (historic) image in the training of educational technologists has been that we are preparing them to create computer programs in which learning tasks are embedded. That is, the program is assumed to 'drive' the learner. Even when we opt for a more learner-controlled or constructivist paradigm, I would claim, the core image is still of 'valuable tasks embedded in objects'. More of this later. For now, I want to argue that there is a trend - to be welcomed - towards a conception of educational technologists' work which is more concerned with the design and management of learning environments, and is more concerned with supporting real-world learner activities than with teachers' idealised conceptions of what learners *should* be doing.

The third and final set of issues is less tightly woven in than the first two. It concerns the status and relations between symbolic and situated knowledge. This is in danger of becoming a tired and overly familiar area (see for example, Anderson, Reder, & Simon, 1996; Brown & Duguid, 1989; Greeno, 1997; Kirshner & Whitson, 1998; Lave & Wenger, 1991; Wenger, 1998). But my focus here is on the *interplay* rather than a *competition* between these forms of knowledge and learning. I will develop this theme in addressing some of the requirements of virtual learning environments, towards the end of the article.

My overall purpose in this chapter is to sketch an emerging image of the role of the educational technologist in the early years of the next century. In doing so, I rashly mix prescriptions and predictions and overstate the case for radical change. The image I am working towards is that of 'architect' of virtual learning environments - building on, and probably deforming, ideas of how the architects of material spaces prepare for, and execute, their work.

DECLINE OF THE COMPLIANT LEARNER

By 'the compliant learner' I mean someone who will, by and large, do what they are told. In many learning situations it is reasonable to expect learners to comply with the instructions or expectations of those who are placed in a position of responsibility for their learning. We can readily think of 'ideal cases' - such as in certain areas of military training, or in the learning of well-defined procedures for dealing with civil emergencies, or in many other areas of high-risk training (Andrews, Waag, & Bell, 1992; Gaddy & Wachtel, 1992; Prince, Chidester, Bowers, & Cannon-Bowers, 1992; Ward, 1988). Many of the core ideas, theories and methods in the field of educational technology, and especially in areas like ISD or instructional design, have origins which were heavily shaped by reasonable assumptions about a compliant learner.

But educational technology has moved on. It is now called upon to find ways of supporting the learning of a great variety of people, quite a few of whom cannot be described as 'compliant'. For example, the recent history of government-funded investment in educational technology in UK higher education shows how misconstruing students' use of learning resources can waste tens of millions of pounds worth of public money and of precious staff time (Dearing, 1997). Evaluative data seems to indicate that, however good the learning software, students will rarely use it unless they are obliged to do so. They will use it if it is part of their normal timetabled activity. They will use it if they need to do so in order to pass some assessed task. But they will not use it just because it is good for them. This is not because they are perverse, lazy or technophobic. Most students use ICT every day – but they use it for their own purposes, just like the rest of us. They use it for emailing their friends, finding interesting material on the web, writing coursework essays and so on. They don't use 'courseware' for the same reason that they don't make as much use as we (their teachers) would like of the university library; they are too busy and it's not on the critical path for any of the significant problems they have to solve each day. Particularly where students are poor and over-assessed, supplementing their income and meeting the next coursework deadline take precedence over 'reading around the subject' or browsing through optional pieces of courseware. The same kind of arguments apply to busy managers, knowledge workers and other creative people for whom very focussed 'just-in-time learning' is all their stressed schedule can afford. Of course I am over-stating the case, but (a) there are few signs that the 'disposable learning time' available to students or workers is increasing – quite the reverse; and, (b) environments for lifelong learning cannot *assume* a compliant learner. Much of today's learning rhetoric is about the value of the autonomous learner and about the need for lifelong learning skills. Among the predispositions and skills of a successful autonomous lifelong learner we may well find an ability to recognise when it is advantageous temporarily to relinquish control over aspects of one's learning. But this must be seen as an occasional eddy in the broad stream of strengthening learner autonomy. And the cold fact remains - we cannot and should not assume that learners' behaviour is under our control. The compliant learner no longer *suffices* as a design image.

TOWARDS A USER-CENTERED EDUCATIONAL TECHNOLOGY

What this means for educational technology, I would claim, is that we need to prioritise the development of technological support for the real-world activities in which our client learners engage. In making this point, I draw on a simple yet too often neglected distinction. This distinction can be made in a number of ways, but I find persuasive the language of the French ergonomist Alain Wisner (Wisner, 1995a; Wisner, 1995b). Wisner calls on us to distinguish between tasks (the prescribed work) and activities (what workers actually do). It is now well accepted in the disciplines of information systems design and software engineering that technology should be built around a well-founded understanding of what people actually do, including new methods such as rapid prototyping and concurrent engineering. Just listening to the managers' accounts of how work *should* be done is a recipe for disaster and leads to unused and unusable software systems[1]. Why should higher education (or other settings in which learners are self-directing) be any different? Of course it is legitimate for managers (or teachers, or trainers) to have views about what learners ought to do. Of course there is something inherently conservative in building technology around existing practices. But I would contend that the biggest problem we are facing is that of learners "voting with their feet". However beautiful our theories or our interfaces, learners are not choosing to spend their time using our products.

Hindsight is a great help when it comes to prediction. But we should have known from more than twenty years of research on student learning in higher education (see for example, Biggs, 1999; Entwistle, 1996; Marton, Hounsell, & Entwistle, 1997) and at least a decade of research on software systems failures (e.g., Flowers, 1996) that we would eventually face this predicament. Now is the time for a user-centered educational technology to

---

[1] See also Bruno Latour who talks about the gap between 'the prescribed user' and 'the user in the flesh' (Latour, 1995, p. 272).

begin working on methods through which we can come to understand the real needs of our target users, and design technology which helps them meet the real challenges they are facing. If it helps them, they will use it.

TASK DESIGN AND THE DESIGN OF LEARNING ENVIRONMENTS

Does this mean that educational technologists no longer need to learn how to design good learning tasks, or have a working knowledge of instructional theory? No. First, let's not forget that it is sometimes perfectly justifiable to design for a compliant learner. Second, well-designed tasks are a *resource* for productive learning activity. Note the claim here. Learners take a task definition and interpret it. Their activity represents a *satisficing* response to their interpretation of the task requirements. Activity and interpretation will both be constrained by the other demands on the learner's time and energy. So task design is still part of the job. But there's a significant shift, which I describe in terms of a need for *reflexive* task design. That is, once we know that learners will interpret and modify the tasks-as-set, engaging in activity to *satisfice* multiple calls upon their time and energy, then we can modify our approach to task design. We can self-consciously allow for the fact that our tasks-as-set will be modified, rather than pretending that tasks and activities are mirror images. We need all the intellectual resources that the cognitive and learning sciences can provide in doing this work of reflexive task design. Unlike the majority of neo-constructivists, we don't have to throw away our scientific heritage.

The bigger shift comes in moving the technology focus. The current paradigm, I would claim, is centered around embedding tasks in technological artefacts. That is, we create courseware in which tasks for the learner are embedded. The courseware drives the learner. We need to shift to building technology around learners' real world activity: to create learning environments which are properly supportive of real world activity.

To summarise: (a) use the best of cognitive science, instructional design theory and so on reflexively to create good learning tasks, but, (b) design technology around a thorough understanding of learner activity.

The Merits of Indirection

It occurs to me that this shift to a somewhat more indirect form of design has parallels in other areas of the educational technologist's work. Table 1 helps explain what I mean.

Design component	To have an effect upon	Which situate	Leading to
Task	Activity		
Space	Place	Learning	Learning outcomes
Organisation	Community		

Table 1. Indirection and the problem space of the educational technologist.

One way of thinking about the educational technologist's problem space is that it has three main elements. We have already discussed tasks and activities. A second element is the technological infrastructure – or, more broadly, the learning environment. I shall take some time to unpick this a little further shortly. But for now I want to draw on a geographer's distinction between space and place. Space is abstract, but a 'place' is concrete and real. "Place" refers to all those attributes of a particular space that make it unique and that differentiate it from other places. There may be good reasons for allowing and perhaps encouraging learners to create their own 'learnplaces', configuring the physical resources available to them in ways they find most comfortable, efficient, supportive, congenial and convivial. But we can't expect them to create their learnplaces from nothing. So a second job for the educational technologist centers on the design of appropriate learning spaces: spaces which can become local habitations[2] for individual learners or for learning communities. Such spaces are the embryonic physical manifestation of the learning environment, in all its nested complexity. Some parts or sub-elements of the learning environment represent familiar challenges – the design and crafting of appropriate cognitive tools for example (Jonassen & Reeves, 1996; Lajoie & Derry, 1993). But others offer new and important challenges – such as the challenges of meshing micro-, meso- and macro- levels of a learning environment within a learning organisation, and working with the multidisciplinary teams responsible for managing and maintaining that learning environment.[3] [See Savenye's chapter for an example.]

---

[2] I take the phrase 'local habitations' from the work of Bonnie Nardi and Kathy O'Day; see Nardi & O'Day (1999).

[3] See Ford (1996) for an account of the complexities of learning environment design and management in a university situation.

It is worth spending a few more moments thinking about this issue of the (physical) learning environment, and especially about the strange transformations of space that are associated with the increasing use of digital network technologies. My emphasis on a user-centered, ergonomically alert, educational technology implies a need to attend to the relations between learners and their environment. What is this environment? For a long time, educational technology has tended to think of a 'learning environment' as a program running on a computer. This is far too restrictive a focus. If we want to design technologies that fit with real user/learner needs, then we must be alert to the broader settings and patterns of activity. Bonnie Nardi and Vicki O'Day (1999) put this very well:

> "The part we often focus our attention on is the technology: computers, networking, applications, handheld information gadgets, instruments, monitors, widgets ad infinitum. We look at the shape, color, texture, and functions of the technologies, and we think creatively about how to make them more usable, appealing, and effective. But it is in *the spaces between these things* - where people move from place to place, talk, carry pieces of paper, type, play messages, pick up the telephone, send faxes, have meetings, and go to lunch - that critical and often invisible things happen. As we look at information ecologies…we need to be mindful of those spaces." (p. 66).

Ethnographies of learning in higher education are beginning to show how a narrow focus on 'the technology' can blind us to much of what students' activity consists of and can mislead us badly about how to design supportive tasks and environments (Crook & Light, 1999; Jones, 1998). So we need to think about the broader physical setting for learners' activity in getting a sense of the space/place in which they work.

But what of the space 'within' their computer? Through the interface to their computer, learner/users also work in a cyberspace, which is populated by objects and people, or at least by representations of them. I will return to this space shortly, to talk a little about the architecture of online learning environments. The point I want to make now is that any plausible conception of 'learning environment' needs to find ways of acknowledging the fusion of physical and digital. 'Real' and 'virtual' don't stand in opposition. Each is part of the other.

The third area to which educational technologists need to find a response (Table 1) is connected with the growing wave of interest and enthusiasm for the social, collaborative or communal aspects of learning. We have some experience in the design of group learning tasks and facilitating group processes. But there are richer prizes to be won. A number of writers talk about building learning communities, (e.g., Riel & Levin, 1990; Wilbur, 1998). In our own work we have shown how ideas from just-in-time learning and the literature on communities of practice (Lave & Wenger, 1991; Wenger, 1998) can be combined to produce requirements for technology to 'build and sustain communities of practice' (Goodyear, 1995; Goodyear,

1996; Goodyear & Steeples, 1993). [The chapter by Marshall and Rossett also provides additional information on communities of practice]. But it may well be the case that communities cannot be artificially created or managed: they need their own dynamic, or organic structure and self-managing processes, if they are to thrive (Smith & Kollock, 1999). We could, however, aspire to help with more formal efforts: laying out frameworks for social organisation perhaps, or setting up and managing appropriate organisational structures within which learning communities stand a chance of functioning productively. Again, part of this work is familiar – we know about organisational forms like universities, courses, classes, seminar groups, etc. We know rather less about how learning communities prosper or are stifled or are stillborn within such organisational forms.

Table 1 tries to bring these elements together. It claims that community, activity and place are the important things, but that we may be wise to work on them indirectly, doing our knowledgeable best to create supportive organisational forms, well-crafted educational tasks and convivial learning spaces.

We are now rather weary of the contest between those who favour the symbolic over the situated, or vice versa. Knowledge can be both symbolic and situated: its acquisition needs to reflect this basic truth. Some knowledge is more readily shared in a declarative or propositional form. Other knowledge is embedded in practice and its tacit nature renders sharing through language rather awkward. Table 2 lists some of the many ways in which these apparently simple oppositions in accounts of knowledge are captured.

Knowledge	v	Skill
Knowing that	v	Knowing how
Understanding	v	Doing
Academic knowledge	v	Practical knowledge
Declarative knowledge	v	Procedural knowledge
Explicit (articulate) knowledge	v	Tacit knowledge
Discursive consciousness	v	Practical consciousness
Theory	v	Practice

Table 2. Recurring distinctions about knowledge.

The variety of terms underscores a simple recurrent theme - that people find a need to distinguish between forms or kinds of knowledge along a small number of dimensions (which are not orthogonal). There is value in making such distinctions, but I want to make two slightly different points: (1) that most instances of complex learning or complex behaviour involve constellations of different kinds/types of knowledge, (2) that some particularly interesting things happen at the intersections or interfaces. I only have space to develop one example of what I mean - which I shall do shortly in talking about the interaction of tacit and articulate knowledge in the context of creating what we call 'shareable representations of practice'.

Table 3 is based on another set of simple binary oppositions. It refers to the 'two worlds' of research and development on computer-mediated communications in education, pointing out that almost all R&D falls into the 'asynchronous text-based' or the 'synchronous multimedia' quadrants of the diagram. Note in passing that the 'asynchronous text-based' quadrant, which is the best explored by educational technologists, is much better aligned to the left hand items in Table 2 than to the right hand items. [See Jonassen's chapter for elaborations and examples of specific items in this table.]

	Synchronous	**Asynchronous**	Strengths	Weaknesses
Text-based	e.g. chat, IRC	e.g. email, CMC	encourages clarity of expression, formalisation of knowledge etc.; indexable, searchable; small data files	time-consuming to produce; hard to capture 'practices'; hard to eradicate or control ambiguity?
Multi-media	e.g. live video-conference	e.g. video-on-demand; video-mail	vivid; rich; allows 'showing' as well as 'telling'; can be easy and quick to produce and 'read'	hard to index & search; large data files
Strengths	supports interactive communication; timely; sense of event & audience	time to reflect; flexible use of time		
Weaknesses	inflexible use of time; may not scale up to large numbers	can be slow or cumbersome		

Table 3. Separate worlds of computer-mediated communications in education.

These two worlds of R&D have had surprisingly little to do with each other. On the one hand, we have the world of asynchronous text-based communication: e-mail, computer-mediated conferencing, etc. On the other hand, we have the world of synchronous multimedia communications: live audio-conferencing, live video-conferencing.

Multimedia communication, in principle, offers a number of benefits. It allows us to demonstrate and show, not just describe in an abstract way. It allows us to incorporate gesture, tone of voice and other cues that are not readily available in text-based communication. It offers richer and more vivid information transfer. For some purposes, people find it easier and quicker to speak than to write, so it can be more time-efficient for the 'sender'. There are not necessarily reciprocal benefits for the 'receiver'.

The use of multimedia communication in synchronous mode also has a number of benefits, such as the possibility of supporting a highly interactive discussion. But synchronicity also has some limitations. It gives little time for the communicating parties to think and reflect, to formulate thoughtful questions and answers. It demands that all the parties communicating should be available at the same time. It can be frustrating when used by large numbers: only a minority can contribute to the discussion; complicated protocols may be needed to support a smooth 'discussion' when it is distributed over a number of sites, etc.

One does not have to dismiss all the advantages of text-based communication and synchronous communication to see that there may be some advantages to the use of asynchronous multimedia communication (see Table 3). This is the starting point for work we have been doing at Lancaster, and elsewhere, through the EU-funded SHARP project (Goodyear & Steeples, 1998; Goodyear & Steeples, 1999). One of the purposes of SHARP is to experiment with ways of supporting members of a distributed community of practice in the activities which flow from a requirement to share, critique and improve each other's working practices. In my view, SHARP is important because it is opening up new ideas for educational technologists to try out, but also because it points a way forward for the kinds of distributed learning environment which we hope to be able to offer to our own MSc students in the next few years.

To be clear: SHARP encourages members of a geographically distributed community of practice to create shareable representations of their working practices through the medium of short digitised videoclips. These videoclips can then be annotated (with text, audio clips or further videoclips) to explain what might otherwise be incommunicable in the raw clip, to articulate tacit knowledge embedded in the practice, and to situate the practice in relation to the 'local habitation' as well as to theoretical ideas which the practitioners encounter in the course of their academic studies. Discourse within the SHARP environment creates a web of annotated multimedia objects, which over time constitutes a repository of reified practice, or an evolving knowledge base for the community (Goodyear, 1995; Wenger, 1998).

VIRTUAL LEARNING ENVIRONMENTS

What is striking about SHARP and similar experimental settings is the relative ease with which fragments of shared virtual learning environments can be set up, and the relative difficulty of creating integrated shared virtual learning environments in which a reasonable range of activities can take place. SHARP is customised to asynchronous use. It has no facilities for synchronous interaction. It is not much good for sharing complex textual objects; so shared writing tasks, or even the critique of other people's writing, is not well supported. Similar remarks can be made about other virtual learning environments. I am aware of none in which it is possible to move seamlessly between synchronous and asynchronous interaction, or to work collaboratively on shared documents and artefacts in both synchronous and asynchronous ways. Among the major challenges for educational technology in the next few years is the specification of requirements and the prototyping and testing of these more open environments. Progress is being made in mainstream areas of technology: in VR and CSCW for example. And some indications of what early (and rather primitive) shared desktop virtual environments may be like can be found in places like Active Worlds (http://www.activeworlds.com) and the blaxxun Online communities (http://www.blaxxun.de).

Figure 1 shows a screenshot from the Contact Consortium's 'architectural competition' for a virtual university (see http://www.ccon.org/).

Figure 1. An early example of a shared virtual learning space (Contact Consortium's 'TheU').

While the interaction and architecture of such environments may be rudimentary, it is worth noting that: (a) we had no conception at all of this kind of technological possibility when we began our Masters programme ten years ago; (b) the pace of change is such that we can reasonably predict creating and using workable versions of such environments within the next three to five years; and, (c) these environments do, in principle, offer possibilities for the seamless transition between the different forms of interaction that I described in the previous section. They are, in principle, places in which live interaction can take place and in which communal repositories of knowledge, reified practice, etc. can be accumulated and used.

ARCHITECTURAL PRACTICE AND VIRTUAL LEARNING ENVIRONMENTS

But what would be our knowledge base for creating convivial on-line learning spaces? As a thought experiment, consider the analogy with architecture.

The Architectural Analogy

One does not need to be a fan of all architecture to see that architects have ways of solving interesting problems. Analogies with architectural practice are not unfamiliar in educational technology. Charles Reigeluth(1983), for example, talked of the instructional designer creating blueprints for instruction. Peter Pirolli (1991) has drawn parallels between computer-aided instructional design in the 1980's and the architectural revolution brought about by the publication of Leo Battista Alberti's *On the art of building in ten books*. Pirolli's analysis (1991, pp. 106-7) is intriguing for a number of reasons. He finds in Alberti's work an important and innovative combination of contributions:

- A re-analysis of ancient writings (in particular, those of the Roman engineer Vitruvius Pollio)
- The extraction of design principles from the classical Roman architecture that he observed throughout Italy
- The formulation of a theoretical basis for the practices of Brunelleschi and other contemporary builders at the start of the Italian Renaissance.

"Alberti's framework was both *systematic and generative* and, more than any other work, was probably responsible for the rapid spread and evolution of Renaissance architecture...thus past history illustrates the importance of abstracting, systematising and disseminating principles of design" (Pirolli, 1991, pp. 106-7, emphasis added).

We can track the growing influence of architectural ideas and practices in a number of places:

1. In software design, Mitchell Kapor's famous manifesto draws on Vitruvius's notion that well designed buildings exhibit qualities of 'firmness, commodity and delight'. He uses these abstractions as the starting points for a theory of software design (Kapor, 1996) (see also Winograd & Tabor, 1996).
2. In the strengthening interactions between VR and architecture - whether the use of VR to design real buildings, or the use of architectural principles to create new virtual spaces (Bertol, 1997; Weisher, 1998).
3. In the emerging digital arts and crafts, and in accounts of the aesthetics and sociology of cyberspace (Holtzman, 1994; McCullough, 1996; Smith & Kollock, 1999).
4. In considerations of virtual space as an organiser of social activity (Anders, 1999; Hillier, 1999; Hillier & Hanson, 1989).

Interestingly, architects themselves may be in the vanguard of applying architectural principles and skills to the design of online learning environments. A good case in point is the work of Anna Cicognani, until recently at the Faculty of Architecture, University of Sydney (Cicognani, 2000). Cicognani takes an architectural perspective on the key design elements that need to be treated in creating an online learning environment:

- Quantitative relationships between information and layers of access
- Organisation of the space into areas of similar functionality
- Possibility of contact and of isolating oneself from others
- Level of user engagement in the design of the space
- User ownership of the space
- Comfort in inhabiting the place (moving around, participating in activities, etc)
- Possibility of transforming and evolving the space for emergent collective purposes

Cicognani (2000) applies these elements to two contrasting case studies, one educational (a virtual classroom) the other from retail finance (a virtual bank) (the Faculty of Architecture's virtual campus can itself be explored at http://moo.arch.usyd.edu.au:7778/).

What appeals to me particularly about architecture as a source of ideas for creating convivial, productive on-line learning spaces is that architecture is about the *crafting of affordances*. Architecture (built space) does not *determine* activity. Bad architecture endangers some kinds of valued activity. Good architecture can nurture it. But the users of built space have proper scope for autonomy.

In addition, I like the way architecture involves a 'reflective conversation with materials'. Good designs emerge through a dialectic between intention and the constraints and affordances of the material. Part-finished and finished designs are available for others to scrutinise and learn from. And we can now draw *directly* upon Donald Schon's intimate understanding of the proper education of architects, in thinking about how to train educational technologists (Schon, 1984; Schon & Bennett, 1996). I think this opens up exciting opportunities for aspects of educational technology training to move closer to being a 'studio subject', in which we can imagine richer forms of discussion that connect evolving artefacts and the abstractions of pedagogy, space and social organisation.

SUMMARY

Current consideration of the working practices and training of educational technologists needs to be informed by due recognition of the increasing salience of lifelong learning and of its accompanying requirement for people to act as autonomous learners. Such thinking also needs to reflect the growing importance of autonomous activity within learning communities, and the growing use of the Internet to create virtual environments for learning communities. If we look at how the relatively autonomous learners to be found in areas of Western higher education are making use of, and ignoring, different kinds of technology, then we may conclude that the practice of educational technology needs to be sensitised to the real needs (and activities) of such learners, rather than relying on official accounts of learners' requirements or of what learners should be doing (the tasks they are given). If this is true in higher education, how much more powerful are the consequences when we consider the much more 'open' world of informal lifelong learning beyond the university level?

To operate in this more open world, I suggest that we need to consider more indirect forms of design. The quality of learnplaces, the conviviality of learning communities, the richness of learning activities: these are key. But we may be mistaken in believing that we can work on these things directly. The practice of architecture offers one source of inspiration for novel and more indirect approaches to design. It may well have a special relevance when we are considering new areas for the application of digital arts and crafts, and when we are considering the affordances of virtual spaces for lifelong learning. With regard to preparing future educational technologists, we should integrate examples of learnplaces and learning communities into their training and offer them opportunities to design their own.

REFERENCES

Anders, P. (1999). *Envisioning cyberspace: Designing 3D electronic spaces*. New York: McGraw Hill.

Anderson, J., Reder, L., & Simon, H. (1996). Situated learning and education. *Educational Researcher, 25*(4), 5-11.

Andrews, D., Waag, W., & Bell, H. (1992). Training technologies applied to team training: military examples. In R. Swezey & E. Salas (Eds.), *Teams: Their training and performance* (pp. 283-328). Norwood New Jersey: Ablex Publishing Corporation.

Bertol, D. (1997). *Designing digital space: An architect's guide to virtual reality*. New York: John Wiley.

Biggs, J. (1999). *Teaching for quality learning at university: What the student does*. Buckingham: Open University Press.

Brown, J. C. A., & Duguid, P. (1989). Situated cognition and the culture of learning. *Educational Researcher, 18*, 32-42.

Cicognani, A. (2000). Architectural Design for Online Environments. In B. Kolko (Ed.), *Virtual Commons: Policy and Community in an Electronic Age* . New York: Columbia University Press.

Crook, C., & Light, P. (1999). Information technology and the culture of student learning. In J. Bliss, R. Saljo, & P. Light (Eds.), *Learning sites: social and technological resources for learning* (pp. 183-193). Oxford: Pergamon.

Dearing, R. (1997). *Report of the national committee of inquiry into higher education*. Middlesex, UK: NCIHE (http://www.leeds.ac.uk/educol/ncihe/).

Duffy, T., & Jonassen, D. (Eds.). (1992). *Constructivism and the technology of instruction*. Hillsdale New Jersey: Lawrence Erlbaum Associates.

Entwistle, N. (1996). Recent research on student learning and the learning environment,. In J. Tait & P. Knight (Eds.), *The management of independent learning* (pp. 97-112). London: Kogan Page.

Flowers, S. (1996). *Software failure*. London: Wiley.

Ford, P., Goodyear, P., Heseltine, R, Lewis, R., Darby, J., Graves, J., Sartorius, P., Harwood, D., & King, T. (1996). *Managing change in higher education: a learning environment architecture*. Buckingham: Open University Press.

Gaddy, C., & Wachtel, J. (1992). Team skills training in nuclear power plant operations. In R. Swezey & E. Salas (Eds.), *Teams: Their training and performance* (pp. 379-396). Norwood New Jersey: Ablex Publishing Corporation.

Goodyear, P. (1995). Situated action and distributed knowledge: A JITOL perspective on electronic performance support systems. *Educational and Training Technology International, 32*(1), 45-55.

Goodyear, P. (1996). Asynchronous peer interaction in distance education: The evolution of goals practices and technology. *Training Research Journal, 1*, 71-102.

Goodyear, P. (1999). Educational technology, virtual learning environments and architectural practice. In D. Ely, L. Odenthal, & T. Plomp (Eds.), *Educational science and technology: perspectives for the future* (pp. 74-91). Enschede: Twente University Press.

Goodyear, P., & Steeples, C. (1993). Computer-mediated communication in the professional development of workers in the advanced learning technologies industry. In J. Eccleston, B. Barta, & R. Hambusch (Eds.), *The computer-mediated education of information technology professionals and advanced end-users* (pp. 239-247). Amsterdam: Elsevier.

Goodyear, P., & Steeples, C. (1998). Creating shareable representations of practice. *Association for Learning Technology Journal, 6*(3), 16-23.

Goodyear, P., & Steeples, C. (1999). Asynchronous multimedia conferencing in continuing professional development: issues in the representation of practice through user-created videoclips. *Distance Education*.

Greeno, J. (1997). On claims that answer the wrong question. *Educational Researcher, 26*(1), 5-17.

Hillier, B. (1999). *Space is the machine: A configurational theory of architecture.* Cambridge: Cambridge University Press.

Hillier, B., & Hanson, J. (1989). *The social logic of space.* Cambridge: Cambridge University Press.

Holtzman, S. (1994). *Digital mantras: The languages of abstract and virtual worlds.* Cambridge Mass: MIT Press.

Jonassen, D., & Reeves, T. (1996). Learning *with* technology: Using computers as cognitive tools. In D. Jonassen (Ed.), *Handbook of research for educational communications and technology* (pp. 693-719). New York: Macmillan.

Jones, C. (1998). *Context, content and cooperation: An ethnographic study of collaborative learning online.* Unpublished PhD, Manchester Metropolitan University, Manchester.

Kapor, M. (1996). A software design manifesto. In T. Winograd (Ed.), *Bringing design to software* (pp. 1-9). New York: Addison Wesley.

Kirshner, D., & Whitson, J. (1998). Obstacles to understanding cognition as situated. *Educational Researcher, 27*(8), 22-8.

Lajoie, S., & Derry, S. (Eds.). (1993). *Computers as cognitive tools.* Hillsdale New Jersey: Lawrence Erlbaum Associates.

Latour, B. (1995). Mixing humans and nonhumans together: the sociology of a door-closer. In S. L. Star (Ed.), *Ecologies of knowledge* . New York: State University of New York Press.

Lave, J., & Wenger, E. (1991). *Situated learning: Legitimate peripheral participation.* Cambridge: Cambridge University Press.

Marton, F., Hounsell, D., & Entwistle, N. (Eds.). (1997). *The experience of learning* (2nd ed.). Edinburgh: Scottish Academic Press.

McCullough, M. (1996). *Abstracting craft: The practiced digital hand.* Cambridge Mass: MIT Press.

Nardi, B., & O'Day, V. (1999). *Information ecologies: Using technology with heart.* Cambridge Mass: MIT Press.

Pirolli, P. (1991). Computer-aided instructional design systems. In H. Burns, J. Parlett, & C. Redfield (Eds.), *Intelligent Tutoring Systems: Evolution in Design* (pp. 105-125). Hillsdale New Jersey: Lawrence Erlbaum Associates.

Prince, C., Chidester, T., Bowers, C., & Cannon-Bowers, J. (1992). Aircrew coordination - achieving teamwork in the cockpit. In R. Swezey & E. Salas (Eds.), *Teams: Their training and performance* (pp. 329-354). Norwood New Jersey: Ablex Publishing Corporation.

Reigeluth, C. (Ed.). (1983). *Instructional design theories and models.* Hillsdale New Jersey: Lawrence Erlbaum Associates.

Riel, M. M., & Levin, J. A. (1990). Building electronic communities: success and failure in computer networking. *Instructional Science, 19,* 145-169.

Schon, D. (1984). The architectural studio as an example of education for reflection-in-action. *Journal of Architectural Education, 38,* 2-9.

Schon, D., & Bennett, J. (1996). Reflective conversation with materials. In T. Winograd (Ed.), *Bringing design to software* (pp. 171-184). New York: Addison Wesley.

Smith, M., & Kollock, P. (Eds.). (1999). *Communities in cyberspace.* London: Routledge.

Ward, G. (1988). *High-risk training: managing training programs for high risk occupations.* London: Kogan Page.

Weisher, P. (1998). *Digital space: Designing virtual environments.* New York: McGraw Hill.

Wenger, E. (1998). *Communities of practice.* Cambridge: Cambridge University Press.

Wilbur, S. (1998). Creating a community of learning using web-based tools. In R. Hazemi, S. Hailes, & S. Wilbur (Eds.), *The digital university: Reinventing the academy* (pp. 73-84). London: Springer.

Wilson, B. (Ed.). (1996). *Constructivist learning environments.* Englewood Cliffs NJ: Educational Technology Press.

Winograd, T., & Tabor, P. (1996). Software design and architecture. In T. Winograd (Ed.), *Bringing design to software* (pp. 10-16). New York: Addison Wesley.

Wisner, A. (1995a). Situated cognition and action: Implications for ergonomic work analysis and anthropotechnology. *Ergonomics, 38*(8), 1542-57.

Wisner, A. (1995b). Understanding problem building: Ergonomic work analysis. *Ergonomics, 38*(3), 595-605.

TABLE OF ABBREVIATIONS

CBT	Computer-Based Training
CSCW	Computer Supported Collaborative Work
ICT	Information and Communications Technology
SHARP	Shareable Representations of Practice
VR	Virtual Reality

ACKNOWLEDGEMENTS

This chapter is a revised and extended version of an invited presentation I gave at the 20th anniversary celebrations of the Faculty of Educational Science and Technology (TO) at the University of Twente, Netherlands in the summer of 1999 (Goodyear, 1999). I would like to thanks friends and colleagues in TO as well as Mike Spector, Norbert Seel and the other participants in the symposium at Bergen for their support and suggestions. I would also like to acknowledge the intellectual contributions of fellow members of the SHARP project team, and the funding of the EU Socrates Open and Distance Learning programme.

JAMES MARSHALL and ALLISON ROSSETT

Chapter 2

KNOWLEDGE MANAGEMENT FOR SCHOOL-BASED EDUCATORS

Keywords: anticipated reciprocity, communities of practice, knowledge management

Abstract. The transition of the workforce from brawn-power to brain-power has prompted organizations to focus on the knowledge created by employees, managers and customers. Knowledge Management (KM) involves recognizing, documenting, and distributing the explicit and tacit knowledge resident in an organization. The Internet can facilitate knowledge sharing communities, support the exchange of tools and resources, and provide new forms of collaborative partnerships. Organizations have already achieved significant performance improvements through KM initiatives. Can educators reap similar rewards? This chapter presents possibilities for knowledge sharing between K–12 educators through exploration of both the content and community dynamics that lie at the heart of knowledge management. Although the ultimate role knowledge management will play in education defies prediction, we identify current trends, key issues, and barriers – real and anticipated – associated with managing knowledge in education settings.

INTRODUCTION

Technology today enables countless interactions between far-flung people. Electronic mail, the World Wide Web, electronic databases, and online discussion groups provide opportunities for communication, argument, friendship, romance, and knowledge sharing and acquisition.

One emerging form of electronic support for distance collaboration is technology-mediated communities of practice. Bassi (1997) defines a community of practice as a network of people who work together and who regularly share information and knowledge. These communities are often self-formed by individuals holding complementary knowledge – knowledge that may be as diverse as information and tools for the teaching of math to resistant youngsters and the secrets and successes for breeding championship West Highland White Terriers. Organizationally speaking, Davenport and Prusak (1998) suggest:

19

J.M. Spector and T.M. Anderson (eds.),
Integrated and Holistic Perspectives on Learning, Instruction and Technology, 19–34.
© 2000 *Kluwer Academic Publishers. Printed in the Netherlands.*

"self-organized groups are generally initiated by employees who communicate
with one another because they share common work practices, interests, or
aims. If their communications prove useful over time, they may formalize the
arrangement, give themselves a group name and establish a regular system of
interchange" (p. 38-39).

Increased access to information and documented knowledge is already
affecting business and government organizations. Knowledge sharing
practices, including the capture of best practices and dynamic online
communities, linked to an organization's core competencies and strategic
mission, are a key component of contemporary successful businesses,
particularly when the business involves knowledge services.

In 1996, there were at least six major international conferences focusing
on knowledge management. The non-profit Knowledge Management
Consortium was founded in 1997 to promote practical, measurable
applications of knowledge management (KM) to business and other
organizations. *Knowledge Management*, a trade publication introduced in
1998, is distributed in print and on the web (see *www.kmmag.com*). The
BixTech Network web site (see *www.brint.com*) is an enthusiastic,
overgrown and rich KM resource. The *iqport* web site (see *www.iqport.com*)
provided an experimental online marketplace where anyone could broker
their own business-related knowledge for sale to other knowledge-seeking
individuals. [See the 1999 Special Issue of the Journal of Organizational
Computing and Electronic Commerce for additional views and resources.]

Excitement about Knowledge Management

The first reason for excitement about knowledge management involves
the knowledge era itself. Peter Drucker (1994) notes that knowledge is no
longer just one more resource in a list that includes labor, capital, and land.
In the information age, knowledge has become *the* resource and the
"knowledge worker" the organization's single greatest asset. The second
reason is that knowledge management is beginning to happen to the intrigue
of leaders across settings, disciplines and geographic barriers and
boundaries.

- The World Bank counts knowledge management as an "urgent
  necessity" for global development, and is spearheading knowledge-
  management initiatives in third world countries (Lakewood
  Publications, 1998).
- IBM's business strategy is replete with KM perspectives,
  emphasizing shared lessons, re-purposed efforts and collaboration
  across the globe.

- Andersen Consulting has leveraged the knowledge of their worldwide workforce through Knowledge Xchange.

A final reason for the burgeoning interest in KM is that it makes sense, although that sense is sometimes more obvious to executives than to the rank and file. While those in favor of KM applaud the idea of capturing the knowledge that resides within people in the organization, not all employees view it with the same enthusiasm.

KM for Schools

An increasing number of schools and educators are finding their way to the Information Highway. The classroom Internet connection is typically used to encourage student exploration, provide access to information, and apply knowledge from diverse sources (Jonassen, Peck & Wilson, 1999). However, use of the Internet for teacher development and community-building still receives spotty though growing, attention.

Watts and Castle (1992) suggest that teachers generally "lack opportunities to share their thinking and to construct new knowledge about their teaching practice" (p. 686). The Internet has the potential to change that; it can link teachers across space and time, facilitate knowledge sharing communities, support the exchange of tools and resources, and provide new forms of collaborative partnerships. Given such an opportunity, would school educators share knowledge, best practices, and experiences through web-based communities of practice? Would educators freely donate the fruits of their labor in the form of lesson plans, activities, and curriculum for the benefit of their fellow colleagues across the country and around the world?

This paper explores these questions by defining the content and community dynamics at the heart of knowledge management and highlighting rich examples from schools and higher education institutions. Although the ultimate role knowledge management will play in education defies prediction, we identify current trends, key issues, and barriers – real and anticipated – associated with managing knowledge in education settings. We also share rich examples.

DYNAMICS OF THE KNOWLEDGE COMMUNITY

While some businesses are already engaged in systematic knowledge management efforts, initiating knowledge management in any organization is a challenge. Research conducted by The American Productivity & Quality Center (APQC) revealed that specific successful practices would typically linger in a company for years, unrecognized and unshared (O'Dell & Grayson, 1998). However, even when recognized, Szulanski (1995) estimates that it takes over two years on average before other sites within a company began to actively adopt the practice, if at all.

Schools provide perhaps an even greater challenge than businesses. To plant and nurture the collaboration that knowledge management promises, attention to the dynamics of the knowledge community is critical. Ensuring access to information, fostering a culture of sharing, enabling exchange of information, support and resources through technology, and prioritizing exactly what knowledge is to be managed all contribute to the success of a knowledge management initiative.

Access to Information

According to Stewart (1997b), it is critical to "connect people to data, experts, and expertise" when they perceive a need (p. 132). The 21st Century Teachers Network (see *www.21ct.org*) attempts to do just that. It profiles each member of its online community, including K–12 educators, university professors, educational technology professionals, and commercial resource providers. Members of the online community can use this directory to identify and access individuals with complementary knowledge at the time of need (see Figure 1).

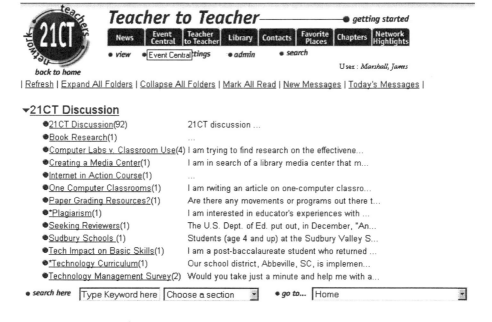

Figure 1. 21st Century Teachers Network Discussion List (www. 21ct.org).

The University of Toronto provides an illustration of another application of technology to community building in higher education. As student teachers enter the classroom for the first time, specific issues, needs, and questions arise. To meet these needs, the University of Toronto established an online community of inquiry for pre-service teachers. The learning environment promotes a sense of community through small group discussions, workshops on cooperative learning techniques, and access to shared electronic databases including frequently asked questions and frequently encountered situations (Brett, 1997).

While providing rich resources and information is critical, there is such a thing as too much of a good thing. For example, given the World Wide Web as a resource, many teachers become awestruck as they attempt to find the proverbial needle (instructional resource) in a haystack (the Internet). Enter much needed knowledge-sharing opportunities such as Blue Web'n (see *www.kn.pacbell.com/wired/bluewebn*). This searchable database of outstanding Internet learning sites has been reviewed by educators and categorized by content, audience, and type (lessons, activities, projects, resources, references, & tools) to provide proven classroom resources for the teacher who is attempting to integrate the Internet into an instructional strategy.

Developing a Culture of Sharing

While profit is not often the motive, prestige and merit may influence how educators feel about giving away for free that which they have come to perceive as their own valuable possession or that which distinguishes them from their peers.

In the online community, the "donator" of information might never know the benefit of his or her contribution, given the potentially large number, and anonymity of, community recipients. Kollock (1999) and Rheingold (1993) suggest the following factors may influence an individual's motivation to contribute to the community:

- Anticipated reciprocity–the possibility of receiving useful help and information in return.
- Enhanced reputation–the chance that one's contributions will effect, ideally elevate, one's reputation within the online community.
- Self-efficacy–a sense that one has some effect on the online community environment.
- Group attachment–a sense of commitment and attachment to the online community.

Are educators in unique need of a systematic approach to encouraging participation? Is hoarding knowledge a particular problem in the school setting? Zimmerman and Greene (1998) admit that encouraging teacher participation in such communities of practice is a challenge; "There may be little incentive for expert teachers to publicly reflect about teaching on a listserv" (p. 1138). Bull and colleagues (1989) believe that benefits must "accrue to users from the public schools if use of the network is to flourish" (p. 27). Sadly, examples of situations where such benefits are commonplace are difficult to find. Rather, it is systems that encourage the opposite behaviors that appear to thrive.

A third-grade educator tells of the culture within her school where attention focused on one particular teacher who is repeatedly held up by the principal as the "star" of the school. This teacher rarely shares resources or instructional materials, let alone casual conversation, with the other staff. In her perception, knowledge is power and therefore she chooses to hoard. The school culture supports, in fact reinforces, this distinction between the teacher who knows and others. This account shows that flawed incentives for sharing are not the exclusive property of the business sector.

Another knowledge-limiting occurrence is the lack of a forum in which knowledge sharing individuals can congregate (Davenport & Prusak, 1998; Stewart, 1998). These authors suggest that venues such as the water cooler and office hallway have historically provided effective forums for knowledge exchange. Opportunities for educators to break the boundaries of their classroom, school, or district and interact with individuals possessing complementary knowledge–their community of practice–are rare. McMahon (1997) asserts that conventional in-service events are inadequate because they "rely on one-shot lecture-style formats that transmit knowledge and skills rather than creating experiences where teachers construct new understandings" (p. 1). Merseth (1992) quotes a novice teacher regarding lack of community and collaboration in the school environment:

> "Teachers are nice and everything, but they do not talk. If you happen to have a free period with someone, sometimes you can talk, but usually you have things to do – and after school everyone leaves A.S.A.P. (except me and about three others). I guess the atmosphere would be even more supportive if we talked more–but the system is not set up in a way to foster this" (p. 682).

Too often, professional development is a "patchwork affair: in inservice day here, and occasional workshop there" (Bull, 1994, p. x). Effective professional development "needs to be a collaborative effort" which breaks the isolation of the classroom and encourages interaction and community (Bull, 1994, p. 26). Davenport and Prusak (1998) concur that instructor-led situations are not venues where knowledge sharing occurs. Optimal knowledge exchange flows through communities of practice within the organization or profession. "Within these webs, people ask each other who knows what, who has previously provided knowledge that turned out to be reliable and useful" (p. 37). Many of the accomplishments can be attributed to people "continually ask[ing] one another who knows how to do things" (p. 37).

According to O'Dell and Grayson (1998), in an open culture that encourages sharing and collaboration, knowledge management will succeed as soon as structural barriers are eliminated and enablers such as technology and facilitators are provided. What about an organization where another culture exists? "If your company's nature is to hoard knowledge, then the best and greatest knowledge management application may not be enough to alter your employees' behavior" (O'Dell & Grayson, 1998, p. 71-72).

Enabling Technologies

Technology is critical to knowledge management, but not sufficient. Daveport and Prusak (1998) put it like this, "It's usually much harder to get organizational consensus for behavior change and new roles than it is for technology, and if you start with technology, the other necessary factors may never materialize" (p. 166).

Although technology can make connections possible, the promise is typically more potent than the reality. The potential of technology to foster a culture of sharing and collaboration is the "over arching goal of many online initiatives" targeted to teacher professional development. However not enough is known about the factors which enhance or deter such relationships from forming (McMahon, 1997, p. 1).

Many teachers already feel isolated, spending the majority of the time in the classroom, with little opportunity to collaborate with peers (McMahon, 1997). To draw teachers into the resources and community KM promises, systems must provide content that will rivet them, answers to problems that vex them, and many opportunities to make their interactions meaningful and personal.

Knowledge Management Priority

Successful knowledge management begins with decisions about what knowledge is worth managing. Davenport and Prusak (1998) suggest that organizations start with high-value knowledge, such as a recognized business problem that relates to knowledge and links to the larger organizational strategy. The University of Toronto focused its KM strategy on an increasingly familiar situation experienced by Teacher Education institutions around the world. The University began with the premise that student teachers entering the classroom for the first time were in need of specific, unique support and that such support would need to be provided at a distance, since teachers were geographically dispersed during student teaching. Faculty wisely elected to avoid remediating or presenting standard course content online. The faculty decided instead to use the power of a collaborative online community to support novice teachers.

One participant demonstrated the value of this community of practice:

> "Perhaps one way we can make everyone feel [like] legitimate participants is to actively encourage peer tutoring and praise... I have a safe, secure environment in which to say 'Stop-I don't understand.' Everyone takes some responsibility in trying to help the struggling member. I feel we cooperate well" (Brett, 1997, p. 26).

The Toronto KM system, targeted both to the typical needs of a first semester student teacher and the unique experiences encountered by each community member, provided a rich forum for support. Additionally, the system has grown over time, as new teachers peruse past experiences, exploring and contributing to the lessons left behind by prior pre-service teachers. Professors can also examine the entries in order to anticipate better the needs of aspiring teachers.

TECHNOLOGY, TEACHERS, AND KNOWLEDGE MANAGEMENT

Typically, knowledge management systems are composed of two complementary parts: one technical, the other social. The technical side seeks to capture, package, and distribute tangible, documented products. According to Horton (1999), this half of the system attempts "to contain a massive amount of information, organize it logically, and make it accessible to the right people, on time."

The social side of the system enables collaboration, connection, and reflection among system users. This is frequently accomplished through shared databases, listserves and chatrooms. A well-establish Harvard program (Merseth, 1992) presents an application of KM as a professional resource for preservice teachers facing the challenges of flying solo in their first teaching assignment. The electronic bulletin board-based support system, Beginning Teacher Computer Network (BCTN), was initiated at Harvard Graduate School of Education in 1987. It provides a forum for encouragement, support, and growth opportunities for first-year teachers by linking graduates of the Harvard teacher education program in their first year of teaching in schools across the United States. Participants use the computer network to "ask questions of one another, share stories of triumphs and failures, seek advice, and offer ideas, reactions, and suggestions" (p. 679).

Exchanges are vivid and diverse, ranging from requests for curricular information to debates about current reform efforts to the broader purposes of education. A typical exchange involved a first year teacher who became disenchanted with the profession following her first semester in the classroom. She openly presented both her situation and her guilt. The other first-year teachers and faculty members responded quickly, resulting in fresh perspectives, support, and praise for the troubled teacher, assuring her that she was not alone in her doubts. One first-year teacher wrote, "Participants like me must reflect on personal experiences and ideas in order to put them in written form, a process that in itself can offer fresh insight into a problem" (Merseth, 1992, p. 680).

Many teacher educators have expressed enthusiasm about the potential for pre- and in-service online education (Breuleux, Laferriere & Bracewell, 1998; Davis, 1998; Riedl & Carroll, 1993; Struck & Fowler-Frey, 1996). While Bates (1995) notes the ready availability of information and resources, Bronack and Kilbane (1998) are intrigued by the current technologies as a "social medium for enabling effective decision making," rather than the historical role as a productivity tool (p. 1191).

Given an online community that is replete with both hard content resources and opportunities for collaboration through discussion and chat, teachers appear to gravitate towards the collaborative and community aspects (Bronack & Kilbance, 1998; Merseth, 1992; Strunk & Fowler-Frey, 1996). These studies found that teachers typically find the connections made with other users, and the resulting support, the most beneficial aspects of their participation in an online community.

Finding Community

Referring to technology infusion in teacher education programs, Davis (1998) remarks that "[b]est practice is being established in a distributed and growing network of higher education institutions and partner schools that will welcome opportunities to assist in the growth of community through discussion and demonstration" (p. 1148). Several examples support Davis' optimism regarding the convergence of teacher education and community building.

TENET

Anderson and Harris (1995) found that community was the critical variable influencing system use on TENET, a statewide educational telecomputing network in Texas. The more individuals were integrated into the online community and the more contacts they could make via the network, the more regular the educator's usage of the system. The extent to which the network users were able to access sought after information and participate in online discussions was of secondary influence when predicting usage. The strong correlation between the number of potential contacts to be made through the system and frequency of system usage illustrates the importance of the social side of knowledge management. McMahon (1997) states that the:

> "proponents of network-based professional development claim that it offers a viable solution to the challenge of providing large numbers of teachers the support they need to develop content expertise and to put new instructional strategies into practice" (p. 1).

A 1990 survey of 550 technology-using educators suggests that for technology-advanced teachers this may be true. The study found that sending e-mail to colleagues, exchanging information on forums and bulletin boards, and accessing databases containing information relevant to students were the most widely used and effective professional development activities enabled through technology. Perceived incentives for using telecommunications as a professional resource included communicating with other educators, accessing information, and combating professional isolation (Honey & Henriquez, 1993).

ESL Online Action Research Project

Pennsylvania's Lancaster Lebanon Intermediate Unit 13 (IU 13) established an ESL (English as a Second Language) Online Action Research Project that used telecommunications for communication between faculty and teacher participants (Strunk & Fowler-Frey, 1996). Each participant was an ESL educator conducting his or her first "action research" project. Action research provides a framework for qualitative investigation by teachers and researchers in complex working classroom situations where all individuals involved in the study are knowing and contributing participants (Hopkins, 1993).

The primary project goal was for participants to realize the benefit of action research as an evaluative tool by doing it themselves, with the support of a professor. The project developed community among practitioners and higher educators, exposing all to a wealth of information and giving them a systematic way to examine their practices, and then to share their perspectives with one another.

The participants and instructors employed online chat sessions, electronic bulletin boards, and electronic mail. Though initially lacking technology expertise, the ten participants overcame their fears and used the technology to support realization of project expectations. One participant noted:

> "I've definitely increased my confidence with using technology. I haven't had as much time as I would like to explore the Internet. However, in my brief browsing I have found a lot of information material; the potential is truly amazing" (p. 31).

This perspective was seconded by six of the ten participants.

Interestingly, participants most often identified the collaborative, social aspects as their favorite project component. "I found my experience with my partner to be the most positive part of the project," (p. 27) and "I feel that I have made a new friend and have enjoyed communicating with her throughout the project. I find that the sharing of ideas greatly facilitates the research process" (p. 26).

Strunk & Fowler-Frey (1996) also highlight the social and connective aspects of the project. In two cases, such support prevented teachers from leaving the project. Participants expressed desire to remain in contact with one another after the project. Obviously, the power of the approach is realized in the interaction between the content and social sides of the project. The content side supports direct learning through the basic action research assignment and subsequent access to resource; the social side enables learning through reflection and the shared experiences of the community.

Dave's ESL Café

Dave's ESL Café (see *www.eslcafe.com*) provides an example of KM's two faces. The Café provides 2,793 ESL-related resources to teachers of English language learners and students learning English as a new language (see Figure 2). The site balances both halves of the KM equation through diverse offerings, from lesson plans and quizzes on the content side, to teacher and student discussion groups on the social side.

As content, the *Idea Cookbook* features 416 "recipes" in 23 different categories comprised of ideas for use in the ESL classroom. Ideas range from how to teach grammar to improving yourself as an ESL teacher. The *Quiz Center* presents 44 quizzes geared to individuals learning English as a Second Language. Grammatical quizzes are most plentiful, followed by

Geography and Science. The *Web Guide* provides links, organized by topic, to over 100 different websites of interest to ESL teachers and students. Site synopses allow teachers to quickly identify sites which are appropriate for their specific needs.

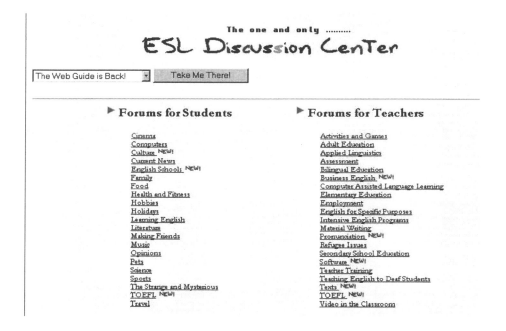

Figure 2. Dave's ESL Café Forums List (www.eslcafe.com).

Resources that support the building of social networks include the Café's address book, which links the community together by recording the name, email, and website address of each Café member. Individuals are registered as a student, teacher, school, or publisher and the address book can be searched by name. ESL Chat Central provides a forum for chat between Café visitors. An interesting approach to the chat feature surrounds the rule presented on opening page: "Please speak ONLY in English!" The site administrator explains the purpose of the rule is to encourage communication among all visitors in a common language and support their developing proficiency in English.

The ESL Discussion Center features discussion boards for both teachers and students. Student topics tend to be general, including health and fitness, travel, or food.

CASENET

CASENET (Bronack & Kilbance, 1998) at the University of Virginia is another example of KM applied to teacher education. This web-based learning environment allows teachers to use the latest technologies to form communities of practice. CASENET focuses on honing educational decision-making skills through "slice-of-life" cases. Occasional face-to-face meetings throughout the semester are bolstered by realistic, school-based cases, discussion groups, journals, and reference materials that occur online.

Instructors believe that the value of CASENET lies in the successful integration of teacher development, the Web, and case methodology. The Web allows for high levels of interaction, unhindered by space or time boundaries. It provides an environment through which multimedia cases can be realistic, providing high face validity to the learner (Herbert & McNergney, 1995). CASENET mirrors the real world through combinations of text, video, and sound.

Yet even in this rich multimedia environment, many participants still placed primary value on the interactive, community-building components of the system. One student's impression follows:

> "The most valuable part of the course is the interaction with preservice and other inservice teachers. Our class discussions and online chats provided the most stimulating experiences. And it is such an eye-opener for preservice teachers and equally educational for inservice teachers to 'see' the different way each of us views a classroom situation" (Bronack & Kilbane, 1998, p. 1194).

EdMAP

KM can also capture the interest of individuals at the district level, especially those charged with disseminating effective practices across the district while holding educators accountable to the required curriculum standards. Computer Curriculum Corporation's new product, EdMAP, has the potential to spread both best practices and adherence to requirements (see *www.ccclearn.com/tools/edmap/index.html*).

EdMAP is a large scale, enterprise-wide database specifically designed for the development and management of instruction and assessment within a school district. Its purpose is to create an environment where teachers throughout a district can plan instruction, collaborate, access resources, and share best practices in instruction. EdMAP's tools include databases of national and state standards, local objectives, model units of instruction and assessment, as well presentation of a district's resources, such as library books, software, or even web sites. A messaging system allows teachers to send their units of instruction to peers electronically across the district. Administrators and teachers collaborate by setting up groups for planning and evaluating lessons, units, and resources. Web-based discussion forums, where educators across the district can discuss topics of interest, are also included.

EdMAP's plan book is where teachers "drag and drop" activities, units, resources, and rubrics to plan their teaching calendars. By establishing "links" to various curriculum components, teachers can plan units, lessons, and resources. This feature enables principals and administrators to generate reports that show coverage of the district objectives. A teacher can also run reports for his or her principal demonstrating accountability for coverage of local objectives or state standards.

EdMAP breaks down the walls and the privacy of the classroom. While more information and sharing is supported, so is increased monitoring and evaluation. How will teachers respond? Without careful attention to the dynamics of knowledge exchange, including incentives, rewards, recognition, security, and reciprocity, participation may be limited. The appeal and the problems associated with such a system must be acknowledged and negotiated, lest the potential be frittered away.

CONCLUSION

Knowledge management has much to recommend it to public education. At its most rudimentary level, knowledge management typically provides useful resources and a forum for dialog among people with similar interests. The teacher education literature suggests that teachers most eagerly embrace the communal aspects of KM systems.

Knowledge management saved Chevron $150 million dollars by connecting building managers to each other's best ideas for energy savings in satellite offices across the world. While the contribution of KM to public schooling may be more difficult to quantify, we believe it has the potential to make equal or more important contributions to schooling. Consider the teacher who sticks with the profession because concerns are echoed and addressed by a kindred spirit across the ocean. Meet the new teacher who locates a way to teach a difficult math concept from distant colleagues via the web. Or the ESL teacher faced with a new student from Laos. That ESL teachers can communicate with others whose greater experience with the Hmong people yield tangible ideas about what to read and do. Finally, consider the veteran teacher who experiences a rejuvenation after examining the lesson database, Blue Web'n, which then stimulates curiosity and action regarding ways to use technology to teach adolescents about history.

For all that knowledge management promises, results are far from guaranteed. Research is needed to further understand the two complementary faces of knowledge management, the social and the product-based components, the frequency with which each is utilized, and the potential for user contributions to one component or the other. Additionally, investigation of factors that compel educators to become active members of online communities, through donation of resources and sharing of ideas, can provide further insight into the efficacy of such KM communities for educators.

Knowledge management is not a panacea for all that ails education, but it offers a starting point for collecting the awesome expertise and energy of teachers and making their ideas, their feelings and their survival strategies more widely accessible.

REFERENCES

Anderson, S. E., & Harris, J. B. (1995, April). *Educators' use of electronic networks: An e-mail survey of account-holders on a statewide telecomputing system.* Paper presented at the meeting of the American Educational Research Association, San Francisco, CA.

Bassi, L. J. (1997, December). Harnessing the power of intellectual capital. *Training & Development, 51,* 25-30.

Bates, J. (Ed.) (1995). *Telematics for flexible and distance learning (DELTA).* Final report. Brussels: European Commission DG XIII_C.

Brett, C. (1997, March). *Communities of inquiry among pre-service teachers investigating mathematics.* Paper presented at the meeting of the American Educational Research Association, Chicago, IL.

Breuleux, A., Laferriere, T., & Bracewell, R. (1998). Networked learning communities in teacher education. In McNeil, S. (Ed.), *SITE 98: Society for Information Technology & Teacher Education International Conference* (pp.1170-75). Charlottesville, VA: Association for the Advancement of Computing in Education (AACE).

Bronack, S. C., & Kilbane, C. R. (1998). CaseNET: Teaching decisions via a web-based learning environment. In McNeil, S. (Ed.), *SITE 98: Society for Information Technology & Teacher Education International Conference.* Charlottesville, VA: Association for the Advancement of Computing in Education (AACE).

Bull, G., Harris, J., Lloyd, J., & Short, J. (1989). The electronic academical village. *Journal of Teacher Education, July-August,* 27-31.

Bull, B.(1994). *Professional development and teacher time: Principles, guidelines, and policy options for Indiana.* Bloomington, IN: Indiana University Education Policy Center.

Davenport, T. H., & Prusak, L. (1998). *Working knowledge: How organizations manage what they know.* Boston: Harvard Business School Press.

Drucker, P. F. (1994, November). The age of social transformation. *The Atlantic Monthly, 275* (5), 53-80.

Herbert, J. M., & McNergney, R. F. (Eds.) (1995). *Guide to foundations in action videocases: teaching and learning in multicultural settings.* Boston: Allyn & Bacon.

Honey, M., & Henriquez, A. (1993). *Telecommunications and K-12 educators: Findings from a national survey.* Center for Technology in Education: New York, NY.

Hopkins, D. (1993). *A teacher's guide to classroom research* (2nd ed.). Bristol, PA: Open University Press.

Horton, W. (1999, April). *WBT and knowledge management, allies or arch-enemies.* Paper presented at the WBT Conference, San Diego, CA.

Jonassen, D. H., Peck, K. L., & Wilson, B. G. (1999). *Learning with technology: A constructivist perspective.* New Jersey: Prentice Hall, Inc.

Kollock, P. (1999). The economies of online cooperation: Gifts and public goods in cyberspace. In M. A. Smith & P. Kollock (Eds.), *Communities in cyberspace.* London: Routledge.

Lakewood Publications. (1998). Third world KM: The best place to start? *Online Learning News* [On-line serial], *1* (39).

McMahon, T. A. (1997, April). *From isolation to interaction? Network-based professional development and teacher professional communication.* Paper presented at the meeting of the American Educational Research Association, Chicago, IL.

Merseth, K. K. (1992, May). First aid for first-year teachers. *Phi Delta Kappan, 73* (9), p. 678-83.

O'Dell, C., & Grayson, C. J., Jr. (1998). *If only we knew what we know.* New York: The Free Press.

Rheingold, H. (1993). *The virtual community: Homesteading on the electric frontier.* New York: Addison-Wesley.

Rossett, A., & Marshall, J. (1999). Signposts on the road to knowledge management. In K. P. Kuchinke (Ed.), *Proceedings of the 1999 AHRD Conference: Vol. 1* (pp. 496-503). Baton Rouge, LA: Academy of Human Resource Development.

Special Issue: Organizational Memory Systems (1999*). Journal of Organizational Computing and Electronic Commerce 9* (2 & 3).

Stewart, T. A. (1998, October 12). Knowledge, the appreciating commodity. *Fortune, 138,* 199-200.

Stewart, T. A. (1997a, June 23). Why dumb things happen to smart companies: Symptoms of bad brainpower management. *Fortune, 135,* 159-160.

Stewart, T. A. (1997b). *Intellectual capital: The new wealth of organizations.* New York: Doubleday.

Struck, S. J., & Fowler-Frey, J. (1996). *ESL online action research. Final report.* Lancaster, PN: Pennsylvania Association for Adult Continuing Education. (ERIC Document Reproduction Service No. ED 406 861)

Szulanski, G. (1996, Winter). Exploring internal stickiness: Impediments to the transfer of best practices within the firm. *Strategic Management Journal, 17,* 27-43.

Watts, G. D. & Castle, S. (1992, May). Electronic networking and the construction of professional knowledge. *Phi Delta Kappan, 73* (9), p. 684-89.

Zimmerman, S. O., & Greene, M. W. (1998). A five-year chronicle: Using technology in a teacher education program. In McNeil, S. (Ed.), *SITE 98: Society for Information Technology & Teacher Education International Conference* (p.1136-39). Charlottesville, VA: Association for the Advancement of Computing in Education (AACE).

WEB SITES

The BixTech Network, www.brint.com

Blue Web'n, www.kn.pacbell.com/wired/bluewebn

Dave's ESL Café, www.eslcafe.com

EdMAP, www.ccclearn.com/tools/edmap/index.html

iqport (no longer available), www.iqport.com

Knowledge Management Magazine, www.kmmag.com

WILHELMINA C. SAVENYE

Chapter 3

REFLECTIONS ON DEVELOPING A WEB-BASED *TEACHING WITH TECHNOLOGY* COURSE

Keywords: distance education, instructional design, instructional technology, teacher technology education, computer-based learning, web-based instruction

Abstract. Institutions that prepare educators have long included in their curriculum courses to help teachers learn to use technology well. However, the definitions of educational technology and specifications as to what teachers most need to know about technology have changed over the years. Courses and texts have gone from focusing primarily on audiovisual aids and media to microcomputers and ever more complex interactive technologies. This chapter begins with a discussion of the issues involved in preparing teachers to most effectively use technology. The planning, development, implementation and evaluation of a fully web-based distance learning course to help teachers integrate these converging technologies into their instruction is the major focus of the chapter. The chapter concludes with reflections on lessons learned and the implications for teacher education of such web-based courses.

INTRODUCTION

A Review of Teachers and Technologies

Institutions that prepare educators have long struggled with exactly what teachers need to know about technology in order to help their students learn well. Yet teachers have sometimes, with good reason, felt that technologies have been foisted upon them, with each new technology seen by society as the latest panacea for all manner of educational, and even societal, problems. Some have even considered teachers to be resistant to using technologies for these reasons (Hannafin & Savenye, 1993; Reiser & Salisbury, 1995).

A look at the history of technological innovations in schools explains some of the dilemma for teachers and teacher educators. Reiser (1987), in his review of the history of instructional technology, notes that we could trace the history of audiovisual devices for learning from as early as Comenius's illustrated textbook, *Orbis Sensualium Pictus* (The Visible

35

J.M. Spector and T.M. Anderson (eds.),
Integrated and Holistic Perspectives on Learning, Instruction and Technology, 35–60.
© 2000 *Kluwer Academic Publishers. Printed in the Netherlands.*

World in Pictures) in the 1650s. In the early part of the century, however, most classrooms still consisted of a teacher, students, and such limited audiovisual aids as maps, charts, and chalkboards. Even early in the century, there were those who thought technological tools would revolutionize classrooms. Reiser (1987), for instance, cites Edison's 1913 pronouncement that books would soon be obsolete in schools, that motion pictures could teach all human knowledge, and that school systems would be profoundly changed in the following ten years.

During the rest of the century, pronouncements that various new technologies would forever change classrooms have appeared at least every decade. Within the past fifty years, training aids such as overhead and film projectors became accepted tools of classroom teachers, though they did not substantially change teaching. Instructional television programs, first delivered via broadcast television and then often via videotape delivery systems, were next seen as technological tools which would change classroom teaching and learning. Computers, first on a small-scale in the 1970s, and then with increasing frequency with the arrival of personal computers in the schools in the 1980s, were next seen as technological "revolutionizers," of teaching and learning. Simpler computer tools in education have been followed by various forms of computer-based instruction, interactive video, multimedia, hypermedia, web-based communication tools, world-wide-web information tools and databases, and distance-education delivery systems. Technologies are increasingly converging, becoming more complex systems of technology. The call is for teachers to integrate these technologies into their teaching, and it is understandable that teachers often feel overwhelmed by rapidly changing technologies and how, precisely, they can best use them to help their students learn.

Teacher-education programs and resources have reflected both the evolving technology systems and changing ideas about what teachers need to learn about technology. Initially, the terms 'audiovisual aids' and 'media' were used to describe technology resources teachers could avail themselves of. For instance, a 1969 book for those who use media equipment, or train teachers to do so, taught the operation of projected optical systems, such as slide, filmstrip, opaque, overhead and motion picture projectors. It also discussed closed-circuit television systems, and basic audio systems, along with how to mount and preserve print visuals (Wyman, 1969). Another such book in 1970 described how to develop "multi-media libraries," which usually consisted of media to be delivered using the above systems (Hicks & Tillin, 1970). Most colleges and universities that prepared teachers included in their curriculum a course on using audiovisual or media technologies.

Soon after the appearance of microcomputers in schools, the approach to educational technologies, and the "media" view began to change. These changing ideas can be viewed through the evolution of published teaching manuals and teacher education programs on technology. For instance, a popular book on planning and producing instructional media included a chapter on developing computer-based instruction and computer-controlled interactive video (Kemp & Dayton, 1985). While such media books and courses still existed, teacher-education books and courses on computers in education began to appear.

In the latter part of the 1980s and early 1990s, media courses were often replaced by computer courses for teachers. Teacher-training books initially focused upon learning the basics of how to use these computers, including how computers worked, how to select computer systems, choosing software, the basics of computer programming, and setting up and maintaining schools and labs to maximize computer access (Coburn et al., 1985).

The next wave of computer education books for teachers began to focus less on how computers worked, and more on how to use computer technologies in education. Several authors helped teachers view a computer as forms of tools, tutors and tutees, terms adapted from Robert Taylor (1980). For instance, learning to use the computer as a tool, teachers would do word processing and use databases, spreadsheets, graphics tools, telecommunications systems and integrated software. Learning to use the computer as a tutor, educators would learn to use, select and evaluate computer-assisted instructional software and computer-managed instructional systems. Learning to use the computer as a tutee, teachers would learn how to help their students learn to program, for instance, in BASIC or LOGO (Flake, McClintock, & Turner, 1990; Lockard, Abrams, & Many, 1990).

More recently, computer-education courses and textbooks have reflected several trends. First, computer education books include more information for teachers on how to integrate technologies into their curriculum. Roblyer and Edwards (2000) for instance, in their book of 15 chapters, conclude with six chapters devoted to using technology in the subject areas of language arts, foreign language, science, mathematics, social studies, art, music, physical education, health and special education.

A second trend in recent computer education books is to include information on learning theories, instructional strategies, and other broader issues, such as equity of access. Geisert and Futrell (1995) for instance, discuss instructional and grouping strategies for computer use. Roblyer and Edwards (2000) include chapters on learning theories and developing technology integration plans that reflect these theories. Equity of access is addressed by Cunningham (1997) and others.

A third trend in technology support materials is that aspects of instructional design are increasingly being incorporated into teacher education for technology. Recent teacher education courses, for instance, recognizing that technology systems alone are not what teachers most need in order to integrate technologies for learning, incorporate at least some discussion of instructional design (Savenye, Davidson, & Smith, 1991). Heinich, Molenda, Russell, and Smaldino (1999) in the many editions of their textbook have long based their discussion of how to teach using instructional media and technologies on what they now term the "ASSURE" model, an adapted instructional design model.

A final trend in computer support materials is the attempt to reflect a recognition that computers fit into broader views of technology, often by using the terms "educational technology" and "instructional technology," rather than computing (Roblyer & Edwards, 2000). This trend may have grown out of the continuing evolution of computer technology systems. Whereas in the 1970s textbooks could comfortably focus on computing, the newer integrated learning systems, multimedia systems, and distance learning and telecommunications systems cannot so comfortably be called simply computers.

One reflection of this final trend is that some of the earlier "educational-media" textbooks for teachers have tackled the convergence of instructional technologies by including discussions of how to integrate emerging computer and distance-learning systems, as well as media technologies in the classroom. In fact, one of the most widely-used books in teacher education, *Instructional Media and Technologies for Learning* includes eight chapters devoted to hardware and software technologies (Heinich et al., 1999). Fully half of these eight chapters discuss computer-based technology systems, including distance-learning systems. This trend may aid technology educators who might previously have felt their courses needed to be about either "media" or "computers."

It must be noted, however, that many computer-technology textbooks still do not necessarily reflect broader views and definitions of the field of instructional technology. Such books still typically reflect the view that instructional technology is hardware and software systems, that is, computers. Schiffman (1995) might call this the media view, as compared with an instructional systems design view. Reiser (1987) notes that instructional technology is really a process, "a systematic way of designing, carrying out, and evaluating the total process of learning and teaching" (p. 12). Seels and Richey (1994) expanded this definition of instructional technology to "the theory and practice of design, development, utilization, management and evaluation of process and resources for learning" (p. 1).

The challenge for teacher-technology educators is to balance the sometimes contradictory, but ever-complex needs of teachers. Definitions of the field, as noted by Reiser and Ely (1997) tend to reflect two sides of instructional technology, the learning resources side and the learning processes side. Teachers need and want concrete skills in using and producing technology resources, which used to mean either media or computers, and now should mean all types of technology resources. At the same time, we believe educators will truly be skilled in integrating rapidly-changing technologies, only if they also are adept at instructional systems design, as well as applying learning theories, instructional strategies, and pedagogical and curricular knowledge to technology integration.

It is hoped that this type of both deeper and broader technology education will enable teachers to become lifelong technology learners. There is no doubt that teachers will need to stay abreast of changing technologies and how to use them to improve student learning, long after their pre-service training (Cunningham, 1997; Heinich et al., 1999; Roblyer & Edwards, 2000). [See chapters by Goodyear and Spector for relevant links to theory].

When asked what the future holds, most teachers and teacher educators agree that technologies will continue to influence schools and societies and that teachers, parents and educational leaders should be those who harness the power of technology to enhance student learning. For instance, in a study of educational technology professionals and students, most respondents responded positively toward statements involving the influence of computer-based instruction on individualization of instruction, and educational technology in schools. Yet they were skeptical about the degree to which computers and technology will assume teachers' roles in delivering instruction (Sullivan et al., 1993), hinting at the conflicting viewpoints educators have regarding the appropriate roles for technology in schools.

The proper and most effective use of technology in schools may continue to become more complicated for educators. In a recent annual edition of *Computers in Education*, some authors noted that technology is here to stay and virtually unstoppable in its evolution to "wired centers of learning" (Withrow, Long & Marx, 2000) and technology is almost irresistible (Oblinger, 2000). Others, however, cautioned that this revolution: has been slow due to many obstacles (Gilbert, 2000); that teaching itself has not changed due to technology, nor should it necessarily change (Cuban, 2000); and, that we must evaluate the effectiveness of technology initiatives (Dede, 2000).

There have been several recent governmental and organizational initiatives in the United States which aid educators and those who prepare teachers to teach with technology. For instance, the International Society for Technology Education (ISTE) in collaboration with other educational agencies, has developed national educational technology standards for students (ISTE, 1998). They also have prepared national standards for technology in teacher preparation. These standards have been adopted in the United States by NCATE, the National Council for Accreditation of Teacher Education, the official body for accrediting teacher preparation programs (ISTE, 1998). These guidelines include foundations for all teachers, as well as standards for basic and advanced programs in educational computing and technology, and in secondary computer science education. Finally, they include guidelines for accrediting institutions which prepare teachers.

Clearly ISTE and others present possible approaches regarding what teachers should learn about technology. Yet controversy remains. Controversy, dilemmas and conflicts may perhaps represent reasons why many teacher-preparation institutions still do not include many required courses for teachers on technology and tend to use that term only to mean microcomputers, with some Internet capabilities. We feel institutions should instead prepare teachers to integrate these converging systems of technologies, with the aid of instructional systems design thinking, into their teaching and into student learning activities.

DISTANCE EDUCATION IN EDUCATIONAL TECHNOLOGY PREPARATION FOR TEACHERS

Colleges and universities are increasingly turning to distance-education techniques and tools to deliver courses. In years past print, then radio, then television were the methods of choice for distance learning. Concurrent with the increasing importance of computers and the Internet for information delivery, there has been a recent explosion in the use of the Internet for delivering both course materials and whole courses at a distance. A discussion of the issues related to distance learning is available in the works of Collis (1996), McIsaac and Gunawardena (1996), Moore and Kearsley (1996), or Simonson, Smaldino, Albright and Svacek (2000). Dede (1991) also discusses the impact of emerging technologies on education. We saw the potential of distance learning for both broadening and deepening our impact on teacher education for technology use through the introduction and delivery of Internet-based technology courses.

Our College of Education at Arizona State University, in its educational technology program, has taken a multi-layered approach to teaching teachers how to integrate technologies into the classroom. This approach reflects to some degree the ISTE standards (1998) and includes both undergraduate and graduate courses that focus on ISTE foundation-level skills for teachers. In undergraduate courses, preservice teachers learn basic computer-technology operations and concepts, along with how to use various productivity tools, computer-based applications, and the Internet. At the graduate level, inservice teachers can continue their technology preparation in several different ways. Teachers may choose to enroll in more advanced courses on computer applications, or on specific tools such as authoring systems, multimedia, the Internet, or distance-learning systems. They may also choose to take a course specifically focused on integrating technology into their teaching, the third ISTE foundational or advanced set of standards. This chapter focuses on a new course, "Teaching with Technology," delivered for the first time at Arizona State University via the Internet.

THE "TEACHING WITH TECHNOLOGY" WEB -BASED COURSE

Background

A team of Arizona State faculty and graduate-student researchers has for several years been investigating factors which facilitate successful student learning via web-based and web-supported courses. We initially conducted a series of formative-evaluation or developmental research studies: one comparing aspects of an instructor-led and a video-based distance learning course for preservice teachers (Savenye & Smith, 1997), and the other on two different sets of web-supported tutorials for engineering students (Savenye, 1998). We are conducting survey studies of faculty who teach using distance learning, as well as studies on enhancing student motivation in distance learning. We are also developing research and theory-based guidelines for developing web-based instruction.

The ultimate goal of our research is to determine not only what is being done in web-based distance learning, but to begin to determine what are the key attributes, or best practices, for fostering learning via the Internet.

Course Development

With our research background in distance learning, and the question of how best to reach working educators who want to learn how to integrate newer technologies into their teaching, our goal was to develop a fully web-based course for inservice teachers. We chose to deliver this course via a web-based distance-learning system, because our university seeks to expand our role in our region and reach out to students not otherwise served. We also hoped to attract students who might later be interested in enrolling in one of our degree programs in educational technology. Our challenge was how to enable educators to learn the newest theories and applications of educational technology, as well as how to apply their knowledge in their own instructional settings.

Development of our semester-long course began in the spring of 1998. The course was initially taught during the 1998 fall semester, was substantially redesigned based on results of a formative evaluation, and has been taught twice since then.

Although we have taught technology courses for teachers many times over the past twenty years, we began development of this course by analyzing the technology knowledge and skills teachers currently need to ensure that the content is up to date. We then determined the overall goals and objectives of the course. As part of a sabbatical project, we visited with faculty from other universities delivering partially or fully Internet-based courses and incorporated their advice into the design of this course. We also considered technology standards for teachers, such as the ISTE standards (1998), and the recommendations of others for what teachers need to learn in integrating technology (cf. Heinich et al., 1999; Lowther & Morrison, 1998; Roblyer & Edwards, 2000).

Our university's Distance Learning Division of our College of Extended Education has been our partner in delivering the course. During the first year Distance Learning chose to use a "custom programming" approach to delivering Internet instructional materials. We wrote the course materials and worked with the Distance Learning programming staff to implement the web-based version of the course. The staff used Internet programming software and languages to build custom courseware wrapped around a commercial discussion software program.

This approach had its advantages. For instance, the instructor did not initially need to learn to set up a web site, as the staff used the instructor's files and converted them to html. The staff also developed the university's system for the discussion board and chat software programs. However, this approach also yielded many drawbacks. For example, the Distance Learning group's staff was small, and it was not able to quickly respond to course revisions, which were often needed as this was the pilot version of the course. In order to quickly respond to student needs, we needed, after all, to learn some web development skills in order to develop a supplementary web site to support the students. We also initially needed to use email communications considerably to deliver course materials and assignments, in addition to standard communications to ensure student learning and satisfaction.

In the next iteration of the course we redeveloped all materials using commercial Internet course software, *CourseInfo* 2.0 by Blackboard, Inc. (1998) which was chosen by Distance Learning for its flexibility and relative cost-effectiveness for a campus of our size. Based on evaluations we have continued to refine this *CourseInfo* -based version of the course.

Course Content

This course provides students with an overview of the most effective ways to teach using various learning technologies. It is designed as an introductory graduate course with no formal course prerequisites. However, some basic competence with computers is required. It is open to students in any graduate program.

The course is primarily designed for K-12 teachers and community college or university instructors. However, each semester several students enrolled in the course are trainers from business and industry, therefore some examples from corporate training supplement the K-12 and higher education examples.

The course begins with a broad view of learning technologies and the research and theory related to using them. Course topics include the advantages and disadvantages of various learning technologies, planning for technology, evaluation, and basic principles of educational technology development. Students then learn how to apply instructional design techniques to integrating technology into their instruction through completion of online discussions, short papers and projects, technology evaluations, a technology integration plan and a final project. The course concludes with a hands-on project in an area of the student's choice.

Students are expected to explore topics of interest to them, to share the results of their learning with their course colleagues, and, in conjunction with the instructor, to tailor the course assignments to further their own learning goals. On several projects students are able to work collaboratively, via the Internet, to complete course assignments and accomplish course objectives.

The Pilot Course

During the first semester we had both an Internet-only section and a campus-based section, however the course has subsequently been delivered in a fully web-based distance-learning format. Fifteen students enrolled in the course initially, although one dropped mid-semester due to work responsibilities. Of the fourteen continuing students, five took the course entirely via the Internet; seven were solely in the campus-based, web-supported section; and two students mixed their method, sometimes attending class, sometimes working only via the Internet, by arrangement with the instructor.

The fully online course section initially included the following components:

- assigned readings in several textbooks to provide the basic information (Heinich et al., 1999; Roblyer & Edwards, 2000);
- standard email communications software for instructors and students; and,
- a web site that is part of Distance Learning's ASU ONLINE offering.

The ASU web site included the following features:

- News feature, which enables instructor to post announcements;
- Assignments feature, which enables the instructor to post, grade and return assignments, and enables students to submit their assignments;
- Test feature, which provides for multiple-choice and short essay testing;
- Link to a Course Information page;
- Link to a Course Syllabus page;
- Discussion component, which provides for flexible threaded asynchronous discussions among all course participants and instructor;
- Chat Room, which allows course participants to meet for synchronous discussions;
- Web Resources component, which was designed to allow course participants to post addresses of useful web sites;
- Calendar component, which was designed to provide information about what topics and assignments are covered during each week in the course.

The pilot course was revised based on the results of an ongoing process of formative evaluation, described in more detail later in this chapter. The course has now been offered for three semesters.

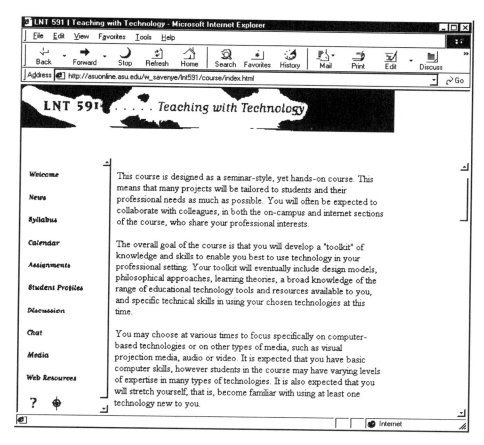

Figure 1. View of the pilot course.

The Revised Teaching with Technology Course

The next two offerings of the course were delivered solely via the Internet. During the second semester twelve students were enrolled in the course, and during the third, eleven were enrolled. Most students tended to come to campus for some other courses, as well, although several did not, due to limited chances to travel from home or because they live in other cities or states.

Distance Learning purchased a site license for *CourseInfo* from Blackboard, Inc. (1998) and we have redeveloped and entered all course materials using this software. The revised course again includes readings in Heinich et al. (1999) and Roblyer & Edwards (2000). However, we have added a third required book, Sullivan and Higgins's *Teaching for Competence* (1983), which teaches basic instructional design and lesson planning. We also added several optional resource readings on visual design, distance learning, and web page design. The new *CourseInfo* -based web site includes the following components:

- Announcements, which enables the instructor to post announcements (called News in an earlier version);
- Course Information, containing information about the "Course Overview," "Course Syllabus and Objectives," "Course Procedures," "Course Requirements and Projects," "Grading Policies," and "System Requirements;"
- Staff Info, with information about the instructor, teaching assistants, and any other staff members;
- Course Documents, containing "Media" (our video clips), "Archives of Previous Weeks' Announcements," and "Handouts;"
- Assignments, in which *CourseInfo* permits a simple listing of assignments, which we have placed into weekly folders;
- Communications, which includes tools to allow students and staff to communicate to individuals or groups using email, view the student roster, view and edit student and group web pages, and communicate using either the Discussion Board or Virtual Chat;
- External Links, designed to allow course participants to post addresses of useful web sites (old Web Resources);
- Student Tools, which includes the "Student Drop Box" for submitting assignments, and tools students can use to change their personal information, and check their grades; and,
- Resources, which will allow students to link to other web sites and information provided by Blackboard to support education.

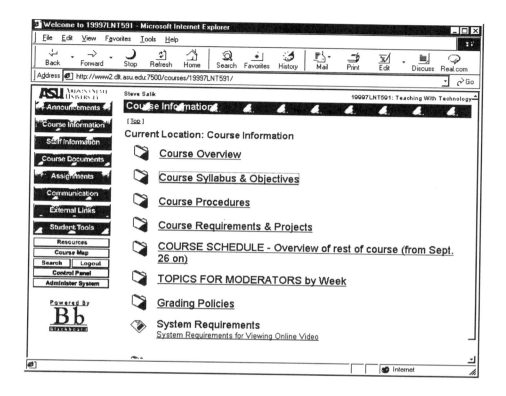

Figure 2. View of the revised course.

The course in its current form focuses primarily on the third ISTE foundational standard, applying technology in instruction, however the term technology is more broadly defined. in the course content than in the ISTE standard. Course content includes:

- Some basic history of the field,
- An overview of the many types of educational technologies available
- How to apply instructional systems design and learning theories to integrating technology,
- How to use visual design principles in developing technology-based materials,
- About using audio and video in instruction,
- How to select and evaluate technology-based products,
- How to integrate computers as tools in their instruction,
- How to evaluate and use multimedia, computer-based instructional software, and telecommunications tools to help their students learn,
- An introduction to the issues involved in distance learning,

- The basics of developing a few instructional technology products, and
- Ethical and legal uses of technology, some views of the future and how to continue their own technology education.

We have continued to expand the resources we provide students. In particular, we have increased the number of video clips available to students, providing them with demonstrations, speakers, and examples. We include many sets of handouts with directions and criteria for doing projects. Finally, we continuously update our educational-technology resource web site. We provide teachers with links, for instance, to sites on pedagogy, on specific technology skills, or on using technology in their subject areas, such as music, science, language instruction or industrial training.

As the course has evolved, course requirements have also been expanded and focused. Students are now required to participate in weekly topic discussions, usually moderated by students in a structured manner. They must complete at least three evaluations of various technology-based learning applications and develop a complete instructional plan to integrate technology into a lesson of their choice. The course continues to culminate with a final independent or collaborative project, which they share with their colleagues.

FORMATIVE EVALUATION OF THE TEACHING WITH TECHNOLOGY COURSE

This technology course for teachers has undergone a continual process of formative evaluation. We have evaluated the effectiveness of web-based online delivery using various methods.

Evaluation Methods

Student Learning Products

During the pilot semester, student grades in the online and the campus section were initially compared. However, the campus section was small and students were allowed to mix their attendance on campus with participation via the Internet, as they needed, therefore the comparison did not prove useful. In general, final grades and grades on mid-course and final projects did not appear to yield discernable differences by section. During subsequent offerings there was no comparative on-campus section.

Each semester students' projects have been reviewed in an effort to determine what students learned as a result of the course and how the course could be improved. Over the course of time, educators' technology-integration plans have become more extensive and have incorporated their additional learning of instructional systems design principles. Similarly, during the pilot semester few students tackled producing instructional technology products of their own. In subsequent semesters they have produced substantial technology-based learning projects. For instance, some have developed web sites to teach adults martial arts, to help parents access school resources, and to teach other educators how to develop web sites. Others produced computer-based and multimedia presentations for young students on birds, on mathematics, and on library skills and writing practices. Still others produced programs for adults on Middle Eastern history, desert survival, distance education and instructional design skills for business trainers. In their evaluations, discussed in more detail below, students indicated that the media and web resources we provided aided them in producing these projects; they also indicated that the support of the instructor and teaching assistant were critical to them in completing the projects. During the latest iteration of the course, educators also developed integration plans to "wrap around" the final technology products they developed.

Student Discussion Evaluating Their Lessons Learned

At the end of each semester the instructor posted a discussion question asking students to write and discuss the lessons they felt they had learned in the course. Generally students indicated they felt positively about what they had learned. Some indicated they learned more about issues related to teaching in general, and most felt satisfied with what they had learned about integrating technology into their teaching. Several indicated they had been "technophobes" prior to the course and were now more aware of the range of technologies available to them. Some said they felt confident they could produce materials, such as web pages and computer-based presentations that were appreciated by their own students and trainees. A few indicated their Internet searches taught them about the surprisingly rich assortment of resources available in their subject area.

Students also described the specific skills they gained, for instance a few had never used telecommunications systems, much less synchronous chat systems, and they expressed enjoyment in their new learning. Several said they were unaware that distance learning could be interactive and could include heated discussions, as well as collaborative work, real videos and ways to easily submit assignments.

Happily, some described the value they found in learning instructional design principles, saying for instance, "It is imperative that instructional strategies/learning objectives are the driving force to course development rather than technology being the driving force... ." Other comments showed an awareness that technology is not synonymous with simply computers. For instance, one said, "I learned that teaching with technology not only applies to computers but several different forms of technology."

These educators' comments also reflected real awareness of the conflicts in teaching with technology. They described, for instance, the need to be a "critical consumer of educational software." Some described the importance of having a "backup plan," in case things go wrong. A few said that although they were at times frustrated by the constraints of technology as students, they themselves would like to try teaching a distance course. Others added that they would like to experiment with uses of distance technologies, adding that such systems might be more effective for teaching advanced, rather than beginning, skills.

Many students described pride in their new skills. For instance, one teacher said that she now felt she knew more than her own school lab technician did. Another said, "If you can believe it, I had never even sent an e-mail before I took this class. I feel I can now teach lessons using technology." A third described an intention to continue to learn, "I have gained the confidence of going into the topics that we discussed in the course at a greater detail...Now I would like to gain more first hand experiences with these technologies to really understand how they can be used."

Student Attitude Survey at the End of the Course

Students also completed a detailed course evaluation, focused on determining the factors that helped them learn and what motivated them to learn. Highlights of the results of particular significance to us were that the students indicated a high level of satisfaction with the course, with most of them rating it as good or better than other courses they have taken at our university. We were also pleased that most students indicated they felt as much or more a part of the class as in other classes. Most said they would take an Internet course again, but not all. Some students said they learned they are better suited to face-to-face classes, and some indicated they felt campus classes were more valuable, if they have a choice. They were unanimous in indicating they valued the final, hands-on development project, and that it should remain a required part of the class. Again, some expressed particular pride in their projects. Problematic areas remained the access to video clips and use of the chat rooms, occasionally some feeling of isolation, and infrequent feedback. Interestingly, there were widely diverging views on the value of textbook readings.

Discussion of Findings from Formative Evaluation

Our findings indicate that students were, somewhat surprisingly, very satisfied with their experience in the *Teaching with Technology course*. This was previously stated in the student comments. However, many issues arose that were a particular struggle for the course instructor as well as students. During the pilot course, programming of materials by the small staff of the campus-wide, distance learning group was problematic. They did their best, but during the pilot semester delays bedeviled the process, even to the point, that the some functions were not usable. In later semesters the use of the *CourseInfo* software enabled us to enter our own content and activities, and to revise them as needed, based on student feedback.

Another result of the custom development approach by the Distance Education computer programmers is that some of the Internet course components were designed using analogies and metaphors that were not suitable for our course. For instance, what programmers, students and instructors conceive of as assignments versus tests was initially problematic. An early version of the "Assignments" component functioned like a "test," and would not allow students to edit or resubmit assignments they had already submitted. Subsequent development using *CourseInfo* has eliminated this problem. However, in contrast, the built-in "test" and "survey" functions of the new software are still somewhat limited in flexibility for instructors and students. For instance, it is difficult to enter student scores from essay tests, although multiple-choice tests can be immediately scored and grades entered. Surveys collate data anonymously by question and do not allow instructors to see which student entered which answer.

Of particular concern to us has been the need to have hands-on projects for teachers who have many different types of hardware and software, in addition to the constraints represented in their off-campus work settings. We have tackled this issue by allowing students a large degree of control in determining the projects they will take on and how they will do them, while providing flexible guidelines and clear evaluation criteria.

Another concern was the need to show students demonstrations of instructional applications, to provide "how-to" technical demonstrations, and to show real-world examples of instructors who have successfully implemented technology into their teaching. We have addressed this need by including video and audio clips in the course. Clips are being developed by digitally taping speakers, demonstrations and "virtual field trips." We will continue to evaluate use of the clips, as they have sometimes been difficult for some students to view.

Providing resources to support student learning has been a continual process throughout the evaluation period. For future courses we are recommending additional revisions to the web course development software, primarily in allowing for categorizable, searchable web addresses in the student web resources function. We would also prefer more flexibility in the student web pages, which now are limited to allowing small bits of biographical information. We envision those pages as true small web sites on which students could post complete projects to share with their colleagues.

As a result of the development and evaluation of this technology course, and our review of research and development literature in preparing the course, we offer several reflections on developing web-based courses for teachers. These are briefly summarized in the section below.

REFLECTIONS ON WEB-BASED COURSE DELIVERY

Course Content Considerations for Internet-Based Delivery

Porter (1997) provides a set of criteria for determining whether a course is suitable for distance delivery. She recommends consideration of a distance delivery format:

- For courses for which there is a ready and appreciative audience, or when individuals might choose the convenience of taking the course at a distance, or when there is no other way to take the course. Distance students also must be somewhat more self-directed than typical campus students.
- For courses which include suitable content. For instance, information-intensive courses might be particularly suitable for web delivery. In contrast, courses which require demonstrations and practice of motor skills might not be as suitable.For courses in which instructor and student interactions can be appropriately planned.
- For course in which the technical tools and instructional materials are easily available and accessible for students and instructor.
- For courses for which high quality can be guaranteed, and for which able, willing and flexible instructors can be chosen (Collis, 1996).
- For courses for which a model of successful course development and delivery is available.

Readers may also refer to McManus (1998) for a discussion of whether or not the Internet should be considered for a course.

Course Design and Evaluation Considerations for Internet Based Delivery

Many models exist for systemically designing sound instruction (cf. Dick & Carey, 1996; Gagné, Briggs, & Wager, 1992; Merrill, Jones, & Li, 1992;

Ragan & Smith, 1996; Reigeluth & Curtis, 1997; Smith & Ragan, 1999). Models also exist for systematically designing more open learning environments (cf. Hannafin et al., 1997; Hannafin & Land, 1997; Hill & Hannafin, 1997) and for the design and evaluation specific to distance-learning technologies (cf. Eastmond & Zieghan, 1995; Eggers & McGonigle, 1996; Hirumi & Bermudez, 1996; Kahn, 1997; Ritchie & Hoffman, 1997; Starr, 1997). In addition, Lewis, Whitaker and Julian (1995), as well as Tiffen and Rajasinghamm (1995), address issues related to the methods, models and analogies used in distance courses.

Technical Considerations for Internet Delivery

Critical to the success of a course are the resources, including hardware, software and technical assistance, available to both students and instructors. Determine whether you plan to use integrated courseware to develop your course, such as *CourseInfo, Web CT,* or *Web Course in a Box.* You might alternately develop a web site to use in presenting information and link to resources and some other type of software, such as *FirstClass* or *Allaire* for the communications features, among them email, threaded discussions and chat rooms. Some colleges and universities are also choosing to contract out the development of web courses, based on instructors' content.

If you develop a web site, how will you develop materials? Consider what type of support staff members are available, or what students might be interested in assisting with development, either as interns, graduate assistants or by developing class projects. We recommend using a team approach. Regardless of the type of site, web pages should be developed based on proven techniques and criteria for good screen design (cf. Grabinger, 1989; Lee & Boling, 1996; Luck & Hunter, 1997).

Decide what types of computer-mediated communication the course will include (Lewis, Whitaker, & Julian, 1995) and determine the technical details of how you will share information via protocols in the shared group (Bull, Bull, & Sigmon, 1997).

Consider the role and function of moderators, either instructors or students, in the discussions. Consider, too, how or whether you plan to use live chat, such as for open office hours, group work, and informally touching base.

Student Considerations for Internet Based Delivery

Moore (1989) discusses the implications of learner expectations in distance courses. Students in our course initially wondered where the "lectures" were. This made us stop and think about their conceptions of the course and how they were receiving information. We chose not to provide "lecture notes" on our site, though the web allows for such documents to be placed on the site. We included readings, video demonstrations, speakers and virtual field trips, and assignment sets, along with weekly asynchronous and occasional synchronous chats. Other instructors have chosen other approaches, such as having students develop information-rich web sites, providing web casting of lectures, providing all lectures notes, or providing computer-based slides with audio to deliver presentations.

We have found it helpful to inform students in web-based courses very early that more self-directed learning may be required of them than they are used to. Students have told us they found it easier, for instance, to delay working on assignments for this course, and ignore the instructor's email messages about their delay, than it would have been in a face-to-face course. They sometimes reported feeling isolated; to combat this we have encouraged more collaboration in our revised versions of the course. We also make an effort to talk with students both via email and phone during the first few weeks of the course about their adjustment to being self-directed learners.

Students also initially will need more time to learn to use all components of an Internet course, if this is their first experience with such a course. In our revised course, we have developed small assignments, with very clear directions, that require students to use each component. This adjustment period takes as much as two or three weeks in a course.

Instructor Considerations for Internet Based Delivery

Many authors note that the role of the instructor changes considerably when teaching via distance learning (cf. Beaudoin, 1990; Gunawardena, 1992; Muffaletto, 1997). Collis (1996) recommends that distance-learning instructors be flexible and willing to try new approaches. Muffaletto (1997) uses an informal discussion area he calls a cafe, in which instructors and students can gather to discuss ideas only somewhat related to course content.

As noted earlier, instructors can expect to spend at least twice their average time preparing to deliver a course via distance delivery, and often three or four times as much. Even after the initial offering, instructors may spend more time teaching the course, due to the limitations of communicating with each student via email, rather than taking care of questions and discussion face-to-face, in a group. Instructors would also do well to determine their technical and pedagogical support for offering the course early in the process.

Finally, our development and evaluation work has yielded several implications for teaching teachers about technology using web-based distance learning courses. These are discussed below.

IMPLICATIONS FOR DELIVERING DISTANCE-LEARNING COURSES ON TECHNOLOGY FOR TEACHERS

Teacher educators are struggling with how best to deliver educational technology instruction to teachers. All indications are that educators will need to develop and maintain their skills in using, selecting, integrating, evaluating and, often, producing, educational-technology products and systems. However, the knowledge and skills they require are likely to continue to expand. Those who analyze trends in educational technology, for instance, stress the importance of instructional design principles and evaluation in developing technology-based learning products, the pervasiveness of computers and telecommunications systems, the increasing impact of distance learning, and the changing role of the teacher (Ely, Freeman, Foley & Scheel, 1995). Others add that independent-learning skills will become more important and that, while technologies may become easier for more teachers to adopt, there may continue to be problems with organizational support, and disagreement about the need for technological literacy (Gentry & Csete, 1995). The ultimate goal is always to help these educators' students learn.

We perceive many challenges before us as we continue to refine this web-based Teaching with Technology course, and to revise and develop other courses in our teacher-preparation track. One challenge facing distance educators is how to prepare our students to be distance learners. One aspect of this challenge is how to ensure that students have the minimal computing and Internet skills required to succeed in the course. Which skills are basic, and which advanced, and for how long into the future? Do we teach basic skills in one course, or several, within a very restricted number of available course credit hours? When do we teach which skills? For instance, which skills should be taught to preservice teachers and which to inservice teachers in our graduate courses? Are there alternate methods for providing these basic skills?

Our university plans to offer optional on-campus workshops on how to use technology. However, for the truly distant students we do not, as yet, have any type of online workshop to prepare them, and, of course, they may not have the skills for even that online course. Some universities are simply requiring that students take such workshops, or demonstrate that they have these skills, before enrolling in online courses. One approach we are taking is to provide information on our supplemental web about other ways teachers could acquire these basic skills. For instance, we are advising teachers about online tutorials, some free and some for tuition. Such tutorials can introduce them to the basics of computing, teach application packages, or provide skills in using email, the Internet and world wide web. We hope, too, that access to such tutorials, and others that we might develop, will aid those teachers who wish to become more proficient in developing computer-based multimedia presentations and basic web pages. This represents another ongoing issue in a web-based class, that is, how, in what currently is a text-intensive medium, to provide hands-on training on producing learning materials.

For now, during the first few weeks of classes we spend extra time helping students who need to learn these skills. However, we hope soon to have resources available for them.

Helping teachers determine the appropriate role of technology is another challenge. Most educators no longer fear that computers will replace them, but many do recognize that their roles may change as they integrate technology. Most, as did our teachers, anticipate using technology to change their instruction. However there are also those who suggest instructional technology will not have much impact on education unless schools themselves undergo considerable structural reform (Honey, Culp, & Carrigg, 1999; Reiser & Salisbury, 1995). We hope in the future to give teachers more experience in grappling with these issues.

How best to help teachers integrate technology is a third challenge. One model for integrating technology is Lowther and Morrison's (1998) NTeQ model. These teacher educators and researchers advise that teachers systematically develop integrated lessons that include activities for using the computer as well as activities to be conducted before and after using the computer. They also suggest that teachers experience these actual lessons, as their students would, in simulated classroom settings. We anticipate trying this approach in our course in some way, with our class students participating in at least some aspects of their own lessons, and those of their colleagues, in simulations.

We have also begun to incorporate another integration approach which holds promise for us. Davis (1999), in discussing ways to globalize education through technology education, recommends that teacher-education programs collaborate with "model technology-rich K-12 schools that can serve as authentic environments for teacher education" (p. 9). We began such collaboration in the form of teachers who served as guest speakers and guest demonstrators in our video clips. Currently one of our students in an highly-technology rich school is developing a video segment and accompanying integration advice, based on her school projects, which she will share with our future students. We plan to extend this type of collaboration in the form of virtual field trips, ongoing discussions with educators in the field, and course projects to be developed in collaboration with teachers and students in schools. This opportunity for collaboration can also be extended to include students who teach in higher education, as well as those who develop training in business and industry.

A final challenge is how to help teachers become lifelong technology learners. We would like them to see our university and its programs, of course, as one of their resources. We intend also in our course and others to provide them with more information about various educational technology professional organizations and conferences, as well as more on general educational technology resources.

We do not claim online learning is always the answer, but this is one method for providing technology education to teachers who might not otherwise be able to engage in it. It is hoped that our course, and the results of studies involving web-based learning for teachers, will provide other teacher educators with some guidance for providing web-based technology instruction for teachers. In the future we also plan to study issues related to computer-mediated communications, sense of presence (Lombard & Ditton, 1997), sense of community (cf. Bull, Bull, & Sigmon, 1997; Moller, 1998), and critical technical issues for students to provide continual information on this area.

REFERENCES

Beaudoin, M. (1990). The instructor's changing role in distance education. *The American Journal of Distance Education 4*(2), 21-9.

Blackboard, Inc. (1998). *CourseInfo 2.0 Instructor's Manual*. Washington, D.C.

Bull, G., Bull, G., & Sigmon, T. (1997, September). Common protocols for shared communities. *Learning and Leading with Technology*, 25(1), 50-53.

Coburn, P., Kelman, P., Roberts, N., Snyder, T. F. F., Watt, D. H., & Weiner, C. (1985). *Practical guide to computers in education* (2nd Ed.). Reading, MA: Addison-Wesley.

Collis, B. (1996). *Tele-learning in a digital world - the future of distance learning*. Boston, MA: International Thompson Computer Press.

Cuban, L. (2000). High-tech schools and low-tech teaching. In Hirschbuhl, J. J., & Bishop, D. (Eds.), *Computers in education: Annual editions, 00/01*, pp. 15-16. Guilford, CN: Dushkin/McGraw-Hill.

Cunningham, C. (Ed.). (1997). *Perspectives: Instructional technology for teachers*. Boulder, CO: Coursewise Publishing.

Davis, N. (1999, Autumn/Winter). The globalization of education through teacher education with new technologies: a view informed by research. *Educational Technology Review, 12*, 8-12.

Dede, C. J. (1991). Emerging technologies: Impacts on distance learning. *Annals of the American Academy of Political and Social Science* (514), 146-58.

Dede, C. (2000). Evaluating the effectiveness of technology initiatives. In Hirschbuhl, J. J., & Bishop, D. (Eds.), *Computers in education: Annual editions, 00/01*, pp. 43-46. Guilford, CN: Dushkin/McGraw-Hill.

Descy, D. E. (1997, November, December). Accessible web page design. *TechTrends*, 3-6.

Dick, W. & Carey, L. (1996). The systematic design of instruction (4th Ed.). New York: HarperCollins.

Eastmond, D., & Ziegahn, L. (1995). Instructional design for the online classroom. In Berge, Z., & Collins, M. (Eds.), *Computer mediated communication and the online classroom*, Vol. 3, pp. 59-80. New Jersey: Hampton Press, Inc.

Eggers, R. M., & McGonigle, D. (1996). Internet-distributed college courses: Instructional design issues. In *Proceedings of Selected Research and Development Presentations at the*

1996 National Convention of the Association for Educational Communications and Technology, 18th, Indianapolis, IN. ERIC Document ED 397 790.

Ely, D. P., Foley, A., Freeman, W., & Scheel, N. (1995). Trends in educational technology 1991. In *Instructional technology: Past, present and future* (2nd Ed.) (pp. 34-60). Englewood, CO: Libraries Unlimited.

Flake, J. L., McClintock, C. E., & Turner, S. (1990). *Fundamentals of computer education* (2nd Ed.). Belmont, CA: Wadsworth.

Gagné, R. M., Briggs, L J., & Wager, W. W. (1992). *Principles of instructional design* (4th Ed.). Fort Worth, TX: Harcourt, Brace.

Geisert, P. G., & Futrell, M. K. (1995). *Teachers, computers, and curriculum: microcomputers in the curriculum* (2nd Ed.). Needham Heights, MA: Simon and Schuster.

Gentry, C. G., & Csete, J. (1995). Educational technology in the 1990s. *In Instructional technology: past, present and future* (2nd Ed.) (pp. 20-33). Englewood, CO: Libraries Unlimited.

Gilbert, S. W. (2000). Making the most of a slow revolution. In Hirschbuhl, J. J., & Bishop, D. (Eds). *Computers in education: Annual editions, 00/01* (pp. 125-139). Guilford, CN: Dushkin/McGraw-Hill.

Grabinger, R. S. (1989). Screen layout design: Research into the overall appearance on the screen. *Computers in Human Behavior, 3,* 173-183.

Gunawardena, C. N. (1992). Changing faculty roles for audiographics and online teaching. *The American Journal of Distance Education* 6(3), 58-71.

Hannafin, M. J., Hannafin, K. M., Land, S. M., & Oliver, K. (1997). Grounded practice and the design of constructivist learning environments. *Educational Technology Research and Development 45(*3), 101-17.

Hannafin, M. J. & Land, S. M. (1997). The foundations and assumptions of technology-enhanced student-centered learning environments. *Instructional Science* 25, 167-202.

Hannafin, R. D., & Savenye, W. C. (1993, June). Technology in the classroom: the teacher's new role and resistance to it. *Educational Technology,* 26-31.

Heinich, R., Molenda, M., Russell, J. D., & Smaldino, S. E., (1999). *Instructional media and technologies for learning.* Upper Saddle River, NJ: Merrill, an imprint of Prentice Hall.

Hicks, W. B., & Tillin, A. M. (1970). *Developing multi-media libraries.* New York: Bowker.

Hill, J. R., & Hannafin, M.J. (1997). Cognitive strategies and learning from the world wide web. *Educational Technology Research and Development 45*(4), 37-64.

Hirumi, A., & Bermudez, A. (1996). Interactivity, distance education and instructional systems design converge on the information superhighway. *Journal of Research on Computing in Education, 29*(1), 1-16.

Honey, M., Culp, K. M., & Carrigg, F. (1999, July). *Perspectives on technology and education research: Lessons from the past and present.* Paper presented at the Secretary's Conference on Educational Technology, Washington, DC, 12-13 July 1999. (http://www.ed.gov/Technology/TechConf/1999/whitepapers/paper1.html)

International Society for Technology in Education (ISTE). (June, 1998). *National educational technology standards for students.* Eugene, Oregon.

International Society for Technology in Education (ISTE). (1998). *National standards for technology in teacher preparation.* (http://www.iste.org/Standards/NCATE/intro.html)

Khan, B. H. (Ed.). (1997). *Web-based instruction.* Englewood Cliffs, NJ: Educational Technology Publications.

Kemp, J. E., & Dayton, D. K. (1985). *Planning and producing instructional media* (5th Ed.). Cambridge, MA: Harper & Row.

Lee, S. H., & Boling, E. (1996). Motivational screen design guidelines for effective computer-mediated instruction. In *Proceedings of Selected Research and Development Presentations at the 1996 National Convention of the Association for Educational Communications and Technology* (18th Ed.) (pp. 401-12). Indianapolis, IN: ERIC Document ED 397 811.

Lewis, J., Whitaker, J., & Julian, J. (1995). Distance education for the 21st century: The future of national and international telecomputing networks in distance education. In Berge, Z., & Collins, M. (Eds.), *Computer mediated communication and the online classroom, Vol. 3* (pp. 13-30). New Jersey: Hampton Press, Inc.

Lockard, J., Abrams, P. D., Many, W. A. (1990). Microcomputers for educators (2nd Ed.). New York: Harper Collins.

Lombard, M., & Ditton, T. (September, 1997). At the heart of it all: The concept of social presence. *Journal of Computer Mediated Communication 3*(2), 1-38. (www.ascsc.org/jcmc/vol3/issue2/lombard.html)

Lowther, D. L., & Morrison, G. R. (1998, March). The NTeQ model: a framework for technology integration. *TechTrends*, 33-38.

Luck, D. D., & Hunter, J. M. (1997, January). Visual design principles applied to world wide web construction. In *VisionQuest: Journeys toward Visual Literacy. Selected Readings from the 28th Annual Conference of the Visual Literacy Association*. Cheyenne, Wyoming, October, 1996. ERIC document ED 408 985.

McIsaac, M. S., & Gunawardena, C. N. (1996). Distance education. In Jonassen, D. H. (Ed.). *Handbook of Research for Educational Communications and Technology* (pp. 403-37). New York, NY: Simon and Schuster McMillan.

McManus, T. (1998). *Special considerations for designing Internet based instruction.* (http://ccwf.cc.utexas.edu/~mcmanus/special.html)

Merrill, M. D., Jones, M. K., & Li, Z. (1992). Second generation instructional design. *Educational Technology, 31*(6), 7-12.

Moller, L. (1998). Designing communities of learners for asynchronous distance education. *Educational Technology Research and Development*, 46(4), 115-22.

Moore, M. G. (1989). Distance education: a learner's system. *Lifelong learning: an omnibus of practice and research, 12*(8), 8-11.

Moore, M. G., & Kearsley, G. (1996). *Distance education: a systems view*. Belmont, CA: Wadsworth.

Muffoletto, R. (1997, March). Reflections on designing and producing an Internet-based course. *TechTrends,* 50-3.

Oblinger, D. G. (2000). Technology and change: impossible to resist. In Hirschbuhl, J. J., & Bishop, D. (Eds). *Computers in Education: Annual Editions, 00/01* (pp. 17-29). Guilford, CN: Dushkin/McGraw-Hill.

Porter, L. A. (1997). *Creating the virtual classroom - distance learning with the Internet.* New York, NY: John Wiley and Sons.

Ragan, T. J., & Smith, P. J. (1996). Conditions-based models for designing instruction. In Jonassen, D. H. (Ed.). *Handbook of Research for Educational Communications and Technology* (pp. 541-69). New York, NY: Simon and Schuster McMillan.

Reigeluth, C. M., & Curtis, R. V. (1987). Learning situations and instructional models. In R. M. Gagné (Ed.). *Instructional Technology Foundations,* 175-206. Hillsdale, NJ: Erlbaum.

Reiser, R. A. (1987). Instructional technology: a history. In R. M. Gagné (Ed.). *Instructional Technology: Foundations* (pp. 11-48). Hillsdale, NJ: Erlbaurm.

Reiser, R. A., & Ely, D. P. (1997). The field of educational technology as reflected through its definitions. *Educational Technology, Research and Development, 45*(3), 65-74.

Reiser, R. A., & Salisbury, D. R. (1995). Instructional technology and public education in the United States: the next decade. *In Instructional technology: past, present and future* (2nd Ed.) (pp. 254-262). Englewood, CO: Libraries Unlimited.

Ritchie, D. C., & Hoffman, B. (1997). *Using instructional design principles to amplify learning on the World Wide Web.* ERIC Document ED 415 835.

Roblyer, M. D., & Edwards, J. (2000). *Integrating educational technology into teaching* (2nd Ed.). Upper Saddle River, NJ: Merrill, an imprint of Prentice Hall.

Savenye, W. (1998, June). *Evaluating the impact of video and web-based distance learning courses.* Paper presented at the annual meeting of EDMEDIA/TELECOM, Freiburg, Germany, June 20-25, 1998.

Savenye, W. C., Davidson, G. V., & Smith, P. L. (1991). Teaching instructional design in a computer literacy course. *Educational Technology Research and Development, 39* (3), 49-58.

Savenye, W., & Smith, K. (1997, February). *Enhancing interaction in an outcomes-based distance learning environment.* Paper presented at the annual meeting of the Association for Communications and Technology, Albuquerque, New Mexico, February 12-16, 1997.

Schiffman, S. S. (1995). Instructional systems design: five views of the field. *In Instructional technology: past, present and future* (2nd Ed.) (pp. 131-144). Englewood, CO: Libraries Unlimited.

Seels, B., & Richey. (1994). The 1994 definition of the field. *Instructional technology: the definitions and domains of the field,* pp. 1-21. Washington, DC: AECT.

Simonson, M., Smaldino, S., Albright, M., & Zvacek, S. (2000). *Teaching and learning at a distance: foundations of distance education.* Upper Saddle River, NJ: Merrill, an imprint of Prentice Hall.

Smith, P. J., & Ragan, T. J. (1999). *Instructional design.* (2nd Ed.). Upper Saddle River, NJ: Merrill, an imprint of Prentice Hall.

Starr, R. M. (1997, May-June). Delivering instruction on the world wide web: Overview and basic design principles. *Educational Technology,* 7-15.

Sullivan, H. J., & Higgins, N. (1983). *Teaching for Competence.* New York, NY: Teachers College Press.

Sullivan, H. J., Igoe, A. R., Klein, J. D., Jones, E. E., & Savenye, W. C. (1993). Perspectives on the future of educational technology. *Educational Technology Research and Development, 41* (2), 97-110.

Taylor, R. (1980). *The computer in the school: Tutor, tool, and tutee.* New York, NY: Teachers College Press.

Tiffen, J., & Rajasingham, L. (1995). *In search of the virtual class: Education in an information society.* London & New York: Routledge.

Withrow, F., Long, H, & Marx, G. (2000). Contemporary technology. In Hirschbuhl, J. J., & Bishop, D. (Eds.). *Computers in Education: Annual Editions, 00/01* (pp. 8-12). Guilford, CN: Dushkin/McGraw-Hill.

Wyman, R. (1969). *Mediaware: selection, operation and maintenance.* Dubuque, IA: Wm. C. Brown.

CATHERINE B. DUNNAGAN and DEAN L. CHRISTENSEN

Chapter 4

STATIC AND DYNAMIC ENVIRONMENTS

The Ambiguity of the Problem

Keywords: computer-based training, decision-making framework, dynamic planning, instructional design

Abstract. The framework for the implementation of effective instruction depends upon three areas of competence: educational foundations, methodology, and process. Traditional methodologies have tried to accommodate both foundations (theory) and process. A serious problem arises in trying to apply static methodologies to dynamic environments. To emphasis this point, we look at lessons learned by instructional designers in the development of one class of technology-supported learning: computer-based training (CBT). Lessons learned cover the 'how', the 'what', the 'who' and the 'why' of CBT development and delivery. The point of this report of lessons learned is to describe conditions that were not considered in traditional methodologies that were associated with sub-optimal outcomes as a basis for our conclusion that static processes were applied to dynamic environments. The result is an ambiguity of methodologies that suggests a need to develop and establish a more dynamic methodology that reflects both the dynamics of learning processes as well as the dynamics of development processes. When these dynamics inform planning and implementation processes, the outcome is likely to be more effective learning.

INTRODUCTION

The implementation of effective instruction depends upon three areas of competence: educational foundations (theory), methodology, and process (Tennyson & Morrison, in press) (see Figure 1). Most current models assume a static environment for the implementation of education and training materials [see especially the chapters by Goodyear and Jonassen in this volume]. Theoretical bases and foundations have been well researched and documented (see, for example, Gagné, 1985). Methodology has been extensively explored, although common and best practices are not necessarily considered and rarely present in published models (Tennyson, 1995). Lastly, the process by which instruction is produced is almost an afterthought and hardly ever documented in the academic literature (Perez &

J.M. Spector and T.M. Anderson (eds.),
Integrated and Holistic Perspectives on Learning, Instruction and Technology, 61–78.

Emery, 1995). Compounding the problem of applying academic theory and conventional wisdom to the design and development of CBT is the constant change in instructional environments. It is a challenge is to keep pace with the many environmental changes, dealing with changing hardware, software, learning situations, and institutional and instructional practices. The time required to create instruction for such a dynamic environment weighs against the use of elaborate and formal methodologies that might be ideally applied to problem solving if one assumes a static time frame and perspective. In addition, practitioners in both academia and industry have been resistant to adopting methodologies offered by the educational research community. [See Goodyear's chapter for an elaboration of this last point; see Kaufman et al. (1996) and Gustafson & Branch (1997) for more about alternative design processes such as rapid prototyping and concurrent engineering.]

Dynamic ID Competencies

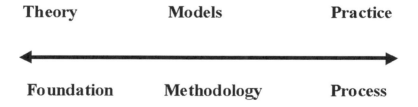

Theory	Models	Practice

Foundation	Methodology	Process

Figure 1. Three areas of competence.

The typical goal of instructors is to provide effective instruction, and institutions and learners demand that it be timely and affordable. The challenge is to utilize available environmental resources effectively within a dynamic environment. The dilemma is that methodologies developed to guide such efforts typically require excessive time, and it is well known that cutting short time spent on planning generally causes further time slippage and cost overruns (Spector, 1995). The problem, then, is to develop flexible methodologies that reflect what we know about learning (foundations, theory, empirical research) and that are responsive to changing learning situations and implementation practices. Figure 1 depicts a continuum along an axis from foundations to methodologies to process, with methodologies playing the mediating role. Associated with such a continuum are competencies that might be clustered into three areas: theoretical knowledge, knowledge of models and heuristics, and practical knowledge [see Wagner's chapter for a discussion of competencies]. We shall argue that instructional design competence requires expertise in all three areas, consistent with Tennyson and Morrison (2000).

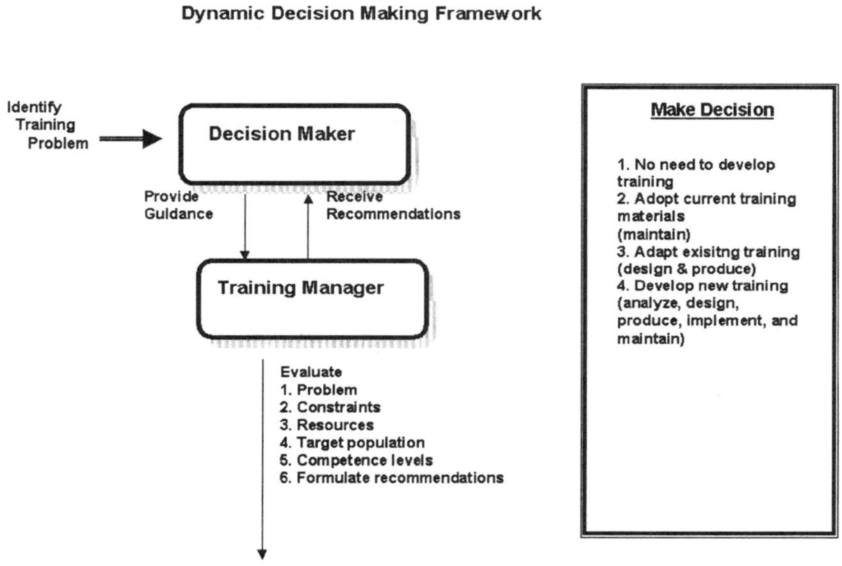

Dynamic Decision Making Framework

Figure 2. Framework for a decision making process.

We proceed from the assumption that the future of instructional design can be enhanced by learning from the past [see chapter 5]. Documentation of lessons learned from the past can obviously help prevent repetition of past mistakes and provide guidance for future developers. Perhaps such lessons might contribute to the development of new methods and praxis (the set of interactions between methodologies and process depicted in Figure 1). Methodologists (e.g., instructional designers) are faced with the continuing challenge of how to deliver timely instruction that provides an ideal solution to learning problems. Future solutions to this challenge can be informed by conducting a situational evaluation, an evaluation that is dynamic in the sense that it is adapted to the situation at hand: which aspect of instructional development is being evaluated; how far along the process is; who is involved in the evaluation; the type of learning environment involved; the target learners and institutions; and so on (see Tennyson, 1995). One way to implement such a situational evaluation is to apply a dynamic framework for decision making, as depicted in Figure 2, which depicts interactions between training managers and instructional designers as well as interactions between decisions to be made and problems to be solved. It is precisely the specifics of such interactions that dynamic planning models should capture and support.

For today's instructional designer, such a decision model provides a dynamic framework for describing conventional wisdom concerning the process of instructional design. This chapter represents an attempt to summarize information on lessons instructional designers have learned in the development of instruction for technology intensive environments. It is not intended to be a complete, definitive list of lessons learned, nor a recap of the latest findings from the research community. From this knowledge, however, future instructional theories might be influenced by the wisdom gained through actual experiences. The primary argument is that practice should inform models and methods, and these relationships are dynamic and changing. The discussion is organized into five sections as follows:

1. HOW: A decision framework paradigm;
2. WHAT: A practical discussion of common factors that influence decision making;
3. WHO: A review of individuals who influence decision making;
4. WHY: A pragmatic guide to the alternatives in implementing instruction; and,
5. CONCLUSION: The collective knowledge on educational foundations, methodology and process, as valuable lessons learned for future developers, who are dealing with both dynamic and static environments.

HOW

The dynamic process proposed herein uses the framework for decision making shown in Figure 2. Experts consider the decision-making (situation evaluation) process to be the most important part of successful training management (Perez & Neiderman, 1992; Richey & Fields, 2000; Spector, 1995; Tennyson, 1995). This section provides a framework to evaluate instructional needs and help answer the question: what kind of training, if any, would be feasible and desirable for a particular problem or need?

The model in Figure 2 depicts a process that many instructional designers have gone through in their careers. The model has been adapted to incorporate typical training problem situations. It is worth noting that this model is consistent with the instructional design competency model advocated by the International Board of Standards for Training, Performance and Instruction (see Richey & Fields, 2000, for the *ibstpi* model). The *ibstpi* model has four domain areas: Professional Foundations, Planning and Analysis, Design and Development, and Implementation and Management. These four areas correlate well with our three competency areas (foundations, methodology and process), with many of the middle two *ibstpi* domains filling in our methodology area; other key activities identified in the *ibstpi* model are easily characterized as foundation competencies or as process competencies. The advantage of our scheme is that it focuses on the kind of activity involved whereas the focus and purpose of the *ibstpi* competencies focus is an individual who is becoming a certified instructional designer.

Both perspectives view the process of designing instruction as ongoing and dynamic. It is worth noting that a process with fixed steps (i.e., a static model) could be ongoing and iterative over time, and would thus be dynamic in a weak sense. The dynamic aspects of instructional design with which we are concerned are stronger in the sense that the nature of the relationships among activities changes over time, requiring different kinds of decision making and situational evaluations. For example, while a designer might repeat a sequence such as assess needs, prototype a solution, and evaluate outcomes, that process is much different depending on whether it occurs at the beginning of a development process or near the end. Differences include the people involved, the way that outcomes are assessed, the purpose of the evaluation, and so on.

The model assumes that there is a decision maker (boss, senior officer, executive) who will approve and/or fund instructional development projects. For example, the training manager and a design staff receive information concerning a problem or need. The task is to analyze the situation, come back to the decision maker, and present recommendations and/or proposed solutions. Subsequent sections contain an elaboration of the components of the decision-making process and associated lessons learned.

Understanding the nature and scope of a training problem is one of the most important authoring activities in instructional design decision making (Spector, 1995). Novices seem to overlook the importance of rigorous evaluation of the problem (Perez & Niederman, 1992). For the most part, inexperienced designers delve right into generating a solution, simply moving directly to micro-level instructional development in either a linear or a haphazard fashion. Experience has demonstrated that thorough evaluation of a training problem is over sixty percent of the total instructional development job (Perez & Niederman, 1992; Rowland, 1992; Seidel & Perez, 1994). The training manager has the responsibility of communicating a problem statement, usually originated by a decision maker. Often, decision makers lack knowledge and/or the ability to define a training problem, yet they control budgets and direction. The training manager provides the interface between the decision maker and the instructional developer and is responsible for meaningful communication of the problem.

At the outset, the developer may receive inaccurate descriptions of the problem, including vague descriptions of training problems, or a description of a situation which really is not a training problem, or such a broad statement of the problem that the solution on such a large scale is unmanageable. The role of the developer is to reduce the problem to a manageable size by proceeding in a systematic fashion through the steps involved in defining the specific problem within a given context. A number of instructional design models provide such guidance, and our Framework for Decision Making Process (see Figure 2) is generally representative (Tennyson, 1995). Most of these models identify the same general sets of activities. However, most fail to emphasize the dynamic aspect of these activities and the implications for project outcomes. Notable exceptions include our own model, Tennyson's fourth generation ISD model (1995), a system dynamics perspective (Spector & Davidsen, 1997), and the *ibstpi* model (Richey & Fields, 2000).

Below are the five steps in the situational evaluation process which we share explictly with Tennyson (1995), and which can found in the other models mentioned earlier. Each step could be considered a candidate for lessons learned. While many of these lessons have been reported in earlier literature (see Montague, 1988, for example), they have been largely ignored. The fact that modern development situations are challenging in new ways, especially on account of the dynamics of instructional development, makes these steps more crucial than ever before. [Chapters by Dijkstra, Goodyear, Marshall & Rossett, and Wagner offer further elaboration.]

1. <u>Identify a clear need/problem in training</u>. This step actually involves a restatement of the problem. As mentioned above, the guidance designers receive may not be clear and comprehensive. The task here is to re-state and identify a manageable problem. The use of objectives and sub-objectives is a traditional method for re-defining a problem. Additional techniques involve user-centered design and can be accomplished using focus groups and delphi techniques (Morris, 1994).

2. <u>Identify relevant constraints</u>. The list of constraints might seem overwhelming but it needs to be made explicit at the beginning of the process or else valuable time and resources will be wasted on apparent solutions which cannot be adopted for various reasons. Again, a detailed list should be prepared to ensure that all issues are addressed. Oftentimes, when the constraints are made explicit, ways to circumvent them become apparent. It is worth noting that some constraints involve required commitments that may consume many resources. For example, it frequently occurs that someone has decided to constrain the solution to a particular delivery mechanism, such as CBT or the Internet, regardless of needs, appropriateness or available budget. The sections, WHAT and WHO, present a partial list of constraints to this process.

3. <u>Identify resources needed to solve training problems</u>. An important planning and management activity in the initial stages of development is identifying where and what resources are available and when they are available. The designer's task is to make a list of which resources will be needed and when in order to solve the training problem, given some expectations about what is available. The training manager's task is to find those resources or indicate as early as possible in the process which resources will not be available. Understanding how various activities influence other activities makes it possible to better anticipate which resources will be needed when. For example, if the activity involves some kind of quality assurance and there are generally few quality control experts available, it is important to understand the consequences of delaying quality checks until later in the development process (e.g., more time iterating between scare quality control and production personnel later in the development process).

4. <u>Identify target population to receive training</u>. This step is one of the most important steps. It is too easy to assume that the target population is homogeneous (Montague, 1988) when in fact important differences may exist. The designer cannot plan effective training and change in outcome knowledge, skills and attitudes without thoroughly understanding the different learners who might be involved. As learning solutions become more readily available to wider audiences (one consequence of web-based training), this task becomes even more difficult. Lessons learned suggest that it is important to identify relevant learner characteristics. For example, a situation may find a diverse population with varying prerequisite abilities (e.g., in an introductory university course) or a population with tightly focused prerequisite abilities (e.g., in advanced pilot training). Learning-centered design practices are again a good solution to insuring that the target population is well understood. It also worthwhile to mention that there may well be

some tension between the perception of institutional sponsors, the targeted learners, and designers on this issue. A difficult task for instructional designers and training managers is to help resolve such differences.

5. Identify who will give the training. This step is often left out of instructional development plans. Evidence of such omission is the failure to create instructor guides until the end of the process or not at all. The person who delivers the training is the person who can make it work or cause it to fail in many cases (Montague, 1988). Often, the people who are asked to manage designers and the training function or train the learners turn out to be subject experts or others with previous experience in the subject or with management but who lack experience as instructors or as training managers. This occurs both in industry and in academia, and is an institutionalized practice in the American defense sector. When situations were simpler, perhaps this practice was acceptable, but as learning situations become increasingly complex and dynamic, this practice brings with it serious consequences that often result in sub-optimal outcomes. The attitudes and training of available instructors greatly influence learning outcomes. The big lesson here is to carefully plan for adequate training and proper motivation for instructors and training managers. An instructor's guide should be developed along with a learner's guide and both should be developed early in the process, rather than at the end (Montague, 1988).

Once the initial situational evaluation process has occurred, the next evaluation process embraces the need to examine alternative decisions, analyze costs and benefits, and make a recommendation along with a detailed implementation plan. Experience has shown that this is a fuzzy decision making process without clear right and wrong answers (Richey & Fields, 2000). This is entirely consistent with out view that instructional design is inherently a complex and dynamic activity system (Spector, 1995). This is also consistent with research pertaining to the nature of instructional design expertise (Perez & Emery, 1995; Perez & Neiderman, 1992; Rowland, 1992; 1995; Seidel and Perez, 1994). Rather than being a discrete, well-defined static process, instructional design is a continuous process of searching for solutions that result in improvements in performance or understanding, if not on the first try, then or the second or third try. Instructional design, in this perspective, is continuously aiming to improve a product, continuously engaged in formative evaluation, rarely completing a product and rarely engaging in summative evaluation.

The following four outcomes are representative kinds of possible training decisions and solutions that might be recommended. It is important to emphasize that circumstances change within and across problem situations. Oftentimes, hybrid or combined solutions are appropriate. Possible decisions to be made or decision outcomes include:

- No need to develop instruction. After restating and identifying the actual problem, it may become obvious that a performance aid or a restructuring of a job may be an appropriate solution. This decision obviates a need to create or change instruction. It is entirely conceivable that a designer might first suggest a performance aid (as a less expensive, "let's try this first" approach) and later recommend instruction (when more is known about the problem situation), again emphasizing the dynamic nature of these activities and decisions.

- Adopt currently available instructional materials. Based upon the situational analysis, the use of existing resources may be indicated. This recommendation would be based upon knowledge that appropriate instruction exists or that new development might be infeasible financially or otherwise, resulting in the need to identify existing instruction. Often, the use of existing instruction is stigmatized as a "not-invented-here" solution. This situation reflects a number of motivational barriers to adoption: reluctance to learn how to deliver another designer's instruction; divergence from the instructor's approach to instruction; inadequate fit with current pedagogy; incompatibility with current equipment; etc. Use of existing instruction is, however, very cost beneficial. At a minimum, results from the analysis of existing instruction and the re-identification of objectives and sub-objectives could result in a more desirable version of the instruction. Once again, a user-centered approach can alleviate this commonly encountered problem. If users (institutional sponsors, designers, and learners) have all been involved in reviewing alternative solutions and collectively arrive at the decision to use a pre-existing solution invented elsewhere, then the resistance is minimized and effective use maximized (Morris, 1994).

- Adapt existing instruction. Adaptation of existing materials allows the designer to capitalize on completed work and yet customize the instruction to suit the target population and instructional context (curricular needs and goals). Variables that adaptation addresses include the special needs of instructors and/or learners, software and equipment requirements, constraints of the curriculum, and any other key resources and constraints associated with solving the training problem. Adaptation of existing instruction should become part of a dynamic planning process, in the sense that when planning a particular solution one ought to consider the likelihood of its being re-used for related purposes in the future. While this may add to short term costs, the additional costs are often justified and not always difficult to defend, especially on large-scale instructional developments that are associated with equipment that is likely to be around for many years, such as with training on aircraft systems that might have a lifetime of twenty or more years with many updates and changes along the way (Spector, Arnold, & Wilson, 1996).

- Develop new instruction. The development of new instruction might well follow an instructional development methodology. Adopting an instructional development model typically represents an investment of both time and funds and frequently meets resistance in smaller scale, non-industrial situations [see Jonassen's chapter]. However, adopting an explicit instructional development model offers flexibility in addressing training problems even though it appears to impose systematically rigid solutions. The flexibility comes in the actual practice and the form of documentation and other design and development aids that can serve well in revisions, updates, and iterations through a complex situation. One can be systematic and remain flexible - this is a management task and challenge for a design team. One can hardly maintain a systemic view required for solving dynamic problems without some degree of discipline associated with systematic approaches (Montague, 1988; Tennyson, 1995).

WHAT

An instructional designer balances a number of factors in making training design decisions (Richey & Fields, 2000; Rowland, 1992; Tennyson, 1995). This collection of factors establishes a context in which the instructional problem is considered and solutions contemplated. Although instructional design is often seen as an individual effort, most regard it as a team effort. Many pressures and factors influence design decisions, including learning effectiveness, delivery mechanisms and hardware, organizational impacts, affective considerations, vendors and markets, political influences and even *zeitgeist*. We identify eight dimensions of success factors in this dynamic environment as follows:

1. Learning Effectiveness. Acceptable instruction results in positive learning outcomes. Given that the focus is on learner needs and abilities, good instruction is that which achieves intended outcomes. Research shows that two primary factors lead to the desired result: student time on task and motivation (Montague, 1988). If learners are not properly motivated to spend time on learning activities, outcomes are likely to be marginal. If learning situations (e.g., job settings or learning environments) do not

lend themselves to spending time on learning tasks, once again less than optimal learning outcomes will occur. Moreover, what works to motivate learners initially may not work over a long period of time. Again the complexities of dynamic planning are evident, further complicating a designer's task [see also chapters by Goodyear and Dijkstra].

2. Delivery. Nearly all agree that meaningful engagement of learners is critical to effective training. Student attention can be engaged with creative use of media. The use of animation, graphics, sound, and so on, can contribute to the creation of engaging instruction, but these should only be used for sound instructional reasons and not merely to exercise the technology as Gagné (1985) argued long ago. Researchers have learned that eye-catching instruction does not necessarily equate to substantive instruction; in some cases, such instruction has caused setbacks in learning (Montague, 1988). What works in general is learner engagement that is relevant to the desired learning outcomes. Occasionally, an indirect approach or an incidental learning paradigm might achieve desired outcomes. In these cases, the learner does not immediately see the targeted learning goal, although the designer has it clearly in mind [see Goodyear's chapter].

3. Hardware. One of the most prevalent mistakes in the history of educational technology is to decide that hardware or equipment or technology is the solution to an instructional problem (Montague, 1988). Experts recognize the need to go through an analysis phase and decision-making process (Perez & Emery, 1995; Richey & Fields, 2000; Rowland, 1992). Only after careful analysis ought one to settle on hardware and delivery mechanisms. Too often, the hardware is selected first, and this serves as a serious constraint to possible solutions, as already mentioned. It is not unusual in such cases to discover that the selected delivery system is no longer in production by the time the need to implement a solution arrives. This is a case where the input from users and sponsors must be severely scrutinized by professional designers.

4. Impact. Instruction can be developed for very specific applications, as a pervasive solution to standard training problems, and sometimes even to promote an institutional image of effect organizational change. Many solutions are only appropriate for a limited time span and/or fall into disuse once their proponent has moved on and advocacy for an approach or solution is lost. If instruction can be generalized, the pedagogy is robust, and the instructional constraints are well-documented, then transportability is possible which can extend the impact of the instruction. Making explicit all of the stakeholders in the process and all of the possible uses and imagined or desired impacts will enable a designer to develop long-range strategic plans. The study of the

organizational impact of instruction and technology is of increasing interest to business and industry, especially with regard to long-range strategic planning [see the chapters by Marshall & Rossett and Wagner].

5. Market. The marketplace for adult training is most certainly changing. Lifelong learning initiatives are occurring more frequently with more support at higher and more global levels [see chapters by Goodyear and Wagner, for example]. Meanwhile, vendors are inclined to claim that their products provide solutions of great generalizability. Vendor knowledge and advice can be helpful; however, the sophisticated planner and designer needs to investigate vendor claims and map needs against solutions, product options, and costs. In the absence of sophisticated design expertise, vendors become the educational technology experts for clients, which can easily lead to single solution approaches to a variety of problems that might be better addressed with a variety of approaches.

6. Affect. Affect in general refers to emotions and feelings as opposed to cognition or intellect. Most problems have both cognitive and affective aspects. In our context, affective considerations include the perceived acceptability and motivational qualities of an instructional solution. Studies show that computer-based instruction can attract and hold the interest of learners (Montague, 1988). In addition, CBT has been shown to work with learners who have not succeeded in learning from traditional classroom delivery methods (Montague, 1988). However, tastes and preferences change, so the designer must again anticipate changes in relevant affective considerations when developing strategic and long-term solutions. Moreover, what is pleasing to users initially may soon become a nuisance (e.g., a system that addresses the user by first name or uses a standard welcome message may become tiresome).

7. Political Influence. All people who are trying to perform their jobs in a bureaucratic organization know the pressures of people with political influence effecting their jobs. Vendors and "hype" often reach the attention of decision-makers and can lead to poor decisions about training. The only advice available is to make a case for the best, most cost effective solution to the training problem. Research evidence shows that computers can make instruction more efficient or effective under the right circumstances.

8. Zeitgeist. The Zeitgeist refers to whatever happens to be the most popular of alternative theories for and approaches to instructional design. The field has been constantly evolving, beginning with behaviorism, followed by cognitivism and Gagné's (1985) nine events model, and now there is a focus on constructivism and situated learning. Professional educational theorists tend to operate with the latest zeitgeist, or instructional design theories; practitioners tend to operate at a less advanced level of theory

with a much higher degree of openness to alternative and hybrid approaches to problems.

WHO

The community at large does not respect or properly value the role of the instructional designer (methodologist) or the unique skills required to develop effective instruction. This trend is changing, since many are beginning to realize the complexities of designing effective instruction in the information age where training can potentially be made available to anyone, anywhere, at any time. Once a training problem is placed in a real life context, decision makers sometimes divert the effort and make costly mistakes (Montague, 1988). In the area of CBT, there are sometimes too many decision-makers. Often, decisions are made by an uninformed person, based upon incorrect or incomplete information, and made with wrongheaded priorities. Because of the complexity of combining management's attitudes, pedagogical perspective and technology, and the instructor/educator's intentions, the learner's interests are often not adequately addressed. The instructional designer will need to recognize and control the decision making process to the extent possible in a dynamic and changing environment. People who influence decisions about CBT training include the following:

- Learner. The satisfactory performance of the learner is the ultimate objective. CBT has been shown to motivate students by engaging their interest, supporting self-paced learning, and offering patience not common to regular teachers. CBT has had reasonable success instructionally. Research shows that learners master the subject as well as in traditional instruction and in the same or less time (Montague, 1988). The more diverse the student population, the less predictable the results. However, CBT can be adaptable and does indulge varied learning styles. Many researchers will even argue that a lot of learning is unplanned, and computers can provide for a rich and varied learning context that supports much incidental learning.
- Technologist. The person well-versed in technology is often sought out to make decisions concerning how technology should be used in instruction. Such a person tends to favor state-of-the-art equipment over the instructional requirements of a system. A classic situation occurs when the platform is selected without regard for the existence of compatible instruction. When the emphasis is on hardware, too little attention is spent on analyzing the cost-benefit of hardware features in relation to course goals.

- Subject matter expert (SME). The conventional instructional development model calls for SMEs as primary content providers. SMEs are selected for their knowledge of a subject area, not usually for their teaching ability or pedagogical knowledge. SMEs rarely influence the upfront instructional decisions; however, if they have any experience in teaching the subject matter, they can significantly improve the instructional product and ultimately, the ability of the learner to master the subject.
- Instructional Designer. The instructional designer understands the methodology to be employed in developing CBT. This person assesses training problems and structures a working solution, employing SMEs where necessary. Although it is not as common as it should be, the instructional designer should be involved at the time when decisions about the choice of hardware, authoring systems and training strategies are made. Typically, the instructional designer will have basic working knowledge of technology and can determine how to combine training needs with an effective delivery environment.
- Educator. The single biggest factor in ensuring success in the use of CBT is the instructor (or learning manager). These people influence whether CBT is perceived as a positive or negative experience. To paraphrase Seidel and Perez (1994), it has been shown that computers can make the learning experience much more exciting, satisfying and rewarding for the instructor and learner; however, none of the potential benefits of CBT are inherent in CBT; they all hinge on the dedication, persistence, and ability of good instructors and courseware developers.
- Researcher. Researchers are known for pursuing the leading edge, rather than defending the status quo. Practitioners are often a generation behind the latest theory. Researchers tend to approach work from a theoretical perspective. Practitioners, in contrast, focus on specific problems at hand and often apply simplified, local or haphazard thinking, leaping over analysis to development.
- Administrator/Purchaser. In many organizations, non-instructional personnel are charged with acquiring hardware, software and instructional tools. Given their priorities and backgrounds, it is not surprising that options selected don't always meet needs.
- Lobbyist. The lobbyist represents a vested interest. Sometimes the lobbyist is a particular vendor or a proponent of that vendor. Strange decisions about CBT have been made because of familiarity with a particular product or vendor. The downside to staying with a familiar vendor, or selecting a product based upon "hype" is that better solutions are not considered. For instance, an authoring system may be enforced

as a standard when other products would be more suitable and cost effective.

- Executive. The ultimate decision-maker is the executive or senior officer. They are most susceptible to lobbyists and often view training problems from a very abstract perspective, detached from practical problems and theoretical foundations. It is the job of the CBT design team to ensure that the executive has a grasp of how they would like to proceed and why. However, the executive can assist the instructors in overcoming institutional and organizational inertia, which might prevent the successful adoption of CBT.

WHY

CBT can increase individualized instruction's effectiveness and efficiency. Why should CBT be used to instruct? What are the dynamics of this basic decision? To answer this question, aspects of unique CBT characteristics, CBT strengths and weaknesses, and human perceptions and affective concerns pertaining to CBT need to be addressed, according to our review of lessons learned from past decisions to use CBT:

- CBT characteristics. Pacing allows control of the timing of the lesson, permitting learners to progress at their own rate. Content variability allows varying the depth and content of the lesson to meet learners' differing entry knowledge and goals. Instructional adaptability permits the method of presentation to be changed according to students' needs and preferences. Learner control allows students to set the pace, content or mode of presentation. Feedback provides comments on learners' performance to assist them in moving at a steady pace toward mastery of the objectives. *Adaptivity* changes a lesson based upon learner performance, to account for varied learning rates. In addition, CBT is easily updated and disseminated electronically.
- Why use CBT to instruct? CBT can promote direct interaction between the medium and the learner. Learners can typically select or formulate answers on an on-going basis, and they usually receive immediate feedback from the system. Consequently, learners' minds can be actively involved, resulting in actual learning occurring and progress towards goals. CBT might be selected as a medium when a combination of the following requirements need to be met: delivering individualized, instructor-free lessons; providing direct interaction between learner and the instructional system; branching to various levels of instruction and different content, based upon learner input; incorporating graphics and animation; providing on-going feedback which requires just in time

record keeping and analysis; using complex or dynamic models, especially when simulating events that might be dangerous, too slow or too fast to observe, too expensive to conduct, or otherwise more feasible to present in the form of an interactive computer simulation.

- CBT frustrations. Initially, learners may be intimidated by computers and fearful of breaking something or looking stupid. Once these fears are overcome, a second area of frustration might be the lesson itself. Information should be presented gradually, allowing the learner to feel in control. It is important to avoid unnecessary and expensive graphics; while these might be initially attractive, they can be tedious when replicated and are sometimes quite costly. Any illustrations drawn on the screen should be rapidly drawn and refreshed and able to be used in multiple scenarios (unless there is an instructional point to having this particular one only at one place for only one purpose). Also, the presentation should be geared to the target audience; avoiding, for instance, "cute" elements that may not be very culturally relevant to a wide audience. The function keys should be identified and easy to understand, with "help" always available for learners. Navigation for the learner should be planned carefully, so the learner doesn't get lost or confused. Finally, responses to the student should be frequent, informative, encouraging and accurate, much as a student would expect a human tutor to be responsive.

CONCLUSION

The ambiguity of the problem lies in the application of methodology in solving instructional problems. Static methodologies are applied to dynamic environments. This application of methodologies has shown that the theoretical bases are not applied consistently in either academic studies or in training environments. In education, the focus tends to be on academic study apart from the dynamics of real world problems, thus establishing a privileged status for solving academic problems in an idealized environment. In training, on the other hand, there is a tendency to focus on the "real work" at hand and to overlook how a solution might be derived from a theoretical perspective or how a theory might suggest an approach to design, development or evaluation. A vocational curriculum in instructional design is project oriented in order to prepare students for the workplace, but the dynamic interchange with theory and research is sacrificed. To further complicate the matter, in the work place emphasis is placed on cost effectiveness more typically than on learning effectiveness. The overall outcome of this situation is that neither the academic curriculum nor vocational curriculum prepares students for professional work as instructional designers as that praxis is now evolving in dynamic working and learning environments of the new millennium.

Figure 3. The ambiguity of the problem.

The theme of this article is that instructional designers work in a very dynamic setting, balancing many factors, involving teams of different persons with different perspectives, trying to satisfy changing expectations. We have reviewed lessons learned from recent practice with the purpose of drawing particular attention to these many dynamic factors. If the fundamental dynamic nature of instructional design is not explicitly recognized in models, it is unlikely that we will systematically prepare designers to be responsive to the challenges of the future. Our framework and perspective intends to combine theoretical foundations with practical concerns. Our framework for a decision making model provides a template that can be used to build a coherent portrayal of instructional design practices and the environment in which this work is conducted. This article combines the authors' collective knowledge of CBT. These lessons learned cover experience over a period from the early sixties to the present. The authors have found that there are no right or wrong answers to the way CBT problems are solved. However, the publishing of these lessons learned should raise questions that will help shape the future of instructional development efforts. Dynamic processes and methods are being used today to help establish effective instructional design praxis and ensure that learning takes place. The explicit recognition of instructional design as a complex and dynamic process and the use of appropriate tools should provide a better foundation for the future.

REFERENCES

Christensen, D. L., Dunnagan, C. B., & Tennyson, R. D. (1998). The future of instructional theory: Lessons learned. *Journal of Structural Leaning & Intelligent Systems, 13(2),* 103-113.

Gagné, R. M. (1985). *The conditions of learning (4th ed.).* New York: Holt, Rinehart, and Winston.

Gustafson, K. L. & Branch, R. M. (1997). *Survey of instructional development models (3rd Ed.).* Syracuse, NY: ERIC Clearinghouse on Information & Technology.

Kaufman, R., Thiagarajan, S., & MacGillis, P. (Eds.) (1996). *Guidebook for performance improvement : Working with individuals & organizations.* San Francisco: Jossey-Bass.

Montague, W. E. (1988). *What works: Summary of research findings with implications for Navy instruction and learning* (NAVEDTRA 115-1). Pensacola, FL: Chief of Naval Education and Training.

Morris, R .C. T. (1994). Toward a user-centered information service. *Journal of the American Society for Information Science,* 45(1): 20-30.

Perez, R. S., & Emery, C. D. (1995). Designer thinking: How novices and experts think about instructional design. *Performance Improvement Quarterly, 8(3),* 80-89.

Perez, R. S., & Neiderman, E. C. (1992). Modeling the expert training developer. In R. J. Seidel & P. Chatelier (Eds.), *Advanced Training Technologies Applied to Training Design.* New York, NY: Plenum Press.

Richey, R. C., & Fields, D. F. (Eds.) (2000). *Instructional design competencies: The standards (3rd Ed.).* Syracuse, NY: ERIC Clearinghouse on Information and Technology & The International Board of Standards for Training, Performance & Instruction.

Rowland, G. (1992). What do instructional designers actually do? An initial investigation of expert practice. *Performance Improvement Quarterly,* 5(2), 65-86.

Seidel, R. J., & Perez, R S. (1994). An evaluation model for investigating the impact of innovative educational technology. In H. F. O'Niel & E. L. Baker (Eds.), *Technology assessment in software applications* (pp.177-212). Hillsdale, NJ: Erlbaum.

Spector, J. M. (on behalf of the Grimstad Group) (1995). Applying system dynamics to courseware development. *Computers in Human Behavior,* 11(2), 325-339.

Spector, J. M. (1996). Creativity and constructivity in learning environments. *Educational Media International,* 33(2), 55-59.

Spector, J. M., Arnold, E. M., & Wilson A. S. (1996). A Turing test for automatically generated instruction. *Journal of Structural Learning,* 12(4), 310-313.

Spector, J. M., & Davidsen, P. I. (1997). Creating engaging courseware using system dynamics. *Computers in Human Behavior,* 13(2), 127-155.

Tennyson, R. D. (1995). Four generations of instructional system development. *Journal of Structural Learning, 12,* 149-164.

Tennyson, R. D., & Morrison, G. R. (2000). *Instructional development: Foundations, process, and methodology.* Columbus, OH: Merrill/Prentice-Hall.

J. MICHAEL SPECTOR

Chapter 5

BUILDING THEORY INTO PRACTICE IN LEARNING AND INSTRUCTION

Keywords: instructional design theory, knowledge ecology

Abstract. A common theme in many instructional design articles is the notion that learning and instructional theories should guide the instructional development process and inform the design of learning environments. This principle may be called the Theory-into-Practice Principle, or TP for short. This prescriptive principle is intended to connect learning theories that are primarily descriptive with instructional design principles that are primarily prescriptive. This paper explores the logic of this principle and the ways that some have attempted to practice TP. My conclusion is that TP sounds fine but is rarely followed with much rigor or success. One set of reasons concerns the vagueness and generality of TP. A second set of reasons concern the exigencies of instruction design practice. I shall also propose answers to two underlying questions: (1) Should TP be revised? and, (2) Should practitioners be encouraged to take TP more seriously?

INTRODUCTION

Instructional design theory is most commonly considered to be primarily prescriptive in nature (Reigeluth, 1983, 1999). Instructional design research is primarily applied research (Gagné, 1985, 1995). Instructional design theory is founded on descriptive learning theories (Kintsch, 1993; Reigeluth, 1983), which typically are derived from much more basic research. Given this perspective, it would be natural to expect that those who plan, implement and manage instructional systems and learning environments want their systems to reflect appropriate theories and research. It is not difficult to find admonitions of the importance of doing this and many who claim to achieve this goal. Many contributors to this volume (e.g., Dijsktra, Goodyear, and Jonassen et al.) argue strongly along such lines, identifying relevant theories and ways them into practical use. Given the continuing and repeated admonitions of the need to put research into practice, one might conclude that this happens all too rarely. Indeed, I believe this is the case. I intend to explore two simple questions in this chapter: (1) Is there a general failure to put theory into practice? and, (2) If so, why?

J.M. Spector and T.M. Anderson (eds.),
Integrated and Holistic Perspectives on Learning, Instruction and Technology, 79–90.
© 2000 *Kluwer Academic Publishers. Printed in the Netherlands.*

In exploring this territory, I will provide a simple framework for the discussion and provide two examples to illustrate some aspects of the landscape. Each of these examples involves research projects that strongly advocated particular theoretical foundations and then proceeded without full regard for those foundations. Not surprisingly, these projects achieved some degree of success. These examples are intended to represent the complexity of the notion of putting theory into practice. Following the discussion of these examples, I shall revisit the problem landscape, suggesting alternative ways to represent the problem space and specific items worth further investigation. I include both learning theory and instructional design theory under the common rubric 'theory'. While this is not common practice, I do so in order to make a clear distinction between theory and practice - practice being what designers and developers actually do in their work settings related to the planning, creation and maintenance of courses and curricula.

FRAMEWORK

The general principle that is elaborated in this chapter is called the Theory-into-Practice Principle (TP). TP has its roots in the definition of the scientific enterprise as a cycle of formulating hypotheses (perhaps deriving them from established theories or unexpected data and using them to construct new or modified theories), deriving predictions and hypotheses concerning as yet unobserved events, making observations, revising hypotheses and theories, and so on. This representation involves an ongoing two-way relationship between that which is theoretical and that which is practical (or that which is observed in the classical scientific model).

Because instructional design is primarily an applied research field, we need to expand this simple experimental framework to include relationships between research fields (both basic and applied). Also, the notion of *individual observations* being used to test and refine hypotheses and theories needs to be expanded to include the notion of *observed practice* being used to refine theories and perspectives. Indeed, the work represented in the other chapters of this volume reflect this latter enterprise quite well. The dynamic relationship between basic and applied research is reflected in Figure 1. This same kind of relationship exists between instructional design theory and instructional design practice. Theory informs and guides practice, which in turn informs and refines theory. [The chapter by Park and Etgen nicely exemplifies the notion of observations informing theory, while the chapter by Seel et al. elaborates how theory guides practice.]

For the sake of this discussion, theory should be broadly interpreted to include both descriptive and prescriptive instructional design theories. Likewise, practice should be broadly interpreted to include all the processes and outcomes typically associated with instructional development and the implementation of learning environments (see Resnick, 1989; Scandura, 1995; Tennyson, 1995). Other chapters in this volume (see, for example, the chapters by Dijsktra and Goodyear) address the concept of a learning environment and the relevant activities of learners, teachers and designers.

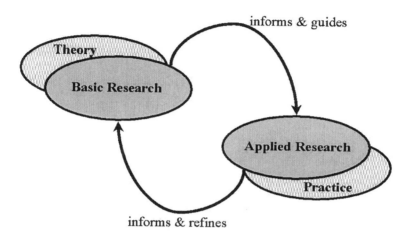

Figure 1. Dynamic relationships between basic & applied research (theory and practice).

It is worth mentioning that a dynamic and ongoing relationship between basic and applied research provides for the possibility of progress in science. Moreover, a parallel relationship between the practice of instructional design and instructional design research provides for the possibility of progress in the planning, implementation, and management of instructional systems and learning environments. Lessons must be learned and used to inform both future practice as well as future applied research. [See the chapter by Dunnagan and Christensen for an extended discussion of this point.] Otherwise, those who design and create learning and instruction must be conceived of as artists and not as artisans or professionals who practice a discipline that systematically improves itself over time. TP assumes the kind of framework depicted in Figure 1.

As an additional part of the background and framework, an elaboration of the meaning of key terms is appropriate. Basic research is generally aimed at answering a scientific question, especially one involving causal relationships, with the general aim of expanding human knowledge in that area or simply satisfying a scientist's curiosity. An example would be finding out whether or not (groups of) people encode, store and retrieve spoken and read text in similar ways. Applied research is generally aimed at finding a solution to a particular problem, such as determining how to minimize cognitive overload in a learning situation that involves learning the names and functions of many pieces of a complicated device. The boundary between these two kinds of research is somewhat fuzzy, but that is not generally problematic.

There seems to be a greater divide between theory and practice, and it is important to interpret these concepts broadly for the purposes of this discussion. I take theory to include descriptive learning theories as well as prescriptive instructional design theories, along with other relevant theories from anthropology, cognitive science, human factors research, organizational research, psychology, and so on. In short, I propose a broad interpretation of 'theory' (Gagné, 1985, 1995; Reigeluth, 1983, 1999; Resnick, 1989; Tennyson & Morrison, 2000). 'Practice' in this discussion includes all the activities that collectively comprise the planning, implementing, evaluating, maintaining and managing of learning environments, instructional systems, and performance improvement solutions in general. Because many persons are typically involved in such efforts, and because the context in which those activities are carried out are critical to their success and impact, it is useful to use the term *praxis* to refer to this larger collection of activities and context (Rowland, 1992; Perez & Neiderman, 1993; Seidel & Perez, 1994; Tennyson, 1995). Some authors have used 'praxis' for this purpose on occasion but the term has not yet caught on in the instructional design literature. I shall use both 'praxis' and 'practice' to refer to the larger collection of situated activities.

MOTIVATION

Is there a widespread failure to translate instructional design theories into instructional design practice? This might appear an easy question to answer, but there are complicating factors. Which instructional design theories should be taken into consideration? What is meant by instructional design practice? What does it mean to translate theory into practice? The most complicated aspect of the question concerns the degree to which attempts to convert theory into practice succeed. It is hard enough to ascertain that learning improvements exist and will generalize to other groups of learners and situations. It is especially difficult to determine whether any observed learning effects and improvements in understanding and performance are attributable to prescriptive instructional design theories. While this is the most important issue raised in this paper, it is well beyond the scope of this discussion to treat this issue in any depth. However, this is arguably the central concern with regard to instructional design research and it does deserve serious and sustained treatment.

That there is a concern to move theory into practice in many fields is no surprise. The educational community has many indicators of this concern, including the quarterly journal *Theory into Practice* published by Ohio State University and the *Theory into Practice Database* developed in 1994 by Greg Kearsley (see http://www.coe.ohio-state.edu/TIP/tip_home.htm) as well as numerous publications by various governmental and research agencies (see Fletcher, 1996; Montague, 1988; O'Neil et al., 1992). This concern exists in our professional community as it does in many others (see, for example, Sternberg, 1986). How well do we meet this goal?

If we take summaries of effective applications of instructional technology as an indication, we might infer that there is indeed a deficiency (see, for example, Christensen et al., 1998; Montague, 1988). If the frequent publication of standards and benchmarks is taken as an indication, then there is again the suggestion that putting theory into practice remains a critical concern (see Richey & Fields, 2000, or The Institute for Higher Education Policy, 2000, for example).

A more detailed argument for both the need and failure to take educational theory into practice can be found in Hopper (1993). Hopper argues that educational research projects should be viewed as experiments in knowledge ecology, which is a concept that fits the dynamic interplay between theory and practice already elaborated. It is possible to read her research as a study of success or failure in putting theory into practice (in the domain of advanced educational technologies), especially since the four large educational research projects she examined proceeded on the basis of explicitly stated theoretical assumptions. The four courseware research projects she examined were: ESCAPE (Engineering Specific Career-planning and Problem-Solving Environment at Prudue University); Context 32 (Intermedia and StorySpace research effort at Brown University); TODOR and Mechanics (AthenaMuse research effort at Massachusetts Institute of Technology), and The Physical Geography Tutor (another AthenaMuse effort at Massachusetts Institute of Technology). The relevant theoretical foundations included both descriptive learning theories and prescriptive instructional design principles, and collectively focused on the perspective of providing rich and flexible experiential learning places for students (see the chapters by Goodyear and Jonassen et al.).

Hopper's perspective has the advantage of introducing criteria into the discussion. How is it determined that projects did or did not succeed in implementing the theoretical foundations upon which those projects were based? The primary criterion Hopper advocates is the continuation of the effort in some form. Success indicators, therefore, include the following:

- the project is still active, sometimes under another name;
- the project fed back results to the theoretical foundations group or researchers who have a related project;
- the project has resulted in a commercial product or full-scale implementation in a practical setting; or,
- the project led to a follow-on effort.

An interesting exercise well beyond the scope of this discussion would be to identify a set of relevant theories (for example those found in Kearsley's Theory into Practice Database), identify a set of development projects associated with those theories, examine the criteria proposed by Hopper (project on-going, project feedback to theoretical work, commercial product or full-scale implementation, or follow-on effort), and then determine how many efforts "died on the vine" without any impact on elaboration of foundations or on practice outside the scope of the project itself. I choose to leave this as an exercise for the reader.

What I propose to do next is to question how we might evaluate success in implementing theory. The theme of the remainder of this chapter is that we do not have clear or specific criteria for determining how theory has influenced praxis. We make such judgments largely on the basis of subjective considerations. If we were to follow this set of criteria (although they are admittedly vague), we might be inclined to judge some projects as failing to put theory into practice. In some cases, such a judgment would be premature and narrow, especially when the dynamic nature of the relationship and broad interpretations for theory and praxis are the focus. Moreover, we might be inclined to rate some projects successful against such criteria when in fact those projects failed to implement relevant theories. I intend to illustrate this point through a discussion of two cases. Thereafter, I argue that we ought to take TP seriously.

TWO ILLUSTRATIVE EXAMPLES

I shall now present two examples of projects that proceeded on the basis of explicit theoretical foundations and then abandoned those foundations midway through the effort. In a sense, these projects decided that they would no longer attempt to put a particular theory into practice, even though in each case the theory was widely adopted and considered highly relevant by both sponsors and clients. The first project (code-named the *Participatory Project* to avoid undue embarrassment) involved a European effort to develop a web-based postgraduate curriculum for orthodontics education. The second project (code named the *Collaboration Project*) involved another European effort to implement collaborative learning in university undergraduate political science education. I should say at the outset that both projects would be judged successful on Hopper's criteria and have been judged successful on criteria established by the European Commission. However, each decided to abandon a relevant theoretical foundation and at least implicitly admitted failure to implement relevant theories.

Participatory Project

The Participatory Project involved four European universities in a collaborative effort to develop, implement and evaluate a web-based curriculum for postgraduate orthodontics education using a problem- and case-based approach. The pedagogical approach used in the traditional instruction was case- and problem-based, and that approach was determined desirable for the web-based curriculum. The design approach was user-centered (Morris, 1994), up to a point. Relevant user communities involved teachers, students, researchers, and sponsoring institutions and agencies.

A masters (*hovedfag*) thesis at the University of Bergen was devoted to an independent usability study of the initial version of the new curriculum with particular attention to the user-centered approach adopted by the project (Makochieng, 1999). This study focused primarily on student users and secondarily on teachers. The Participatory Project adopted a user-centered design approach in its first year, partly to help harmonize the different interests and perspectives of the four participating universities (Bergen, Göteborg, Munich, and Thessaloniki) and partly to help harmonize the different interests of researchers, students, system designers, and teachers. It is specifically the user-centered design approach of this effort that will be considered in a bit more detail.

According to the user-centered design approach adopted, representatives of the user populations would be involved in successive and iterative prototyping efforts, proceedings in these four steps (Makochieng, 1999):

1. paper-based prototypes;
2. presentation software-based prototypes;
3. initial web-accessible interface and database; and,
4. refined version to be the basis for a commercial development.

The project in fact used this approach for the first two steps. At this point, Makochieng's (1999) satisfaction surveys indicated high expectations and high satisfaction with the project on the part of both teachers and students, even though students had seen very little of the initial prototype. As the effort progressed, an implementation decision was made to use the same database software for the remaining two steps. This software and the associated development turned out to be expensive and consumed the majority of resources remaining for the effort. As a consequence, user involvement in the design was dropped because there were insufficient funds to support that involvement and because there was insufficient time due to greatly extended timelines for the third step. Makochieng's surveys indicated a significant drop in levels of satisfaction and expectations at the end of the third step.

By the time the project reached the fourth step, there was active student resistance and teacher skepticism with regard to the effort. However, no one doubted the good faith and hard work exerted by project leaders and project loyalty remained high (Makochieng, 1999). The curriculum was subsequently revised without any direct student input and minimal teacher input. Critical design decisions in the fourth phase were made by software specialists and researchers and not by teachers. There were no additional design reviews by students or teachers after step 3. Instead, those sessions turned into training sessions - how to make the best of the new system, rather than how to improve that system.

Publicly, the project maintained its commitment to the user-centered design approach and to the theory of participatory design (Floyd et al., 1989). Internally, those involved admitted that they had made decisions as best they could to make effective use of remaining resources. No one took responsibility for the critical change in plans at step 3 to use the same expensive database software for the final two phases, nor did the project formally make a connection between this decision and subsequent lack of support from teachers and students. The university failed to embrace the new curriculum in spite of strong support from the previous Dean, from project researchers and database designers, and from the central university administration that offered additional funding support. In short, the decision to abandon the user-centered approach led to low support from two relevant constituencies (students and teachers) and was most likely connected with the failure of the involved faculty to follow-through as originally planned.

Based on Hopper's criteria, the project was successfully because there was a funded follow-on effort, because there was internal feedback through Makochieng's thesis concerning the costs of the user-centered approach and consequences of abandoning it, and because there is commercial interest in developing the database. That the project failed to implement a particular theory in a practical setting mitigates against this apparent success. This potentially delivers a mistaken message with regard to the relevant theory (participatory design). The message that could be derived is that participatory design is too expensive and too slow to accommodate real-world efforts. The message that should be derived is that sticking with a commitment to participatory design will result in higher likelihood of ongoing support by user communities.

The point I wish to make is that it is far from clear how to make sense of such apparent successes or failures with regard to the dimension of putting theory into practice. The broader perspective I wish to encourage suggests that this particular effort failed to put the theory of participatory design into practice and that the abandoning of a user-centered approach led to a decline of support for the effort, just as the theory predicts (Makochieng, 1999). However, it remain fuzzy whether or not TP was achieved and with what degree of success.

Collaboration Project

The Collaboration Project brought together a diverse group of educators and researchers from five institutions in four European countries who share a common interest in simulations and games. The Collaboration Project is developing, testing, evaluating and implementing simulation scenarios in response to the urgent need to provide Europeans with an effective means of harnessing the power, creativity and richness of cultural diversity to address the challenges facing Europe.

The relevant theoretical foundation for this effort is collaborative learning (Salomon, 1993) in the context of situated learning (Lave, 1988). The project claims on its home page that the effectiveness of distributed telematics simulations in providing a supportive, holistic learning environment is working, as predicted by relevant theories, as shown by an increasing appreciation for the complexity of international issues, by greater sensitivity to cultural and linguistic differences, and by a greater understanding of the different perspectives that nations bring into negotiating situations. Participants report learning to accept responsibility for their own learning and for their team's success; moreover, they gain experience in working together to accomplish shared goals and in conflict resolution.

The project fails to report just how these improvements are determined, however, The measures collected only provide support for increased involvement as opposed to increased understanding. Since the goals are quite soft (e.g., greater sensitivity to cultural differences), it is not surprising to find self-reports by participants on those items since the project goals are made explicit to all involved. In short, this project cannot clearly demonstrate that it achieves its goals. [See the chapter by Seel et al. for a more rigorous attempt to validate outcomes.]

Moreover, the scenarios around which the distributed, technology-facilitated negotiations proceed do not lend themselves to collaboration in the sense proposed by Salomon. There are different negotiating teams representing different countries, and within those teams, there are various sub-groups and roles. Participants do not rotate through those roles and teams as they might in a non-collaborative but still cooperative setting. However, the real-world sense of relying on some other person's expertise and good judgment is artificially imposed in these scenarios and the associated simulation environment. While the scenarios appear realistic and authentic, they lack genuine authenticity since decisions for Europe are not being made. Moreover, there has been no effort to demonstrate that the improvements transfer in any noticeable way outside the context of the learning environments. [See Dijkstra's for the instructional significance of distinguishing reality from representations of reality.]

In summary, this project appears to put a relevant learning theory into practice. That it does so is questionable, although it certainly appears to do so. With regard to Hopper's criteria, there have been follow-on funded efforts. However, there is as yet no commercial derivative product nor an adopted standard curriculum. Moreover, the relevant research community in this case appears to only consider confirmatory evidence, so feedback from practice to theory is basically non-existent or highly questionable. As with the previous project, when one examines the theory-into-practice dimension in this quite credible effort, it, too, turns out to be unclear as to which theories were instantiated and with what results.

CONCLUSION

I selected these two projects since they were both examples of efforts much in line with the kind of holistic approaches to learning, instruction and technology that are the theme of this volume. These are credible research projects with demonstrated results. The researchers are distinguished and dedicated. I suppose that many other efforts to directly implement theories in practice and demonstrate benefits can be found. Hopper examined four in great detail. We might easily compile a list of 400 in the last few years. We ought to ask ourselves what we have learned from these efforts. The lessons-learned literature does not provide clear or definitive answers. Those things that have indisputably been demonstrated to have the most impact and to clearly account for the most variance in learning were established many years ago (e.g., small class size, a variety of engaging activities, and so on). Those lessons are not new. We have new names for many things. Gagné (1985) identified an important learning event that he called gaining attention. More modern writers say that contextualized learning is what matters (see various chapters in Reigeluth, 1999). The differences in such positions when each is examined dispassionately and in detail are quite minor. Yet we are confronted with new theories and perspectives at an alarming rate. Serious scholars have difficulty in keeping up with the published literature. The public at large remains largely skeptical (Spector, 1998).

Is TP confused? Are our expectations confused or ill-founded? Ought we abandon or modify TP? My suggestion, after this admittedly limited review, is that we ought not to abandon TP. What we ought to do is adopt more appropriate attitudes with regard to theory and praxis. What is happening at an increasing rate is that advocacy is replacing inquiry. The TP framework presented at the beginning of this chapter assumed that inquiry was the fundamental process and that understanding was the fundamental product. The advocacy model proceeds on the assumption that the fundamental process is change and the fundamental product is verification or confirmation of one's position. As the learning focus has shifted towards more holistic concerns (larger groups of learners interacting in a variety of ways with more global goals), the research has shifted from more quantitative methods to more qualitative methods. Both methods can be applied superficially or with rigor. However, when the concern shifts from inquiry to advocacy, research tends to be subordinated to political or other concerns. Some will argue that this is as things should be and that advocacy cannot be entirely or neatly separated from inquiry.

Regardless, what is appropriate is an open acknowledgement that theoretical positions within an inquiry or an advocacy context should be held with an appropriate degree of uncertainty. Likewise, positions with regard to practical outcomes and what works best should be held with similar degrees of uncertainty. We generally know less than we are inclined to admit about almost any topic. If we do not accept appropriate degrees of uncertainty, then the dynamic relationships between theory and praxis are jeopardized and progress becomes sporadic and intermittent, based on catastrophic failures rather than on progressive steps towards improved understanding. If we fail to establish rigorous methods of inquiry, then we are not likely to make steady progress in developing methods to improve understanding in complex domains. [Those methods illustrated in the chapters by Park & Etgen, Savenye, and Seel et al. provide constructive models of inquiry aimed at improving such understanding.]

REFERENCES

Center for Working Life, the Royal Institute of Technology, Stockholm, Sweden and the University of Aarhus, Denmark.

Christensen, D. L., Dunnagan, C. B., & Tennyson, R. D. (1998). The future of instructional theory: Lessons learned. *Journal of Structural Leaning & Intelligent Systems, 13(2)*, 103-113.

Fletcher, J. D. (1996). Does this stuff work? Some findings from applications of technology to education and training. *Proceedings of Conference on Teacher Education and the Use of Technology Based Learning Systems.* Warrenton, VA: Society for Applied Learning Technology, 1996.

Floyd, C., Mehl, W. M., Reisin, F. M., Schmidt, G., & Wolf, G. (1989). Out of Scandinavia: Alternative approaches to software design and system development. *Human-Computer Interaction*, 4(4), 253-350.

Gagné, R. M. (1985). *The conditions of learning (4th ed.).* New York: Holt, Rinehart, and Winston.

Gagné, R. M. (1995). Learning processes and instruction. *Training Research Journal, 1*, 17-28.

Hopper, M. E. (1993). *Courseware projects in advanced educational computing environments.* Unpublished doctoral dissertation. West Lafayette, IN: Purdue University.

Lave, J. (1988). *Cognition in practice: Mind, mathematics, and culture in everyday life.* Cambridge, UK: Cambridge University Press.

Makochieng, O. (1999). *Effects of information technology on the learning process: Formative evaluation of a technology based curriculum for postgraduate orthodontics education.* Unpublished *hovedfag* thesis. Bergen, Norway: Department of Information Science, University of Bergen.

Montague, W. E. (1988). *What works: Summary of research findings with implications for Navy instruction and learning* (NAVEDTRA 115-1). Pensacola, FL: Chief of Naval Education and Training.

Morris, R .C. T. (1994). Toward a user-centered information service. *Journal of the American Society for Information Science*, 45(1): 20-30.

O'Neil, H. F. Jr., Allred, A., & Baker, E. L. (1992). *Measurement of workforce readiness competencies: Review of theoretical frameworks* (CSE Technical Report No. 343). Los Angeles: University of California, Center for Research on Evaluation Standards and Student Testing.

Perez, R. S., & Neiderman, E. C. (1992). Modeling the expert training developer. In R. J. Seidel & P. Chatelier (Eds.), *Advanced Training Technologies Applied to Training Design.* New York, NY: Plenum Press.

Reigeluth, C. M. (Ed.) (1983). *Instructional design theories and models: An overview of their current status.* Hillsdale, NJ: Erlbaum.

Reigeluth, C. M. (Ed.) (1999). *Instructional design theories and models: A new paradigm of instructional theory*, Vol II. Mahwah, NJ: Erlbaum.

Resnick, L. B. (Ed.) (1989). *Knowing, learning, and instruction.* Hillsdale, NJ: Lawrence Erlbaum.

Richey, R. C., & Fields, D. F. (Eds.) (2000). *Instructional design competencies: The standards (3rd Ed.).* Syracuse, NY: ERIC Clearinghouse on Information and Technology & The International Board of Standards for Training, Performance & Instruction.

Rowland, G. (1992). What do instructional designers actually do? An initial investigation of expert practice. *Performance Improvement Quarterly*, 5(2), 65-86.

Salomon, G. (1993) (Ed.). *Distributed cognitions: Psychological and educational considerations.* New York: Cambridge University Press.

Scandura, J. M. (1995). Theoretical foundations of instruction: Past, present, and future. *Journal of Structural Learning*, 12(3), 231-243.

Seidel, R. J., & Perez, R S. (1994). An evaluation model for investigating the impact of innovative educational technology. In H. F. O'Niel & E. L. Baker (Eds.), *Technology assessment in software applications* (pp.177-212). Hillsdale, NJ: Erlbaum.

Spector, J. M. (1998). President's corner. *Journal of Courseware Engineering*, 1, 1-4.

Sternberg, R. J. (1986). Intelligence applied: Understanding and increasing your intellectual skills. San Diego, CA: Harcourt Brace Jovanovich.

Tennyson, R. D. (1995). Four generations of instructional system development. *Journal of Structural Learning, 12,* 149-164.

Tennyson, R .D., & Morrison, G. R. (2000). *Instructional development: Foundations, process, and methodology.* Columbus, OH: Merrill/Prentice-Hall.

The Institute for Higher Education Policy (2000). Quality on the line: Benchmarks for success in Internet-based distance education. Washington, DC: The Institute for Higher Education Policy.

ELLEN D. WAGNER

Chapter 6

LEVERAGING TECHNOLOGY IN THE SERVICE OF LIFE-LONG LEARNING

Keywords: competency model, computer-based learning, coopetition, employee development, knowledge management, performance management

Abstract. This paper describes issues associated with the implementation of a technology-mediated performance diagnosis and prescription system. The system called *Kompetansenettet*, benchmarks individual user competencies against performance standards defined for job-specific or learning area-specific competencies. While *Kompetansenettet* has been designed as a professional development tool for individuals, it also gives organizations a means of focusing professional development investments in areas likely to provide better value for the organization. The discussion includes an elaboration of a competency-based approach as opposed to a knowledge-based approach.

INTRODUCTION

Technology continues to transform the way that business is conducted in today's global marketplace. Interest in electronic commerce is at an all-time high. Messaging, document transfer and transactional processing are increasingly commonplace, even in small companies. Virtual warehousing has completely altered inventory management practices. Marketing activities are a mainstay of corporate web applications. Clearly, knowing how to effectively deploy technology in the workplace has become a mission-critical business skill.

Electronic learning (Wagner 1998), increasingly called "e-learning" (Trondsen, 1999) refers to the wide range of technology applications that provide learners with the means to increase their knowledge and improve their skills when and where they need improvement. Trends in several distinct arenas have strongly influenced e-learning's growth and development. First, there are issues pertaining to technology infrastructure. The ubiquitous availability of information technologies has made e-learning a viable alternative for even the smallest organizations. Second, increasingly complex, competitive workplace needs for information, learning and

J.M. Spector and T.M. Anderson (eds.),
Integrated and Holistic Perspectives on Learning, Instruction and Technology, 91–102.

performance support are resulting in increased demands for better access to a company's intellectual assets, when and where these resources are needed most.

INFORMATION TECHNOLOGIES: INFRASTRUCTURE FOR E-LEARNING

One of the most obvious attributes of e-learning is its dependence upon technology. The infrastructure needed to distribute electronic learning resources has reached a sufficient number of (potential) users to create a burgeoning market for programs and services.

Some of the specific developments leading to the widespread availability of technology include the following (Wagner, 1999):

- *Platform-independent data transmission protocols.* Given the tremendous developments in networking protocol interoperability (e.g., UNIX users can share data with Microsoft Windows users, who can, in turn, share that information with Macintosh OS users, who can, in their turn, share information with OS/2 users), concerns of networking now focus less on the tools of system networking and more on the intent of interpersonal networking.
- *Improved browser technology, and features such as Java-enabled client-server interactivity.* Readily accessible new media, such as online multimedia and hypermedia, offer computer users of all proficiency levels gateways to an array of full-motion, fully animated, interactive, and responsive information resources.
- *Content Objects and Knowledge Content Distributors.* A content object is a modular data unit that encapsulates information to describe and present a concept, skill, operation, or procedure [see Dijsktra's discussion of knowledge and Jonassen's transmissive model of instruction in this volume]. A categorization schema, called a meta-data structure, defines an object's descriptive attributes (e.g., whether it is text, animation, audio or video information; the size and type of file; the topic being presented in the object, the performance that the object is intended to elicit, and so on). The meta-data structure makes it possible to combine powerful database capabilities with online search and file retrieval capabilities so that specific content objects can be identified, located and retrieved. Known as *Knowledge Content Distributors* or *KCD*s (Masie, 1998), these content object/meta-data tools operate as "wholesalers" of online and digital learning content from multiple vendors, providing user organizations with the ability to mix and match learning products. In practical terms, this means that users can select and compile the precise content objects that they specify.

- *Improved "backend" database technologies.* Combined with the browser and KCD features noted above, programs employing full-scale database "back-ends" make it possible for even small businesses to leverage the power of real-time online transactional processing. They also make it possible to offer adaptive, fully individualized professional development resources that respond to a user's profiled needs and interests by establishing search and sort protocols that access only the information that is relevant to that user's profile.
- *The ubiquitous availability of commercial Internet Service Providers (ISPs).* The burgeoning number of commercial Internet Service Providers and the competition among them has dramatically affected the access to service, types of service, costs for service and provision of user support that Internet users have come to expect.

DEMANDS FOR WORKPLACE PERFORMANCE IMPROVEMENT

Success in today's economy requires an organization to develop specific competencies related to thriving in the midst of change. These competencies could include employees' ability to think critically, to solve problems and to anticipate new possibilities (Rothwell, 1996). Growing workplace demands for information, instruction and training resources that are available when and where they are needed is driven by individuals' requirements for "just-in-time, just-for-me" learning and performance support tools [see Goodyear's discussion of compliant versus autonomous learners in this volume]. The presence of a growing online learning and performance support marketplace marks this shift in the balance of power away from providers to the individual learner. It is easy to understand why there is growing impatience with traditional methods of designing, delivering and managing learning experiences that are increasingly out of touch in a "wired world."

While training is an important tool for improving employee knowledge and skills, conventional classroom-based training may be insufficient for providing the full range of continuous, individualized performance improvement interventions (Ellis et al., 1999). Training has traditionally been something which is "done to" learners, implemented to react to a performance deficiency. Specific outcomes need to be achieved, so learners are expected to conform to a path dictated by either the designer of the learning experience, the instructor for the learning experience, or both. Typically, it has not been a goal of training to meet the individual needs of the learner. Traditional training design does not address the need for flexibility required to meet an individual's learning needs. Nor do traditional training delivery mechanisms allow for training to be available at the time it may be needed by any given individual. [See chapters by Jonassen et al. and Goodyear for further elaboration of these points.]

E-learning provides learners the means to proactively pursue information and performance support resources unconstrained by training design or delivery mechanisms. E-learning tools can offer individualized learning profiles. It can diagnose skill gaps and prescribe professional development activities ensuring the link between learning events and on-the-job practice. Individuals can monitor their own progress and determine what the next step in their professional development should be. Training is available when and where those resources are needed by the learner.

INFLUENCES OF KNOWLEDGE MANAGEMENT

The knowledge management movement is likely to have significant impact on e-learning programs in the next few years. Knowledge management refers to the way that organizations generate, communicate and leverage their intellectual assets. Knowledge management is proving to be an essential source of competitive advantage in the information economy. [See Marshall & Rossett in this volume for additional discussion of knowledge management.]

While organizational size and complexity have accelerated the need to consciously manage knowledge across time and space, relatively little has been done to increase an individual's personal capacity to absorb information and create new knowledge. The central challenge is to better manage the flow of information through and around the "bottlenecks" of personal attention and learning capacity.

Sieloff (1999) suggests a number of strategies for facilitating attention management to deal with information overflow including:

Know what you don't need to know. Organizations need to accommodate the knowledge needs of individuals without forcing everyone else in the organization to master the same body of information. Of course this places a heavier meta-cognitive burden on learners to determine what they do not need to know in addition to what they need to learn.

"Just-in-time, just enough" delivery of knowledge resources reduces the required inventory that an individual must hold in store. It is no longer necessary to expose individuals to the full array of information resources that may be available. Instead, it is increasingly important to profile the knowledge needs of individuals and to link them to the resources needed to engender specific capabilities.

Use trusted intermediaries. Universal access to content, whether represented as objects, links or frames, can literally destroy the context from which content is drawn. This, in turn, compromises an individual's ability to assign meaning, create associations and link new information with already held knowledge (Ormrod, 1998). It also makes it difficult to filter content for importance (Jonassen & Grabowski, 1993). Technology-mediated intermediaries (such as online advisors, intelligent search tools, literature summary services and learning management systems) help establish, maintain and monitor frameworks that can define (situational) context. Even so, online communities of practice, knowledge advisors and learning mentors are playing increasingly important roles in helping individuals to filter and to assign meaning to the array of elements that may be contained in a content object library.

Precision distribution provides individuals with content objects and context for interpretation. The degree of precision for accessing content objects is a function of the quality and robustness of schemas used to organize and arrange data files and define access and retrieval strategies. Significant work has been undertaken by such groups as the Aviation Industry Computer-Based-Training Committee (AICC), the IEEE Learning Technology Standards Committee, the Educause Instructional Management Systems (IMS) Project, and the World Wide Web Consortium (W3C) to address the notion of system-level interoperability (Richards, 1998).

COMPETENCY MODELS

Competency models first appeared in the 1970s in US business settings as an employee selection strategy (Lucia & Lepsinger, 1999). A competency model is a collection of related descriptions of the behaviors of an excellent performer. Each competency statement contains a set of related skills, knowledge and attitudes that characterize the excellent performer. For an example of instructional design competencies, consistent with the framework presented here, see Richey & Fields (2000).

A variety of discovery audit techniques, including Delphi forecasting, focus groups, workplace observations and interviews with multiple stakeholders, are used to define and predict the essential attributes of an individual that results in a superior performance on the job. By identifying the attributes of outstanding employees in given job roles, criteria can be used to establish performance standards for review of existing employees, and to establish hiring standards (or expectations or guidelines – the term used to describe the performance attributes varies, as does the degree of rigor used to identify or define attributes associated with specific job roles).

Competency models are used by organizations to plan tactics for implementing the organization's strategic vision. The tactics center around a set of competency models that articulate the collection of abilities, skills and competencies required of its' employees if the organization is to realize their vision. Given these sets of competency models, the organization can assess the competencies of its' existing employees. It can plan to address key gaps in the competencies through training, hiring, influencing government and university policy, and so on. Competency models provide the means to align human resources policies with the long term strategic planning as well as ongoing, periodic reassessment and re-calibration of the organization's human resources. Human resources planning becomes the occasion to identify and capitalize on strategic opportunities.

Standards/expectations/guidelines expressed in a competency model for a particular job or performance category can be used in a variety of ways, including employee selection and job performance evaluation. They can also provide employees with a mechanism for converting the description of attributes to expressions of essential skill areas. On this basis, employees are able to compare their skills with those expected of the outstanding performer. Thus, competency models support the employees' efforts to create professional development strategies so that on an organizational level, the overall level of skills and competencies is raised.

BENEFITS OF COMPETENCY MODELS

Competency models benefit organizations and employees because they:

- Help organizations drive strategic change by modeling the organizations' vision of success;
- Allow organizations to set training, hiring, and policy goals to meet the human resources requirements of the strategic vision;
- Help organizations manage to strategic plan by enabling managers to monitor the essential performance requirements of a given job at any given time;
- Align employee behaviors with organizational strategies and values;
- Help clarify job and work expectations for employees and their managers; and,
- Support self-improvement by giving employees benchmarks against which to see how he or she measures up to company expectations.

COMPETENCY-BASED LEARNING

Sieloff's (1999) personal knowledge management heuristics support the notion of helping individuals target their personalized learning and performance support needs. Competency-based learning (CBL) offers such a strategy. It links assessment instruments with an articulated competency model of the excellent performer. CBL thereby provides the means to benchmark an individual's competencies against specific standards of competency demonstration. When used in combination with a knowledge content distributor, individual learners are then linked to learning objects in the form of courses, modules and lessons that will help build capacity in empirically targeted areas.

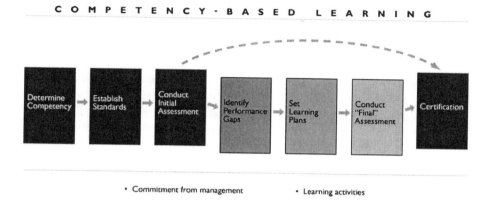

Figure 1. A competency-based learning model.

It should be noted that while the model depicted in Figure 1 appears linear, this linearity pertains only to notion of the general logical flow from determining competencies to establishing standards to conducting initial assessments, and so on. Implementing such a model and then developing associated training and certification involves much iteration and is not such a linear process. Competency-based learning emerges from research and best practices dealing with motivation and achievement (see, for example, McCombs, 1992; Richey & Fields, 2000). It is predicated on the practice of using competency models to articulate performance expectations associated with specific categories of jobs.

Competency-based learning works by linking skills and competencies (as described in a competency model) to those learning resources that will help the individual build targeted skills and competencies (e.g., traditional classes, white papers, URL links, videos, CD-ROM/multimedia training and Web-based training). In addition to providing employees the means of determining where (deficient) skills can be strengthened, CBL also provides a means of ensuring recognition of skill mastery that has been achieved but not formally acknowledged through formal training or education.

Competency-based learning is a strategy for maximizing the effectiveness and impact of training and performance support programs and resources. Where competency models define the scope of skills expected of a high performing employee, Competency-based learning provides the means of linking employees with the essential learning resources they need to build targeted skills.

KOMPETANSENETTET: COMPETENCY-BASED LEARNING IN PRACTICE

Kompetansenettet[1] is an online learning management system that is being implemented in Norway under contract with *Næringslivets Hovedorganisasjon* (NHO), the Confederation of Norwegian Business and Industry. Its intent is to help users (adult learners) improve their job performance by focusing training and education activities on building essential, job-specific knowledge, skills and attitudes rather than emphasizing mastery of a body of knowledge that may or may not be applied on the job.

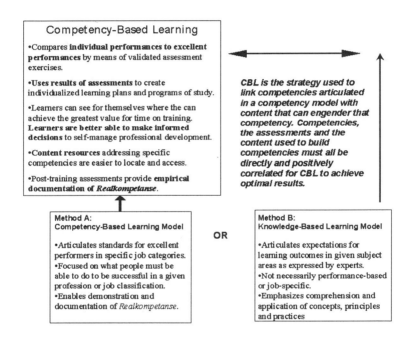

Figure 2. Competency-based learning - a strategy for linking competency models to content.

The genesis for implementing *Kompetansenettet* came from government, labor and industry leaders calling for the provision of professional development opportunities for up to 10% of a worker's time on-the-job. This represents a growing trend to provide more opportunities for lifelong learning worldwide, although Scandinavian and other Northern European countries are most aggressive about national strategies for lifelong learning.

---

[1] *Kompetansenettet* is a customized implementation of Informania, Inc.'s WebLearn Plus® learning management system.

As part of the strategy for responding to this Norwegian directive, businesses are looking toward and expect technology-mediated training to meet the needs of workers while minimizing the impact of time away from the workplace pursuing training opportunities. Both NHO and *Landsorganisasjonen*, the Norwegian Confederation of Trade Unions (LO), have indicated their interest in using *Kompetansenettet* to document "*realkompetanse*" – the professional knowledge, skills and attitudes developed over time that are not otherwise sanctioned or acknowledged by official learning credentials or certifications.

Kompetansenettet was designed to make active use of competency models to define the scope and focus of knowledge, skills and attitudes attributed to excellent performers in a given job category or learning area (Klemp, 1980). In the pilot implementation of *Kompetansenettet*, existing web-enabled courseware available from multiple vendors was reviewed, analyzed and mapped to relevant elements of appropriate competency models. Wherever possible, competency models were validated using third party data sources (e.g., professional certification guidelines, "best practices" data from professional associations, etc.) to enhance their validity and their generalizability.

As originally conceptualized, *Kompetansenettet* compared an employee's job-specific knowledge, skills and attitudes with standards of performance established by excellent performers in those same job-specific knowledge, skill and attitude arenas represented in the competency models registered in *Kompetansenettet*. *Kompetansenettet* users complete assessment exercises – situated, scenario-based examples of problems or situations likely to be encountered on the job - in relevant learning areas to see how they compare to standards of performance defined in the *Kompetansenettet* competency models. Assessment results give a user a metric for comparing his or her competencies for his or her job with those competencies as expressed in the *Kompetansenettet* competency models. Assessment results help diagnose a user's strengths and greatest opportunities for improving his or her job-related knowledge skills and attitudes. *Kompetansenettet* uses the results of assessments to prescribe an individualized learning plan. The learning plan consists of content objects (typically online courseware or modules within courses) that correlate with competencies expected of a high performing employee in specific job classifications.

While *Kompetansenettet*'s unique value lies in its ability to apply competency-based learning strategies and tactics to improve workplace performance, *Kompetansenettet* also needed to offers robust search and retrieval capabilities to be an effective means of managing all forms of web-enabled learning content. This is a response to two real-world contingencies: the first is the relative lack of web-enabled content, and the second is that, of web-based instructional content that is available, the vast majority is knowledge-based content rather than competency-based content. In a knowledge-based learning model, content is organized around topic or subject attributes rather than around discrete performances expected of excellent performers as described in a competency model.

Kompetansenettet's search and retrieval functionality is enabled by means of meta-data tags that index all data elements in the system. Meta-data tags for content mapped to competencies registered in *Kompetansenettet* use several categories of meta-data tags, including those that specify FORMAT attributes, SUBJECT attributes, and COMPETENCY attributes. Content that is not correlated to a specific competency contained in a registered model typically only display FORMAT and SUBJECT meta-data tags. Whether or not content correlates directly to a registered competency model, use of the FORMAT and SUBJECT meta-data tags increase the number of content index terms/access points, making it easier for users to locate relevant content resources.

The results of research and practice in similar kinds of technology-mediated performance improvement systems indicate that a number of other issues are likely to surface that will underscore the challenges of implementing competency-based learning programs using web-enabled learning technologies. These issues include the following:

Knowledge-based learning designs or competency-based learning designs? The CBL design featured in *Kompetansenettet* establishes a direct, positive correlation among:

- The competency standards for a degree or certification programs;
- The assessments developed to benchmark an individual's competencies against those standards; and,
- The modularized learning resources – "learning objects" – that will build learning capacity in the competency arena identified by the assessment tests.

The vast majority of content that is currently available from universities, publishers and commercial course providers are still based on the "knowledge model" as constructed by subject matter experts. In this model, content is organized around topic or subject attributes rather than around discrete performances expected of excellent performers. While this shift from the "Subject Matter Expert" approach to the "Expert Performer" approach will ultimately result in greater availability of modular, reusable learning objects, content providers who are accustomed to producing fully integrated courses will be asking why they should change the way that they organize learning content.

Dealing with "Coopetition." Coopetition is a term that combines the terms 'cooperation' and 'competition'. An example of a *coopetition* can be found by considering the challenges faced by courseware providers who are accustomed to developing their products for sale using the standard knowledge based approach to course design. What happens if a content provider chooses NOT to create modularized content that can be deployed in a CBL application? Will their competitors (who do accommodate modularization) be better prepared to re-purpose their content for multiple uses?

Competency articulation for knowledge-oriented programs. The articulation of competency standards works well in vocational or professional educational programs. How well can a competency-based learning model be used to define the expectations for a general educational program? How can the valuable content of knowledge-based approaches be retained and reused in meaningful ways? The meta-tagging scheme suggested earlier is a step in this direction.

Assessing "realkompetance." How can an individual (or an organization) be assured that the assessments available via *Kompetansenettet* or another competency-based system are valid, reliable and predictive? What varieties of assessment experiences (e.g. objective tests vs. reflective tests? multiple choice or "point and click" graphical response items? simulations, reflections recitations, or demonstrations?) will be required to ensure that the full range of competencies in any given competency model cover the full range of simple to complex learning and performance expectations? The acceptance of sponsoring organizations, as well as individual learners, are both required to insure the success of such competency-based approaches.

CONCLUDING REMARKS

This discussion has provided a brief overview of issues to be addressed when adding Competency-based learning to an organizational repertoire of performance improvement skills. Competency-based learning offers a useful strategy for responding to the challenge presented by intellectual asset management. A case study describing the implementation of a national technology-mediated, competency-based learning initiative has been described to illustrate some of the issues encountered when implementing the vision of competency-based learning designs in practice.

Much serious work remains to be done in order to make competency-based approaches and models a widespread and accepted approach to support and sustain lifelong learning in the digital era. Providing learners with additional meta-cognitive support for instruction and re-purposing valuable knowledge objects from knowledge-oriented approaches to the form of knowledge content distributors are but two of the many difficult issues remaining. The growing interest in and support for adult learning in workplace settings makes it imperative that such issues are systematically addressed and resolved.

REFERENCES

Ellis, A. L, Wagner, E. D., & Longmire, W. (1999). *Managing web-based training.* Alexandria, VA: American Society for Training and Development.

Jonassen, D. H., & Grabowski, B. L. (1993). *Handbook of individual differences, learning and instruction.* Hillsdale, NJ: Lawrence Erlbaum Associates

Klemp, G. O. (Ed.) (1980). *The assessment of occupational competence.* Washington, DC: Report to the National Institute of Education.

Lucia, A. D., & Lepsinger, R. (1999). *The art and science of competency models: Pinpointing critical success factors in organizations.* San Francisco: Jossey-Bass/Pfeiffer.

Masie, E. (1998, April). Emerging acronyms spell market change. *Computer Reseller News.* April 27, 1998, p. 59.

McCombs, B. L. (1992). *Learner centered psychological principles.* Washington, DC: American Psychological Association, in collaboration with the Mid-continent Regional Educational Laboratory.

Ormrod, J. E. (1998). *Educational Psychology: Developing Learners, 2nd Ed.* New York: Merrill Prentice Hall.

Richards, T. (1998). *The Emergence of open standards for learning technology.* San Francisco, CA: Macromedia, Inc. (http://www.learnativity.com/standards.html)

Richey, R., & Fields, D. (Eds.) (2000). *Instructional design: The standards.* Syracuse, NY: ERIC-IT Clearing House.

Rothwell, W. J. (1996). *Beyond training and development: State of the art strategies for enhancing human performance.* New York: American Management Association.

Sieloff, C. (1999, September). *Why knowledge management projects fail.* Presentation made at the 1999 Meeting of Knowledge Management, September 17, 1999, San Francisco, CA.

Trondsen, E. (1999, September). *Learning on demand.* Presentation at the Stanford Research Institute: Learning On Demand Workshop, Palo Alto, CA. September 14, 1999.

Wagner, E. D. (1999). Beyond Distance learning: Distributed learning systems, in H. Stolovich & E. Keeps (Eds.), *Handbook of Human Performance Technology, 2nd Ed.*, pp, 626-648. San Francisco: Jossey Bass.

Wagner, E. D. (1998). Are you ready for electronic learning? In *Learning without limits, (2nd Ed.) (*pp. 7 – 13). San Francisco: Informania, Inc.

DAVID H. JONASSEN
JULIAN HERNANDEZ-SERRANO
IKSEON CHOI

Chapter 7

INTEGRATING CONSTRUCTIVISM AND LEARNING TECHNOLOGIES

Keywords: affordance, collaborative learning, constructivism, distributed cognition, effectivity, meaning making, mindtools, submissive learning, transmissive teaching

Abstract. This chapter seeks to demonstrate how constructivism and its associated theories (e.g., activity theory, distributed cognition, situated learning, etc.) can be used as lenses for examining the potentials of technologies to promote meaningful learning. The systematic application of technologies for instruction began after World War II. In the beginning, technologies were employed to help teachers and designers communicate more effectively with learners. In recent years, technologies have been reconceived as contexts, productivity tools, and thinking tools (Jonassen, 1997), rather than media for communicating knowledge (see Goodyear's chapter for more on this point). How has that change transpired?

INTRODUCTION

We begin this chapter with a brief review of the assumptions about and beliefs underlying the use of instructional technologies. In the past decade, the cognitive revolution of the 1960s and 1970s has acceded to a theoretical revolution that is being driven by constructivism and a number of associated theories, including situated, socio-cultural, ecological, everyday, and distributed conceptions of cognition (Jonassen & Land, 2000). These theories and perspectives represent a paradigm shift for educators and designers with dramatic implications for the roles for technologies in supporting learning processes. After describing how these theories conceptualize learning, we will describe how a number of contemporary technologies can be used to support these new conceptions of learning. Other chapters in this volume also provide good examples of effective integration of technology into meaningful learning environments of the kind that we advocate here.

J.M. Spector and T.M. Anderson (eds.),
Integrated and Holistic Perspectives on Learning, Instruction and Technology, 103-128.
© 2000 *Kluwer Academic Publishers. Printed in the Netherlands.*

INSTRUCTIONAL TECHNOLOGIES, TRANSMISSIVE TEACHING, AND SUBMISSIVE LEARNERS

Systematic instructional design emerged during World War II as a process for producing reliable training. Rooted in behavioral psychology, communications theory, and information processing theory, instructional design focused on developing instruction that emphasized the conveyance of ideas supported by structured and appropriate practice and reinforcement. These approaches presume that learning involves a process of knowledge transmission and reception that results in observable changes in learner behavior. What are the assumptions behind these beliefs?

This kind of traditional instruction is often called transmissive instruction, because it assumes that information and ideas can be transmitted from teachers and/or teaching systems to learners. Transmissive instruction is based on a simplistic communications model of instruction (see Figure 1) that continues to prevail in many settings. The transmissive instructional model assumes that improving learning is primarily a function of more effectively communicating ideas to learners by improving the clarity of the instructional messages being transmitted. If teachers communicate (transmit) clearly to students what they know, then students will interpret the messages correctly and acquire knowledge by processing the information into internal representations that are similar to those of the transmitter. Therefore, teaching is a process of conveying ideas to students. Better teachers are better communicators. Transmissive instruction also assumes that because teachers, designers, and/or subject experts have studied ideas longer, they understand them better and are therefore better able to make appropriate representations and to communicate (transmit) these effectively.

From an ontological perspective, transmissive instruction assumes that knowledge is a kind of object that can be conveyed and possessed by individuals. Epistemologically, transmissive instruction assumes that knowing involves students receiving, processing, and interpreting what teachers tell them.

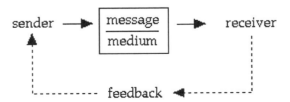

*Figure 1.*Communications model of teaching.

Transmissive instruction further assumes that effectiveness in learning is a function of communicational efficiency and so instruction discounts the intentions of learners in fulfilling instructional goals related to performance goals and objectives. Is this really what it means to be a student? If so, what does it mean to learn or to intentionally study?

In many modern societies, being a student is a culturally accepted responsibility and an expected part of the maturing process. It is a right and responsibility of passage into adulthood — a way of inculcating socially accepted beliefs. According to Merrill, Drake, Lacy, Pratt, and the ID2 Research Group (1996):

> "Students are persons who submit themselves to the acquisition of specific knowledge and skill from instruction; learners are persons who construct their own meaning from their experiences. All of us are learners, but only those who submit themselves to deliberate instructional situations are students." (p.6)

The transmissive model of education relies on students submitting themselves to the acquisition of knowledge. The unstated implication is that students who are more submissive in that knowledge acquisition process are better students. It is worth noting that Merrill and the ID2 Research Group do not necessarily associate submission with passivity. They are making the point that most humans are naturally learning all kinds of things nearly all the time. To be a student for them implies that one recognizes an authority in some area and has committed oneself to study with that authority in some disciplined and structured manner. To be a successful student, in their view, implies a high level of engagement in order to acquire the knowledge and skill possessed by some recognized authority. This model has prevailed for centuries and must result in some positive outcomes in terms both of learning and socialization. However, our argument is that the transmissive model of instruction is not a generalizable model and does not account for all learning and instruction. Moreover, it fails to account for the most interesting kinds of instruction to support learning in and about complex domains that are now possible with advanced technology. Alessi's chapter concerning the issues associated with building versus merely using instructional simulations make the inadequacy of the transmissive model quite clear.

Another shortcoming of the transmissive model is that it fails to account for students who may be highly motivated but who fail to see the relevance of submitting to a process which might seem unlikely to them to lead to the understanding or enlightenment they seek. In short, some students may (and often do) legitimately decide to acquire something other than that possessed and defined by a recognized authority. The theories discussed in the remainder of this chapter recognize that some students may not be sure why they should submit themselves to instruction or why they need to acquire knowledge that appears irrelevant, useless, or meaningless to them at the time. What does it mean for such non-submissive (or non-compliant, in Goodyear's terminology) persons to study? Clearly it is possible for these people to be students and to become successful in advancing their understanding about some selected topic. It is our argument that constructivism, properly articulated, accounts for both kinds of students, and is, therefore, an improved and consistent way to conceive of all learning.

In instructional design processes, behavioral and information processing psychologists have focused their efforts on amplifying the communication (submission-transmission) process by adding practice and feedback. Behaviorists argued that if learning were marked by a change in behavior, then that behavior had to be shaped through reinforced and structured practice. As a result, various practice strategies (e.g., drill, mnemonics, mathemagenics, algorithimization, automization, and many others with cognitive explanations) have been appended to the communication process (see Figure 2) to strengthen the students' abilities to simulate the knowledge and skills of their teachers. An especially interesting practice strategy that bridges the transmissive model and the constructivist approach is a completion strategy that gradually requires learners to construct more parts of solutions to increasingly complex problems (backward chaining). This assumption is implicit in the practice of scaffolding and much of the cognitive apprenticeship literature. In a sense, these various elaboration strategies amount to an implicit recognition of the limitations and inadequacies of the transmissive model.

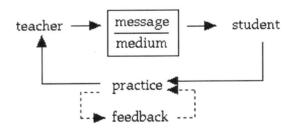

Figure 2. Practice with feedback added to the communications model of teaching.

Throughout the 1970s and 1980s, cognitive psychologists provided internal, mentalistic explanations for these learning processes. In a sense, cognitive psychology opened the black box of the mind. Numerous cognitive theories evolved to describe those mental processes. However, the elaborated communications model with practice and feedback was clearly successful in selected and simpler domains. Moreover, cognitive psychologists had difficulty in providing clear and convincing accounts for many mental processes, such as recognizing a familiar face or identifying the composer by listening to a piece of music. Additionally, many cognitive psychologists continued to accept a simple communications model so long as a few intervening mental boxes were added and elaborate practice/feedback strategies were included. As a result, in spite of the many achievements and improvements introduced by cognitive psychologists in the last thirty years, the transmissive model continued to dominate the field of instructional design.

CONSTRUCTIVIST CONCEPTIONS OF LEARNING

During the 1990s, we have witnessed arguably the most substantive and revolutionary changes in learning theory in history. What made this revolution more substantive than the cognitive revolution of the 1960s and 1970s are the shifts in the underlying ontology, epistemology, and phenomenology of learning. Contemporary situated, socio-cultural, and constructivist conceptions of learning are built on different philosophical foundations than communications theory, behaviorism, and cognitivism. We have entered a new age in learning theory. Never in the relatively short history of learning theories (one hundred plus years) have so many theoretical foundations shared so many assumptions and common foundations (Jonassen & Land, 2000). Never have alternative theories of knowledge and learning been so consonant in their beliefs and the methods they imply. These theories are no longer the alternative; they represent the dominant paradigm of learning.

Constructivism is an ontology, epistemology, and phenomenology that is built on a sense of individual and social responsibility, a recognition of the variety and dynamic nature of beliefs, a commitment to self-determination, and the perspective that understanding is what learners seek. Humans interact with and experience their environment and naturally seek to understand those interactions by developing their own theories in action and sharing them with others. We naturally work to make sense of experiences based on prior experience and knowledge and use that newly constructed knowledge to generalize to new experiences. Constructivism basically argues that this view of the human as a natural learner should inform the design of learning environments because it best fits what people, in fact, do.

Constructivism is best viewed as an amalgamation of several theories, including especially socially shared cognition, situated learning, everyday cognition and everyday reasoning, activity theory, ecological psychology, distributed cognition, case-based reasoning, and Deweyian pragmatism (Jonassen & Land, 2000). While an elaboration of these theories is beyond the scope of this chapter, we briefly highlight three fundamental shifts in thinking that are entailed by these theories.

Meaning Making

First, learning is primarily and essentially a process of meaning making, not one of mere knowledge transmission. This basic perspective is based on observations of human activities. What do people do? Humans interact with other humans and with artifacts in the world and naturally and continuously attempt to make sense of these interactions. This is the point of departure for activity theory (Wertsch, 1998). Meaning making is a process of resolving the dissonance between what we know for sure or believe that we know and what we perceive, what we would like to know, or what we believe that others know. On this view, meaning making or learning results from a puzzlement, perturbation, expectation violations, curiosity, or cognitive dissonance. Resolving this dissonance ensures some ownership of the knowledge that is constructed by the learner. Knowledge that is personally or socially constructed is necessarily owned by and attributed to the meaning makers because it was constructed by the meaning makers, not acquired from someone else. When learners clearly recognize that they are personally and socially involved in making meaning and constructing knowledge, then it is much more likely that they will become actively engaged in all aspects of learning (e.g., participating in and contributing to a community of practice as opposed to merely efficiently completing specific tasks, however complicated and challenging). So, when encountering a puzzlement or problem, learners formulate and articulate an intention to make sense of the situation or phenomenon and then engage in some kind of interaction, hopefully consciously reflecting on the meaning of those interactions. Supporting these formulation, articulation and reflective processes is one way that instructional design then changes in response to a constructive perspective.

Ontologically, it should be clear that knowledge is not something that is directly transmitted. Rather, knowledge is something that must be constructed, and this is most naturally and most effectively done with peers and others, which is why socially situated learning and distributed cognitions figure so prominently in much of the constructivist literature. Moreover, knowledge is not a simple thing, since it is constructed and usually shared. It is a dynamic process, subject to multiple revisions, elaborations, representations, interpretations, and so on. In one sense, this conception of knowledge is more like the understanding sought by Socrates in Plato's dialogues.

The underlying epistemological revolution here is the rejection of dualistic beliefs that mind and behavior are separate phenomena. Rather, mind and behavior and perception and action are wholly integrated. We cannot separate our knowledge of a domain from our interactions in that domain. Nor can we consider the knowledge that is constructed from the activity outside the context in which we constructed. This is the basic perspective found in activity theory (Engeström, 1993), and it serves to underline the false dichotomies that Goodyear also identified in his chapter.

Social Aspects of Learning

Second, contemporary learning theorists focus increasingly on the social nature of the meaning making process, as already strongly suggested. Behavioral and cognitive theories focused on the individual as the primary mediator of and unit of analysis for learning. They argue that information is processed, stored, retrieved, and applied by individuals who are able to compare their representations with others. Knowledge is in the head. However, just as the physical world is shared by all of us, so is some of the meaning that we make from it. Humans are social creatures who rely on feedback from fellow humans to determine their own existence and the veridicality of their personal beliefs. Language theorists and philosophers have long recognized the social nature of language and the impossibility of a completely private language [see Wittgenstein's *Philosophical Investigations*, for example]. Likewise, social constructivists have believed for many years that meaning making is a process of social negotiation among participants in an activity. Learning in this perspective is dialogue, a process of internal as well as social negotiation. Learning is inherently a social and a dialogical process (Savery & Duffy, 1996).

Distributed Cognitions

The third fundamental shift in assumptions relates to the locus of meaning making. Many psychologists cling to the belief that knowledge resides only in the head. Humans are the only information processors who can make meaning from experience or anything else. However, as we engage in communities of practice, our knowledge and beliefs about the world are influenced by that community and their beliefs and values. Through legitimate peripheral participation (Lave & Wenger, 1991), we absorb part of the culture that is an integral part of the community, just as the culture is affected by each of its members. As we engage in communities of discourse and practice, our knowledge and beliefs are influenced by those communities. So is our identity formation, which is also a major outcome of learning. Not only does knowledge exist in individual minds and in socially negotiating minds, but it also exists in the discourse among individuals, the social relationships that bind them, the physical artifacts that they use and produce, and the theories, models, and methods they use to produce them. Knowledge and cognitive activity are distributed among the culture and history of their existence and is also mediated by the tools they use.

Ontolologically, knowledge is not something that can be solely possessed by an individual. The assumption of the transmissive model that knowledge is something that an individual can possess is impoverished, however well that model may have worked for however many years. Once again, constructivism provides a richer and more general account of learning, knowledge, and human activity than what was offered by previous accounts of learning.

One implication of this aspect of the constructivist perspective is that when we investigate learning phenomena, we are obligated to consider not only the performances of the individual and groups of learners, but also the socio-cultural and socio-historical setting in which their performance occurs as well as tools and mediation systems that learners use to formulate and exchange ideas, support reflection and make meaning (see Figure 3).

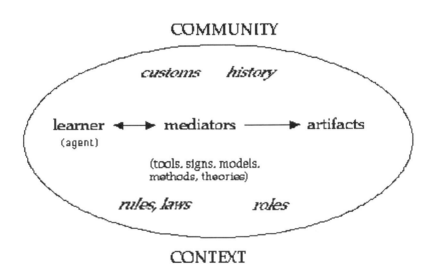

Figure 3. Learning in context.

We have already argued that, from a constructivist perspective, learning is a process of knowledge construction. The construction process is best understood as learners or learning agents employing a variety of tools in the production of artifacts (papers, tests, theories, projects, etc.). The tools (theories, methods, sign systems, etc.) that learners use in the construction process affect the nature of their conscious activity as well as the artifacts mental or physical that they construct). In the latter part of this chapter, we describe a number of technologies that can be used to mediate the learning and construction process. This activity theory conception of learning (Engeström, 1993; Leont'ev, 1974) also claims that this construction process is mediated by the socio-cultural and socio-historical context in which the construction is accomplished. The history, customs (formal and informal rules), and roles that different actors play in the context also shape the construction and learning process. The ways that tools are used and learning occurs in different contexts differ. What activity theory teaches us is that learning is a far more complex social and intellectual activity than is conceived by information processing theories. Learning is not merely a matter of internally processing percepts but rather an interaction of those percepts with conscious activity and context.

WHAT IS LEARNING FROM A CONSTRUCTIVIST PERSPECTIVE?

We have briefly reviewed transmissive conceptions of learning and constructivist critiques of those conceptions. Constructivists, believe that meaning making (i.e., meaningful learning) involves willful, intentional, active, conscious, constructive practice that includes reciprocal intention—action—reflection cycles (see Figure 4). Intentionality, activity, and reflection are essential to meaningful learning, especially in complex and new domains. Although individuals may learn some things incidentally and even accidentally without intention, action, and reflection, those learning instances will not be transferable without action and reflection (Duffy & Jonassen, 1992; Rieber, 1989). Let us address each of these in turn.

Humans are distinct from primates in their abilities to articulate an intention and willfully plan to act on it. As argued before, constructive learning normally results from a question, curiosity, a perturbation, an expectation failure, or some other dissonance between what is perceived and what is understood. When that dissonance occurs, learners seek to understand the phenomena in a way that resolves that dissonance. That learning, we argue, is oriented by an intention to resolve the dissonance, to answer the question, satisfy the curiosity, or figure out the system. Articulating intentions is a conscious process. It requires the learner to reflect on what is known and needs to be known.

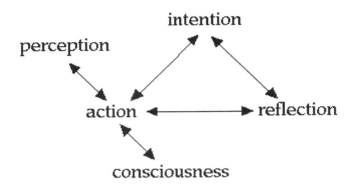

Figure 4. Learning processes and interactions from a constructivist perspective.

Actions are the central learning mechanism. Actions can be physical, mental, and social all at once and are typically comprised of perception-action processes. Ecological psychology claims that learning results from the reciprocal perception of affordances from the environment and actions on the environment (Gibson, 1977; Young, Barab, & Garrett, 2000). So learning activity involves perception-action processes (as noted by the links between perception and action in Figure 4. Activity theory (Jonassen, 2000b) claims that actions and consciousness are completely interactive and interdependent. We cannot act without thinking or think without acting (therefore the link connecting action and consciousness in Figure 4).

Although learning is frequently conceived of as an active process (clearly the ID2 group accepts this much), the meaning of activity is not always clear. Activity theory and ecological psychology provide a clear explanation of what 'active' means. In addition to regulating activity, reflection on these perceptual and conscious actions is necessary for constructing meaning. While perceiving and experiencing their environment, humans intentionally act on it. The perception-action and consciousness-action processes engaged in by experience are the basis for reflection. Those reflections become an important part of the experience that is used to help explain new experiences and generate fresh intentions. Conscious activity is guided by intentions and reflections which are informed by consciousness. The dialectic between reflections and intentions also accounts for metacognitive activities and self-regulatory efforts engaged in by learners. The richness of the constructive perspective makes it a powerful and useful tool in designing instruction for complex domains precisely because it allows us to view learning as an integrated and holistic collection of processes and activities.

In the remainder of the chapter, we describe a number of technologies that can support the intention-action-perception cycles of knowledge construction. We examine these technologies for their affordances and for how learners can use them to act on and mediate the construction process.

WHAT ARE TECHNOLOGIES?

Historically, learning technologies have been conceived as machines that are used as conveyors of knowledge. Instructional designers encoded knowledge and intelligence into the machine and used the machine to mediate the conveyance of knowledge from the teacher to the student. Technologies have been used as conveyors because educators believed that they were efficient and that they provided reliable contexts for learning. However, this conception of learning technologies is inconsistent with the constructivist assumptions and beliefs that we have stated about learning, and when one examines how current technologies are in fact used, one discovers that they can be used for much more then mere conveyers (see Park & Hannafin, 1993, and Alessi's chapter, for example).

We have defined conscious learning from a constructivist perspective as the reciprocal interaction between intentions, actions, and reflections of learners. In order to carry out those actions, humans use tools and signs to mediate their actions. Technologies are tools for supporting and amplifying human activity. Technologies shape the way people act and think. From an activity theory perspective, technologies may include not only physical apparatus and tools but also theories, models, or methods for mediating human activity. Technologies alter the activity and are, in turn, altered by the activity.

So from a learner-centered, constructivist perspective, learning technologies are tools for mediating the practice of learning. As such, they are tools for representing (reflecting and constructing) learner understanding, tools for socially co-constructing and re-constructing meaning, and intelligent formalisms that amplify learners' thinking. When used as tools for mediating learning, the learning that students do with the technology will more likely be assimilated into their cognitive repertoires, especially in complex and new domains. How do we understand the relationship between learners and learning technologies? If we examine the potential of any learning technology from the learners' perspectives, then we must consider the affordances and effectivities of each technology. That is, technologies should be examined for the effectivity-affordance relationships that they have with the learning activities they are mediating. The affordances of any technology are the properties of that environment that enable the effectivities of the technology, the abilities of the learner to take learning actions. In the remainder of this chapter, different technologies will be examined for the affordances they provide learners for effecting learning activities. Other chapters in this book offer extended and elaborated examples of specific technology affordances in richly constructed learning environments.

TECHNOLOGIES THAT SUPPORT CONSTRUCTIVE LEARNING?

Table 1 lists technologies that can be used to support constructive learning. We do not argue that these are the only technologies capable of affording constructive learning. These are the technologies that have the most obvious affordances (see, for example, Dede, 1996; Savery & Duffy, 1996).

Technology	Learning Approach
Computer Supported Collaborative Work	Learning by Working
Electronic Performance Support Systems	Learning by Performing
Virtual Reality Simulations and Microworlds	Learning by Experimenting
Intentional Information Searching	Learning by Exploring
Videography	Learning by Visualizing
Multimedia/Hypermedia Construction	Learning by Constructing
Knowledge-Building Communities - Computer Supported Collaborative Learning	Learning by Conversing
Mindtools - Cognitive Tools	Learning by Reflecting
Constructivist (Problem-/Project-based) Learning	All of the above

Table 1. Technologies for supporting constructive learning.

Computer-Supported Collaborative Work (CSCW) – Learning by Working

Technologies that can be used to facilitate, augment and redefine social interactions among members of a community of practice fall into the realm of computer-supported collaborative work (CSCW) (Koschmann et al., 1996). CSCW makes use of groupware and other technologies that support group work for the sake of achieving higher levels of productivity within a group. These technologies require advanced computer workstations with an array of multimedia and communication hardware and software, as well as a highly integrated network system that supports sophisticated levels of local and remote interactivity.

Most CSCW systems provide a shared workspace that allows a larger community of workers to think critically by inquiring, reflecting, sense making, arguing and building knowledge (individually and within the community) with the goal of co-constructing an object (Jonassen, 2000a). CSCW tools provide a structure that facilitates learning to use the tools as well as the protocols for contributing effectively within group.

For any particular group interaction, any participant may opt to inspect another participant's screen, receive and send comments and data to others, modify the objects of work, and confer with group members who may be across the office, in another building or on another continent. For all these situations, CSCW tools provide a structure that inherently scaffolds group work by providing structure and sequence to the collaborative endeavor. CSCW supports interactive data sharing and the ability to view a co-participant's computer screen. In addition, it provides project management tools, access to external resources (electronic libraries, Internet, etc.) and group decision support systems. CSCW provides for the automatic distribution of the objects of work and related modifications, as well as electronic conferencing tools that support virtual meetings. These are the technological affordances of CSCW.

CSCW affords the co-construction of knowledge and products without the need for formal instruction. CSCW provides an environment in which participants learn to work within a group by using the CSCW tools, thus contributing to the group goal—the creation of objects of work. Consistent with activity theory, the object of work consists of both the knowledge that is co-constructed and the artifacts of that conscious activity. Those are the effectivities of CSCW. That is, with powerful tools that scaffold work, workers can learn to work without instruction. CSCW tools make possible more effective work activities, that is, constructing products. That is the ultimate outcome of constructive learning.

Electronic Performance Support Systems: Learning by Performing

According to Gery (1991), Electronic Performance Support Systems (EPSSs) can electronically:

> "provide whatever is necessary to generate performance and learning at the moment of need [so it can be] universally and consistently available on demand any time, any place, and regardless of situation, without unnecessary intermediaries involved in the process" (p. 34).

Based on learners' needs, EPSSs are designed to provide various types of information, such as interactive advice, explanations, demonstrations, descriptions, interactive training, simulations, feedback, directions, coaching, procedures, etc. EPSSs include advisory or expert systems for problem structuring, decision support, analysis, or diagnosis; interactive productivity software such as spreadsheets, text processors, and job aids; applications software for performing specific job tasks or functions; and help systems, among other features (Gery, 1991). These tools scaffold performance. That is, individuals can perform without being taught. They learn from performing, once again constructing knowledge without the benefit or necessity of formal instruction. Just-in-time learning is perhaps the most constructive form of learning.

Within an EPSS, learners engage various effectivities that can promote meaningful learning. Given a complex problem situation, learners can ask questions, or request help, support, explanations, and advice from the EPSS while successfully performing a task. Some EPSSs even monitor user activities and offer unsolicited advice (e.g., so-called software wizards). However, users typically get useful information from an EPSS when they ask the right questions, and this can happen only if they develop the necessary higher order thinking processes such as articulating, analyzing, reflecting, testing, monitoring, and evaluating what they know and what they don't know (Dillon, 1986; Miyake & Norman, 1979). So, EPSSs afford meaningful learning activities. When learners apply the requested information from the EPSS, they are actively involved in meaningful learning because they are responsible for performance and the learning required to achieve it; so learners can elaborate on or analyze the new information, integrate or relate to previous knowledge, anchor new knowledge to previous experience, and evaluate it (King, 1989, 1992; Schank, 1995). Learners can model experts' behaviors and even internal processes, such as reasoning, decision-making and problem solving, by interacting with EPSSs containing experts' knowledge. Learners can take systems-initiated information (e.g., advice, help, assessment, feedback, etc.), analyze the context, and reflect and update their performance. Therefore, learners can perform better as well as learn better by interacting with EPSSs; it is emergent (need-based) learning by performing with just-in-time support.

There are several affordances for meaningful learning in EPSSs. First, EPSSs have various input-mechanisms that allow learners to ask questions, get support, and seek advice. These features enable learners to reflect on their own knowledge and to become ready to acquire new knowledge for achieving goals. Second, EPSSs have just-in-time service features that enable learners to learn at the moment of need. These features provide a variety of information to learners when they are most motivated to learn, leading them to more meaningful learning and better performance. Third, EPSSs have modeling features that provide advice, examples, demonstrations, and even reasoning processes to solve problems as the real experts do. Lastly, EPSSs have various modes of presenting information (such as text, graphics, visual images, audio, motion video, etc.) that enable learners to capture information with the most effective mode depending on the situation.

Virtual Reality/Microworlds: Learning by Experimenting

Microworlds are "primarily exploratory learning environments, discovery spaces, and constrained simulations of real-world phenomena in which learners can navigate, manipulate or create objects, and test their effects on one another" (Jonassen, et al., 1999, p. 157). That is, microworlds are simplified models of parts of the world (Hanna, 1986) or constrained versions of reality which enable learners to manipulate variables and experiments within the parameters of some systems. The term 'microworld' was coined by Papert (1980) to describe explorative learning environments such as those provided by Logo. Nowadays, various other examples are available, such as: *Interactive Physics* for simulating Newtonian mechanics; *SimCalc* for simulating calculus concepts; *Geometric Supposer* for simulating geometric concepts; and many more. Virtual Reality provides immersive environments that function like microworlds to the extent that it provides a controlled real-world environment where people explore and experience almost the same things that they can do in the real world. Virtual reality provides a high fidelity simulation of the world that allows users to interact with the virtual environment in a manner similar to how users do it in the real world.

Learners effect these environments in different ways. Learners can design their own experimental environments by creating objects and conducting experiments by manipulating variables and controlling parameters/factors. Through these activities, learners engage higher order thinking skills, such as generating hypotheses, designing experiments and testing them, observing and analyzing experimental results, regenerating alternative hypotheses, etc. Eventually, this will lead them to construct their own understanding of the underlying principles of the microworld through the exploration of the experimental phenomenon and by (re)building their own mental model of the world they are experimenting with. They can build concrete understandings by visualizing abstract concepts after conducting various experiments.

In Interactive Physics, for example, learners can design their own experiments by modeling Newtonian phenomena by creating objects, showing grids, rulers, axes, vectors, masses, etc., and selecting various ways to measure the effects of changes in the variables. Then, they can conduct experiments by manipulating factors such as gravity, air resistance, elasticity of bodies, etc., and observe and measure the results such as changes in velocity, acceleration, momentum, and other forces. In virtual reality/microworlds learners can also practice the newly acquired skills and knowledge without the unfortunate results of actual failures. Therefore, they can learn safely by simply doing and experimenting in the environments provided by virtual reality/microworlds.

There are several affordances for meaningful learning in these environments. First, a microworld contains a simplified model that is part of the complex, real world which affords a reduction in cognitive load. Also, by containing features for controlling the complexity of the models, it allows users to learn meaningfully according to their learning progress. Second, microworlds have manipulation-observation features that allow learners to manipulate parameters and observe certain variables/factors in various ways (e.g., meters, graph, etc.). These features are very effective in engaging learners in critical thinking by allowing them to generate, speculate, and test hypotheses. Lastly, virtual reality/microworlds deliver a certain level of realism of the world they are based on. This allows learners to interact with the virtual reality/microworld in a manner similar to the way they would do in the real world by immersing learners in the environments thus achieving meaningful learning.

Intentional Information Searching – Learning by Exploring

There are tools that promote learning by exploring especially on the World Wide Web (WWW). These tools support learners' intentional information searching goals by helping them articulate their intentions, focusing the learners' attention into effective information searches, finding useful sources of information on the WWW, and keeping the learners on-task and away from sources of information that drives them away from the learning goal. In addition, these tools help learners interpret the information they find on the WWW while constructing knowledge bases. All that learners require is the appropriate hardware (computer, basic communication equipment, etc.), software (WWW browser, access to search engines, etc.) and basic WWW search skills.

Intentional Information Searching represents a constructivist environment. After declaring an intention to build knowledge (a desire to know), the learner must collect and interpret the information that relates to the declared intention. This process promotes meaning making by constantly forcing the learners to interpret the information they are finding on the WWW in response to their intentional search and determining how relevant it is to their intended purpose (Jonassen, 2000a).

Learners effect their learning in different ways as they approach the WWW. They must have already defined an information need (develop an intention). It is necessary for them to clearly articulate that information need and purpose. It is the learners' purpose that drives the learning by developing search strategies that allow them to find information through social communication in computer-mediated collaborative work environments, build temporary repositories of information with a search engine (search results page) that is organized around a purpose that is congruent with the learner's intentions, or configure an intelligent agent according to the learner's needs and intentions. Once the learners receive the information, they need to critically inspect the information contained, verify the author's professional credentials, and evaluate any possibilities for biases; in other words, they need to ensure that the information they are getting is valid. Considering the enormous amount of information available through the WWW, learners should pursue a strategy of triangulation, whereby they need to obtain additional WWW sources that touch upon the issue of interest and report the information with the same level of accuracy (Jonassen, 2000a).

At the other end, the tools that learners use for satisfying their information needs provide numerous affordances:

- a door to the complex world of information in the Internet by facilitating a point of entrance to computer chat rooms, asynchronous conferences and other forms of electronic social communication;
- access to numerous WWW search engines for searching by category, scaffolding the learner's search by using the existing structure within a search engine (e.g., Education => K through 12 => Curriculum => WWW Projects: Activity Structures) or by searching with keywords, facilitating the dynamic creation of unique repositories of information with links to specific resources that respond to the learner's intentions (e.g., *Search the Web:* Curriculum AND "Technology applications"); and,
- access to intelligent agents that permit automatic searches, and information evaluation and collection according to patterns that responds to the learners' preferences and needs.

In each case, the result of the intentional search allows learners to develop another web page with a collection of links to existing web pages with the information that responds to the learner's search needs and goals accompanied by brief summaries of the contents of these pages, or a written report with citations that refer to these web pages.

Videography: Learning by Visualizing

Videography (Jonassen, et al., 1999) refers to the use of video equipment for video recording, editing, and replaying, including video cameras, monitors/televisions, videocassette recorders (VCRs), editors, and microphones. Today, this equipment is so small, cheap, and efficient that it is affordable and usable by all. Video cameras (or camcorders) are small recording systems that include a lens for visually capturing images, a video pickup tube for converting the image into a monitor, a cassette transport system, a video tape recorder for encoding electronic signals of the visual image into video cassettes, and a small viewer or monitor for viewing the images being recorded or replayed. VCRs (or a camera's replay function) decode magnetic signals from videotapes into electronic signals and send them to monitors/televisions. Video editing programs allow for the arrangement of disconnected scenes from different videotapes into a coherent sequence.

These tools afford different activities for learners. Learners can watch authentic, complex problems that need to be solved, engage in the problems deeply, identify and adapt goals, seek important cues from the rich stories being played, build and justify their expectations or solutions, compare their solutions to others, and revise their understanding (e.g., Anchored Instruction, CTGV, 1992; Science in action, Goldman et al., 1996). Learners can also construct their own understanding of ideas by producing video programs for a video press conference, newsroom, talk show, documentary, video theater, etc. Learners can take on the role of directors, producers, camera operators, set designers, and actors. In these creative activities, learners engage in a variety of meaningful interactions, including:

- analyzing problems, issues and topics;
- studying various perspectives, characters and related information;
- generating questions and answers that represent their understanding about the ideas;
- making plans about the program in a way that express their intention and understanding about ideas; and,
- writing scripts, rehearse, videotape and organizing the scenes.

In short, learners become more active, constructive, intentional, and cooperative. They also can model complex skills, behaviors or even internal processes (such as decision making, questioning, or a problem resolving process) of experts by watching video models. Additionally, they can reflect on and correct their performance and thinking processes by watching themselves perform (direct and self-constructed feedback).

Multimedia/Hypermedia Construction - Learning by Constructing

Multimedia is the incorporation of more than one medium into some form of communication. Hypertext refers to a non-sequential, nonlinear method for organizing and displaying text that enables learners to access the information contained within it in ways that is most meaningful to them. Hypermedia is hypertext with multiple representation forms (text, graphics, sounds, video, etc.) (Jonassen, 2000a). One of the most conspicuous examples of hypermedia is the World Wide Web (WWW). Allowing learners to represent what they are learning through the use of multimedia/hypermedia tools will help them integrate this information with their existing knowledge and provide ways of synthesizing that information into a meaningful communication. Learners require access to a multimedia computer equipped with the necessary hardware to incorporate the media, and software to edit it and complete a production.

The production of multimedia/hypermedia by students promotes important constructive learning. After having declared an intention to build knowledge, and having collected and interpreted the information that relates to the declared intention, multimedia/hypermedia tools help learners build new understanding by providing them with affordances to represent what they are learning. In order to accomplish that, learners must focus their intentions by critically evaluating the underlying structure of the collected information, generate model cases from it and develop arguments to justify the hypermedia design used to represent what they have learned (Jonassen, 2000a).

Learners learn as a result of authoring multimedia/hypermedia materials in ways that best represent their perspectives or evolving understanding of the subject matter into a design to be shared with others (see Alessi's chapter for a discussion of this in the context of constructing simulations). Once a sufficient amount of information has been collected, the learners' goal then becomes representing that into a multimedia document. That means that learners have to make choices about what topics to represent and in what form they should be represented so that their understanding is conveyed best (text, video or audio clip, etc.). They need to construct relationships among the topics by linking them. And they have to design an interface to their knowledge base for others to inspect. This is not a simple linear process but one in which multiple goals emerge and are pursued until satisfied depending on the dynamics of the learners' intentions. While engaged in these knowledge-building activities, learners may also develop project management, research, organizational, representation, presentation, and reflection skills.

Multimedia/hypermedia construction tools and web authoring tools provide affordances to learners by allowing the construction of representations of abstract ideas into an easily inspectable knowledge base.

These tools permit learners to structure what they are learning in the form of nodes (chunks of text, pictures, video clips, and so on), and links that connect these nodes in meaningful ways. These tools afford the learners with the ability to transform the collected information into multiple representations, allow them to keep what's important and drop what is not, segment information into nodes, link the information segments by semantic relationships, and in general allow them the flexibility to represent their ideas as they see fit.

By having learners engage in the knowledge building process and supporting that process with appropriate multimedia/hypermedia tools, the learners will become designers instead of passive learners, and knowledge constructors instead of knowledge users (Jonassen, 2000a). Learners will work on creating representations of their own understandings, and this will afford them a sense of involvement and vested interest that will help them sustain their intentions for further knowledge construction and learning.

Knowledge-Building Communities: Learning by Conversing

Sometimes the goals of a particular learner can best be met through collaboration within a larger community of like-minded learners. There are a number of technologies, called Computer-Supported Collaborative Learning (CSCL), that can be used to support these knowledge-building communities. Knowledge-building communities afford conversation social interaction (Kolodner & Guzdial, 1996). CSCL affords learners with a type of understanding that leads to learning by having learners work together and socially co-construct a common understanding. For example, a school environment that supports collaborative learning is the Living Schoolbook Project at Syracuse University (http://lsb.syr.edu/lsbweb/index.html).

By having to negotiate sense making with a larger community of learners, the critical thinking skills of inquiry, reflection, sense making, argumentation and knowledge building (individually and within the community) are afforded. In addition, CSCL promotes a high sense of learner ownership of their contributions (a sense of accomplishment) by seeing how they influence the group's learning; ownership motivates learning and further participation (Kolodner & Guzdial, 1996).

In learning environments that incorporate CSCL technologies, learners affect their environment by participating within a group's discussions. Once there is an intention to participate in a discussion, the learner may ask questions, as well as respond to other participant's questions. The learner may also need to elaborate on and interpret responses and respond to others. This way, learners provide and are exposed to multiple perspectives, thus promoting the critical examination of concepts, ideas, issues or dilemmas. By having to articulate and explain their ideas, learners make ideas more concrete and precise. While articulating their arguments and raising learning issues, the community of learners is driven to reach a consensus about the knowledge being built.

CSCL software affords learners continuous social discourse (conversing) while sustaining the knowledge building community. It provides an interface that promotes collaborative interaction and tools for sharing learner-built representations of concepts. It provides communication combinations — synchronous, asynchronous, local and remote —that allow learners to share their arguments. It facilitates the process of transformative conversation by allowing learners to ask questions and follow up on inquiries over different occasions (time-space). In addition, it provides support to the collaboration process by offering a shared record-keeping space where intentions are articulated, which is available for inspection by members of the community. An example of CSCL is Computer-Supported Intentional Learning Environment (CSILE); it supports the dialectical process by providing content and rhetorical spaces.

By forming knowledge building communities through CSCLs, learners are exposed to the subject matter and acquire the social skills necessary for participating in future knowledge communities (virtual and real). It is expected that learners will apply what is learned from their collaboration using CSCL to other situations; this will not only increase knowledge-building communities but also create favorable attitudes toward them. By having a high sense of ownership on the discussion, learners will be more motivated to persevere in the knowledge building process and thus become better collaborators and inquirers.

Mindtools-Cognitive Tools: Learning by Reflecting

Mindtools are "computer-based tools and learning environments that have been adapted or developed to function as intellectual partners with the learner in order to engage and facilitate critical thinking and higher-order learning" (Jonassen, 2000a). Computer applications that are used or developed to facilitate critical thinking in learning can be classified as Mindtools. These include (but are not limited to) semantic organization tools, dynamic modeling tools, visualization tools, and so on.

Semantic organization tools include databases and semantic networking tools. Databases are record keeping systems that were designed to allow users to store, classify, and retrieve information. Semantic networking tools are applications that help users to draw spatial representations of concepts and their interrelationships representing the users' knowledge structures (Jonassen, Beissner, & Yacci, 1993).

Dynamic modeling tools include spreadsheets, expert systems, and system modeling tools. Spreadsheets are numerical record-keeping systems that were originally designed to help users (like accountants) with accounting operations (summing, subtracting, and balancing). Expert systems are artificial intelligence programs designed to simulate expert reasoning in order to facilitate decision making for all sorts of problems. System modeling tools are applications allowing users to build models of dynamics systems and test the models by simulation.

Visualization tools are applications that help learners to interpret abstract concepts, numeric data, and invisible phenomena and to represent it visually by converting the original information into visible representations.

Mindtools afford the organization, representation, and expression of what learners know. Learners correct, update, and reorganize their knowledge or mental models based on critically thinking about the content (or objects) and thinking about their own knowledge. For example, when using databases, learners define "fields" (that describe the class or type of information in the domain) by identifying their goals and features of information, build records (that describe objects) by collecting and inserting information into the fields, and reorganize information by sorting it and making new links among the fields in order to answer queries and to discovery new relationship among the fields. With semantic network tools, learners also evaluate information to build visual-verbal representations of their own ideas or what they learn by using nodes (concepts or ideas) and links (statements of relationship); they continuously reorganize the information. With spreadsheets or systems modeling tools, learners can build and represent their mental models of dynamic systems or complex phenomena that contain mathematical or logical relationships, simulate them by manipulating variables or components, and observe the results. In expert systems, learners evaluate a current problem situation, seek rules that will provide advice about that situation, and reflect on the structure of knowledge by simulating it. Learners can reason visually in certain domains with visualization tools by manipulating the representation of the idea and articulating the underlying principles. With Mindtools as intellectual partners, learners become active designers of objects, constructors of their own knowledge, and critical and reflective thinkers.

Mindtools have two critical affordances that lead learners to meaningful learning. First, Mindtools provide various formalisms for representing what people know. Language is one typical formalism to express and communicate ideas; but sometimes ideas are hard to represent verbally. The fields, records, and query functions that link new relationships between fields and make new criteria for sorting information in databases; cells, mathematical functions defining relationship between cells and their structure in spreadsheets; visual maps of relationships between ideas in semantic networks; visual symbols and causal-loops in system modeling tools; and rule based expert shells in expert systems are all examples of formalisms that allow users to represent and to communicate meaningfully their knowledge. Second, most Mindtools have manipulation-feedback features that amplify the cognitive process of learners. Databases have query functions that enable learners to manipulate relationships between fields and to sort records with different criteria. System modeling tools or spreadsheets have functions that enable learners to select and manipulate variables and to present the results in various ways. Visualization tools also allow learners to observe the results visually by manipulating factors. These manipulation-feedback processes engage learners in deep reflection that promotes meaningful learning. However, the primary affordance of Mindtools is critical thinking. Using Mindtools engages learners in critical thinking; they cannot build Mindtool knowledge bases without thinking critically.

Constructivist Learning Environments – Integrating Affordances

Learning environments can be built that integrate most of the other technologies that have been described, which is a key point of this chapter and indeed an underlying theme of this book. Constructivist learning environments (CLEs) are case-, project-, or problem-based environments that engage learners in articulating, solving, and reflecting on their solutions of a problem or project space, including a representation of the problem, descriptions of the context in which the problem occurs, and the ability to manipulate and test various solutions to the problem (Jonassen, 1999). Additional affordances include case-based stories about different aspects of the problem solution, information resources, cognitive tools that scaffold the performance of required tasks, collaboration tools that scaffold group decision making, idea sharing, and co-construction of shared knowledge. Each of these affordances scaffold different steps in the problem solution. The activities that are being scaffolded are also important parts of the sense-making process.

An example of such a CLE is one we developed for an operations management course on how to conduct aggregate planning (Jonassen, Prevish, Christy, Stavurlaki, 1999). In this environment, we presented two companies engaged in aggregate planning. In each problem, learners begin by entering into a conversation with employees of the firm as well as reading and listening to internal correspondence within the organization. These conversations help to establish the organizational and operational climate of the businesses, that is, establish the problem context. The narrative format for representing the problem context is realistic and illustrates the attitudes and beliefs of stakeholders in the organization. Learners can get historical sales information, available inventory, demand, human resources, and technology. The problem for the learner is to predict demand and sales and to determine the appropriate levels of technology, inventory, and human resources to maintain. Students' solutions are worked out on a complex and multifaceted spreadsheet (the cognitive tool for this performance). Students manipulate the factors such as production rates, employees hired, or employees fired. These values are integrated into aggregate planning formulas to allow learners to test the effects of any manipulation. They continue to manipulate the variables until they have achieved what they believe to be the maximum levels.

The related cases include several similar planning cases and include stories about how those similar companies accommodated demand, technology needs, sales, human resources, and inventory problems in their companies. By presenting related cases in learning environments, learners are provided with a set of experiences to compare to the current problem or issue. Learners retrieve from related cases advice on how to succeed, pitfalls that may cause failure, what worked or did not work, and why it did not.

The aggregate planning CLE provides a variety of information resources about the aggregate planning process that help the students to understand the process and its business procedures well enough to solve the problem. Students are provided text documents, graphics, and sound resources about the process.

The aggregate planning cases may be engaged individually or in groups. In group situations, either synchronous decision making conferences or asynchronous conferencing may be used. Solving problems like these is an essential component of synchronous conferences, we believe. Synchronous conferences are more productive when learners are engaged in an intentional problem-solving process.

CLEs incorporate most of the other constructivist applications of technology in the solution of complex and ill-structured problems. Ill-structured problems are difficult to solve because the solutions and solution paths are not obvious. CLEs scaffold the solution processes and the reflection on them. In order to construct them, it is necessary to understand the activity systems in which work is normally accomplished and to provide affordances for the activities necessary to solve those problems those authentic environments.

CONCLUSIONS

In this chapter, we have reconceptualized the meaning of learning as intention-action-reflection cycles. These action cycles represent ways that learners effect their knowledge and their environments. They are guided and regulated by articulating intentions and reflecting on their actions.

In this chapter, we have also reconceptualized technologies very broadly as affordances for learner activity. That is, learning technologies provide affordances for intentional thinking. The role of technologies in learning can best be understood by analyzing the effectivity-affordance relationships between the technologies and the ways they are used, that is, the kinds of actions taken with them. We have analyzed a variety of technologies for the ways that they can be used to construct understanding (effectivities) and for their affordances that support those activities. We hope that this chapter and other examples discussed in this book help make clear the richness of a constructivist approach to learning and the various ways that technology can be integrated in meaningful learning environments. The general notion that ties these issues together is a holistic view of human activity and it is that perspective which can and will drive the design of learning environments for the foreseeable future.

REFERENCES

Dede, C. (1996). The evolution of constructivist learning environments: Immersion in distributed, virtual worlds. In B. G. Wilson (Ed.), *Constructivist learning environments: Case studies in instructional design* (pp. 165-175). Englewood Cliffs, NJ: Educational Technology Publications.

Dillon, J. T. (1986). Student questions and individual learning. *Educational Theory, 36,* 333-341.

Duffy, T., & Jonassen, D. H. (1992). *Constructivism and the technology of instruction: A conversation.* Hillsdale, NJ: Erlbaum.

Engeström, Y. (1999). Activity theory an individual and social transformation. In Y. Engeström, R. Miettinen, & R.L. Punamäki (Eds.), *Perspectives on activity theory* (pp. 19-38). Cambridge: Cambridge University Press.

Gery, G. J. (1991). *Electronic performance support systems.* Tolland, MA: Gery Performance Press.

Gibson, J. J. (1979). An ecological approach to visual perception. Hillsdale, NJ: Lawrence Erlbaum Associates.

Hanna, J. (1986). Learning environments criteria. In R. Ennals, R. Gwyn, & L. Zdravchev (Eds.), *Information technology and education: The changing school.* Chichester, UK: Ellis Horwood.

Jonassen, D. H. (1999). Designing constructivist learning environments. In C. M. Reigeluth (Ed.), *Instructional design theories and models: A new paradigm of instructional theory* (Vol II.) (pp. 215-240). Mahwah, NJ: Lawrence Erlbaum Associates.

Jonassen, D. H. (2000a). *Computers as mindtools for schools: Engaging critical thinking.* Columbus, OH: Prentice Hall.

Jonassen, D. H. (2000b). Revisiting activity theory as a framework for designing student-centered learning environments. In D.H. Jonassen & S.M. Land (Eds.), *Theoretical foundations of learning environments* (pp. 89-121). Mahwah, NJ: Lawrence Erlbaum Associates

Jonassen, D. H. & Land S. M. (2000). *Theoretical foundations of learning environments.* Mahwah, NJ: Lawrence Erlbaum Associates

Jonassen, D. H., Beissner, K., & Yacci, M. A. (1993). *Structural knowledge: Techniques for representing, conveying, and acquiring structural knowledge.* Hillsdale, NJ: Lawrence Erlbaum Associates.

Jonassen, D. H., Peck, K. L., & Wilson, B. G. (1999). Learning with technology: A Constructivist perspectives. Columbus, OH: Prentice Hall.

Jonassen, D., Prevish, T., Christy, D., & Stavurlaki, E. (1999). Learning to solve problems on the Web: Aggregate planning in a business management course. *Distance Education: An International Journal, 20*(1), 49-63.

King, A. (1989). Effects of self-questioning training on college students' comprehension of lectures. *Contemporary Educational Psychology, 14*, 366-381.

King, A. (1992). Facilitating elaborative learning through guided student-generated questioning. *Educational Psychologist, 27*, 111-126.

Kolodner, J., & Guzdial, M. (1996). Effects *with* and *of* CSCL: Tracking learning in a new paradigm. In T. Koschmann (Ed.), *CSCL: Theory and practice* (pp. 307-320). Mahwah, NJ: Erlbaum.

Koschmann, T., Kelson, A. C., Feltovich, P. J., & Barrows, H. S. (1996). Computer-Supported problem-based learning: A principled approach to the use of computers in collaborative learning. In T. Koschmann (Ed.), *CSCL: Theory and practice* (pp. 83-124). New Jersey: Mahwah.

Leont'ev, A. (1974). The problem of activity in psychology. *Soviet Psychology, 13*(2), 4-33.

Merrill, M. D., Drake, L., Lacy, M. J., Pratt J., & the ID2 Research Group (1996). Reclaiming instructional design. *Educational Technology, 36*(5), 5-7.

Miyake, N., & Norman, S. A. (1979). To ask a question, one must know enough to know what is not known. *Journal of Verbal Learning and Verbal Behavior, 18*, 357-364.

Papert, S. (1980). *Mindstorms: Children, computers, and powerful ideas.* New York: Basic Books.

Park, I., & Hannafin, M. J. (1993). Empirically-based guidelines for the design of interactive multimedia. *Interactive Multimedia Design, 41* (3), 65-85.

Rieber, L. P. (1989). Computer-based microworlds: A bridge between constructivism and direct instruction. *Educational Technology Research and Development, 40* (1), 93-106.

Savery, J. R., & Duffy, T. M. (1996). Problem based learning: An instructional model and its consructivist framework. In B. G. Wilson (Ed.), *Constructivist learning environments: Case studies in instructional design* (pp. 135-150). Englewood Cliffs, NJ: Educational Technology Publications.

Schank, R. C. (1995). *Engines for education.* Mahwah, NJ: Lawrence Erlbaum Associates.

Wetrsch, J. (1998). *Mind as action.* Cambridge: Cambridge University Press.

Young, M. F., Barab, S., & Garrett, S. (2000). Agent as detector: An ecological psychology perspective on learning by perceiving-acting systems. In D. H. Jonassen & S. M. Land (Eds.), *Theoretical foundations of learning environments* (pp. 147-171). Mahwah, NJ: Lawrence Erlbaum Associates.

ACKNOWLEDGEMENT

This chapter was completed while I was a visiting faculty member in the Department of Information Science at the University of Bergen. My thanks to them for their support.

NORBERT M. SEEL
SABINE AL-DIBAN
PATRICK BLUMSCHEIN

Chapter 8

MENTAL MODELS & INSTRUCTIONAL PLANNING

Keywords: accommodation, assimilation, causal explanations, cognitive apprenticeship, conceptual models, instructional planning, mental models

Abstract. Important educational implications have been drawn mainly from two movements in epistemology: *constructivism* and *situated cognition*. Whereas *constructivism* is relevant for instruction primarily on a meta-theoretical level, the concept of *situated cognition* has strong educational implications for instructional practice. A central assumption of situated cognition is that people construct mental models to meet the requirements of (learning) situations to be cognitively mastered. Research on how to influence the construction of mental models has been criticized by several authors from a theoretical and methodological perspective. This chapter asks: Has descriptive research on mental models in instructional contexts provided results that can serve as a foundation for prescriptions to facilitate or improve the student's construction of mental models? We first discuss the characteristics of learning situations that necessitate the construction of mental models. Our next step is a search for theoretically sound conceptions of instruction that either impel students to construct mental models for themselves or which adaptively guide and direct the students in the process of model construction. We report on an exploratory study which investigated: (a) the applicability of cognitive apprenticeship for designing effective learning environments; (b) the effect of providing an initial conceptual model on learner construction of mental models during instruction; and, (c) the long-term effectiveness of a multimedia learning program on acquired domain-specific knowledge and the stability of initially constructed mental models. Finally, we address what happens when there are no relevant learner preconceptions available.

INTRODUCTION

Over the past several decades, important educational implications have been drawn mainly from two movements in epistemology: *constructivism* and *situated cognition* (Anderson et al., 1996; Reynolds, Sinatra & Jetton, 1996). Whereas constructivism refers to a particular philosophical position that is relevant for education and instruction primarily at a meta-theoretical level (Dinter, 1998; Dinter & Seel, 1994), the concept 'situated cognition' has strong educational implications because it might provide numerous prescriptions for instructional practice. As Reynolds and colleagues (1996)

J.M. Spector and T.M. Anderson (eds.),
Integrated and Holistic Perspectives on Learning, Instruction and Technology, 129–158.
© 2000 *Kluwer Academic Publishers. Printed in the Netherlands.*

have pointed out, situated cognition evolved from artificial intelligence and cognitive science to capture the broader situational context of learning and communication. Theories of situated cognition aim to account for how individuals learn in conceptually organized environments which contain: (1) the external world to be understood; (2) the individual's perceptions and internal representations of this world; and, (3) the individual's symbolic interactions with it. In this context, learning is defined as the individual's ability to construct meaning by extracting and organizing information from environments. Thus, cognitive processes that occur as an individual interacts with a given environment are at the core of situated cognition, and, consequently, learning, thinking, and reasoning are made up of interactions between learners and situations in the world. According to the terminology of practical philosophy, situations include all environmental states and conditions to which subjects are exposed and which are not available as self-constructed models. However, this definition involves a dichotomy, since external situations are separated from mental constructions. Therefore, the question arises of how the suggested interactions between a learner and a physical or social situation may occur. The answer of those who advocate situated cognition is that the learner constructs a *mental model* in order to simulate relevant properties of the situation to be cognitively mastered.

Mental models emerged in the 1980s as a central theoretical construct to capture situated cognition and qualitative reasoning. Incidentally, there are cognitive psychologists who consider mental models to be the best organized representations among declarative learning results (Glaser, 1990; Shute, 1994). More specifically, it has been argued that comprehension and reasoning in specific situations (e.g., in schools and real-life situations) necessarily involve the use of mental models of different qualities (Greeno, 1989). The idea of mental (or internal) models is based on the presumption that an individual who intends to give a rational explanation for *something* must develop practicable methods in order to generate adequate explanations from his knowledge of the world and his limited information processing capacity. Thus, the individual constructs a *model* that both integrates the relevant semantic knowledge and meets the requirements of the situation to be explained. Accordingly, this model 'works' (*sensu* Craik, 1943) when it fits both the subject's knowledge base, and the explanatory need, with regard to the concrete situation or context to be mastered cognitively. That is, internal or mental models serve a twofold epistemological function: They represent and also organize the subject's knowledge in such a way that even complex phenomena become plausible.

Reality does not provide a discernible fixed, and finished shape that can be mapped by the human mind. Rather, it is the other way around. The mind projects order onto the diversity of world phenomena. Accordingly, mental models *reflect* the structure of the external world because they are constructed to structure it, and not to reproduce or copy a given external structure. However, the human mind is not free to arbitrarily impose any possible structure onto the world, but rather the external world imposes on the mind. Thus, mental models are constructed with regard to the subject's affordances within specific environmental contexts. Model-based reasoning occurs when an individual mentally manipulates an environment in order to simulate (in the sense of thought experiments) specific transformations which may occur in real-life situations. Then, mental models "run in the mind's eye" (Vosniadou & Brewer, 1994) to readily produce qualitative inferences with respect to the situation to be cognitively mastered. This is the reason that several researchers prefer to use the term "situation model" (Greer, 1997; Morrow, Bower & Greenspan, 1989).

From an instructional point of view, the suggestion can be made that mental models are constructed from the significant properties of external situations, such as learning environments in schools, and the subject's interactions with these well-designed situations. Accordingly, from its very beginning we can find a strong instructional impetus in research on mental models. This has been expressed by Johnson-Laird (1989) as follows:

> "What is at issue is how such models develop as an individual progresses from novice to expert, and whether there is any pedagogical advantage in providing people with models of tasks they are trying to learn" (p. 485).

Snow (1990) integrated mental models into a comprehensive conceptual framework and identified the learning-dependent mental model progression as a specific kind of transition mediating between preconceptions or misconceptions, which describes the initial states of the learning process, and the causal explanations, which are described as the desired end state of learning (see Figure 1).

In view of these conceptions, our research group has recently analyzed more than 240 publications (published from 1983 to 1999) addressing mental models in different fields of interest, such as logic and qualitative reasoning, spatial cognition, human-computer-interaction, and text processing. More than 20% of these publications were explicitly concerned with the issue of what extent the construction and progression of mental models could be facilitated or improved through instruction. However, a more specific analysis confirmed the observation made by several researchers that research on mental models, especially in instructional contexts, is not theoretically sound and presents substantial methodological deficiencies (Seel, 1999). Accordingly, the research on mental models has been criticized in the past from both a conceptual and a methodological point of view. First, several authors (e.g., Rips, 1987; Wilson & Rutherford, 1989) established that the research on mental models harbors considerable conceptual confusion due to an inflationary use of a specific concept, weaknesses of its' theoretical foundation, and shortcomings of formal precision. Secondly, several authors (Royer, Cisero & Carlo, 1993; Snow 1990) have criticized that mental model research has regularly been done piecemeal and in small scale, specialized contexts, whereby the assessment primarily was concerned with the diagnosis of malfunctions of mental models in limited learning situations. Accordingly, these authors concluded that the mental model research of the 1980s is instructionally irrelevant, and Jih and Reeves (1992) continued to criticize this research for not providing prescriptive device for the instructional design of learning environments.

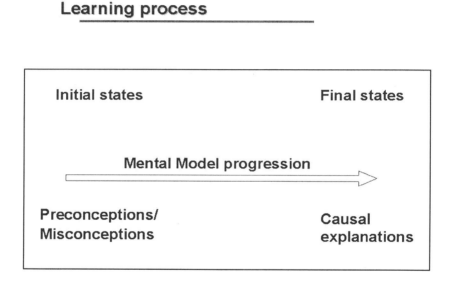

Figure 1. The general progression of mental models (Snow, 1990).

With respect to this criticism we focus in this article on the following question: Has descriptive research on mental models in instructional contexts provided results that can provide a foundation for prescriptions to facilitate or improve the construction of mental models by learners in specific learning situations? To answer this question requires that we clarify what characteristics of learning situations necessitate the construction of mental models. The next step involves the search for theoretically sound conceptions of instruction for designing learning environments that either impel students to construct mental models for themselves in an exploratory manner, or which adaptively guide and direct the students in the process of model construction.

INSTRUCTIONAL PREREQUISITES FOR THE CONSTRUCTION OF MENTAL MODELS

Because most regular class work is concerned mainly with the accumulation of domain-specific knowledge, instruction alone does not imply in general the construction of a mental model. Accumulation of knowledge is certainly an important form of learning, but there are other things that also must be achieved in the course of school learning. So, for example, another important form of learning is that of restructuring one's knowledge - that means to reformulate the very basis of understanding of a given topic in consequence of new concepts and experiences. Furthermore, there is the fine tuning of behavior, the sharpening of adequate skills and understanding to that of the expert - smooth, efficient, effortless. And last but not least, there are mental efforts to understand complex structures and systems, thereby constructing appropriate mental representations to model and comprehend these structures and systems. Certainly, this kind of learning may also involve the accumulation of domain-specific knowledge, but its main purpose consists in the construction of causal explanations with the help of appropriate mental models. It is a mode of accommodation rather than of assimilation (Seel, 1991). Consequently, the construction of a mental model in the course of learning often necessitates both a restructuring of the underlying representations and a reconceptualization of the related concepts. We maintain that there is no need for a mental model as long as the learner can assimilate the learning material into the structures of prior knowledge. Therefore, we consider a substantial *resistance to assimilation* to be prerequisite to the construction of a mental model, and we believe that the degree of this *resistance to assimilation* heavily depends on the complexity of the topics to be learned. This assumption also has implications with regard to motivation insofar as such resistance may evoke - to some extent - epistemological curiosity due to cognitive dissonance or even conflict (Eckblad, 1981).

This argument is based on the assumption that the student is provided with learning material whose content or structure is inconsistent or dissonant with preconceptions acquired in previous learning situations. Johnson-Laird (1989) differentiated between three different sources for constructing mental models, namely: (a) the learner's ability to construct models in an inductive manner, either from a set of basic components of world knowledge or from analogous models that she already possesses; (b) everyday observations of the outside world; and, (c) other people's explanations. Our argumentation focuses definitely on the third possibility. This corresponds with the mainstream of instructional research on mental models that is based on two assumptions: First, it is possible to infer, from the performance in specific tasks, the quality of a mental model that subjects construct at the beginning or in the course of the learning phase. Secondly, it is effective to provide externally model-relevant information before or during learning in order to help students to construct adequate mental models (Mayer, 1989; Seel & Dinter, 1995).

As in the popular study of Kieras and Bovair (1984), the following method has been often applied, first after the initial training in which the subjects have to generate an initial mental model, and then after an experimentally varied learning phase, the subjects perform specific tasks considered indicative of successful learning and model construction. In accordance with Johnson-Laird's (1989) idea of investigating whether there is any pedagogical advantage in providing people with models of the tasks they are trying to learn, numerous researchers (e.g., Anzai & Yokoyama, 1984; Kieras & Bovair, 1984; Mayer, 1989) provided their subjects with a *conceptual model* of the topics to be learned. Following Norman (1983), a *conceptual model* can be understood as a specific kind of a representation which is constructed in accordance with didactic principles in order to illustrate the main components and relationships of a complex system with the help of graphical diagrams or object-based replica. The globe as well as the well-known illustrations of human memory are good examples of conceptual models (see Norman, 1983). There are researchers who are convinced of the effects of graphical diagrams or even "helpful video" on the construction of mental models, insofar as they consider these instructional media to be effective with regard to the creation of dynamic images that constitute the frame of reference for the construction of mental models (Hegarty & Just, 1993; Sharp et al., 1995). However, this presupposes that the learner is sensitive to characteristics of the learning environment, such as the availability of certain information at a given time, the way the information is structured and mediated, and the ease with which it can be found in the environment (see, for example, Anzai & Yokoyama, 1984).

Meanwhile there are several studies (Mayer, 1989; Seel, 1995) which have demonstrated that the presentation of a conceptual model affects the construction of a task-related mental model depending on the stage in the learning process at which a conceptual model is presented. A presentation at the beginning of the learning process seems to increase both the quality of comprehension during the learning process and the quality of causal explanations by the end of the learning process. According to these findings, we presume in our current research that a conceptual model provided at the beginning of a lesson facilitates the construction of an adequate mental model for cognitively mastering the demands of the learning situation. However, when we adopt Snow's (1990) conceptualization that mental models mediate between preconceptions (defined here as the initial states in the learning process) and causal explanations (defined here as the desired final states in the learning process), we can distinguish between different possibilities of how an externally provided conceptual model can interact with preconceptions:

The structure or content of the conceptual model is compatible with existing preconceptions. In this case, it will be assimilated immediately. As suggested in previous comments, there is no need for a mental model and learning corresponds in a broader sense with the accumulation of knowledge.

The conceptual model does not fit with existing preconceptions, neither structurally nor in content. In this case, a cognitive conflict or at least an assimilation resistance may arise. However, as research on conceptual change indicates, when a preconception is concrete, coherent, and strongly anchored in the learner's world knowledge, it may be resistant to change (Chinn & Brewer, 1993; Slotta et al., 1995). Thus, a substantial change in such an anchored preconception may demand tremendous efforts in order to convince the learner of the necessity of a conceptual change.

The learner has no relevant preconception in mind. That means the subjects are provided with learning material which is definitely new to them. In this case, the provided conceptual model will be adopted and function as the "*a priori* understanding" of the learning tasks, discussed here in terms of an initial mental model that serves at least the function of an advance organizer (Ausubel, 1968). We can also assume that learning occurs as a combination of accumulation of knowledge and a successive consolidation of the mental model. Dependent on both the learner's capabilities and the complexity of the learning situation to be mastered, various degrees of instructional efforts are necessary.

As several experiments of my research group indicate (Seel, 1995; Seel & Dinter, 1995) model-based learning depends on the learner's domain-specific knowledge and related cognitive structures, the nature of the material to be learned and the modality in which the contents to be learned are presented and delivered by media. Last but not least, it depends on the characteristics of the learning environment and the methods of teaching, which will be the focus of the following section.

TEACHING THAT HELPS TO CONSTRUCT MENTAL MODELS

Clearly, there might exist learning environments that can initiate learning in the sense of free explorations by invention, but in instructional contexts (especially in schools) we regularly operate with well-prepared and predesigned learning environments that constrain the student's learning processes to various extents. Generally, there are three different opportunities to enhance exploratory learning and problem solving through instruction aiming at:

- self-organized discovery learning,
- externally guided discovery learning, and
- receptive meaningful learning.

With respect to the construction of mental models, *self-organized discovery learning* is reasonable only if the learner has previously achieved adequate metacognitive skills to guide the problem-solving process effectively. As a matter of fact, this approach can be rather pretentious, which even an expert could sweat over sometimes. So for most novice students, *self-organized discovery learning* is closely associated with learning by trial-and-error insofar as an initial model must succeed with a procedure called "fleshing out" (Johnson-Laird, 1983, p 452) that continuously examines whether a model can be replaced with an alternative model or not. This procedure, which corresponds to a *reductio ad absurdum*, is at the core of mental modeling in general. However, in *self-organized discovery learning* the learner has to continuously search for information in the given learning environment in order to complete or stabilize an initial mental model. In this case, the creation of the mental model corresponds with an "a priori understanding" of the material to be learned. However, Briggs (1990) demonstrated in a case study that an instructional strategy aiming at discovery learning may dramatically increase the probability of stabilizing faulty initial mental models. Consequently, a substantial conceptual change does not take place, and relatively stable intermediate states of causal understanding often precede the instructionally intended conceptual mastery (Galili, Bendall & Goldberg, 1993).

Guided-discovery as well as expository strategies of teaching may be helpful in reducing the likelihood that faulty mental models will be constructed in the course of learning (Seel, 1995). In the case of *guided-discovery learning,* the teacher usually first develops a relevant problem-solving context for the students, and then may formulate a problem task. She may also provide a strategy for the problem solving process or for the evaluation of a solution. For these purposes particular teaching aids my be utilized, such as "product-oriented" or "process-oriented" strategies in order to assist the learner in accomplishing the tasks and problems to be mastered. The first strategy aims at the comprehension of regularities in numerous situations with a similar structure, whereas the second strategy aims at the improvement of metacognitive control and self-regulation (Seel & Dinter, 1995).

In the case of *receptive meaningful learning*, the teacher explicitly directs the mental model progression. As a first step, an explicit and consistent conceptual model that should direct the learner's comprehension of the learning material and that may evoke a substantial change of preconceptions is presented. As pointed out, the idea of providing students, especially novice learners, with a well-designed conceptual model has instructional appeal for several authors in the field of mental model research (see, for example, Kindfield, 1993; Norman, 1983). It is often easier for a novice learner to assimilate a causal explanation (provided through a conceptual model) rather than to induce one individually. In this case, the provided conceptual model will be functionally incorporated in the thinking process, and related information can be progressively integrated in a more or less consistent manner.

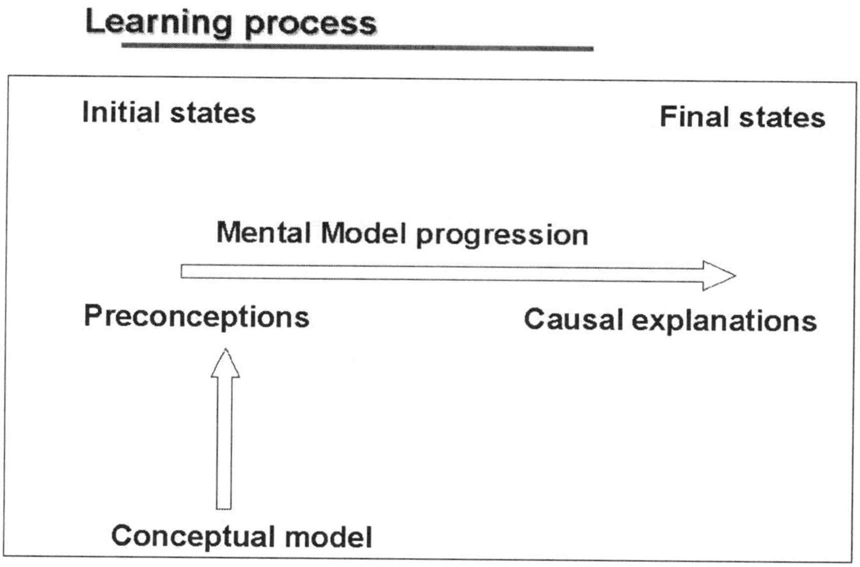

Learning process

Figure 2. The mental model as created through the conceptual model.

Every instructional psychologist knows the central ideas of both the expository and guided-discovery teaching strategies are rooted in the work of Ausubel (1968) and Bruner (1966). Today we can find several theoretical approaches, such as Spiro's "random access instruction", Schank's "goal-based scenarios" or the cognitive apprenticeship approach (Collins et al., 1989), that correspond closely with Ausubel's and Bruner's ideas. Therefore, it is relatively easy to classify the different instructional strategies and methods into the broad categories of expository teaching versus guided-discovery teaching. From our point of view, Ausubel's approach of expository teaching, Wittrock's approach of generative teaching (Kourilsky & Wittrock, 1992), and the cognitive apprenticeship approach of Collins,

Brown and Newman (1989) belong to the first class of instructional intervention, whereas the approaches of "random access instruction" (Spiro et al., 1991), "anchored instruction" (CTGV, 1997) and "case-based learning" with "goal-based scenarios" (Schank et al., 1993/94) belong to the second class of discovery teaching. With regard to the initial discussion about situated cognition, these various models can be described to some extent through the "contextual + complex + authentic + social" formula for learning situations. It is not possible here to do justice to these various models of situated learning, but it seems clear that among them the cognitive apprenticeship approach corresponds best with the principles described for the construction of mental models through instruction, due to the fact that this approach implies *modeling* (as providing an expert's conceptual model) as a central component of teaching.

COGNITIVE APPRENTICESHIPS AND MENTAL MODELS

Methods of cognitive apprenticeships try to integrate learning into realistic (authentic) activities of expert practice, referring to the social, physical, and psychological context of teaching and learning in a constructivist sense. Accordingly, the state of the art literature on situated cognition and learning refers to methods of traditional apprenticeship as the most important instructional strategy (Collins, Brown, & Holum, 1993):

> "In ancient times, teaching and learning were accomplished through apprenticeship. [...] Apprenticeship was the vehicle for transmitting the knowledge required for expert practice in fields from painting and sculpting to medicine and law. It was the natural way to learn" (p. 6).

This argumentation is rooted in classical philosophy where teaching and learning are considered to involve the methodical interaction of two or more partners through which at least one of them acquires practical, poetic, or theoretical skills. Teaching aims at the transference of these skills, and thus, it applies primarily appropriate semiotic acts to guide the student for the acquisition of skills. Thus, learning corresponds to the acquisition and comprehension of such skills, and often proceeds on a trial and error basis, insofar as the learner tries to achieve mastery of a particular skill through repetition. Here both, the demonstration of a skill and the imitation of it is precisely that which distinguishes teaching and learning from mere training. In addition to simple practice through repetition, there is also a strong relationship between teaching and learning to comprehension and knowledge.

Collins and colleagues (1989) argued that effective learning environments could be characterized through 18 features belonging to four broad *dimensions*, namely content, methods, sequencing, and the sociology of teaching. We will now focus on the dimension of methods, which is the most important for our experimental research program. Six successive teaching methods are distinguished: *modeling, coaching, scaffolding* (fading), *articulation, reflection* and *exploration* (see Figure 3). We explain these methods now by using expressions from our multimedia learning program which will be discussed in more detail in the next section.

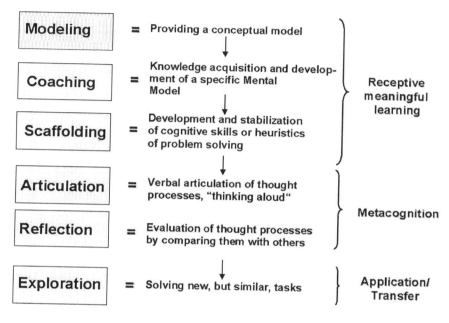

Figure 3. The cognitive apprenticeship dimension method and its six components.

EFFECTIVE TEACHING METHODS

In *modeling*, the instructor demonstrates a problem's solution, and the students acquire a conceptual model of this process by observing the instructor's approach. In our implementation, we've broken this method into 5 steps. Initially, a process is presented which the student is already familiar with, such as the water cycle. We identify the major elements in the water cycle, their stages, the streams of transition between stages, and the forces driving the transitions. Secondly we develop a systemic model of this process, that is a simple diagram in order to offer a visual representation of our model (see Figure 4). Third we introduce the new instructional concept such as the economy, and again we indicate the fundamental elements, stages, streams, and forces. Finally, we develop a new systemic model for the economy, using the same approach as the water cycle model including identification of elements, stages, transitions and forces to represent the flow of money and goods between households and companies. So with each investigation of analogous processes, our model of the economy becomes more complete. Finally, we compare and contrast the two models to find similarities and differences. This process is repeated using successive examples, further refining our economic model each time. This procedure is strongly related to expository learning and elaborating a cognitive structure from a subsuming concept as Ausubel (1968) investigated.

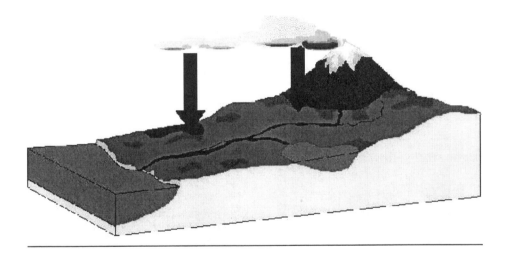

Figure 4. A model of the water cycle applied in the MFS program.

In *coaching*, students are supervised and given guidance as they try to find solutions to a given task in an adaptive manner. We've also broken this method into five steps: A particular aspect of the economy is described, and how this fits into a feed-back-circuit is examined. Then another aspect of the economic system is described, and the student is asked to perform a systemic analysis of it. Finally, feedback to his analysis is offered.

In *scaffolding*, students are offered process-oriented assistance to improve their cognitive skills for problem solving. The heuristics of *scaffolding* consists of the decomposition of a complex problem into sub-problems and the construction of analogies between the sub-problems. We've implemented this in three steps: (1) a question is posed whose answer is slightly beyond the student's current base of knowledge; (2) the student tries to answer the question by drawing new conclusions and observations from what the student already understands; and, (3) the student is then presented with various expert strategies for solving the problem, whereby the student picks the path which most closely resembles his or her thinking process. The approaches are then explained in further detail, allowing him to see how his own strategy could be enhanced.

Articulation is the process of "thinking aloud" while working on a task, and *reflection* is the comparison of the problem solving procedures applied by the learner and the expert respectively. Collins and colleagues (1989) maintain that these methods contribute greatly to the development of reflective thinking and metacognitive control of learning. For our purposes, they have been integrated into a "teach-back" procedure (1991) in a social learning situation.

Cognitive Apprenticeship: Sequencing

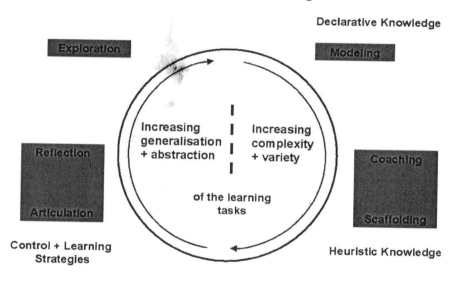

Figure 5. A detailed view of the cognitive apprenticeship model.

In *exploration*, the student independently applies the problem solving procedures learned to new, but similar, tasks. By doing this, the student's cognitive problem solving skills are to be improved. In the case of our experimental research program, the improvement is focused on a single class of tasks, in other words, a near transfer within the field of economics with higher complexity.

In the next section we will introduce our multimedia experimental research program which was built based on the cognitive apprenticeship approach described.

THE 4M PROJECT

The learning environment which we have constructed for realizing the cognitive apprenticeship principles is, to a large extent, a multimedia environment. Therefore, we have named the project simply the "4M project"[1] (MultiMedia and Mental Models). It is explicitly geared towards investigating the learning-dependent progression of mental models, both over an extended period and in a complex field of study. The cognitive apprenticeship approach has been previously applied in several experimental studies in various domains (Casey, 1996; Farmer, Buckmaster, & Legrand, 1992; Lajoie & Lesgold, 1989; Niegemann, 1995; Pieters & deBruijn, 1992; Volet, 1991), where it has proved successful in promoting student's higher order thinking skills as well as in shaping the social interactions between teachers and students to goal-oriented problem solving. However, there has been remarkably little investigation of complex learning tasks that take many hours or even weeks to accomplish. What goes on during that time? Whatever it is, it is slow, effortful, continuous, often unconscious, sensitive, and fragile. There is no magic dose of knowledge in the form of a pill or lecture. Merely a lot of slow, continual exposure to the topic, probably accompanied by several bouts of restructuring the underlying mental representations and reconceptualizing the concepts, plus many hours of accumulating and assimilating many facts.

Accordingly, we have chosen the subject matter domain of economics and dynamic economic systems due to their complexity. To focus within the field of economic systems, we have selected two topics to be taught through the instructional software program *Multimedia Financial Systems (MFS)*: the financial politics of the Federal Bank of Germany, including (a) the whole financial system, and (b) the approaching European monetary union because the introduction of the *Euro* (money) provides the wider context for German financial politics. Both topics are concerned with highly complex systems. After a series of evaluation studies (Al-Diban & Seel, 1999; Seel et al., 1998), we know that the multimedia program *Multimedia Financial Systems (MFS)*, which we have developed and refined since 1994 fulfills the criteria of modeling complex systems. As already mentioned, this program has been designed in accordance with the principles of the cognitive apprenticeship approach. It is geared to students in grade 12, and takes over six hours on the average to effectively complete the instructional process.

Figure 6 provides an overview of the program's structure as well as an assessment of the mental model progression at various junctures.

---

[1]   Since 1994 we gratefully acknowledge financial support for this research from a grant provided by the German Research Assocation (Deutsche Forschungsgemeinschaft) with Grant-No. Se 399/4. The research group consists currently of Sabine Al-Diban, Wolfram Lutterer, Katharina Schenk and Ralf Siegel.

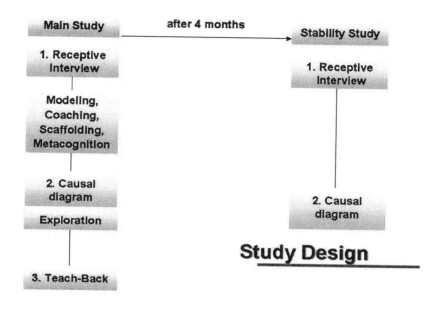

Figure 6. An overview of the program structure and the design of the study.

The Research Assessment Methods

We assessed the learner's mental models at three different stages during our long term exploration study: (a) Prior to the study, with the help of a guided interview technique; (b) within the study, after the realization of the metacognitive methods of *articulation* and *reflection,* with the help of causal diagrams (i.e., a special assessment procedure discussed in detail by Seel, 1999); and, (c) after the study, by means of cooperative learning in a "teach back" procedure (Sasse, 1991). After a period of four months we again applied a receptive interview technique and used causal diagrams to assess learners' mental models in a stability test.

So far, we have carried out four empirical studies in order to investigate the effectiveness of the multimedia program MFS. These studies were exploratory due to the novelty of research in this field of interest. They were designed as replication studies that aimed at both the empirical evaluation of the MFS program and the assessment of mental modeling during the course of learning. The results of these investigations are reported in Al-Diban and Seel (1999) and Seel and colleagues (1998). In the fourth study we extended the research focus on the learning-dependent progression of mental models by especially investigating the long-term stability of constructed mental models. Therefore, several students have been tested again four months after working on the MFS program. The related problem of *change measurement* as it is linked to the learning-dependent change of cognitive dispositions is discussed by Seel (1999).

We will focus now on the fourth replication study, which was concerned with the investigation of the stability and change of mental models over the course of learning directed in accordance with the principles of cognitive apprenticeship.

The Research Design

When we began to develop the multimedia program MFS, it soon became evident that the prescriptions of Collins et al. (1989) concerning the different methods of cognitive apprenticeship were too broad and unspecified to be realized effectively at once. Rather, we had to invest some time and effort in finding theoretically sound explanations and effective realizations of that which the original authors of the cognitive apprenticeship approach possibly had in mind. In accordance with both Seel's (1991) theory of mental models and with experimental results from studies on schema acquisition from single examples (Ahn, Brewer, & Mooney, 1992), we experimentally varied the apprenticeship methods of *modeling* and *scaffolding* by contrasting a deductive strategy of explanation-based learning with an inductive strategy of example-based learning. Both variants of *modeling* center, in the same way, around the introduction of an expert's macroeconomic model, providing a good example for complex dynamic systems which contain at least two variables at two different times that are causally related:

$$Y(t) = f(Y(t-1), ..., Y(t-k)).$$

The system's dynamics are attributed to the fact that states and interventions at a former time affect the state of Y at the time *t* (Hübner, 1989). In this way, the numerous interrelated elements and sectors of a dynamic system can be integrated into aggregates (i.e., components). In macroeconomic models, such aggregates are firms, households, wealth creation etc. They are characterized by similarity within a given sector and dissimilarity between different sectors. At the component level, various processes are present, such as the supply of produced goods and the demand for purposes of consumption or net investments. These processes are usually described through linear equations. In Figure 7, a simple model of an open national economy is described.

Dynamic Model of an Open National Economy

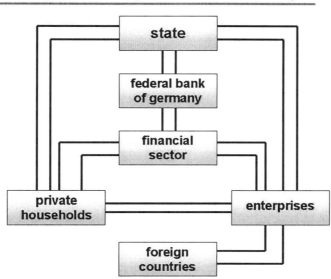

Figure 7. A dynamic model of an open national economy as used in MFS.

This dynamic model gives a good example of the type of conceptual models that are used in the multimedia program MFS and constituted the instructional foundation for the investigation of change and stability of the learner's mental models.

In *coaching* we applied various result-oriented teaching aids in order to assist learners with the completion of various analogous learning tasks. Independent of the aforementioned experimental variation, we designed *scaffolding* with process-oriented support in order to teach the heuristic purpose of the deconstruction of complex tasks into subtasks and solving them via analogy. More detailed information about teaching strategies can be found in previous articles from our research group (e.g., Al-Diban & Seel, 1999; Seel et al., 1998) and in chapters by Spector, Park and Etgen, and by Sayenye in this book. In the related studies we found evidence that the metacognitive components of *articulation* and *reflection* can not be realized effectively in a computer program (Casey, 1996). We therefore integrated both components jointly into a "teach back" procedure, which simultaneously served as a basis for the assessment and demonstration of the learner's mental models in progression. More specifically, we applied a backward strategy in *reflection* in order to focus the learner's attention onto the problem solving strategy common to all of the tasks presented in MFS.

In the section *exploration,* the students were asked to transfer the new domain-specific knowledge and skills to solve tasks of a different nature, where no external support was provided. For example, the subjects had to solve tasks about the consequences of European money policy, whereby they could use all available teaching aids in the program (conceptual models, animations, illustrations, etc.).

Methods

In this exploratory study we investigated: (a) the effects of providing a conceptual model at the beginning of the learning process on the construction of a corresponding mental model; and, (b) the long-term effectiveness of the multimedia learning program on both the acquired domain-specific knowledge and the stability of the initially constructed mental models. In order to assess any significant changes of domain-specific knowledge and of the constructed mental models, we used a pre/post-test design with multi-stages of testing with different test procedures. Declarative knowledge and causal models must both be learned and demonstrated for satisfactory completion of the learning cycle. Declarative knowledge was assessed with a special test developed by Beck (1993). For the assessment of mental models we applied the technique of "verbal protocols". This was done in two phases: first at the beginning of the learning phase by means of a cognitive interviewing technique, and again after *articulation* and *reflection*, where *causal diagrams* were used for assessing causal explanations in accordance with Snow's (1990) reasoning. We again assessed the quality of the learner's mental models at the end of the learning process with the help of a "teach back" procedure. The long-term stability of the mental model was tested again on the second occasion with causal diagrams, so that we could achieve a high degree of comparability.

More than 150 subjects have been tested with regard to their performance in various versions of MFS. In our last exploratory study on the stability and change of mental models, 19 high school grade 12 students (10 females and 9 males) took part, 7 of them voluntary took part on the additional test of diagnosis of mental models.

Some Selected Results

To check the students' prior knowledge and preconceptions before working with the learning program, they were asked to causally explain which effects several decisions of the Federal Bank of Germany (e.g., lowering of the discount rate and the Lombard rate) may have on the macroeconomics of Germany. So far only a few subjects were able to give even partial explanations to the initial task, and most of them could not even give any plausible answers at all. Therefore, we were not surprised to observe that the students had a strong tendency to adopt the explanations provided by the expert's conceptual models in the *modeling* component of the program. Moreover, we observed that the learners also applied the expert's conceptual models in order to solve the tasks involved in the *coaching* and *scaffolding* components (Seel et al., 1998).

We hypothesized that the inability of the subjects to answer the initial questions could be explained by a lack of domain-specific prior knowledge, but this proved to be wrong, since the subjects had, on average, a relatively good prior knowledge about economics. Table 1 gives an overview of the results of the standardized pre-, post-, and stability tests (four months after working with MFS) of the subject's domain specific knowledge following the procedure of the Knowledge Test of Beck (KTB). According to the experimental design, the different treatments realized during the acquisition phases with MFS all led to a significant improvement of the domain-specific knowledge.

Time of assessment	M	SD
Pretest	14.4	2.5
Posttest	16.6	3.6
Stability (after 4 months)	16.8	3.2

Table 1. Stability of acquired declarative knowledge (Means and Standard Deviations, N=19).

Significant differences could only be found with regard to the comparisons between the pretest and posttest as well as between the pretest and stability test. There was no significant difference between the posttest and stability test (p = .76). Thus, we can conclude that the domain-specific knowledge was acquired within the learning phase and was stable and constant over a period of about four months.

Furthermore, as a validation procedure, the KTB offers a five step differentiation into subscales, using Bloom's Taxonomy of educational objectives (knowledge, comprehension, application, analysis and evaluation; 1972). By doing this, a detailed impression of possible changes in the learner's domain-specific knowledge is inherently provided with the KTB. We used this tool to find more detailed information about possible changes of the student's declarative knowledge. In this way we were able to detect a significant improvement of knowledge in the subscale "comprehension". At first glance, the impact of the program on the "comprehension" of economic facts and relationships supports the assumption that the multimedia program MFS strongly influences the learner's causal understanding of economics. In the next step we examined this assumption with regard to the qualitative mental models that have been constructed by the students while working with MFS.

In order to investigate the stability or change of mental models we applied qualitative methods of assessment, that have been used in previous studies such as receptive interviews and causal diagrams, so that we could compare results of this case-study with our former research concerning the quality of the learner's mental models (quasi-experimental design). The use of causal diagrams especially indicated an increasingly dominant role of causal patterns which was anticipated in the students answers after having completed the instructional program MFS. This is also postulated by Snow (1990) for the progression and change of mental models during the learning process which leads to more sophisticated models.

Therefore, in order to capture the mental model progression, our qualitative diagnosis consisted of two steps in accordance with the chosen methods in addition to the KTB. First, a receptive interview took place in the pretest, based upon general concepts about politics in the field of economics. This has mainly been applied to investigate the subjects' individual problem spaces. Second, we applied the technique of causal diagrams and related "structure-spreading-techniques" (Seel, 1999) in the posttest and stability test in order to assess the long-term quality of the students' causal explanations of dynamic economic systems. The following two cases demonstrate some typical examples.

Subject #206 scored 11 points in Beck's knowledge pretest, 13 points immediately after the learning phase (Figure 8), and she improved to 14 points in the stability test (four months after having completed the learning phase with MFS - Figure 9). These results describe a relatively low domain specific knowledge base. The scores in other tests were average. By contrast, in the stability test this learner was able to recall 5 out of 6 economical sectors taught in MFS and relate them to each other. She began with a sketch and continued with 10 distinct examples that were obviously strongly influenced by her personal experiences. Several statements showed that this learner was making mental reference to the systemic model which was presented in MFS. Nevertheless, on the whole a deeper understanding of multi-causal and systemic aspects of the domain could be observed. The causal diagram which this learner produced in the stability test indicates similar results concerning her concepts of economy as she demonstrated a substantial knowledge of multi-causal and systemic relations. In fact, this diagram was even more detailed in regard to the relevant causes, aims, and involved processes than the causal diagram produced in the posttest. Four months later, subject #206 was not only able to reproduce important factors of the economic systems but she also made several attempts to run through various economic elements in the 'mind's eye', considering positive and negative influences of several processes and their causes and consequences. Adapting the provided conceptual model this learner developed an increasingly idiosyncratic mental model to integrate individual experiences and economic knowledge for better understanding of dynamic economic systems.

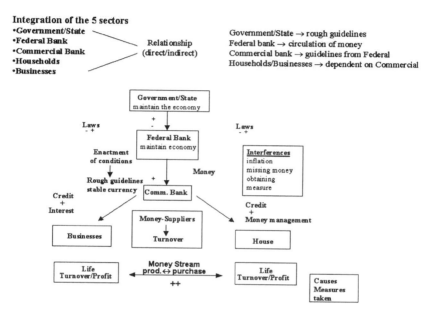

Figure 8. Subject #206 – Posttest causal diagram assessed after the MFS learning program.

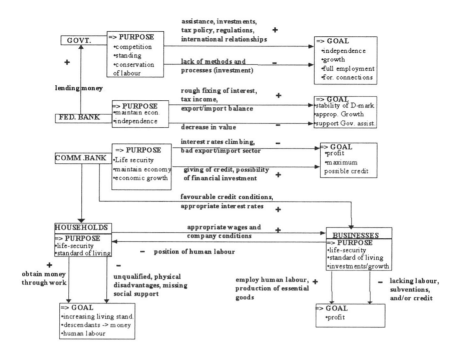

Figure 9. Subject #206 – causal diagram assessed 4 months after the MFS learning program.

Subject #401, our next example (Figures 10 - 13), scored 14 points on the knowledge pretest, 17 points on the posttest, and improved by another 3 points to 20 points on the delayed stability test. Although this person reached an above-average level in declarative knowledge we can note that the reconstruction of mental models in the stability test was intra-individually less successful. However this subject recalled five of six economical sectors and established relationships between these sectors through five examples and additional explanations. First, he wrote down the terms that he considered important for further comprehension. Like subject #206, his examples also referred closely to personal experiences. The verbal protocols of the interviews revealed multi-causal and systemic comprehension similar to that of subject #206, but the complexity of the explanations of subject #401 was slightly higher.

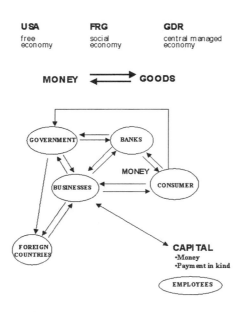

Figure 10. Subject #401 – Preconception about the economic system by a receptive interview.

As his causal explanations were causal-generalizing, the systemic comprehension of this subject included systemic-procedural relationships. After the learning process subject #401 reproduced causal diagrams of economic cycles that were causally very similar to the representations taught by MFS (Figures 12 - 13). Furthermore, this learner gave suitable examples where appropriate. A general analysis of the causal diagrams shows that his representation included essential factors and important relationships of economic cycles. The components he described were clearly structured. He reported, for example, on four financial political objectives and nine methods for reaching these objectives through interventions in financial politics. These methods were further divided into five stimulating and four repressing interventions. In the stability test, the receptive interview assessed a conceptual model of the national economy which corresponded closely with the one at the beginning of the MFS program (Figure 7). In contrast, the preconception model (Figure 10) shows less exact relations between the sectors. These facts seem to indicate the subject's integration of the provided conceptual model into his 'subjective problem space'.

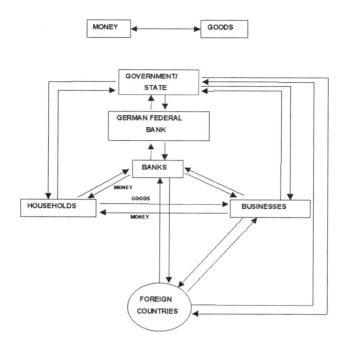

*Figure 11.*Subject #401 – Conception of the economic system 4 months after MFS.

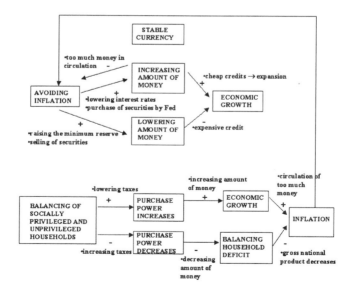

Figure 12. Subject #401 – Posttest causal diagram assessed after MFS.

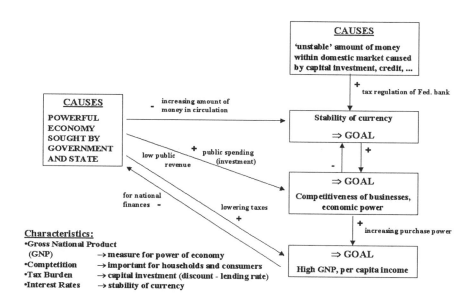

Figure 13. Subject #401 – Causal diagram 4 months after MFS.

DISCUSSION

Mental models can be considered a central theoretical construct of the situated cognition approach, since it is assumed that the learner constructs a mental model in order to simulate relevant properties of the situation to be cognitively mastered. An instructionally far-reaching assumption of the situated cognition approach is that these cognitive artifacts are not fixed structures in the mind, but are rather constructed when needed - for example, in order to master a new learning situation with its specific demands. In accordance with this, numerous studies in the research field of conceptual change (Dole & Sinatra, 1998) indicate that students dynamically modify and restructure their knowledge bases when externally provided information is evaluated as more plausible and convincing than the prior knowledge. This depends to a large extent on the externally provided information in the form of a conceptual model, aimed at the facilitation and improvement of constructing an appropriate mental model to master the learning situation and its cognitive demands.

Taking into account the fact that instruction in general aims at the construction of stable knowledge structures and even more importantly at elaborated skills, we investigated how permanent and stable those mental models are which have been generated after a learner's early exposure to an appropriate conceptual model. Therefore, the investigations of our quasi-experimental research confirm these assumptions, insofar as most of the subjects integrated the expert's conceptual models provided in the *modeling*-component into their "subjective problem spaces". This observation corresponds in part with our assumption that if no relevant preconceptions are available, learners tend to adopt the conceptual models provided in order to construct an idiosyncratic mental model of the tasks they are trying to learn. Accordingly, the subjects in our exploratory study drew causal diagrams which indicated strong but varying degrees of similarity to the provided conceptual models. We have also ascertained that causal diagrams are an adequate method of assessing mental models; at the same time, we are aware of the difficulty of accurately deducing an abstract concept like a mental model from a drawing.

The results of our previous investigations also indicated that most students applied their initially constructed mental models to mastering the learning tasks of the subsequent components *coaching* and *scaffolding*. That means that the initially constructed mental models of the learners became stable although they evidently changed after the learning period in accordance with the requirements of the situation.

Thus, mental models are acquired with the significant properties of learning situations and the subject's interactions with them. Moreover, effective mental models are stored in memory as an effective means for having mastered a specific situation, but they will never function as mere patterns to be rotely reproduced in another situation ('sleeping copies'). As our stability test shows, mental models have been generated on the basis of former experiences with similar situations and have served to help master the new situation. In other words, we consider mental models temporary structures created by an individual when confronted with a new situation that cannot be mastered with available conceptual structures. Accordingly, we do not suppose a factual persistence of a stagnant mental model over time, but rather more plausible a situation-dependent reconstruction of previously generated mental models. This fits in with the observation of our subjects' slightly changed mental models after four months. Obviously, these mental models, assessed through causal diagrams, have met the requirements of the new situation, which in turn closely resembled the former learning situations. With regard to situated cognition prescriptions for instructional practice, the construction of an appropriate mental model can also be understood as a constructivist learning process.

Our research thus far can only offer a snapshot of a huge and complex learning phenomenon. We still have to confirm and differentiate our principles and results, and to do more research in this very interesting field, therefore we are currently performing a more extensive systematic study to find better answers to more challenging questions.

Finally, a brief comment concerning the effectiveness of the multimedia-program MFS which we have designed in accordance with the principles of the cognitive apprenticeship approach. After four empirical studies, there is no question that this approach can serve as solid foundation for the instructional design of multimedia - but only with regard to the expository methods *modeling, coaching,* and *scaffolding*. Evidently, the subjects acquired a significant amount of domain-specific knowledge, and possibly more important, there was a substantial improvement of analytical reasoning skills. However, with regard to the metacognitive components *articulation* and *reflection*, our investigations confirm Casey's (1996) verdict:

> "The only way to get learners to truly verbalize and thoroughly surface internal processes seems to be through a cooperative learning environment. Interaction with the computer can provide a great deal of information on why learners make the choices they make, but computer-based intelligence seems pale in comparison to the open peer dialogue we observed learners having during the testing of CI [Convection Initiation, a multimedia training course]." (p. 83).

REFERENCES

Ahn, W. K., Brewer, W. F., & Mooney, R. J. (1992). Schema acquisition from a single example. *Journal of Experimental Psychology: Learning, Memory, and Cognition, 18* (2), 391-412.

Al-Diban, S., & Seel, N. M. (1999). Evaluation als Forschungsaufgabe von Instruktionsdesign. Dargestellt am Beispiel einer multimedialen Lernumgebung. *Unterrichtswissenschaft, 27* (1), 29-60. [Evaluation as a research problem of instructional design.]

Anderson, J. R., Reder, L. M., & Simon, H. A. (1996). Situated learning and education. *Educational Researcher, 25* (4), 5-11.

Anzai, Y., & Yokoyama, T. (1984). Internal models in physics problem solving. *Cognition and Instruction, 1,* 397-450.

Ausubel, D. P. (1968). *Educational psychology: A cognitive view.* New York: Holt, Rinehart Winston.

Beck, K. (1993). *Dimensionen der ökonomischen Bildung. Meßinstrumente und Befunde.* Nürnberg: Universität (Abschlußbericht zum DFG-Projekt 'Wirtschaftskundlicher Bildungs-Test [WBT]. Normierung und internationaler Vergleich).

Bloom, B. S. (Hrsg.) (1972). Taxonomie von Lernzielen im kognitiven Bereich. Weinheim: Beltz. [Taxonomy of educational objectives. Handbook I: Cognitive domain.]

Briggs, P. (1990). The role of the user model in learning as an internally and externally directed activity. In D. Ackermann & M. J. Tauber (Eds.), *Mental models and human-computer interaction, Vol 1* (pp. 195-208). Amsterdam: Elsevier.

Bruner, J. S. (1966). *Toward a theory of instruction.* Cambridge, MA: Harvard University Press.

Casey, C. (1996). Incorporating cognitive apprenticeship in multi-media. *Educational Technology Research and Development, 44* (1), 71-84.

Chinn, C. A., Brewer, W. F. (1993). The role of anomalous data in knowledge acquisition: A theoretical framework and implications for science instruction. *Review of Educational Research, 63* (1), 1-49.

Cognition and Technology Group at Vanderbilt (CTGV) (1997). *The Jasper project. Lessons in curriculum, instruction, assessment, and professional development.* Hillsdale, NJ: Lawrence Erlbaum.

Collins, A., Brown, J. S., & Holum, A. (1993). Cognitive apprenticeship: Making thinking visible. *American Educator, 15* (3), 6-11, 38-46.

Collins, A., Brown, J. S. & Newman, S. E. (1989). Cognitive apprenticeship: Teaching the crafts of reading, writing, and mathematics. In L. B. Resnick (Ed.) (1989), *Knowing, learning, and instruction* (pp. 453-494). Hillsdale, NJ: Erlbaum.

Craik, K. J. W. (1943). *The nature of explanation.* Cambridge: Cambridge University Press.

Dinter, F. (1998). Zur Diskussion des Konstruktivismus im Instruktionsdesign. *Unterrichtswissenschaft, 26* (3), 254-287.

Dinter, F. R., & Seel, N. M. (1994). What does it mean to be a constructivist in I.D.? An epistemological reconsideration. In J. Lowyck & J. Elen (Eds.), *Modelling I.D.-research* (pp. 49-66). Leuven: Proceedings of the first workshop of the SIG on instructional design of EARLI.

Dole, J. A., & Sinatra, G. M. (1998). Reconceptualizing change in the cognitive construction of knowledge. *Educational Psychologist, 33* (2/3), 109-128.

Eckblad, G. (1981). *Scheme theory. A conceptual framework for cognitive-motivational processes.* London: Academic Press.

Farmer, J. A., Buckmaster, A., & Legrand, A. (1992). Cognitive apprenticeship: Implications for continuing professional education. *New Directions for Adult and Continuing Education, 55,* 41-49.

Galili, I., Bendall, S., & Goldberg, F. (1993). The effects of prior knowledge and instruction on understanding image formation. *Journal of Research in Science Teaching, 30* (3), 271-301.

Glaser, R. (1990). The reemergence of learning theory within instructional research. *American Psychologist, 45* (1), 29-39.

Greeno, J. G. (1989). Situations, mental models, and generative knowledge. In D. Klahr & K. Kotovsky (Eds.), *Complex information processing* (pp. 285-318). Hillsdale, NJ: Lawrence Erlbaum.

Greer, B. (1997). Modelling reality in mathematics classrooms: The case of word problems. *Learning and Instruction, 7* (4), 293-307.

Hegarty, M., & Just, M. A. (1993). Constructing mental models of machines from text and diagrams. *Journal of Memory and Language, 32,* 717-742.

Hübner, R. (1989). Methoden zur Analyse und Konstruktion von Aufgaben zur kognitiven Steuerung dynamischer Systeme. *Zeitschrift für Experimentelle und Angewandte Psychologie, 36* (2), 211-238.

Jih, H. J, & Reeves, T. C. (1992). Mental models: A research focus for interactive learning systems. *Educational Technology Research and Development, 40* (3), 39-53.

Johnson-Laird, P. N. (1983). *Mental models. Towards a cognitive science of language, inference, and consciousness.* Cambridge: Cambridge University Press.

Johnson-Laird, P. N. (1989). Mental models. In M. I. Posner (Ed.), *Foundations of cognitive science* (pp. 469-499). Cambridge, MA: The MIT Press.

Kieras, D. E., & Bovair, S. (1984). The role of a mental model in learning to operate a device. *Cognitive Science, 8,* 255-273.

Kindfield, A. C. H. (1993). Biology diagrams: Tools to think with. *Journal of the Learning Sciences, 3* (1), 1-36.

Kourilsky, M., & Wittrock, M.C. (1992). Generative teaching: An enhancement strategy for the learning of economics in cooperative groups. *American Educational Research Journal, 29* (4), 861-876.

Lajoie, S. P., & Lesgold, A. (1989). Apprenticeship training in the workplace: Computer-coached practice environment as a new form of apprenticeship. *Machine-Mediated Learning, 3*, 7-28.

Mayer, R. E. (1989). Models for understanding. *Review of Educational Research, 59* (1), 43-64.

Morrow, D. G., Bower, G. H., & Greenspan, S. (1989). Updating situation models during narrative comprehension. *Journal of Memory and Language, 28*, 292-312.

Niegemann, H. M. (1995). Zum Einfluß von "modelling" in einer computergestützten Lernumgebung: Quasi-experimentelle Untersuchung zur Instruktionsdesign-Theorie. *Unterrichtswissenschaft, 23* (1), 75-87.

Norman, D. A. (1983). Some observations on mental models. In D. Gentner & A. L. Stevens (Eds.), *Mental models* (pp. 7-14). Hillsdale, NJ: Erlbaum.

Nussbaum, J., & Novick, S. (1983). Alternative frameworks, conceptual conflict and accommodation: Toward a principled teaching strategy. *Instructional Science, 11*, 183-300.

Pieters, J. M., & deBruijn, H. F. M. (1992). Learning environments for cognitive apprenticeship: From experience to expertise. In P. A. M. Kommers, D. H. Jonassen & T. Mayes (Eds.), *Cognitive tools for learning* (pp. 241-248). Berlin: Springer.

Reynolds, R. E., Sinatra, G. M., & Jetton, T. L. (1996). Views of knowledge acquisition and representation: A continuum from experience centered to mind centered. *Educational Psychologist, 31* (2), 93-104.

Rips, L. J. (1987). Mental muddles. In M. Brand, & R. M. Harnish (Eds.), *The representation of knowledge and belief* (pp. 259-286). Tucson: University of Arizona Press.

Royer, J. M., Cisero, C. A., & Carlo, M. S. (1993). Techniques and procedures for assessing cognitive skills. *Review of Educational Research, 63* (2), 201-243.

Sasse, M. A. (1991). How to t(r)ap users. In Ackermann, D. & Tauber, M. J. (Eds.), *Mental models and human-computer interaction, Vol 2*. Amsterdam: Elsvier.

Schank, R.C., Fano, A., Bell, B., & Jona, M. (1993/94). The design of goal-based scenarios. *Journal of the Learning Sciences, 3* (4), 305-345.

Seel, N. M. (1991). *Weltwissen und mentale Modelle*. Göttingen: Hogrefe.

Seel, N. M. (1995). Mental models, knowledge transfer, and teaching strategies. *Journal of Structural Learning and Intelligent Systems, 12* (3), 197-213.

Seel, N. M. (1999). Educational diagnosis of mental models. Assessment problems and technology-based solutions. *Journal of Structural Learning and Intelligent Systems, 14* (1), 153-185.

Seel, N. M., Al-Diban, S., Held, S., & Hess, C. (1998). Didaktisches Design multimedialer Lernumgebungen: Theoretische Positionen, Gestaltungsprinzipien, empirische Befunde. In G. Dörr & K.L. Jüngst (Hrsg.), *Lernen mit Medien. Ergebnisse und Perspektiven zu medial vermittelten Lehr- und Lernprozessen* (S. 87-119). Weinheim: Juventa.

Seel, N. M., & Dinter, F. R. (1995). Instruction and mental model progression: Learner-dependent effects of teaching strategies on knowledge acquisition and analogical transfer. *Educational Research and Evaluation, 1*(1), 4-35.

Sharp, D. L. M., Bransford, J. D., Goldman, S. R., Risko, V. J., Kinzer, C. K., & Vye, N. J. (1995). Dynamic visual support for story comprehension and mental model building by young, at-risk children. *Educational Technology Research and Development, 43* (4), 25-42.

Shute, V. J. (1994). Learning processes and learning outcomes. In T. Husén & T. N. Postlethwaite (Eds.), *The international encyclopedia of education, Vol. 6*, (pp. 3315-3325). Oxford: Pergamon & Elsevier Science Ltd.

Slotta, J. D., Chi, M. T. H., & Joram, E. (1995). Assessing students' misclassification of physics concepts: An ontological basis for conceptual change. *Cognition and Instruction, 13* (3), 373-400.

Snow, R. E. (1990). New approaches to cognitive and conative assessment in education. *International Journal of Educational Research, 14* (5), 455-473.

Spiro, R. J., Feltovich, P. J., Jacobson, M. J., & Coulson, R. L. (1991). Cognitive flexibility, constructivism, and hypertext: Random access instruction for advanced knowledge acquisition in ill-structured domains. *Educational Technology, 31* (5), 24-33.

Volet, S. E. (1991). Modelling and coaching of relevant, metacognitive strategies for enhancing university students' learning. *Learning and Instruction, 1* (4), 319-336.

Vosniadou, S. & Brewer, W. F. (1994). Mental models of the day / night circle. *Cognitive Science, 18,* 123-183.

Wilson, J. R., & Rutherford, A. (1989). Mental models: Theory and application in human factors. *Human Factors, 31,* 617-634.

ACKNOWLEDGEMENT

Very special thanks to the ambitious work and patience of Bettina Couné who prepared the Power Point slides and Ellis Whitehead who arranged the video presentation of the 4M-Project.

FRANK ACHTENHAGEN

Chapter 9

REALITY, MODELS AND COMPLEX TEACHING-LEARNING ENVIRONMENTS

Keywords: complex learning, computer-based instruction, instructional modeling, mastery learning, vocational education

Abstract. Complex teaching and learning environments are a result of a number of factors, including the increasing complexity of entrepreneurial processes and the greater diversity of the workforce, especially in Europe. In meeting the new challenges associated with increasing complexity, linearized and chopped up pieces of curricula are less and less effective. New modes of teaching and learning that help to develop deep comprehension of the systems character of these complex and dynamic processes are necessary. This chapter reports on the construction, implementation and evaluation of a complex teaching-learning environment that uses advanced technology to support requirements in the German dual system of apprenticeship.

DEFINING THE PROBLEM: CHALLENGES IN LIFE AND IN THE WORKPLACE INTERPRETED AS "MEGATRENDS"

The actual discussion of problems of the labor market, and, consequently, of vocational and occupational education and training as preparation for employment, is influenced by current environmental challenges. These challenges influence independently or in combination the shape of jobs and labor organizations. Nearly all industrialized countries are confronted with these challenges in a comparable way, and the long-term consequences, especially for teaching and learning procedures, cannot be easily drawn. For this reason, Buttler (1992) proposed the term "megatrends" to characterize these challenges (see also Achtenhagen, 1994; Achtenhagen, Nijhof & Raffe, 1995).

Overall categorical labels may help to characterize the "megatrends" influencing vocational education and employment opportunities. The megatrends may be labeled as demographic shifts resulting from:

- changes in population levels, migration of populations, and decreased applicant availability for certain skilled jobs;

159

J.M. Spector and T.M. Anderson (eds.),
Integrated and Holistic Perspectives on Learning, Instruction and Technology, 159–174.
© 2000 *Kluwer Academic Publishers. Printed in the Netherlands.*

- internationalization of economies resulting from globalization;
- international mergers & acquisitions;
- the information explosion including increased availability of research results;
- increased use of new information and advanced communications technologies.

Benefits and at the same time consequences of these trends provide new possibilities for system optimization, a flattening of the organization hierarchical system, and new forms of organizational coordination (Achtenhagen & Grubb, in press).

In response to these "megatrends" recent research has shown that enterprises are trying to combine working tasks, thereby creating more complex tasks, in order to compensate for the shortage of highly qualified personnel and to react adequately to international business requirements. [The same phenomenon is occurring in the US defense sector due to a period of continued downsizing and restructuring that has created a comparable situation.] More complex work tasks provide enterprises with opportunities to incorporate recent research results on education and learning, to fully exploit the advantages of modern organizational structures, and to recruit employees who have different and changing value and motivational systems.

The new responsibilities and tasks in the worksite are more complex compared to the traditional tasks in the following manner:

- work tasks may cover a rich and varied content;
- work tasks may include a large number of variables with different degrees of embedded transparency;
- work tasks may comprise a network with many interrelationships;
- work tasks vary over time in a non-linear manner; and,
- many work tasks are *polytelic*, introducing the problem of primary and secondary impact of decisions which have to be made with regard to the initial task and problems.

This complex business environment calls for new forms of employee treatment and management. The development of individual employee competencies and personalities has become a major goal of leading firms. [See the chapters by Marshall & Rossett and Wagner for an elaboration.] Research on vocational and occupational education and training has had to react to these challenges. Young people must be better prepared to actively and consciously fulfill new complex tasks at the worksite. Education must also develop and stabilize their personalities and attitudes. That means that vocational educators have to develop in themselves and their students:

- a way of thinking in terms of overlapping, complex dynamic structures;
- a broad conceptual understanding of the economic, technical and social contexts of work tasks and activities;
- cognitive abilities (such as ill-structured problem solving and metacognitive reasoning), emotional maturity, and the necessary inner strength and perseverance required for success in new business environments; and,
- social competencies such as the ability to effectively co-operate and communicate with many different kinds of persons.

Educational research, therefore, has to describe and explain thoroughly the tasks and problems associated with complex learning, and then to analyze, construct, implement and evaluate teaching-learning processes in a new way by fully exploiting the advantages of instructional technology. A decisive prerequisite for the success of these research activities is that they are not treated by isolated steps but are carefully embedded in new goal and content structures. [This emphasis on integrating and embedding learning activities in larger contexts is a central theme echoed in many other chapters of this volume, especially those of Dijkstra, Goodyear, Jonassen and colleagues, Marshall and Rossett, Seel and colleagues and Wagner.] The development of complex teaching-learning environments for vocational education also urges adequately reformulated curricula.

These problems are herein discussed using examples from the German dual system of apprenticeship for the commercial, administrative and public services, in which about 62% of all German employees are working.

REALITY OF VOCATIONAL AND OCCUPATIONAL EDUCATION AND TRAINING

The German dual system of apprenticeship is organized in the following manner. Every German has to enter a recognized apprenticeship program after completion of nine years of compulsory school (the attendance of the Gymnasium frees a student from this regulation). It is the student's responsibility to identify, apply for and become accepted at an apprenticeship program that trains for one or more careers. Apprenticeships normally start in August and last for three years. Student apprentices have to work and be trained for three to four days per week in their individual training firm and to attend one or two days per week vocational school, *Berufsschule*, on a part time basis.

In response to the "megatrends" and their undeniable consequences for the *Berufsschule*, the author was asked by the Lower Saxonian Ministry for

Education to run a research & development project[1] for the apprenticeship of industrial clerk (*Industriekaufmann*) which is quantitatively and qualitatively one of the most important training programs. The Ministry wanted to get a solution for the following problems and problematic situations:

a. Both enterprises and commercial schools are confronted with the increasing complexity of the business environment and their consequences for instruction and training.

b. New ways of teaching, training and learning need to be proposed and developed for this specific apprenticeship (industrial clerk, *Industriekaufmann*).

c. There is an increasing heterogeneity of apprentices in the vocational classroom. One consequence of the "megatrends" is an increase in the average age of apprentices. Nine years of compulsory schooling is now only the minimum; more and more apprentices attend schools for a longer time, including students with *Abitur* (received after 13 years of schooling) who try to enter an apprenticeship before going to the university.

d. There is an increasing heterogeneity of training firms. In Germany, an apprenticeship is seen as a very worthwhile educational track, and a lot of political effort is given to finding a program for each student who wants to enter one. Because of popular demand, new firms continually appear in the training market that have little or limited knowledge regarding effective training and sometimes lack adequate equipment or resources needed for high quality learning and training.

e. The Ministry changed the curriculum structure for vocational schools to overcome the traditional linearized structure of goals and content into learning "areas". The change in curriculum resulted in a loss of applicability and validity of existing teacher preparation programs and subsequent teacher resistance to the Ministry's reforms.

The goal of the research and development project was to find solutions for these problems. We, therefore, started the work by formulating four assumptions:

1. Linearized and piecemeal curricula, and the corresponding teaching-learning processes, do not support effective and responsible teaching and learning. This statement is valid with regard to all modes of teaching and learning following

---

[1]   The project was also financed by the German Research Foundation (Ac 35/15-1).

new theoretical approaches especially in light of recent discussions on constructivism. [See also the chapters by Dijkstra, Goodyear, and Jonassen and colleagues.]

2.   New modes of teaching and learning are necessary to develop an adequate and deep understanding of the systematic character of complex and dynamic processes in the worksite and private life. [See the chapter by Dunnagan and Christensen for an elaboration of ignoring this important factor.]

3.   Complex teaching-learning environments can be structured to model teaching and learning in a new way by using new technology. The importance of defining the problem space and individual meaning making should be embedded in newly structured curricula.

4.   The teachers need new and/or alternative materials and technical support to replace their traditionally used transparencies and methods.

Year of Birth	1998: Apprentices in Northeim	1998: Apprentices in Osterode
1971	1	
...		
1975	1	
1976		
1977	2	
1978	3	1
1979	4	3
1980	1	7
1981	3	6
1982		6
Sum	15	23

Figure 1. Distribution of apprentices by age and location.

The research and development project started in 1997. The team consists of 8 university researchers, 12 teachers and 2 headmasters from two different commercial schools, one district inspector and one civil servant form the State Ministry for Education. The Chamber of Industry and Commerce and the trainers from the firms involved were informed by special seminars and fully agreed with the project goals. There were two different field phases in 1998 and 1999. As the evaluation results for the two years (in different classrooms) were similar, only those results for 1998 are reported here. Some of the practical-political conditions of the project shall be demonstrated before discussing the content domain and educational assumptions.

The high heterogeneity of apprentices with regard to age and (school) socialization, which greatly impacts the teaching and learning efficiency of the vocational classroom, is illustrated by Figure 1. Figure 2 illustrates the heterogeneity of the training firms that train vocational apprentices. It seems evident that it is very hard or nearly impossible to exploit the practical experiences of the apprentices for classroom teaching if they are trained within such different branches and firms. This is because the goals and content of the instruction must be run on a very abstract level which reduces individual applicability and interest to a great extent.

Heterogeneity of training firms	Number of apprentices
Municipal utilities	4
Power stations	3
Clothing industry	2
Packaging material	9
Air conditioning industry	2
Transport systems	2
Accumulator	2
Plaster	3
Others	11
Sum	**38**

Figure 2. Heterogeneity of training firms.

The problem (anticipated by the Ministry of Education) of negative consequences for instructional processes due to such heterogeneity were clearly confirmed given the starting points illustrated by Figures 1 and 2, which are typical for the majority of commercial schools in Germany. Based on these and other data, we hypothesized the following:

- The complexity and diversity of the worksite complicate apprentice understanding and comprehension.
- The heterogeneity of the training firms involved complicates teaching-learning processes in the commercial schools.
- The heterogeneity of prior knowledge, previous school careers and age of the apprentices complicates the training and learning conditions of the individual apprentice.
- The new structure of commercial curricula complicates the teacher's orientation within and the structuring of the necessary teaching-learning processes.

MODELS FOR SOLVING TEACHING-LEARNING PROBLEMS IN COMMERCIAL SCHOOLS

We decided to develop solutions for teaching-learning problems in the commercial schools on three levels, which are naturally strongly related to each other: (a) the curriculum level; (b) the didactic level; and, (c) the instructional design level, especially constructing a complex teaching-learning environment. Each of these is discussed in the next three sections.

The Curriculum Level

One of our central assumptions is that curricular embeddedness is one necessary prerequisite for the successful use of complex teaching-learning environments. The newly developed State curricula prescribe, as the introductory curriculum unit of 60 lessons, the topic "the enterprise as a complex economic and social system." Figure 3 shows 9 out of the 16 learning areas with the corresponding amount of lessons for the students to be taught over 3 years (1 elementary and 2 professional stages; only the first professional stage has hours assigned in this case).

The State curriculum urges all of the following:

- a high level of knowledge (with small standard deviations);
- stability of knowledge over time;
- comprehension and appreciation of a model enterprise as support for teaching-learning processes;
- promotion of interest, motivation and emotion; and,
- promotion of a constructive collaboration within vocational classrooms.

No.	Learning Areas	Elem. Stage (hours)	Prof. Stage 1 (hours)	Prof. Stage 2 (hours)
1	The enterprise as a complex economic and social system	60		
2	Financial accounting as an instrument for registration of economic transactions	60		
3	Customers' orientation and marketing	60		
4	Purchasing and logistics	60		
5	Handling of orders	40		
6	Information and communication technologies in firms	40		
7	Employees in the firm		60	
8	Organisation and control of work processes		60	
9	Cost accounting as an instrument for registration and assessment of work processes and results		60	

Figure 3. Overview of learning areas for the industrial clerk apprenticeship.

The Didactic Level

The intermediate level between the curriculum and concrete methods and the medium-oriented level (e.g., that of complex teaching-learning environments) is the didactic level. Didactic, here and according to the German and Scandinavian tradition, has a positive connotation compared to United States usage[2]. The main focus is to develop a teaching and learning strategy that is useful for overcoming the artificial constraints of the classroom environment.

To address student variability in prior years of school attendance, age and maturity level we instituted a mastery learning approach. It was not the goal to override the results of the very different socialization processes. This is impossible. We do believe that it might be possible to structure the teaching-learning environment so that at the end of the first curriculum unit all apprentices attain a comparable mastery level of knowledge and, hopefully, also of motivation.

The mastery learning approach has its roots in the reform pedagogy of the 1920s. Proponents of mastery learning, including Carroll (1963), Keller (1968) and Bloom (1971), reported on a concept that radically broke with the

---

[2]   Things are changing, however, as Westbury, Hopmann & Riquarts (1999) try to claim a comprehension of the European didactic tradition in the US.

traditional view of school achievement which normally follows, or has to follow, a bell curve. The Keller plan advocates a personalized system of instruction which requires mastery of material before a student can move ahead. Carroll (1963) and Bloom (1971) focused on the time variable emphasizing that the degree of learning is a function of the quotient "time allowed for learning" and "time needed for learning". In this equation "time allowed for learning" includes both time and motivation. "Time needed to learn" includes time, quality of instruction, and the ability to understand instruction.

The mastery learning approach is designed to bring a high percentage of students (e.g., 90%) to a mastery level of achievement compared to the normal bell curve distribution. All mastery approaches, therefore, rely on tutorial and other methods of individualizing instruction. Block (1971) defines the main factors for use in mastery learning to be student selection, defining and measuring mastery, formative evaluation, learning correctives, frequency of use of the feedback-correction procedures, and allocation of learning-instructional time.

In 1987 and 1990 research on the outcomes of the mastery learning approach was published in the *Review of Educational Research*. According to our judgment, these debates do not consider the main point of success or failure, namely: are the teachers in a "normal" classroom able to cope with and to control the quality and the quantity of goals and content to be taught and learned individually? Our answer is an emphatic 'no'. We believe it is understandable that the mastery learning results reported in the research literature do not show an entirely clear picture. Consequently we decided to construct a computer-based virtual enterprise which contains all goals and content needed for the first learning area ("the enterprise as a complex economic and social system") using a mastery model. By employing a computer-based model, all goals and content are given in the same manner for all students and their achievement can be monitored and interpreted more clearly. Learning time can be exactly administered for the solution of clearly defined tasks and problems.

The presentation of goals and contents by the virtual enterprise was accompanied by formative student evaluations and remedial teaching and learning support. As the goals and content are fixed, the apprentices had the opportunity to attain content mastery by lengthening their learning time.

A special problem of mastery learning needs to be mentioned. This approach suffers the negative consequence of limited social acceptance. As nearly all educational institutions follow the bell curve distribution of student achievement, it seems unbelievable that 90% or more of students should be able to master a subject. If such a success is reported, teachers are suspected of failing a given level of standards at least in regard to distributing their student grades. In short, we have become accustomed to using grades to select and differentiate as well as to reflect mastery, and, as a consequence, we arbitrarily limit the number of persons allowed to master particular tasks and curricula. This arbitrary social or political constraint can and should be changed, especially in vocational education. [The US defense training community has long recognized the validity of this argument.]

For the German apprenticeship system, we observe different evaluation criteria compared to the academic track. For the intermediate and final examinations, which are externally run by the Chambers of Industry and Commerce, all firms expect that their apprentices will get the best grades possible. They, therefore, provide additional learning time and supplemental instructional courses that repeat the content of the commercial schools. One might interpret these procedures as a "mastery learning" approach which is strongly related to the formal examinations. We use the mastery learning model in our virtual enterprise from the very beginning, starting in the first week of apprenticeship instruction in the commercial school.

The Instructional Design Level

We followed a modified instructional design approach developing a multimedially-represented virtual enterprise named "Arnold & Stolzenberg". Figure 4 shows the planning model - a modified version of proposals from Seel (1999) and from Achtenhagen (in press).

For the development of the virtual enterprise we brought together ideas from different research areas:

- using ideas of situated learning - especially anchored instruction and goal-based scenarios [see the chapters by Goodyear and Jonassen and colleagues];
- using ideas out of business administration - especially modeling an enterprise as a complex and dynamic systems structure [see the chapters by Dunnagan and Christensen, Marshall and Rossett, and Wagner]; and,
- using ideas out of the fields of subject-didactics (as they are discussed in Germany) - especially didactic modeling [see the chapter by Seel and colleagues].

The main point here is that we have to differentiate two modes of didactic modeling. The first mode involves modeling reality. The second mode involves modeling models of reality from a didactic perspective [see the discussion of a similar concept in Alessi's chapter]. By neglecting this twofold process of didactic modeling, many instructional design arrangements fail to achieve their goals (Achtenhagen, in press).

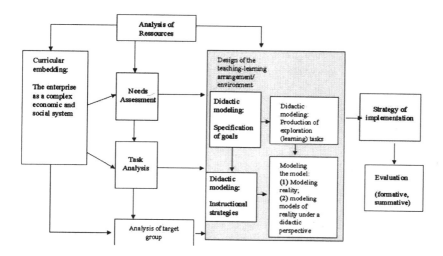

Figure 4. Components of instructional design under a planning aspect.

The virtual enterprise "Arnold & Stolzenberg" has a strong resemblance to a real enterprise "Arnold & Stolzenberg" which is a British firm close to Göttingen that has about 500 employees and produces industrial chains for one fourth of the world market. To create the virtual enterprise, we filmed within the enterprise, interviewed and filmed employees, detailed the organizational structure and production processes, and modeled the business figures such as cost accounting structures and balances according to actual figures. All this material was used to create a CD-ROM to present all necessary information for treating goals and content of the first curriculum unit.

The Complex Teaching-Learning Environment

The goals and content presented by the virtual enterprise are demonstrated in Figure 5. For structuring the navigation through the virtual enterprise the apprentices have to solve "exploration tasks". The first exploration task is to determine the earliest possible date for the delivery of a certain amount of industrial chains. The task is given by a video sequence where an apprentice gets a call with the corresponding question (see Figure 6).

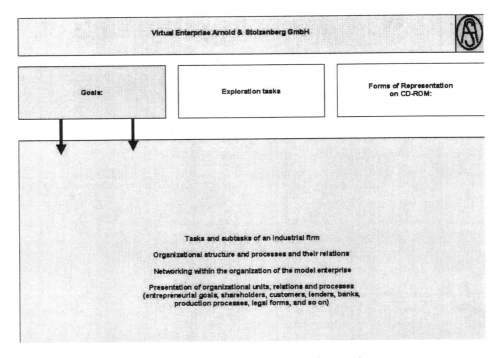

Figure 5. Goals and content of the virtual enterprise.

Each apprentice in the classroom then has to navigate through the virtual enterprise to collect all necessary information via pictures, diagrams, videos, texts, and simulated computer terminals, in order to answer the exploration task question. After having worked out the right solution, the student comes to a video which closes the first exploration task and demonstrates how the answer is given to the client. All navigation steps, their sequence, and the time for working with a special screen are determined by protocols. As students need different amounts of time for finding the right solution, completion times for the first task will vary. Immediately after having successfully completed the first task, a new task in a different format and mode of representation is given to the student. The second task has to be solved in the same lesson. As the first classroom unit consists of three lessons, only a few students manage both tasks within school time. As all students have to deliver the right solution to the second task at the next classroom session, they are required to work at home or at their workplace in the firm, which was previously agreed to by their superiors. The same procedure takes place if the students need more time for other tasks to be solved. Throughout the exploration tasks, each failure is automatically recorded and new exploration is encouraged. Apprentices (students) are able to take the CD-ROM to their homes or firms to continue working on lessons.

During the second exploration task, the client is phoning to ask: "Why didn't you deliver?" and the overall navigation has to be repeated, modeling the Total Quality Management concept of the real firm. Later, a third exploration task is given in which apprentices have to solve computer-driven tasks in their individual real training firms by determining all necessary information for their actual products and business processes, which are totally different from those of the virtual enterprise and the real Arnold & Stolzenberg enterprise. The actual results, together with a presentation of their firms and products, have to be presented to the whole classroom in the presence of their trainers.

The program for the whole 60 lessons was not only run with regard to declarative and procedural knowledge but also with special attention to strategic knowledge - always with a large amount of individualized remedial instruction. As stated above, the quality and quantity of goals and content was controlled by the "virtual enterprise" computer-based system and additional instructional materials.

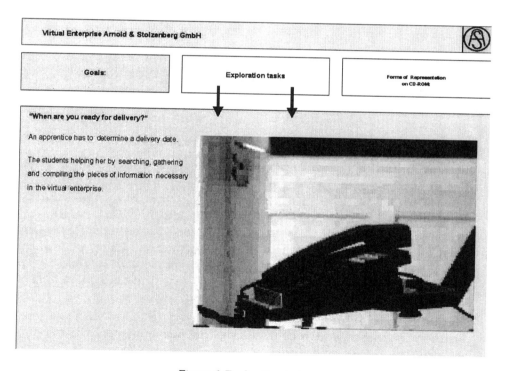

Figure 6. Exploration task.

Evaluation

We administered many evaluation instruments over the course of this study. Here, only selected results are reported. Figure 7 demonstrates the needs for mastery learning. One can see the large differences for the first trial where only 14% of students with the lowest prior school attendance, but 75% of those with the highest came immediately to the right solution. We interpret this result as a consequence of the large heterogeneity of apprentices; this probably would lead to different subgroups within one classroom which we tried to overcome by our virtual approach.

Prior schooling	Years of schooling	N = 38	First exploration task: % of solution: 1ˢᵗ Trial
Abitur with business knowledge	13	4	75%
Abitur without business knowledge	13	4	75%
Fachhochschulreife (for the attendance of a Polytechnic)	12-13	5	20%
0-level (with the right to enter the Gymnasium) with business knowledge	12	7	29%
0-level (with the right to enter the Gymnasium) without business knowledge	10	8	14%
0-level	10	10	20%

Figure 7. Needs for mastery learning

Figure 8 shows selected effects of the administration of a set of test items of the official Chamber examinations over the last five years. Apprentices had to solve items by using information provided by the virtual enterprise and by pressing buttons to indicate the right answer. Incorrect answers required students to navigate again through the virtual enterprise. We observe for the first trial the differences in results according to school socialization, but highlight also the effects of remedial learning by the percentage of correct values for the third trial.

Prior schooling	Years of schooling	N =38	1st Trial %	2nd Trial %	3rd Trial %
Abitur with business knowledge	13	4	83%	95%	99%
Abitur without business knowledge	13	4	71%	93%	99%
Fachhochschulreife (for the attendance of a Polytechnic)	12-13	5	68%	97%	100%
0-level (with the right to enter the Gymnasium) with business knowledge	12	7	64%	93%	95%
0-level (with the right to enter the Gymnasium) without business knowledge	10	8	49%	81%	90%
0-level	10	10	58%	88%	97%

Figure 8. Effects of remedial learning

We also could see by other evaluation procedures that our mastery learning approach did not restrict the learning possibilities of the students with more highly developed prior knowledge. These students exploited chances to learn and demonstrated additional knowledge of goals and content to a mastery level of 90%. This is a decisive political argument. We can show that we are able to promote learning in those students with lower prior knowledge while also supporting students with higher entry level knowledge through this mastery model.

CONCLUSION

The construction, implementation and evaluation of a complex teaching-learning environment which is developed using advanced technology provides new possibilities to foster effective teaching and learning. The example provided from the field of vocational education and training demonstrates the importance of instructional technology for the "megatrends" and their consequences for teaching and learning. Multimedia-based, complex teaching-learning environments that are thoroughly embedded in adequately developed curricula and run according to sense-making didactic programs seem to provide one effective possibility to react to new challenges. Such environments appear capable of and vital to strengthening the role of formal education and training. In the future, experimental research and control studies for the stability of the observed effects are planned.

REFERENCES

Achtenhagen, F. (1992). The relevance of content for teaching-learning processes. In F. K. Oser, A. Dick & J. L. Patry (Eds.), *Effective and responsible teaching – the new synthesis* (pp. 315-328). San Francisco: Jossey-Bass.

Achtenhagen, F. (1994). How should research on vocational and professional education react to new challenges in life and in the workplace? In W. J. Nijhof & J. N. Streumer (Eds.), *Flexibility in training and vocational education* (pp. 201-247). Utrecht: Lemma.

Achtenhagen, F., Nijhof, W. J., & Raffe, D. (1995). *Feasibility Study: Research scope for vocational education in the framework of COST social sciences.* European Commission, Directorate General: Science, Research and Development. Social Sciences, COST Technical committee, Vol 3. Brussels, Luxembourg: ECSC-EC-EAEC.

Achtenhagen, F. (in press). Criteria for the Development of Complex Teaching-Learning Environments. *Instructional Science.*

Achtenhagen, F., & Grubb, W. N. (in press). Vocational and occupational education: Pedagogical complexity – institutional diversity. In V. Richardson (Ed.), *Fourth Handbook of Research on Teaching.* Washington: AERA.

Block, J. H. (1972). *Mastery Learning.* New York: Holt, Rinehart & Winston.

Bloom, B. S. (1971). Mastery learning. In J. H. Block (Ed.), *Mastery Learning* (pp. 47-53). New York: Holt, Rinehart & Winston.

Buttler, F. (1992). Tätigkeitslandschaft bis 2010 [Structure of jobs until 2010]. In F. Achtenhagen & E. G. John (Eds.). *Mehrdimensionale Lehr-Lern-Arrangements* (pp. 162-182) [Multidimensional teaching-learning arrangements]. Wiesbaden: Gabler.

Carroll, J. B. (1963). A model of school learning. *Teachers College Record, 64,* 723-733.

Keller, F. S. (1968). Good-bye teacher! *Journal of Applied Behavioral Analysis, 1,* 79-84.

Seel, N. (1999). Instruktionsdesign: Modelle und Anwendungsgebiete [Instructional Design: Models and Applications]. *Unterrichtswissenschaft, 27,* 2-11.

Westbury, I., Hopmann, S., & Riquarts, H. (Eds.) (1999). *Teaching as a Reflective Practice – the German Didaktik Tradition.* Mahwah, NJ: Erlbaum.

STEPHEN ALESSI

Chapter 10

BUILDING VERSUS USING SIMULATIONS

Keywords: declarative learning, discovery learning, model building, procedural learning, simulation design, skill training, system dynamics

Abstract. The educational use of simulation encompasses two very different approaches: learners using simulations created by others, and learners building simulations themselves. At a general level it is tempting to say that the former (using simulations) applies more to procedural learning while the latter (building simulations) applies more to declarative learning. But what of the specific cases, the exceptions, and most importantly the common situation where both procedural and declarative learning must occur? This paper addresses two questions. First, what are the conditions which suggest choosing one approach (using versus building) over the other, or a combination of both? Second, what should be the characteristics of the learning environment to support each approach? Answering the first question requires analyzing the characteristics of the knowledge, the learners, and the learning processes that must occur. Answering the second question requires analyzing the characteristics of modeling, of simulations, and of learning environments needed to foster the approach and the desired learning processes.

INTRODUCTION

When people speak or write about educational simulations they usually have some specific type of simulation in mind. However, educational simulation has become a diverse field encompassing everything from children's simulation-games, to curricula based on student modeling (Mandinach & Cline, 1994), studying sciences using laboratory simulations, to commercial airline pilots learning to fly new aircraft using physical simulators costing millions of dollars. Simulation has also come to encompass large networked simulations, such as for military battlefield training (Andrews, Dineen, & Bell, 1999; Dewar at al., 1996; Neyland, 1997), and some new technology approaches which, though they go by different names, are in many cases simulations: virtual reality (Psotka, 1995; Milheim, 1995), microworlds (White, 1995), and goal-based scenarios (Collins, 1994; Schank & Cleary, 1995). I define an educational simulation as a program that incorporates a model that the learner can manipulate and for which the learning objective includes understanding the model. That is a

J.M. Spector and T.M. Anderson (eds.),
Integrated and Holistic Perspectives on Learning, Instruction and Technology, 175–196.
© 2000 *Kluwer Academic Publishers. Printed in the Netherlands.*

more generous definition for simulation than is used by many other educators.

The theories and design models that have been advanced for educational simulation usually encompass certain types of simulation, such as simulations for scientific discover learning (de Jong & van Joolingen, 1998), the System Dynamics approach to student modeling (Davidsen et al., 1995), or Harry Pappo's recent text on simulations for skill training (Pappo, 1998). Furthermore, some types of simulations are still designed in a totally atheoretical fashion or based solely on functional issues, such as the military and aviation industry approach, which is to make the simulator look and work exactly like the real aircraft.

There are many ways to subdivide the simulation field based upon these various program types and approaches. We could do so based on platforms and scale of the simulations, on the type of underlying mathematical models used, on various educational strategies or philosophies implicit in them. I would like to address what I consider to be the most broad or general variable distinguishing approaches to educational use of simulations, namely, whether learners are themselves *building* models or simulations as a way to expand their knowledge, or whether they are learning by *using* simulations previously created by other people. I'll also address another critical issue, though it is not independent of the build-use distinction, rather, it is highly correlated with it. That is whether the knowledge sought is *procedural* or *declarative*. For the latter term (declarative knowledge) you might prefer to substitute conceptual, propositional, or verbal knowledge. I will use *declarative* knowledge in this chapter.

The sequence of this chapter is as follows. I'll begin with some elaboration of what I mean by building versus using simulations. Second, I'll discuss the relationship between the building versus using distinction and the procedural versus declarative knowledge distinction. Third, I'll suggest some conditions for when a learning environment should include simulation-building activities and when it should include simulation-using activities. Fourth, I'll discuss the characteristics a learning environment should have to support learning by building simulations and learning by using simulations.

USING SIMULATIONS

The fields of education and training include many examples of learning by using simulations. Most examples are small-scale simulations which run on microcomputers. The simulations used in science education typically fall into two categories. Some are *scientific discovery learning* simulations (de Jong & van Joolingen, 1998). They contain a well-developed model of some set of science concepts and principles, for example the area of Mendelian genetics, as in the well known *Catlab* simulation (Kinnear, 1998). A learner's task is to generate hypotheses about genetic principles, test them, and refine them. The goal of scientific discovery learning is usually declarative knowledge. Scientific discovery learning is not only used for learning the physical and biological sciences, but also in the social sciences and in business education. Funke (1991), for example, reviews 28 simulations in areas such as business economics and urban planning.

In contrast to scientific discovery learning, laboratory simulations (e.g., EME Corporation, 1999) allow learners to perform experiments as they would in a lab, such as determining an unknown substance, doing a titration, or comparing the acceleration of various objects when dropped. The procedures are generally well defined. The learning in laboratory simulations is usually a combination of procedural knowledge, such as the steps in a titration, and declarative knowledge, such as the concepts of acidity, alkalinity, and neutralization.

Not all simulations fit neatly into these two categories, of course. For example, many simulations have been created by the *CoVis* (Learning through Collaborative Visualization) project at Northwestern University (Edelson, Pea, & Gomez, 1996) which place their emphasis on helping learners visualize scientific phenomenon such as atmospheric and oceanic effects. For example, learners may generate world maps showing temperature changes due to global warming. Some might argue whether this is an example of educational simulation. I define a simulation as any program which incorporates an interactive model (one which can be repeatedly changed and rerun) and where a learning objective is for students to understand that model, whether through discovery, experimentation, demonstration, or other methods. By that definition, many of the *CoVis* visual modeling programs are simulations.

Physical simulators make up a significant portion of the professional training field. Large physical simulators are used for training in aviation, power plant operation, emergency vehicle operation, dentistry, surgery, police work, nursing, and other professional occupations. It is increasingly common for television news programs to include stories about the use of simulation technology in such fields of training, evidence to their increased use.

BUILDING SIMULATIONS AND MODELS

Some clarification of terms is necessary at this point. I use the term *model* when referring to the mathematics or logic which underlies a simulation, and *model building* or *modeling* to mean the creation of such a model. A model may be in your head, a diagram on paper, or a computer program. In contrast, I will use the term *simulation* when referring to a computer program which includes such a model *and* includes an interface allowing users to easily interact with the model, examining its various inputs and outputs. Building simulations includes building models and programming them along with a user interface. Thus, although this chapter's title refers to building simulations, building models is a part of it.

Educational simulation and model building began in the 1960's with Jay Forrester's development of the System Dynamics approach (Forrester, 1961, 1968, 1969, 1971) and creation of the *Dynamo* programming language for modeling on mainframe computers (Pugh, 1983). In the 1980's and 1990's new microcomputer-based modeling tools were created which were much less expensive and easier to use. These included *STELLA* (High Performance Systems, 1987), *PowerSim* (PowerSim, 1999), *Extend* (Imagine That, 2000), *Model-It* (Jackson et al., 1995, 1996), and *SimQuest* (van Joolingen and de Jong, 1997). The availability of these tools led to more widespread application of modeling in school curricula. The use of Forrester's System Dynamics approach in the 1960's and 1970's was limited to higher education because of the need for mainframe computers. However, in the 1980's and 1990's, educators of pre-college students have increasingly applied System Dynamics to education in the sciences and other areas. In 1983 Nancy Roberts and her colleagues wrote a textbook (Roberts, Anderson, Deal, Garet & Shaffer, 1983) intended for teaching pre-college students the System Dynamics approach using *MicroDynamo* (Pugh-Roberts Associates, 1982), a microcomputer version of Dynamo created for Apple and IBM microcomputers. Subsequent examples of such work include the *STACI*[N] project (which stands for the Systems Thinking and Curriculum Innovation Project – Networked) of Ellen Mandinach and Hugh Cline at ETS (Mandinach & Cline, 1994) and the National Science Foundation's *CC-STADUS* (Cross Curricular Systems Thinking and Dynamics using STELLA) and *CC-SUSTAIN* (Cross-Curricular Systems Using *STELLA*: Training And In-Service) projects (Zaraza & Fisher, 1997; Zaraza, Joy, & Guthrie, 1998), all of which are based on *STELLA*, a more visually oriented version of *DYNAMO* which is available for both the Macintosh and Windows operating systems. The University of Michigan's Highly Interactive Computing Project was the source of *Model-It* (Jackson et al., 1995), a more user-friendly modeling program intended for younger audiences. The *CoVis* project at Northwestern University (Edelson, Pea, & Gomez, 1996) has included models built by students as well as professional scientists, using more general tools such as common spreadsheet programs and image analysis software.

Not all educational modeling is based upon System Dynamics or digital visualization. For example, *How to model it: Problem solving for the computer age* (Starfield, Smith, & Bleloch, *1990*) teaches a variety of mathematical approaches to modeling including ordinary algebra, graphing, queuing theory, decision trees, and logical if-then analysis.

All of these projects and approaches are based on the principle that through modeling, students learn about a content domain by personally doing research and recreating the domain's basic concepts and principles, rather than reading about them. A further aspect of the modeling approach is the contention that it results in students developing more transferable thinking and problem solving skills.

THE *USING* TO *BUILDING* CONTINUUM

Not all educational simulations can be classified neatly into *using* them versus *building* them. They form a continuum (Figure 1) with one end emphasizing the use of simulations and the other end emphasizing building simulations or models. Figure 1 indicates approximately where some of the content areas and simulation-based learning projects lie on this continuum. There are many examples of professional training which lie on the far left (using simulations) end of the continuum, such as high-fidelity simulators for flying (both commercial and military aircraft), driving (including cars, trucks and various military ground vehicles), and other professional training (such as, surgery, dentistry, and power plant operation). Trainees, whether they be airline pilots or surgeons, do not build or modify such simulations; they just use them. Building these high-fidelity simulators is a very expensive and difficult endeavor, requiring large teams of mechanical and electrical engineers, programmers, content experts, and other professionals. But more importantly, it is doubtful that any educational benefit would accrue from a surgeon or an airline pilot trying to build such simulations.

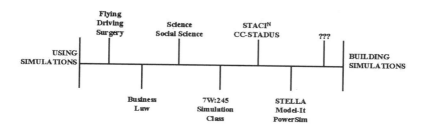

Figure 1. The continuum of using versus building simulations.

Business education makes considerable use of microcomputer-based simulation-games (Faria, 1998) for learning about management, negotiation, planning, marketing, and the like. *Capitalism* (Interactive Magic, 1996, 1997) is a well known example. Law education also uses microcomputer-based simulations such as *The Interactive Courtroom* (Practising Law

Institute, 1996). These do not require dedicated hardware such as aircraft and surgery simulators. Although such microcomputers simulations are pre-built, they can sometimes be modified. Learners may not be able to modify the internal code of the computer programs, but in some cases may modify parameters which change the simulation model in significant ways. This may be considered simulation building in only a trivial way, which is why I indicate it as an example near the left end of the continuum.

I place learning in the sciences (social, physical, and biological) a little more towards the middle. The majority of science curricula incorporate the use of commercially produced microcomputer simulations, much like those for business and law education. They too, in many cases, allow modification of parameters which change a simulation's underlying model. However, learning in the sciences also includes simulation building. In school curricula where students regularly use simulations of the scientific discovery variety, students sometimes go on to create their own versions, generally based upon what they learned from (and perhaps did not like about) the commercially-available simulations. The previously mentioned *CoVis* project was designed with the intention of learners investigating scientific phenomena by using databases of scientific data in conjunction with visualization software and models already created by scientists. However, the open-ended nature of the modeling tools used in the *CoVis* project allows students to modify the original models or build their own.

Curricula which teach about simulation and modeling, such as my own graduate course on educational simulation design (Alessi, 2000b), lie in the middle of this continuum. In teaching instructional design students to develop simulations, I have them begin by studying existing simulations, both commercial examples and ones built by other instruction design students in previous semesters. The simulations developed by other students have the advantage of being 'inspectable' at the source code and model level, as well as being 'runnable'. The extent to which students choose to study other designers' simulations is up to them, beyond an initial assignment to get them going. The students then spend as much as half of the semester (about 8 weeks) creating a simulation model. This process includes a combination of doing research on their chosen phenomena, and modeling the phenomena with *STELLA*. Next they transfer their *STELLA* model into an authoring system, such as *Authorware* (Macromedia, 1999), in which they can create a complete simulation learning environment that other people can study. The distinction between a model and a simulation should be stressed here. The model is a *STELLA* program that embodies the mathematical and logical relationships. It usually does not include an instructional interface or supports for learning (such as coaching). The simulation is a fully functional program that embodies the model and also includes a user interface and features which support learning strategies. Fully functional simulations can be constructed using modeling software such as *STELLA* and *PowerSim*, but good user interfaces and supports for learning are much easier to create using more general authoring software. The key point is that a course on simulation design generally demands a combination, almost equal parts, of students using simulations and students building simulations.

As we move to the *building* end of the continuum, the examples are more complex. The *STACI^N*, *Model-It*, and *CC-STADUS* projects all rely on students studying the models of others as a part of developing their own models. In their description of the *STACI^N* project, Mandinach & Cline (1996) describe this as a sequence of four stages requiring increasingly more independent student work. They call the first stage *parameter manipulation*. In that stage, students manipulate the variables of existing simulations created by others. It is essentially *using* simulations in order to learn about their internal models and characteristics. The second stage is called *structural manipulation*, in which learners modify the logical or mathematical model. This involves changing computer program code, or if using *STELLA*, changing the flow diagram and its associated equations. The third stage is called *constrained modeling*. During that stage, students begin to construct their own simple models. The fourth and last stage is known as *epitome modeling*. In that stage, students engage in the entire process of creating models, sometimes fairly complex ones. It includes doing research on the phenomenon, creating a draft model, evaluating the model, and revising the model until its output reflects reality, in other words, until the model is valid.

The *Model-It* project has been more focused on the physical and biological sciences, especially topics like ecology. In contrast, both the *STACI^N* and *CC-STADUS* projects encompass a variety of school curriculum, although the majority of examples discussed in their reports are from the physical, biological, and social sciences. In Figure 1, learning in the sciences was depicted as toward the left (simulation using) end of the continuum. That is because the predominant paradigm in teaching those subjects emphasizes students using commercially created materials. The *STACI^N* and *CC-STADUS* projects utilize a more constructivist paradigm, within which simulation building is a more common approach.

The question marks (???) on the right end of the continuum imply that there are few, if any, pure examples of building simulations. Most examples of educational simulation lie at various middle points on the continuum. Although software such as *STELLA*, *PowerSim*, and *Model-It* were created for student modeling, they are almost always used in conjunction with students studying models created by other people.

WHERE'S THE DEBATE?

I don't wish to imply that there is a debate between educators favoring the *use* of simulations versus those favoring the *building* of simulations or models. There has been little debate on the topic. Curiously, such a debate exists for other types of software. For example, there have been claims that people learn more by creating multimedia programs than by studying them, by creating expert systems rather than by using them (Jonassen, 2000), or by creating games rather than by playing them (Rieber, 1994). In the simulation field, different educators use them in very different ways and don't appear to pay much attention to the others. Proponents of System Dynamics study and teach system modeling and (if their publications can be taken as any indication) seem unconcerned with the designers building physical simulators, case-based scenarios, or any of the other learning environments which are based on simulations to be run and studied. Similarly, the latter group seems just as unconcerned with the model building approach and the people who are engaged in it. Perhaps this is a good sign, reflecting a general acceptance of the many different approaches in the simulation field. However, I contend that there should be some debate. I say that not because I think one or the other is better in some general sense. Rather, I say it because each approach is better for different learning goals, and the combination of both using and building simulations will be the best choice for learning environments that have multiple goals, as most of them do.

THE RELATIONSHIP BETWEEN BUILDING VERSUS USING SIMULATIONS and DECLARATIVE VERSUS PROCEDURAL LEARNING

When we inspect the various curricula in which learners either use simulations or build simulations, the general observation, illustrated in Figure 2, is that, (1) when learning goals are primarily *procedural* (flying an airplane, doing a titration) the learners *use* simulations built by other people; and (2) when learners are *building* simulations the goals are primarily *declarative*. Those two statements should be analyzed carefully because they have opposite directionality. In statement 1, I say that when the goals are *procedural* the learners generally *use* simulations. But the converse is not at all true. That is, it is *not* the case that when learners are using simulations the goals are mostly procedural. Procedures, the *goal*, implies using simulations, the *method*. The goal implies the method. But for statement 2, the opposite is the case, the method implies the goal. In learning environments where students *build* simulations (the method) the knowledge being learned is usually declarative (the goal). The converse is again not true. The goal of learning declarative knowledge does not appear to require the method of building simulations.

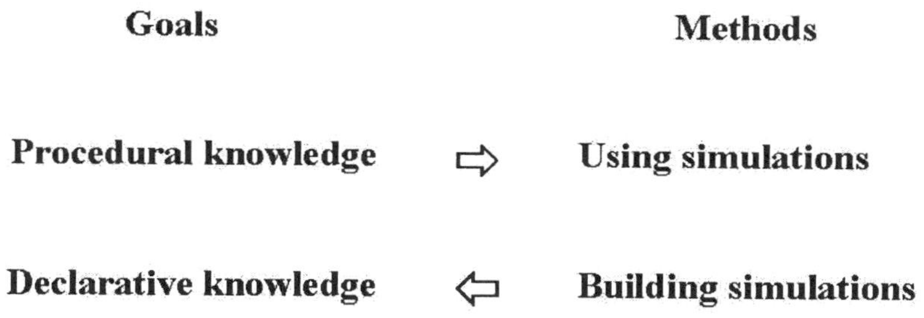

Goals   **Methods**

Procedural knowledge   ⇨   **Using simulations**

Declarative knowledge   ⇦   **Building simulations**

Figure 2. The relationship of different learning goals and simulation methods.

By implication, people rarely learn procedures by building procedural-type simulations. Similarly, using simulations is not exclusively applied to learning procedural knowledge, but also to learning declarative knowledge. In general, building simulations is the more *constrained methodology*, applying when there is declarative knowledge to be learned. Similarly, procedural knowledge is the more *constrained goal*, generally requiring the use of simulation, not the building of simulations. In contrast, using simulations appears to be the fairly *unconstrained method*, appropriate for both procedural and declarative knowledge, and declarative knowledge is the more unconstrained *goal*, benefiting from both learners using and learners building simulations.

I am not aware of any exceptions to this in the simulation training field, although they are certainly possible. For example, although it might not make sense for airline pilots to design and build simulators, it might be useful for chemistry students to build a simulated apparatus for doing a laboratory experiment. Indeed, professional chemists must often design and build novel devices for control and measurement in their research studies.

In the paragraphs above I have discussed learning which is *either* procedural or declarative. However, the more important and quite common situation is when the learning goals include both procedural and declarative knowledge. This is often the case when science laboratory simulations are being used. [Indeed, a recurrent theme in this volume is that many learning situations involve such complex objectives that are not easily or naturally separated into discrete units of instruction.] For example, there is conceptual knowledge that must be understood if the procedures, such as performing a titration, are to make any sense. Most laboratory simulations assume that the student knows the conceptual information. Unfortunately, it is likely that a significant proportion of students *lack* the prior conceptual knowledge and as a result are not truly understanding why certain procedures should be performed. For the procedures of a titration to make any sense, learners must understand how acids and bases neutralize each other.

EFFICIENCY VERSUS DEPTH OF KNOWLEDGE

Another aspect of the building versus using continuum is the common educational dilemma of choosing between efficiency of learning and depth of learning. Building a simulation is assumed (and I believe the assumption is usually true) to result in deeper knowledge. By deeper knowledge, I mean knowledge which can be used, in contrast to *inert* knowledge (Greeno, Smith, & Moore, 1993; Renkl, Mandl, & Gruber, 1996), which is difficult or impossible to use outside of the immediate instructional situation. The activities of model building require a learner to use and manipulate the knowledge, not just observe or repeat it. This is likely to improve not only recall of the relevant knowledge, but its application and transfer. The dilemma, of course, is that building a simulation, like building a multimedia program or an expert system, is very time consuming. Learners must use a variety of resources to investigate the subject matter. They may need to interview experts. They must learn to use modeling software and create a model with it. They must evaluate the model, such as by entering historical data and assessing whether the output conforms to reality. Based on the results, they must refine the model. When my students are first learning to use *STELLA* for modeling, I regularly observe the same problems that other teachers of System Dynamics observe. The students confuse levels with rates of change. They do analytic analyses rather than systemic analyses. They insert crude fixes (fudge factors) to make their models work. They do not test sensitivity to extreme conditions or to variations in the time increment. Their models are unnecessarily complex and do not have a close correspondence to reality. I could go on and on. The point is, to learn modeling (whether System Dynamics or any other approach) is very difficult and time consuming, even for sophisticated graduate students. But when done, even though their models may still need improvement, their understanding of the phenomena being studied is very deep and transferable. They can use the knowledge in a variety of contexts. That is so because they have already been using the knowledge, as they had to manipulate it to make it function in a modeling program. They often had to go back to primary sources and to experts to figure out what they had missed, as exemplified by models producing nonsensical output. This process leads to very good understanding of the knowledge and the ability to use it, teach it to others, and transfer it to other situations.

In contrast, learning by studying another person's model may not result in the same quality of knowledge, but it is much more efficient. This is not to say that the knowledge is useless or inert. Studying by using a simulation is quite different than studying a book, listening to a lecture, or doing a computer drill. In a scientific discovery simulation, for example, the learner is performing experiments, varying input variables in a systematic fashion, observing and recording output, and (if the simulation is designed well) reflecting on the results. Just *using* a simulation is a very active process, similar to doing research and creating new knowledge. Furthermore, doing experiments in a pre-built simulation is almost always more efficient than creating a new simulation. Good simulations will generally include a variety of supports for learning (such as coaching, hints, and feedback) and for self-initiated learning strategies (such as providing laboratory notebooks or questions to spur reflection). Finally, figuring out the underlying model of a simulation is almost always easier than figuring out how to program the same model.

Summarizing to this point, there are two very different approaches to the use of simulations for learning: students building them and students using them. Building simulations takes much more time and effort, but is believed (although there is little research to back the belief up) to result in better and more useful knowledge. In general, building simulations, or modeling, has been applied to declarative knowledge and mostly in the physical and social sciences. In contrast, procedural knowledge is almost always addressed by using simulations and rarely (perhaps never) with modeling or simulation building. Training in the professions often deals with complex, expensive, and dangerous procedural learning and when that is the case, the use of large physical simulators is often the preferred approach. Academic learning, primarily between the ages of 5 and 21, includes a combination of declarative and procedural learning, suggesting the need for both simulation approaches. I now suggest recommendations about when and how to use these two approaches. Several of these recommendations may be fruitful areas for research.

CONDITIONS UNDER WHICH *USING* SIMULATIONS MAY BE MORE BENEFICIAL

Having taken the view that both using and building simulations are beneficial learning activities, it follows that the designer of a learning environment should always address the question of which approach is applicable for a particular project. I'll begin with conditions that suggest learners use of simulations rather than building them. These conditions are not in a preferred order because I don't think there is one.

The first condition is when skilled performance is the objective of training, especially when the performance involves expensive devices or potentially dangerous activities. Obvious examples are operating aircraft, other vehicles, power plants, and machinery. Less obvious but equally valid examples are performing surgery or other medical procedures, and running or maintaining mechanical or information systems on which large numbers of people depend. Physical simulators are often used to meet these needs. Physical simulators include not only vehicle simulators, such as for aircraft, but other realistic devices connected to and controlled by computers, such as special mannequins for simulations of medical diagnosis, cardiopulmonary resuscitation, dentistry, and surgery. Increasingly, virtual reality devices will be designed to facilitate this type of training.

A second condition is when learning requires interpersonal interactions. We call simulations of this type *situational* simulations (Alessi & Trollip, 1991). For example, even though business managers know all about supply and demand, setting prices, and labor negotiation, they do not always apply that knowledge successfully in real business situations. One reason is that they do not operate independently in the business environment. There are many elements of interaction including competition, cooperation, and interdependence, all of which are affected by the complexity of human emotion, personality, and behavior. Business is the largest subject area employing situational simulations, but others include simulations for teachers (especially classroom behavior management), counselors and therapists, politicians, military leaders, and parents. All of these share an important characteristic. You may know some basic principles that theoretically will maximize your success, but the other people in the situations are similarly applying principles to maximize *their* success, which is often mutually exclusive with yours.

A third condition is when the system to be learned is very complex and contains many variables (Funke, 1991). Each of the simulation-games in the growing *Sim City* family contains hundreds of variables (Maxim, 1996a, 1996b, 1998). Although they are marketed as games, several of these programs are valuable tools for studying ecology (*Sim Earth*), business management (*Sim Farm*), and urban planning (*Sim City*). It would not make sense to have learners try to build simulations of such size or complexity. They could only succeed with small subsets (two or three variable) and would not learn nearly as much about complex systems as they would by using the commercially developed programs.

A fourth condition is when instructional time is limited. In that situation you must strike a compromise between the competing goals of learning depth and learning efficiency. Although it sounds nice to say that learning should not be rushed and we should provide the time necessary for proper mastery, reality often does not afford us that luxury. This is especially true for adult learners. They not only must abide by the requirements of employers and other circumstances, they are also more demanding that their time be used efficiently.

A fifth condition, related to the previous one, is when the target learners have no prior experience in building models or simulations. Their first encounter with model building will require considerable time and guidance. It should only be undertaken if the time, facilities, and expert support are present to make the experience a successful one.

The sixth condition is when learners will soon be *building* simulations and using simulations is a precursor to that. Almost all modeling curricula (such as *STACI^N* and *CC-SUSTAIN*) begin with demonstrating to learners the modeling process and allowing them to manipulate and experiment with other people's models before undertaking their own.

CONDITIONS UNDER WHICH *BUILDING* SIMULATIONS MAY BE MORE BENEFICIAL

Next I consider the conditions that suggest learners will benefit more from building simulations. Once again, these are not in any preferred order and such an order probably does not exist.

The first condition is when learning conceptual information in systems with a small number of primary variables (perhaps 2 to 20) which account for the majority of variance in system behavior. That is, a system may contain many variables, but only a few are needed to make accurate predictions and explanations. A good example is the predator-prey relationships in animal communities, one part of the study of ecology and population dynamics. Many variables affect animal populations (such as the weather and diseases) but when a predator-prey relationship exists between two animal species, the population size of each species is the variable having the most dramatic effect on the population size of the other. Many physical and social science systems taught in schools and universities fit into this category. The best understanding of such systems will probably result from building the models and simulations.

The second condition is when learning about systems where expert knowledge is itself somewhat imprecise and hypothetical. Good examples are learning about the ozone hole or global warming. There are considerable differences of opinion among scientists concerning what is causing the ozone hole, whether it will expand or contract, and what the consequences will be. Similarly, there is great debate about whether global warming is occurring, its causes, its consequences, and how to reverse it. A danger with having learners only *use* models of such phenomenon is that they will accept the models as fact rather than theory. Using such models may be a good precursor to building their own (as discussed in the sixth point of the previous section), but appreciation of the complexities and the different points of view will be facilitated much more by model building.

A third condition is when a primary learning goal is *solving a problem* within a system, rather than simply understanding the system. Although problem-solving activities (such as hypothesis formation and testing) may be facilitated by simulation use, learners are afforded much more flexibility to pursue their own hypotheses and potential solutions when they are building models. Pre-existing simulations invariably include assumptions about what hypotheses and solutions are plausible and prevent learners from pursuing ones that do not conform to the original designers assumptions. When students are building their own models they are only constrained by their own assumptions.

The fourth condition, similar to the third, is when the primary learning objective is not the subject area at hand (biology, for example), but instead, is more general thinking and problem-solving skills. These include making and questioning assumptions, generating and testing hypotheses, collecting and analyzing data, and evaluating potential solutions to problems. It also includes learning to use various thinking and problem-solving tools including mathematics, logic, and visualization. Once again, simulation use can contribute to such goals and can be a good first step towards their attainment, but simulation building affords much more flexibility to learners, allowing them to pursue directions that another person (the designer of an existing simulation) may never have envisioned.

The fifth condition suggesting greater benefits from simulation building (and which stands in direct contrast to the fourth and fifth conditions of the previous section), is when time is *not* constrained and when learners either have prior experience or when this will be their first in a sequence of many model building experiences. This is the situation when a long-term curriculum is being built upon a modeling approach, such as the *STACI^N* or *CC-SUSTAIN* curriculum projects. When that is the case, learners may spend considerable time in their initial model building efforts, but efficiency will be accrued with each new application of modeling to another problem or subject area. This is usually most appropriate in academic environments (K-12 and university education). However, it is beginning to be recognized as valuable in some areas of professional education as well, such as business administration (Senge, 1990).

The sixth condition is when learning a procedural skill depends directly on some conceptual understanding of basic principles underlying the procedure, in which case simulation building acts as a precursor to simulation use. A good example involves diagnostic simulations (Johnson & Norton, 1992). In diagnostic simulations the learner must figure out the problem occurring in a system and in some cases fix the problem. The system may be a car engine, a sick patient, or an electronic circuit. Good diagnosticians do not follow cookbook rules. They understand the underlying principles of the system, be it electronics, biology, or the operation of internal combustion engines, and apply that knowledge to diagnosis and repair. If a system is not too complicated (that is, it does not have too many variables), it will be beneficial for learners to develop a deep and complete understanding of the system's principles through modeling, and then progress to learning diagnosis and repair through simulation use.

CONDITIONS EQUALLY FAVORING SIMULATION BUILDING AND SIMULATION USE

The twelve recommendations above seem straightforward enough. However, there are many situations in which an argument can be made for either simulation building or simulation use. For example, with much learning in the sciences (physical, biological, and social), the learning goals include not only the immediate content, but also more general thinking skills such as the scientific method (generating and testing hypotheses, controlling variables, and so on). In many cases the current scientific theories are precise and widely agreed upon, while in other cases they are imprecise and hotly debated. Some of the systems are very complex, with a large number of important variables, while other systems are fairly simple. Under these mixed conditions, should learners be using simulations or building them?

Although this question needs considerably more analysis and research across a wide variety of content areas, I would suggest that selecting the appropriate approach depends upon which thinking skills and methods are relevant. If a primary goal is learning the experimental method (which would include generating hypotheses, formulating tests, controlling and manipulating variables, and collecting data), then *using* scientific discovery simulations may best allow learners to focus on those skills. If the primary goal is developing skills such as observation, theorizing, visualization, distinguishing causation from correlation, or seeking parsimony, then modeling may be more likely to facilitate the goals.

Based on the previous discussion, I contend that when an instructional designer is considering simulation as an appropriate strategy for a learning environment, an important decision for the designer to carefully address is whether to create an environment in which learners use simulations, build simulations, or do both. Few designers even consider that decision. Instead, they consistently apply the approach (simulation use or simulation building) with which they are most familiar.

Elsewhere I have explicated a theory of simulation and a model for simulation design that progresses through six stages, as illustrated in Figure 3 (Alessi, 2000a). The first stage is to begin with the theory of simulation, which has the four components of knowledge attributes, learner attributes, simulation attributes, and the representation of knowledge.

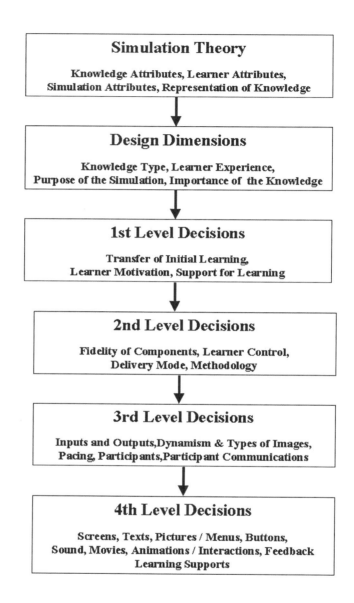

Figure 3. A model for simulation design based on a theory of simulation.

That theory suggests four relatively independent design dimensions, the type of knowledge (procedural or declarative), the prior experience of learners (a continuum from novice to expert), the purpose of the simulation (whether it is being used for learning or for assessment), and the importance of the knowledge (by which I mean, the severity of the consequences following errors or the value of benefits which follow from success).

These dimensions, in turn, inform progressively more detailed levels of design and design variables, all the way down to designing the appearance and functionality of every picture, button, sound, and user action. The designer's decision to have learners use versus build simulations is, I believe, a decision that should be made in Level 2, the fourth box of Figure 3. That is because it should be a function of the type of knowledge, the learners' prior knowledge, the type of transfer (near or far), and several other components of the first three phases. Deciding whether to have learners use or build simulations is a decision about the learning methodology, which appears in the box for 2nd Level Decisions.

Following a decision to use one or both of the approaches, the designer must subsequently make a multitude of detailed design decision. Which design issues are more important and which are less important is a function of the decision to have learners use simulations versus build them. This chapter concludes with some suggestions concerning which characteristics of learning environments (and their design) are most important for the simulation use approach versus the simulation building approach.

CHARACTERISTICS OF ENVIRONMENTS TO SUPPORT LEARNING BY *USING* SIMULATIONS

Once a designer decides that learners will be *using* simulations, the most important characteristic of the simulation environment is its fidelity (Alessi, 1988). Saying fidelity (the level of realism) is important is not the same as saying that fidelity should be high. Quite the opposite is often the case. An educational simulation must not only imitate reality, it must simplify it. When learners use a simulation created by somebody else, they are generally disoriented and confused at first. Those and other learning difficulties can be diminished if a designer implements dynamic fidelity, whereby the realism and complexity of various simulation elements begins at a low level and increases gradually. The change in fidelity may be based upon user choice, user performance, instructor choice, or situational variables such as whether a collaborative learning approach is being employed.

Simulation fidelity is not a single overall environment characteristic or design decision. Rather, the designer must differentially choose the fidelity of presentations, of the underlying model, of user actions, and of the time-scale, to name a few (Andrews, Carroll, & Bell, 1995). In simulations for procedural learning, the fidelity of user actions and feedback are more critical. In simulations for declarative learning, fidelity of the model and presentations are more critical. Higher fidelity will tend to be more important when a simulation is being used for assessment, when learners have more prior knowledge, and when transfer of learning is the primary goal. In contrast, when designing simulations for novice learners and for initial learning of skills or knowledge, lower fidelity may be better. For simulations to support scientific discovery learning, a primary consideration is how many and what variables to include in the underlying model.

Fidelity is not the only characteristic of importance when learners are using simulations. The delivery mode (which may be a microcomputer, a virtual reality room, or a large scale physical simulator, to name just a few) and locus of control (meaning, to what extent the learner, the program, or an instructor controls sequence and other instructional events) are other important characteristics decided upon in Level 2 decisions. At Level 3, the decision of what inputs and outputs to provide is most critical. At Level 4, the micro level of design, many decisions are important, but the features that support learning and learning strategies (Veenman & Elshout, 1995; Alessi, 2000b) are the most critical characteristics.

Finally, another essential characteristic of the learning environment is features which enhance learner engagement with the simulation. Interesting and clear tasks or scenarios can enhance engagement. For example, learner engagement during scientific discovery simulations can be facilitated with suggested investigations or research questions. Engagement when using large-scale physical simulators is enhanced when users are given clear and interesting goals or problems. For example, an airline pilot in a 747 simulator may be given the task of coping with frequent turbulence during a long flight from New York to Los Angeles.

Summarizing, the most important characteristics of a learning environment to support learning by using simulations include proper levels of fidelity for the various components, an appropriate delivery mode, a balance of user and program control, features to support learning and learning strategies, and features to maximize learner engagement.

CHARACTERISTICS OF ENVIRONMENTS TO SUPPORT LEARNING BY *BUILDING* SIMULATIONS

When the designer is creating an environment for learners *building* simulations, characteristics related to Level 2 decisions are much less important. The reason is simply that the learners will themselves make most of those decisions, not the designer. When the learner is building a simulation, the locus of control rests almost entirely with the learner. Similarly, fidelity levels are selected by the learner, constrained only by the characteristics of the modeling software being used. The delivery mode is almost always the same, a microcomputer with modeling software, so that too is not much of an issue.

Characteristics determined at Level 3 are similarly of low importance. Learners doing modeling have almost complete control over the choice of inputs and outputs, methods of visualization (within the constraints of the modeling software), and pacing. However, the environment characteristics relevant to *participants* and *participant communication* are important and are decided upon by designers. I will discuss them below, under the topic of collaborative learning.

The characteristic of support for learning and learning strategies again stands out as the most important consideration among 4th Level decisions. Everyone who has taught simulation design affirms that it is a difficult, frustrating, and time consuming process. Learners encounter many roadblocks and need frequent help. A learning environment for modeling must include scaffolding (such as, working with partial models), coaching (expert assessment of students' models and provision of advice), and metacognitive support (such as, encouragement for learners to evaluate and improve their draft models). Although learning support features are also important in environments where learners are using simulations, the success of environments in which learners build simulations will depend on them even more.

Next, environments for simulation building require support for the concepts and procedures of modeling, and for learning the modeling software employed. The third is relatively straightforward. The first and second, as discussed earlier, are very challenging for people who have never done modeling. A significant amount of guidance, scaffolding, and feedback are necessary from experts.

Lastly, collaborative learning is a critical characteristic for environments in which learners build simulations. Collaborative work among learners with differing levels of experience is one method to provide the scaffolding and other support discussed in the previous paragraph. Collaborative work has other advantages for simulation building. It alleviates the problem caused by the time-consuming nature of simulation building, discussed earlier under the efficiency versus depth of knowledge tradeoff. Collaborative work provides metacognitive support as members of a group critique and improve each others ideas. Finally, the multifaceted activities of simulation building (doing research, organizing data, programming, evaluation) benefit from the variety of skills and knowledge different learners bring to a project.

Summarizing, the most important characteristics of environments for learners building simulations are supports for learning and learning strategies, support for the modeling and programming process, and collaborative learning and work.

CONCLUSION

Few designers make a deliberate and carefully considered choice about which approach to simulation, building versus using them, will best facilitate their goals for learners. Most designers have had experience with the simulation use approach and so almost always employ it. A smaller number of designers are modeling enthusiasts and tend to favor that approach. Designers should take greater advantage of both approaches and their combination. Furthermore, learning environments should be designed in appreciation of the learning needs associated with each approach. Simulation researchers, for their part, should concentrate more effort on examining the characteristics of learning environments which support each of the simulation approaches, in order to provide designers with a more scientific basis for quality learning environment design.

REFERENCES

Alessi, S. M. (1988). Fidelity in the design of instructional simulations. *Journal of Computer-based Instruction, 15*(2), 40-47.

Alessi, S. M. (2000a). Simulation design for training and assessment. In H. F. O'Neil, Jr., & D. Andrews (Eds.), *Aircrew training and assessment: Methods, technologies, and assessments.* Mahwah, NJ: Lawrence Erlbaum.

Alessi, S. M. (2000b). Designing educational support in System Dynamics based interactive learning environments. *Simulation & Gaming, 31*(2), 178-196.

Alessi, S. M., & Trollip, S. R. (1991). *Computer-based instruction: Methods & development (2nd Ed.).* Englewood Cliffs, NJ: Prentice Hall.

Andrews, D. H., Carroll, L. A., & Bell, H. H. (1995). The future of selective fidelity in training devices. *Educational Technology, 35*(6), 32-36.

Andrews, D. H., Dineen, T., & Bell, H. H. (1999). The use of constructive modeling and virtual simulation in large-scale team training: A military case study. *Educational Technology, 39*(1), 24-28.

Collins, A. (1994). Goal-based scenarios and the problem of situated learning: A commentary on Andersen Consulting's design of goal-based scenarios. *Educational Technology, 34*(9), 30-32.

Davidsen, P., Gonzalez, J. J., Muraida, D. J., Spector, J. M., & Tennyson, R. D. (1995). Applying system dynamics to courseware development. *Computers in Human Behavior, 11*(2), 325-339.

De Jong, T., & van Joolingen, W.R. (1998). Scientific discovery learning with computer simulations of conceptual domains. *Review of Educational Research, 68*(2), 179-201.

Dewar, J. A., Hodges, J. S., Bankes, S. C., Lucas, T., Vye, P., & Saunders-Newton, D. K. (1996). *Credible uses of the distributed interactive simulation (DIS) system.* Santa Monica, CA: The Rand Corporation.

Edelson, D. C., Pea, R. D., & Gomez, L. (1996). Constructivism in the collaboratory. In B.G. Wilson (Ed.), *Constructivist learning environments: Case studies in instructional design.* Englewood Cliffs, NJ: Educational Technology Publications.

EME Corporation. (1999). *Burette.* [Computer program]. Stuart, FL: EME Corporation.

Faria, A. J. (1998). Business simulation games: Current usage levels - An update. *Simulation & Gaming, 29*(3), 295-308.

Forrester, J. W. (1961). *Industrial dynamics.* New York: John Wiley & Sons, Inc.

Forrester, J. W. (1968). *Principles of systems (Second preliminary edition)*. Cambridge, MA: Wright-Allen Press, Inc.

Forrester, J. W. (1969). *Urban dynamics*. Cambridge, MA: The M.I.T. Press.

Forrester, J. W. (1971). *World dynamics*. Cambridge, MA: Wright-Allen Press, Inc.

Funke, J. (1991). Solving complex problems: Exploration and control of complex systems. In R. J. Sternberg & P. A. Frensch (Eds.), *Complex problems solving: Principles and mechanisms*. Hillsdale, NJ: Erlbaum.

Greeno, J. G., Smith, D. R., & Moore, J. L. (1993). Transfer of situated learning. In D. K. Detterman & R. J. Sternberg (Eds.), *Transfer on trial: Intelligence, cognition, and instruction* (pp. 99-167). Norwood, NJ: Ablex.

High Performance Systems. (1987). *Stella*. [Computer program]. Lyme, NH: High Performance Systems.

Imagine That, Inc. (2000). *Extend*. [Computer program]. San Jose, CA: Imagine That, Inc.

Interactive Magic. (1996). *Capitalism*. [Computer program]. Research Triangle Park, NC: Interactive Magic.

Interactive Magic. (1997). *Capitalism Plus*. [Computer program]. Research Triangle Park, NC: Interactive Magic.

Jackson, S., Stratford, S. J., Krajcik, J., & Soloway, E. (1995, March). *Model-It: a case study of learner-centered software for supporting model building*. Proceedings of the Working Conference on Technology Applications in the Science Classroom, The National Center for Science Teaching and Learning, Columbus, OH.

Jackson, S., Stratford, S. J., Krajcik, J., & Soloway, E. (1996). Making dynamic modeling accessible to pre-college science students. *Interactive Learning Environments*, *4*(3), 233-257.

Johnson, W. B., & Norton, J. E. (1992). Modeling student performance in diagnostic tasks: A decade of evolution. In J. W. Regian & V. J. Shute (Eds.), *Cognitive approaches to automated instruction*. Hillsdale, NJ: Lawrence Erlbaum.

Jonassen, D. H. (2000). *Computers as mindtools for schools: Engaging critical thinking*. Upper Saddle River, NJ: Merrill.

Kinnear, J. (1998). *Catlab*. [Computer program]. Stuart, FL: EME Corporation.

Macromedia. (1999). *Authorware 4*. [Computer program]. San Francisco, CA: Macromedia.

Mandinach, E. B., & Cline, H. F. (1994). *Classroom dynamics: Implementing a technology-based learning environment*. Hillsdale, NJ: Lawrence Erlbaum.

Mandinach, E. B., & Cline, H. F. (1996). Classroom dynamics: The impact of a technology-based curriculum innovation on teaching and learning. *Journal of Educational Computing Research*, *14*(1), 83-102.

Maxis. (1996a). *Sim City*. [Computer program]. Walnut Creek, CA: Maxis.

Maxis. (1996b). *Sim Farm*. [Computer program]. Walnut Creek, CA: Maxis.

Maxis. (1998). *Sim Earth*. [Computer program]. Walnut Creek, CA: Maxis.

Milheim, W. D. (1995). Virtual reality and its potential applications in education and training. *Machine-Mediated Learning*, *5*(1), 43-55.

Neyland, D. L. (1997). *Virtual combat*. Mechanicsburg, PA: Stackpole Books.

Pappo, H. A. (1998). *Simulations for skills training*. Englewood Cliffs, NJ: Educational Technology Publications.

PowerSim. (1999). *PowerSim*. [Computer program]. Bergen, Norway: PowerSim.

Practising Law Institute. (1996). *The Interactive Courtroom*. [Computer program]. New York: Practising Law Institute.

Psotka, J. (1995). Immersive training systems: Virtual reality and education and training. *Instructional Science*, *23*(5-6), 405-431.

Pugh, A. L. (1983). *DYNAMO user's manual: including DYNAMO II/370, DYNAMO II/F, DYNAMO III/370, DYNAMO III/F, DYNAMO III/F+, DYNAMO IV/370, and Gaming DYNAMO. 6th ed.* Cambridge, MA: M.I.T. Press.

Pugh-Roberts Associates. (1982). *Micro-DYNAMO*. [Computer program]. Reading, MA: Addison-Wesley.

Renkl, A., Mandl, H., & Gruber, H. (1996). Inert knowledge: Analyses and remedies. *Educational Psychologist, 31*(2), 115-121.

Rieber, L. P. (1994, April). *An instructional design philosophy of interaction based on a blending of microworlds, simulations, and games.* Paper presented at the Annual Meeting of the American Educational Research Association, New Orleans, April 4-8.

Roberts, N., Anderson, D., Deal, R., Garet, M., & Shaffer, W. (1983). *Computer Simulation: A System Dynamics Modeling Approach.* Reading, MA: Addison-Wesley.

Schank, R., & Cleary, C. (1995). *Engines for education.* Hillsdale, NJ: Lawrence Erlbaum.

Senge, P.M. (1990). *The fifth discipline: The art and practice of the learning organization.* New York: Doubleday Books.

Starfield, A.M., Smith, K.A., & Bleloch, A.L. (1990). *How to model it: Problem solving for the computer age.* New York: McGraw-Hill.

Van Joolingen, W. R., King, S., & de Jong, T. (1997). The SimQuest authoring system for simulation-base discovery environments. In B. du Boulay & R. Mizoguchi (Eds.), *Knowledge and media in learning systems* (pp. 79-87). Amsterdam: IOS.

Veenman, M. V. J., & Elshout, J. J. (1995). Differential effects of instructional support on learning in simulation environments. *Instructional Science, 22*(5), 363-383.

White, B. Y. (1995). *Discrete models, computer microworlds, and scientific inquiry: An alternative approach to physics education.* San Francisco: American Educational Research Association

Zaraza, R., & Fisher, D. (1997, August). *Introducing System Dynamics into the traditional secondary curriculum: The CC-STADUS project's search for leverage points.* Paper presented at the 15th International System Dynamics Conference, Istanbul, Turkey, August 19-22.

Zaraza, R., Joy, T., & Guthrie, S. (1998, July). *Modeling in the educational environment – Moving from simplicity to complexity.* Paper presented at the 16th International System Dynamics Conference, Quebec, Canada, July 20-23.
[This and the previous reference are available on the CC-SUSTAIN Web site: http://www.teleport.com/~sguthrie/cc-stadus.html.]

OK-CHOON PARK and MICHAEL P. ETGEN

Chapter 11

RESEARCH-BASED PRINCIPLES FOR MULTIMEDIA PRESENTATION

Keywords: cognitive theories, instructional design, information modality, multimedia, object representation

Abstract. Four basic principles of multimedia presentation were derived from empirical findings and examined in terms of several different theories of cognition. The first principle suggests that combining different types of information with variation of either perceptual modality (e.g., visual and auditory), representational forms (verbal and nonverbal), or both is desirable, while the second principle states that one should keep presentations of related information integrated physically and/or temporally. The third principle asserts that the pace, continuity, and complexity of information must be considered, while the fourth principle maintains that coupled verbal and pictorial information must match in terms of semantic characteristics to be effective. The limitations of the proposed principles stem from the incomplete consideration of all studies and theories relevant to multimedia presentation, as well as the effect of individual differences upon the variables involved in the principles.

INTRODUCTION

Development of multimedia products has explosively increased for the last ten years as evident in the many CD-based products at software sellers, book stores and World Wide Web sites on the Internet Because of the perceptually attractive, realistic and engaging attributes of multimedia programs and technical advancements in development and delivery, this trend will continue. However, most of these programs, including CD-based games and educational programs, appear to be developed focusing on aesthetic or sensational appeal rather than the instructional effectiveness of different multimedia features. The purpose of this paper is to derive principles for the presentation of multimedia information based on relevant research findings and cognitive theories.

Recent development of multimedia programs has centered on the concept of interactive hypermedia, that is, multimedia databases that allow one to navigate one's own course through the information network. However, a long history of empirical research with many different mechanisms for

J.M. Spector and T.M. Anderson (eds.),
Integrated and Holistic Perspectives on Learning, Instruction and Technology, 197–212.
© 2000 *Kluwer Academic Publishers. Printed in the Netherlands.*

presentation (i.e., television, film, books, tape recorder, computer, etc.) tend to demonstrate a consistent picture of information processing within multimedia environments, separate from the navigational issues associated with hypermedia. Therefore, this paper will focus on the underlying principles for multimedia presentation independent of how it is delivered (i.e., with or without hypermedia links on a computer), as distilled from a review of older and more recent empirical studies. To begin with, we will clarify our conceptualization of multimedia and other relevant terms.

Multimedia is characterized as the delivery of complementary information in two or more different modality formats. Complementary information is that which pertains to the same concept, but arises from different types of representational forms (e.g., text, graphics, and sound). The modality format refers to the way in which information is presented and perceived (e.g., visual and auditory). Information presented in the same modality format can be conveyed and processed in different representational forms (i.e., verbal and nonverbal). For example, the perceptual modality of a written text and picture are both visual, but the representational form for processing written text is verbal, while that of picture is nonverbal. However, the semantic meaning of the text and picture may be identical.

This paper is concerned with the four types of information primarily used:

(a) text - modality format is visual and representational form is verbal;
(b) narration – auditory and verbal;
(c) graphics – visual and nonverbal; and,
(d) sound – auditory and nonverbal.

We are primarily interested in the effect of the interactions between the different combinations of information types upon task performance.

Previous attempts have been made to provide guidelines for the presentation of interactive multimedia, but they often fall short of their utilitarian goal due to a proliferation of principles and vacuous content. For instance, Park and Hannafin (1993) created a long list of principles based upon a framework that included psychological, pedagogical, and technological foundations. The resultant principles are sometimes repetitive and too general, and often difficult to implement. Our approach differs from Park and Hannafin (1993) in several ways. First, we consider the processing of multimedia information without delving into the realm of hyper-interaction between computer and user. As such, our empirical evidence may or may not necessarily involve computer-based presentation, but may use other delivery media. Additionally, we distill from the literature only four broad, but applicable and straightforward, principles for the presentation of multimedia information. These principles will help to insure an optimal method for presenting multimedia information independent of the delivery mechanism, therefore providing a basic set of guidelines for developers and designers to follow.

PRINCIPLES FOR MULTIMEDIA PRESENTATION

Four general principles for the presentation of multimedia information were derived from the empirical literature. Each of the principles is first stated and then followed by supporting research evidence. Finally, cognitive theories supporting the principle and research evidence are discussed.

Principle I:

The combination of information types that vary by either modality formats (i.e., visual plus auditory), representational forms (i.e., verbal plus nonverbal), or both is more effective than a non-combined information type. Combinations that vary along both dimensions are optimal (e.g., picture - visual and nonverbal - plus narration - auditory and verbal).

Empirical Findings. This principle has been supported by studies on various tasks that range from the recall of simple line figures (Ishi & Yamauchi, 1994) and concrete words (Kobus, Moses, & Bloom, 1994; Lewandowski & Kobus, 1993) to the comprehension of complex narratives (Dean, Garabedian, & Yekovich, 1983; Kruley, Sciama, & Glenberg, 1994; Glenberg & Kruley, 1992; Verdi, Peterson, Webb, Stock, & Kulhavy, 1993; Stock, Kulhavy, Webb, Pridemore, & Verdi, 1993) and geometry problem solving (Mousavi, Low, & Sweller, 1995; Sweller, 1988, 1989, 1993, 1994).

Ishi and Yamauchi (1994) examined the effect of multiple-modality presentation on the recall of line-figures. In this study, subjects either studied a textual description of a line figure or a textual description accompanied by a graphical representation of the figure. Recall was assessed by asking the subjects to draw the figures using the arrows on a computer keyboard. The authors found that more items were correctly recalled when the subjects studied the figure in the text and picture than in the text alone.

Kobus, Moses, and Bloom (1994) examined the recall of words taken from Snodgrass and Vanderwart (1980) that were presented concurrently in multiple combinations. Subjects were divided into seven groups dependent upon the combination of: text, narration, picture, text/narration, picture/narration, picture/text, and picture/narration/text. They found that the picture and picture/narration/text groups recalled equally as many words and significantly more than other groups. It is unclear as to why the picture group was able to perform equally as well as the picture/narration/text group, and better than other verbal-nonverbal combinations. A possible explanation may be that the verbal label evoked by the stimuli may not have matched well with the label given by the experimenter. Any conflict in labeling on the part of the picture/narration/text group could have been dampened by the use of multiple formats. Of course, there could also be methodological problems with the study.

Lewandowski and Kobus (1993) studied accuracy and reaction time in a lexical decision task as well as the recall of words presented contiguously in the different combinations of information types. For the lexical decision task, subjects were asked to press keys on a computer keyboard for either a "yes" or "no" decision depending upon the category membership of the presented stimuli. Words were either presented as written text, narration, or a combination of text and narration in which both words could be the same or different. The authors found that there was no difference between the text and the combination of text and narration for the measure in the lexical decision task, but subjects did show significantly slower reaction times and less accuracy in the narration. Subject's recall of words presented in the combined form was significantly greater than that in text or narration alone, but only when the words were related to the lexical decision task. The results from these studies suggest that information presented in multiple forms is recalled better than that presented in a single form, and multiple-forms presentation seems especially advantageous when the information is presented within a meaningful context.

The research with more complex information further explicates the above principle of multimedia presentation. Dean, Garabedian, and Yekovich (1983) studied the effect of combined information types on recognition and recall of reading passages. In this experiment, subjects studied four semantically similar passages, with a shift of information type from text to narrative on the last passage for half the subjects. On a recall test, the non-shift group exhibited a proactive interference effect, with declining recall over the course of the experiment. However, the shift group showed a distinct release from the proactive interference effect, with a similar degree of recall for the last passage as for the first passage. The same result has been shown for both the recall of words and the comprehension of complex information.

Kruley, Sciama and Glenberg (1994) used a divided-attention paradigm to study how unrelated information interferes with the processing of narratives. In the experiment, subjects read passages that either were or were not accompanied by a related picture. But prior to reading, subjects performed a spatial task and were told that they either should or should not retain the spatial information while reading the passage. The spatial information was consistently available to those who were not to retain it during reading.

All subjects answered questions about the passages and spatial information after reading. Results showed significant main effects of picture presence and type of spatial task on comprehension. Those who did not have to retain the spatial information outperformed those who did, and those who were shown the picture outperformed those who were not. In addition, spatial task performance was poorer for those who had to retain information, especially for those who did so while reading a passage with a picture. In another experiment, subjects were required to complete a verbal task during text comprehension that either did or did not require retention of a list of digits. This experiment differed from the first one in that the presentation of the digits was auditory. Results again showed that comprehension was better overall for those who had a picture present during reading, but performance on the digit task was not affected by picture presence. These results indicate that a visual-spatial retention task will interfere with the interpretation of text-relevant pictures during the reading of passages, but a verbal retention task will not.

Glenberg and Kruley (1992) examined how graphics help text comprehension when readers are confronted with anaphor resolution. For the first experiment, subjects read passages containing anaphors that were either physically near or far (within the text body) from their referents, and with or without accompanying graphics of the passage topic. They found that the subjects who had no picture maintained similar reading times for both near and far anaphors, but answered fewer questions correctly about the far anaphors than the near. The groups with graphics read the near anaphor sentences faster than the far, and also answered fewer questions correctly about the far anaphors than the near. Overall, the subjects who had graphics read faster and answered more questions correctly than those who did not have graphics. The second experiment changed the information presentation to the moving window method, in which only one word or phrase is exposed at a time. Results mirrored those of the first experiment, with the picture group outperforming the no-picture group. These findings indicate that graphics do aid in the comprehension of text and the resolution of anaphors.

Mousavi, Low and Sweller (1995) examined the effects of different modality and representation forms on geometry-problem solving. In the first and second experiments, subjects received geometry problem statements and graphics concurrently by one of three methods: (a) multiple-mixed modality with mixed representation form (text – visual/verbal, narration – auditory/verbal, and picture – visual/nonverbal); (b) same modality with different representation form (text – visual/verbal and picture – visual/nonverbal); and, (c) mixed modality with mixed representation form (narration– auditory/verbal and picture –visual/nonverbal). The group receiving mixed modality with mixed representation form was significantly superior to the others in problem completion time, but was not different on the number of unsolved problems. For the third and fourth experiment, subjects were given the information by one of four methods: (a) same modality with different representation form (text and picture) concurrently;

(b) mixed modality with different representation form (narration and picture) concurrently; (c) same modality with different representation form (text then picture) serially; and, (d) mixed modality with different representation form (narration then picture) serially. The results showed the main effect of modality on time required to solve the problems, with those subjects who received information in a mixed modality (with different representation form) superior to the same modality groups regardless of presentation order. Again, the number of unsolved problems was not different. The final two experiments served to clarify the mixed-modality effect by accounting for other factors that may alter the subject's cognitive load. Results from all experiments provided evidence that mixing the modality of presentation leads to faster problem solving, though not necessarily to improved problem solving.

Theoretical Support. The theoretical support for this principle comes from both applied and theoretical researchers. From the perspective of human factors psychology, Wickens (1992) proposed a multiple resource theory of attention. This theory states that there are certain cognitive resources available for information processing, and these resources vary along three dimensions: processing-code (verbal or spatial), perception modality (auditory or visual), and processing-stage (early or later). According to this theory, the heightened performance effects with mixed-modality and mixed- representation forms are due to the effective use of different resources for processing information. Information processing is maximized when it consumes resources of different dimensions and diminished when it consumes resources from the same dimension because the cognitive resource capacity for processing information in each dimension is limited.

From a cognitive psychological perspective, Paivio (1986) proposed a dual-coding theory which states that there are two theoretically distinct symbol systems (verbal and nonverbal) in memory, containing mental representations that preserve properties of perceived information. The verbal system deals directly with linguistic input and output, while also serving a symbolic function with respect to nonverbal objects, events and behaviors. The nonverbal system acts upon modality-specific images for shapes, sounds, actions, skeletal/visceral sensations, and other nonlinguistic information. These representations are perceptually similar to the objects and events that they denote. Connections can be formed between semantically–related or similar representations in these two systems, as well as within the systems. The system connections allow for the naming of graphics or the imagining of text. Therefore, presentation in a mixed modality and representation form is optimal due to the facilitative effects of the cognitive connections between verbal and nonverbal information and the complementary or reinforcing effects of verbal information for nonverbal information and vise versa. [For more information on mental models see chapters by Seel et al., Achtenhagen and Alessi.]

Principle II

The integration of information both physically and temporally is optimal, though temporally preceding verbal information with pictorial can also be effective.

Empirical Findings. Many studies suggest that verbal and visual information presented contiguously in time and/or space improves learning and performance over non-contiguous presentation (Bagget, 1984; Chandler & Sweller, 1992; Glenberg & Kruley, 1992; Mayer & Anderson, 1991, 1992; Mayer & Sims, 1994; Mayer, Steinhoff, Bower, & Mars, 1995; Mousavi, Low & Sweller, 1995). The importance of physical and temporal contiguity in multimedia presentation has been investigated using a variety of tasks: recalling concrete elements and factual information (Bagget, 1984; Verdi. Peterson, Webb, Stock & Kulhavy, 1993; Stock, Kulhavy, Webb, Pridemore, & Verdi, 1993), solving physics or mechanical problems (Mayer & Anderson, 1991, 1992; Mayer & Sims, 1994; Mayer, Steinhoff, Bower, & Mars, 1995), and comprehending technical documents (Chandler & Sweller, 1992).

Bagget (1984) examined the creation of associations between narration and graphical information using a lecture-oriented film that introduced the pieces of an assembly kit with voice-over. Subjects were divided into seven groups according to the presentation order of the information formats: narration before picture by either 21, 14 or 7 seconds; narration and picture simultaneously; and picture before narration by either 21, 14, or 7 seconds. Retention was assessed immediately and after one week by a cued-recall task in which the subject provided a verbal label to the items shown in the graphics. For the immediate test, the groups which saw the picture 7 seconds before the narration and simultaneously with the narration outperformed all other groups. The same two groups showed the best performance on the delayed retention test. The performance differences were most salient between the subjects who saw the picture before the narration and those who heard the narration before the picture. These results suggest that the optimal presentation for graphics and narration is either graphics concurrently with, or slightly before narration.

Studies by Stock and associates (Verdi, Peterson, Webb, Stock, & Kulhavy, 1993; Stock, Kulhavy, Webb, Pridemore, & Verdi, 1993) suggest that when presenting verbal and graphical information serially, the graphical should precede the verbal. In the Stock experiment (Stock et al., 1993), subjects studied a geographical text and maps presented in different orders. Subjects who studied the map before the text recalled significantly more geographical facts about regions on the map and were more accurate in a map reconstruction task. In the Verdi experiment (Verdi et al., 1993), the authors attempted to clarify whether the presentation-order effect shown in the previous study was a result of the information format (verbal vs. nonverbal) or the semantic characteristics of the information (verbal information that describes spatial relationships vs. graphical information that directly represents relationships). Subjects studied a carefully-normed verbal description of a geographical region (intended to be the equivalent of a map) and facts about the region. No differences were found between presentation orders on either task. This result supports the contention that the presentation order effect (shown by Stock et al., 1993) must have been due to the interaction of the presentation order with the information format rather than with the semantic characteristics. These studies show that graphical-before-verbal presentation can be instructionally effective due to differential processing of graphical and verbal information in memory.

Mayer and Anderson (1991) investigated the effects of temporal contiguity within Paivio's (1986) dual-coding theory in the learning of mechanical device models. In the first experiment, subjects saw an explanative animation of a bicycle pump either concurrently with or after listening to an explanative narration. Subjects were required to complete a creative problem-solving task following the learning phase. Those who saw the animation concurrently with the narration gave significantly more correct solutions than those who saw it serially after the narration. The second experiment was divided into two parts, with part "a" replicating the first study, but with the addition of a recall measure. Part "b" compared the performance of the concurrent group with three new groups: narration only, animation only, and a no stimuli (control) group. On part "a", results again showed the same pattern for the concurrent and serial groups on the problem solving, but there were no significant differences in the recall of information. On part "b", the concurrent group outperformed all other groups on problem solving, but not the narration-only group on the recall test.

Mayer and Anderson (1992) again investigated temporal contiguity within Paivio's dual-coding theory with the addition of 8 new groups which were based upon the order of presentation of animation (A) and narration (N): concurrent (A+N, A+N, A+N), four versions of serial (ANANAN, NANANA, AAANNN, and NNNAAA), animation only (AAA), narration only (NNN) and a control group. All groups completed a recall test and a problem solving task following the learning phase. The concurrent group outperformed all others on the problem solving task, but did not differ from any other group except the control on the recall task. The same pattern of results was found in the second experiment with the same groups but a different learning task (brakes instead of a pump).

Mayer and Sims (1994) investigated the interaction effects between presentation order of animation and narration and an individual-difference variable (spatial ability). The results showed the superiority of concurrent presentation over serial presentation again, but only for subjects with high spatial ability. For low spatial ability subjects, the main effect of presentation order was not significant. The authors found similar results when they changed the learning task to the human respiratory system, with the exception of the low spatial-ability control group performing worse than the concurrent and serial low spatial-ability groups. These results suggest that differences in the presentation order of verbal and spatial information do not affect learning to a large degree when the subject has low spatial ability.

Mayer, Steinhoff, Bower, and Mars (1995) investigated the effect of physical contiguity in the presentation of text and graphics. A passage explaining the formation of lightning was presented with either a picture accompanied on the same page with appropriate annotations, or a picture presented on a different page without annotations. Subjects who studied the integrated materials generated 50% more creative solutions than those who studied non-integrated materials. They also noted that the effect of physical integration was greatest for those students with low meteorological experience. These results suggest that physical integration facilitates learning.

Chandler and Sweller (1992) examined the comprehension of a technical document (numerical control machine programming) as a function of the integration of text and applicable diagrams. Subjects were trained with either an integrated or the conventional nonintegrated manual, and then completed a ten-item test which covered the important materials in the manual. Results showed that the integrated group outperformed the nonintegrated group. In the second experiment, Chandler and Sweller (1992) utilized empirical articles from psychology journals that had either integrated or separate text and diagrams. They found that those subjects who read the integrated article were able to answer more comprehension questions correctly than those who studied the separate article. These results suggest that physical integration of graphical and verbal information is preferable to nonintegrated information, verbal or graphical.

Theoretical Support. Many of the applied and cognitive psychological positions explain the first part of the principle, but no theory clearly supports the second part of the principle that preceding verbal information with pictorial is as effective as or can be more effective than the concurrent presentation of verbal and pictorial information. Paivio's (1986) dual-coding theory suggests that when multimedia information is presented in a physically and/or temporally integrated form, it increases the number of referential connections between verbal and graphical information and produces better information processing. But according to Pavio's theory, non-contiguous presentation, including graphical-before-verbal, may result in the reduction of referential connections (Asp, 1979) and should not be as effective as concurrent presentation.

Wicken's (1992) theory posits that physically and/or temporally integrated text and graphical information could be processed effectively, though not as well as narration plus graphical information. Other work by Wickens (Wickens, 1992; Carswell & Wickens, 1987) on the proximity compatibility principle in system design has specifically suggested that related information must be temporally and spatially integrated to maximize performance. Therefore, it too does not explain why graphical-before-verbal presentation can be beneficial.

Bagget's (1984) "bushy and skimpy" theory provides a somewhat suitable explanation as to why graphical information can precede verbal information and still produce effective information processing. She suggested that graphical information is "bushy", or can become associated with a great deal of other information, whereas verbal information is "skimpy". According to her study, the number of learning-appropriate connections is greatest when graphical information precedes verbal information by several seconds. However, Bagget's theory does not consider the effect of physical integration and provides only a partial explanation for the study results supporting the above principle.

Principle III

The pace, continuity, and complexity of information presentation must be adjusted according to student cognitive ability and task characteristics.

Empirical Findings. The pace, continuity and complexity of information presentation have not been well-studied in multimedia research. However, some empirical and anecdotal evidence suggests that all three aspects of presentation are important for learning. Mayer, Bove, Bryman, Mars, and Tapangco (1996) conducted a series of experiments to examine the learning effects of information complexity with materials describing the eight steps of lightning formation. Subjects were shown either a series of graphics with concise summary captions, a series of graphics with concise summary captions plus a full explanatory text, or the full explanatory text only. Those who saw the graphics with concise summary captions recalled more of the eight steps of lightning formation than the other groups. They also solved more creative transfer problems than those who received the full explanatory text only, although they solved the same number of problems as those who received the graphics with concise summary captions plus the full explanatory text. These results suggest that greater complexity, represented by the detailed explanations given in the full explanatory text, can be an impediment to learning and problem solving.

Pace is defined as the amount of information presented per unit of time. Wright, Huston, Ross, Calvert, Tolandelli, Weeks, Raeissi, and Potts (1984) defined pace as the rate of scene and character change, and they varied it along with continuity in their study. Low continuity programs contained several scenes that were independent of one another, whereas high continuity programs showed only connected scenes (as in a story). Their results showed that slow-paced/high continuity programs were more effective than other programs in promoting the recall of information from the video. Although this experiment did not include complexity as a variable, it would likely have an impact on both pace and continuity.

The relationship between complexity of material and presentation pace should be inverse if other conditions remain equal (i.e., if the information is more complex, the presentation pace should be slower), whereas the relationship between complexity and continuity should be monotonic (i.e., if the information is more complex, it should be more connected). If these values are mismatched, subjects may be either overwhelmed by information, or under-whelmed and bored. Perhaps the mismatched interaction between these variables is a possible cause of the instructional ineffectiveness of some hypermedia programs (Carmel, Crawford & Chen, 1992). Combinations of these variables in specific ways seem to mirror some of the browsing strategies outlined by Carmel, Crawford and Chen (1992). For instance, their "scan-browsing" strategy is similar to Wright et al. (1984) low continuity/fast pace, and, in these two studies (Carmel et al., 1992; Wright et al., 1984), subjects learned very little from their respective instructional programs. It is unclear as to why there is a lack of systematic research on the interaction between all the three variables (i.e., complexity, continuity, and pace), especially with the explosive growth of computer-mediated instruction.

Theoretical Support. The theoretical support of this principle is not as systematic as for other principles due to the lack of empirical findings. Baddeley's (1992) theory of working memory provides a suitable explanation with his insistence that there is a short-term storage characterized by a tripartite system: a central executive and two subsidiary components, the articulatory/phonological loop and the visuospatial sketchpad. The central executive functions like an attentional system that is responsible for delegating or differentiating information processing resources and directing the activities of the subsystems. The articulatory/phonological loop consists of two sub-components that represent and process verbal information: phonological storage and articulatory rehearsal processes. The phonological storage process codes incoming verbal information by sounds or articulatory properties before storage. The articulatory rehearsal process re-codes information presented visually into a phonological representation by way of a mechanism similar to sub-vocal speech. The visuospatial sketchpad basically represents and processes information in an analog spatial form, typical of mental imagery.

Braddeley's (1992) theory of working memory suggests that information processing is least effective when the presentation pace is fast, continuity is low, and complexity is high. In such a situation, information contents are disjointed and working memory capacity is easily exceeded. However, information presented with a slow pace, high continuity, and reasonable complexity can be processed effectively because working memory is not overloaded. According to Bradeley, a slow pace and high continuity can permit a higher degree of complexity, and a reasonable level of complexity maintains a high level of student interest without excruciating detail.

Principle IV:

Information presented in verbal and graphical formats should match in terms of representing proposition-specific and relational information.

Empirical Findings. Proposition-specific information describes or concretizes a particular concept or idea. For example, a proposition-specific sentence about glaciers may state that the walls of Himilayan glaciers can vary in thickness from 600 to 1000 feet (Waddill & McDaniel, 1992). Relational information organizes and/or connects concepts or ideas. For example, a relational sentence about Himilayan glaciers may state that the plasticity of the ice allows glaciers to grow to a thickness of as much as 1000 feet Relational information is often in the form of either causal or contrastive relationships (Waddill & McDaniel, 1992).

The matching of information elements presented in different formats along the proposition-specific/relational dimension seems to play a major role in comprehension (Waddill, McDaniel, & Einstein, 1988; Waddill & McDaniel, 1992; Mayer & Gallini, 1990). The distinction between proposition-specific and relational material may also shed light upon the problem of when animation, as opposed to static images, is the most useful graphical presentation format (Park & Hopkins, 1993). Waddill and associates (1988, 1992) proposed that narrative (i.e., story-like, with no reference to modality) and expository (i.e., explanatory statement-like) texts are processed and remembered somewhat differently, with subjects accumulating much more relational information from narrative texts and proposition-specific information than from expository. Waddill, McDaniel, & Einstein (1988) investigated the effect of graphics representing either relational or proposition-specific information upon the comprehension of a text about either a fairy tale or a mountain range. Results suggested that graphics effectively increased recall only when the picture matched the text on the proposition-specific relational dimension, no matter what the subject matter. A second experiment showed that specific instructions to attend to certain types of information increased recall of that information, but the congruency effect of the picture and text remained the same.

Waddill and McDaniel (1992) examined the effects of proposition-specific and relational graphics on the recall of text that was specifically created so as to convey proposition-specific or relational information. They again found that the subjects who read passages with graphics that focused upon proposition-specific details recalled significantly more of the details than the control or relational groups, whereas the subjects who read passages with graphics that focused upon relations between concepts recalled more relational information than the control or proposition-specific groups. The control group performed as well as the proposition-specific picture group on the questions of relational information, and as well as the relational-picture group on the questions of proposition-specific information. All groups recalled equal amounts of non-target information. The results of both studies suggest that the combination of graphical information and text produces greater recall than that of text alone, though this effect is mediated by the relationship between the two types of information.

Mayer and Gallini (1990) also studied the proposition-specific/relational information, although they used different terminology. In three experiments, students learned about automobile brakes, bicycle pumps, and electric generators using a device model. In each experiment, subjects read explanative passages that were accompanied by either explanative illustrations (proposition-specific information), non-explanative illustrations (relational information), both types, or no illustration. Among low-prior knowledge subjects in the first experiment, the group that received both types of illustrations recalled the most integrated conceptual information, and out-performed all other groups on a problem-solving task. Additionally, all groups performed similarly on the recall of proposition-specific information and a recognition test. Among high-prior knowledge subjects, no differences were found on any of the measures. The second and third experiments replicated the first using different knowledge domains.

Theoretical Support. Paivio's (1986) dual-coding theory explains why the proposition-specific/relational match between graphical and textual information is important. Due to the spreading activation that is characteristic of associative networks, information which does match along that dimension is more likely to create more referential connections between the verbal and nonverbal memory systems than information which does not match. Bagget's (1984) "bushy and skimpy" theory also suggests that semantic connections between different types of information in memory increase as the nature of the information becomes semantically closer. Bushy graphics are more likely to form multiple associations with verbal information if they both are on the same semantic level.

Principle	Short Elaboration
I. Combine information types	Combining information types that vary by modality, representational forms, or both is more effective than a non-combined information type.
II. Integrate physically and temporally	Integrating information physically and temporally is optimal.
III. Adjust to student ability and characteristics	The pace, continuity, and complexity of information presentation must be adjusted according to student cognitive ability and task characteristics.
IV. Make verbal and graphical formats consonant	Information presented in verbal and graphical formats should match in terms of representing proposition-specific and relational information.

Table 1.Summary of key principles.

LIMITATIONS OF THE PRINCIPLES

The proposed principles are limited because the optimal value of the variables involved in the principles can vary widely depending upon individual differences. Studies have shown that spatial ability (Mayer & Sims, 1994), information coordination ability (Yee, Hunt, & Pellegrino, 1991), and prior domain knowledge (Mayer & Gallini, 1990) all modify to some extent the principles proposed above. For example, subjects with poor spatial ability will not be able to utilize graphical information to the same degree as those with good spatial ability. Those with poor coordination ability may not be able to advance through information at the same pace as others, and may have trouble coordinating information which is functionally integral for most people. For subjects who have had much experience in a domain, many of the variable parameters do not seem to have as much influence upon performance. Without sufficient complexity though, advanced subjects could easily become complacent in a learning situation and therefore neglect new information.

Unfortunately, the influence of individual differences is difficult to assess and incorporate into the design of information presentation and instruction (Cronbach & Snow, 1977; Jonassen & Grabowski, 1993; Gagné, 1967). Park (1997) shows that adaptive instruction requires a different design approach from non-adaptive, uniform instruction and is difficult to implement. The design and implementation of adaptive instruction becomes more sophisticated and complex as more individual-difference variables (e.g., ability, prior knowledge, motivation, etc.) and instructional variables (including multimedia components) are taken into account.

However, four principles proposed in this paper provide guidelines for designing basic instructional strategies for the presentation of multi-media information, regardless of whether or not the instructional situation requires adapting the instructional process to individual students' learning needs. Once the basic strategies are designed on the basis of these principles, specific procedures for accommodating various types of individual differences and other instructional variables (e.g., subject domain characteristics, instructional delivery systems, and other situational factors) can be integrated in the application of the principles.

REFERENCES

Asp, S. (1979, April). *How does the mode of presentation affect story comprehension?* Paper presented at the Annual Meeting of the American Educational Research Association, San Francisco, CA.

Baddeley, A. D. (1992). Working memory. *Science, 255,* 556-559

Bagget, P. (1984). Role of temporal overlap of visual and auditory material in forming dual media associations. *Journal of Educational Psychology,* 7-6, 408-417.

Carmel, E., Crawford, S., & and Chen, H. (1992). Browsing in hypertext: A cognitive study. *IEEE Transactions on Systems, Man & Cybernetics, 22(5),* 865-884.

Carswell, C. M., & Wickens, C. D. (1987). Information integration and the object display: An interaction of task demands and display superiority. *Ergonomics, 30,* 511-527.

Chandler, P., & Sweller, J. (1992). The split-attention effect as a factor in the design of instruction. *British Journal of Educational Psychology, 62,* 233-246.

Cronbach, L. J., & Snow, R. E. (1977). *Aptitudes and Instructional Methods: A handbook for research on interactions.* New York: Irvingston.

Dean, R. S., Garabedian, A. A., & Yekovich, F. R. (1983). The effect of modality shifts on proactive interference in long-term memory. *Contemporary Educational Psychology, 8,* 28-45.

Gagné, R. M. (1967). *Learning and Individual differnences.* Columbus, OH: Merrill.

Glenburg, A. M., & Kruley, P. (1992). Pictures and anaphora: Evidence for independent processes. *Memory & Cognition, 20,* 461-471.

Ishi, H., & Yamauchi, H. (1994). A study of cognitive loading in dual-coding theory. *Perceptual and Motor Skills, 79,* 458.

Jonassen, D. H. & Grabowski, B. (1993). *Handbook of Individual Differences, Learning and Instruction.* Hillsdale, NJ: Erlbaum.

Kobus, D. A., Moses, J. D., & Bloom, F. A. (1994). Effect of multi-modal stimulus presentation on recall. *Perceptual and Motor Skills, 78,* 320-322.

Kruley, P., Sciama, S. C., & Glenburg, A. M. (1994). On-line processing of textual illustrations in the visuospatial sketchpad: Evidence from dual-task studies. *Memory & Cognition, 22,* 261-272.

Lewandowski, L. J., & Kobus, D. A. (1993). The effects of redundancy in bimodal word processing. *Human Performance, 6,* 229-239.

Mayer, R., & Anderson, R. (1991). Animations need notations: An experimental test of a dual-coding hypothesis. *Journal of Educational Psychology, 83,* 484-490.

Mayer, R., & Anderson, R. (1992). The instructive animation: Helping students build connections between words and pictures in multimedia learning. *Journal of Educational Psychology, 84,* 444-452.

Mayer, R., Bover, W., Bryman, A., Mars, R., & Tapangco, L. (1996). When less is more: Meaningful learning from visual and verbal summaries of science textbook lessons. *Journal of Educational Psychology*, 88, 64-73.

Mayer, R., & Gallini, J. (1990). When is an illustration worth ten thousand words. *Journal of Educational Psychology*, 82, 715-726.

Mayer, R., & Sims, V. K. (1994). For whom is a picture worth a thousand words? Extension of a dual-coding theory of multimedia learning. *Journal of Educational Psychology*, 86, 3 89-40 1.

Mayer, R. E., Steinhoff, K., Bower, G., & Mars, R. (1995). A generative theory of textbook design: Using annotated illustrations to foster meaningful learning of science text. *Educational Technology Research and Development*, 43, 31-43.

Mousavi, S. Y., Low, R., & Sweller, J. (1995). Reducing cognitive load by mixing auditory and visual presentation modes. *Journal of Educational Psychology*, 87, 319-334.

Paivio, A. (1986). *Mental representations: A dual-coding approach*. New York: Oxford University Press.

Park, I., & Hannafin, M. J. (1993). Empirically-based guidelines for the design of interactive multimedia. *Educational Technology Research and Development*, 41, 63-85.

Park, O. (1997). Adaptive instructional systems. In D. H. Jonassen (Ed.), *Handbook of research on educational technology and communication.* Academic Press.

Park, O. & Hopkins, R. (1993). Instructional conditions for using dynamic visual displays: A review. *Instructional Science,* 21, 427-449.

Snodgrass, J. G., & Vanderwart, M. (1980). A standardized set of 260 pictures: norms for naming agreement, familiarity, and visual complexity. *Journal of Experimental Psychology: Learning, Memory and Cognition,* 6, 174-215.

Stock, W. A., Kulhavy, R. W., Webb, J. M., Pridemore, D. R., & Verdi, MP. (1993, April). *Map and text learning: The privilege of economical representation.* Paper presented at the Annual Meeting of the American Psychological Society, Arpil 19093, Chicago, IL.

Sweller, J. (1988). Cognitive load during problem solving: Effects on learning. *Cognitive Science*, 12, 257-285.

Sweller, J. (1989). Cognitive technology: Some procedures for facilitating learning and problem solving in mathematics and science. *Journal of Educational Psychology*, 81, 457-466.

Sweller, J. (1993). Some cognitive processes and their consequences for the organization and presentation of information. *Australian Journal of Psychology*, 45, 1-8.

Sweller, J. (1994). Cognitive load theory, learning difficulty and instructional design. *Learning and Instruction*, 4, 295-312.

Verdi, M. P., Peterson, S. E., Webb, J. M., Stock, W. A., & Kulhavy, R. W. (1993, April). *Creating maps from perceptual and verbal stimuli: Retrieving text and recreating maps.* Paper presented at the Annual Meeting of the American Educational Research Association, April 1993, Atlanta, GA.

Waddill, P. J., McDaniel, M. A. (1992). Pictorial enhancement of text memory: Limitations imposed by picture type and comprehension skill. *Memory and Cognition, 20,* 472-482.

Waddill, P. J., McDaniel, M. A., & Einstein, G. O. (1988). Illustrations as adjuncts to prose: A test-appropriate processing approach. *Journal of Educational Psychology*, 80, 457-464.

Wickens, C.D. (1992). *Engineering Psychology and Human Performance.* New York: Harper Collins Publishers, Inc.

Wright, J. C., Huston, A. C., Ross, R. P., Calvert, S. L., Rolandelli, D., Weeks, L. A., Raeissi, P., & Potts (1984). Pace and continuity of television programs: Effects on children's attention and comprehension. *Developmental Psychology, 20*, 653-666.

Yee, P. L., Hunt, E. B., & Pellegrino, J. W. (1991). Coordinating cognitive information: task effects and individual differences in integrating information from several sources. *Cognitive Psychology*, 23, 615-680.

SANNE DIJKSTRA

Chapter 12

EPISTEMOLOGY, PSYCHOLOGY OF LEARNING AND INSTRUCTIONAL DESIGN

Keywords: concept learning, categorization, image schemas, instructional design, experientialism, knowledge acquisition, naturalistic epistemology, problem solving

Abstract. This chapter addresses the implications of epistemology and the psychology of problem solving and learning for the design of instruction. First, renewed interest in experientialism, influenced by studies of basic-level concepts, is discussed. Second, the relationship between naturalistic epistemology and the psychology of problem solving and learning is outlined. Third, the implications for the design of instruction are clarified. The chapter makes clear that the connection from epistemology to problem solving and learning ("psychology") and instructional design is not a matter of simple applications of "assumption" to "process" to "intervention." The chapter concludes with a few remarks on learning environments, developmental education, and evaluation.

EPISTEMOLOGY AND THE DESIGN OF INSTRUCTION

During the last fifteen years, the meaning of epistemology and implications for the design of instruction have been studied and discussed (see, for example Jonassen, 1992, and also the chapters by Jonassen et al. and Goodyear in this volume). There has been renewed interest in genetic and naturalistic epistemology and in the use of these ideas for the education of the child. (Piaget, 1970; Von Glasersfeld, 1996). Lakoff (1987) reviewed many studies of concept learning, the conclusions of which he used to answer fundamental questions such as: What is reason and what is knowledge? What is a conceptual knowledge system and how do human beings develop and change their knowledge? What is the function of perception and interaction with the real world in the development of knowledge? These answers have a number of features, based on which Lakoff distinguished two categories of answers, which he labeled experientialism or experiential realism and objectivism. From these two large categories, Lakoff developed a preference for the first category of answers (experientialism) as especially relevant to developmental learning. Jonassen (1992) followed Lakoff and related the epistemological issues to

J.M. Spector and T.M. Anderson (eds.),
Integrated and Holistic Perspectives on Learning, Instruction and Technology, 213–232.
© 2000 *Kluwer Academic Publishers. Printed in the Netherlands.*

the design of instruction. Instead of experientialism he used the label constructivism.

Piaget (1937, 1970) supposed that the growing intelligence of young children involved constructing images of the world around them; that is to say, more or less stable conceptions of objects are developed from experience with objects. Piaget further supposed that knowledge is a process. Knowledge is the adaptation of thought to reality and reflects interactions between knowing subjects and objects. Because of a process of continuing adaptation, this means that the result of knowledge development, once it can be expressed in verbal terms, is subject to change and is often only temporarily valid from the perspective of the child as well as from the perspective of others.

Drawing especially from studies by Rosch (1978) on concept learning, Lakoff (1987) summarizes the main features of human thought and knowledge which characterize experientialism as follows:

- dependence on physical experience;
- employment of imagery and metaphor to represent external reality;
- use of gestalt properties, such as the general shape and appearance of objects; and,
- dependence on the overall structure of the conceptual system (ecological structure).

After Lakoff (1987) gave an overview of the main assumptions of both experientialism and objectivism, he described their common assumptions as follows:

- the acceptance of the existence of a real world, both external to human beings and including the existence of human experience;
- a certain correspondence between aspects of reality and human conceptual systems;
- the assumption that some conceptual systems give a better "coverage" of reality than others; and,
- the belief that knowledge is relatively stable, at least for some period of time.

These assumptions are general and abstract. Much emphasis is given to the perception of reality, experience, mental imagery and categorization. The identification of the set of common assumptions suggests that the recent polarizing debates between so-called constructivists and objectivists are somewhat over-done, and that radical extremes on both sides are ruled out of the mainstream discussion. Radical constructivists who stress only individual perception and end up with a purely subjectivist and individualistic interpretation are led to solipsism and do not reflect the intention or beliefs of the founders and leaders of that theoretical perspective. Likewise, those radical objectivists who stress only external realities and completely disregard individual differences in perception and knowledge construction do not reflect the intention or beliefs of the founders and leaders of that theoretical perspective. Both sets of assumptions, those that are common and those that prevail in experientialism will be elaborated in the next section.

EXPERIENCE, IMAGERY AND CATEGORIZATION OF OBJECTS

Human beings experience reality by perceiving and by manipulating it. These processes, which are directly observable soon after the child is born, are necessary for the development of the conceptions of objects ("things") and space (Piaget, 1937). The interpretation of these processes (perception, manipulation of objects, etc.) and their results (beliefs, creation of artifacts, etc.) are of importance for the help and guidance that is given to the child, although some parents and teachers are unable to make these matters explicit. The first sentence in Piaget's (1937) book reads:

> "La première question qu'il vienne de se poser, pour comprendre comment l'intelligence naissante construit le monde extérieur, est de savoir si, durant les premiers mois, l'enfant conçoit et perçoit les choses, commes nous le faisons nous-mêmes, sous formes d'objets substantiels, permanentes et de dimensions constantes" (p. 9).

This can be roughly translated as follows: "The first question that one must pose in order to understand how the developing intelligence of a child constructs the external world is to know how a child, during the first few months, conceives and perceives things, as we do ourselves, in the form of substantial objects that are persistent and that have constant dimensions." The sentence shows that Piaget supposed that the mind constructs the external world and that during the first months of life the child develops a conception of "things" as substantial and permanent objects with constant dimensions.

In the first years of the child's life, concrete objects are isolated. The availability and the possibility to act and play with these objects is especially important. With the development of language, children become able to denote these concrete objects and possible actions with them. In subsequent years of development, the concept of "thing" remains central. The label 'thing' here is used broadly to include objects, entities, events, and situations. Two processes are critically important: imagination and categorization of things.

Image Schemas and Imagination

Based on their shape and function, some objects can easily be distinguished and categorized, such as chair and table, cow and horse, crow and butterfly, rose and tulip. In her research on categorization, Rosch (1978) labeled the categories to which these objects belong as the basic-level categories. The objects in these categories are isolated in interactions with the external environment, gestalt perceptions and motor movements. At the basic level, children, and human beings in general, can easily distinguish discontinuities in the external world and form images of basic-level objects. Lakoff (1987) argued that at the basic level our experience becomes pre-conceptually structured. Human beings "have general capacities for dealing with part-whole structure in real world objects via gestalt perception, motor movement and the formation of rich mental images." (p. 270). Before any concept is formed basic experiential structures are available. These are labeled kinesthetic image schemas, such as the "container" schema, the "part-whole" schema, the "source-path-goal" schema.

These and other schemas develop from physical experience, that is to say interaction with the external environment. These schemas make concepts meaningful: buses and trucks are vehicles, a tree has leaves, water flows into a bathtub, etc. These schemas are a necessary condition for understanding pictures of objects. Schemas are also used at about the age of four in fantasy stories, such as a tree as a "house" for animals. Later, from about the age of nine, children become able to relate a model (or sign) of an object to the real object. For example, a schematic layout of a classroom or a map of a town is related to the actual classroom or to the streets and houses in the actual town. Then a "mental" walk can be made by observing the map and using the "source-path-goal" schema. A few years later, children also start to imagine "abstract" objects such as artificial or imposed structures, such as the structure of longitude and latitude to describe a specific location on the earth. Also, sometimes with and sometimes without the help of adults, children imagine models of objects, such as molecules and atoms to describe the structure of matter. Children further become able to imagine and understand systems of objects, such as the solar system. While the components of such abstractions may be concrete objects, the systems themselves represent a kind of abstraction. The general assumption is that to understand information and problem-solving procedures, a human being relies first on basic-level, kinesthetic image schemas built up from interaction with basic-level objects. Later, when these schemas are no longer valid, the knowledge needs to be changed.

Categorization

The basic-level concepts correspond to the experiential, pre-conceptual structures and are formed first. They refer to the basic-level categories and objects within these categories, such as man and woman, table and chair, car and bus, house and church, and many others. Within a couple of years the child can point at them and give their names. Children develop mental images or mental prototypes of typical examples of objects in a category. From about nine years of age, concepts at other levels (subordinate and superordinate) are developed.

For this development to occur (effectively and efficiently), instructional guidance is necessary in order to help children to structure reality in such a way that it is more internally consistent (for purposes of individual meaning-making -- see Jonassen et al. in this volume) and also more externally consistent with the view of experts (for purposes of social sense-making -- see Goodyear's chapter). Objects or a representation of objects are encountered. Based on their features, they are described, and if they have certain recognized features, children and adults categorize the objects. The result of this process of categorization is the development or construction of a concept. This may be a cognitive construct; or, it may consist of conceptual knowledge comprised of mental images of objects; or, it may simply be thought of as the name of the objects in a category, the features of which are relevant for categorizing and making logical connections. Experiential schemas, such as the "container" and the "part-whole" schemas that develop from gestalt perception, physical experience, imagery and metaphors are crucial for conceptual development. These schemas are basic for the development of the meaning of concepts. During the child's development, the process of categorizing shows differences, but for most children this process reaches its final stages at the start of adolescence when concepts can be described formally. There are many ways to categorize objects depending on different needs and circumstances. Categories are basic to our thinking, perception and action. Presumably, knowledge of different relationships among objects and features of objects, interpretation of changes in objects and relationships, and the design and construction of new objects is only possible if appropriate conceptual knowledge has been developed.

This development process is often encountered when analyzing misconceptions, and it suggests a sequencing of instruction that acknowledges such development [see, for example, the chapters by Alessi and Spector in this volume]. To a certain point in the development of knowledge the schemas and metaphors are productive, but if they are unable to further support the development of knowledge they will hinder it (Bereiter, 1999). If manipulation of the reality and predictions of future events lead to new phenomena and to errors, the students can no longer rely on the schemas and their conceptions should be replaced by scientific knowledge. Asking the "right" instructional questions will lead to new observations and to change of existing conceptions.

IMPLICATIONS OF EPISTEMOLOGY FOR INSTRUCTIONAL DESIGN

Renewed interest in the nature of thought and knowledge found in naturalistically oriented epistemology and phenomenologically oriented psychology caused changes in the assumptions, models and rules for instructional design. Instructional systems design models were especially criticized (see Duffy & Jonassen, 1992, and Jonassen et al. and Goodyear in this volume). Designers were urged to develop "constructivistic learning environments," the features of which should include the following:

- acquisition of knowledge that is realized through active construction of knowledge objects;
- learning that is situated in a relevant and realistic context;
- alternative interpretations and a variety of possible meanings are provided;
- minimizing misconceptions using a variety of different contexts; and,
- learning that is fostered as a social process with feedback from teachers and peers, and cooperation among students.

These rules are widely accepted and will not elicit much opposition from designers and teachers. The problem with these rules, however, is that they are too general for designing usable instruction.

The general and abstract epistemological assumptions about thought and knowledge and the description of the processes of image schematizing and categorization reviewed earlier do have meaning for and should inform the design of instruction. However, those who are involved with education and training require an explicit technology (a process involving models and rules). Moreover, and especially significant as a result of emphasis on the construction of knowledge objects, both designers and teachers need models and rules to help guide students in developing hypotheses and theories and in solving their own design problems. It should be evident that this latter set of learning tasks and goals is much more challenging than more directive and confined learning tasks and goals. While a naturalistic epistemology certainly enriches our understanding of the world, it significantly complicates the design of meaningful instruction.

Now instructional designers need to know which features the design should show and how to develop appropriate instructional materials to support learning. The development of an instructional technology from naturalistic epistemological assumptions and from the perception of objects (description of relevant imagery and categorization) is not a simple "translation" from theory to practice. Before such a technology for the design of experientially-based instruction can be made explicit, attention has to be paid to such things as the following:

- the storage and availability of information and problem-solving methods;
- the use of these by students in education and training situations;
- the variety and nature of instructional communications;
- representations of reality in instructional settings; and,
- the integration of problem-solving situations in which new knowledge can be developed and skills can be practiced and automated.

INFORMATION AND PROBLEM-SOLVING METHODS

The exploration of the environment and the perception of objects with all our senses characterizes human behavior and our understanding of the world. This experiential orientation is crucial for successful adaptation to the environment and for survival. This experientially oriented way of behaving continues throughout our lifetimes. As a consequence, and as many others in this volume have argued, exploration and experiential understanding should be used in education and training whenever possible and in the best ways possible so as to promote and enhance a genuine sense of lifelong learning.

At a certain moment in the history of mankind, the need for exploring and understanding and for communicating those explorations and understandings led to a new development, namely, the possibility to represent objects in pictures and picture languages (Seel & Winn, 1997). Such representations were of tremendous social and scientific importance. From then on, human beings were able to discuss the "same" objects and construct shared meanings, which then became the fabric of society. In later centuries, written script (non-pictographic language) was developed and ways to reason evolved and were studied. Still later, during the Renaissance, systematic observation of objects and their changes led to conceptual knowledge and theories. Also, technologies for preparing food and shelter, for defense and for transport became part of human culture and society. Today, human beings make use of a substantial amount of information and procedures belonging to many cultures to solve problems. Information and problem-solving procedures are mainly stored in libraries, and continually extended by additional exploration, research and development. Because the amount is so huge, it is impossible for a person to acquire all this information and problem-solving methods as personal knowledge and skills. Thus, a selection must be made with regard to what is necessary to address in education for the acquisition of general and specific knowledge and skills. Earlier it was indicated that a key instructional design task involved sequencing of materials. This became more difficult due to the experiential perspective. It should now be obvious that the other major instructional design task, the selection of materials to support learning, has also become enormously more complicated due to the "information explosion." While the world of experience becomes richer and richer in terms of available information and knowledge, the world of instructional design becomes more and more complicated.

One of the results of scientific research and development projects is the publishing of new information and problem-solving methods. Each working day, 20,000 scientific publications are realized, and every five to seven years the content of the empirical sciences is changed almost entirely (Rüttgers, 1999). This means that our knowledge and skills should be adapted and updated regularly, and this is yet another challenge for those who would design instruction to support lifelong learning. At all levels of education and training, refresher courses are necessary to keep up with these developments, and this represents a new challenge for instructional designers.

Because the knowledge base in most domains is now so large, newcomers to a domain often require assistance in finding structure and relevant information. The structure of these distributed knowledge bases is partly determined by the structure and content of the subject matter - this is a remnant of truth from the objectivist heritage. The new challenge for education is to help students acquire an integrated body of knowledge and skills in a domain that can be deployed in subsequent school and work settings in meaningful and productive ways. For this general purpose it is necessary that students develop knowledge and skills from the manipulation of objects in such a way that they will understand how objects (entities, situations, events) are categorized and why they change, how to design new objects, and what the manipulation of the design means for the construction of these. These activities typically require coaching by an instructor or mentor.

Existing and new information and methods are the result of systematic interactions with reality, including explorations of phenomena, observations of features of objects, experiments to find regularities, and the design of associated objects and artifacts. These systematic activities can be collectively labeled problem solving, and the way interactions are accomplished constitute problem-solving methods or procedures. For the persons involved, these activities lead to the development of knowledge and skills and to improved understanding of reality. Many studies support this claim that problem solving fosters the development of new knowledge and methods (e.g., Anderson, 1982; Duncker, 1945; Polya, 1954). Obviously, results can be repeatedly used and improved, consistent with the spirit of the scientific method and much in line with recent emphasis in information science on the creation of reusable objects. Therefore, problem solving means learning, not as an isolated part of a learning process such as conditioning or configuring, but as an integrated and purposeful behavior that leads to better understanding and to new designs (Gagné & Merrill, 1990). The problems which result in new information and methods are grouped into three main types: (1) problems of categorization; (2) problems of interpretation; and, (3) problems of design (Dijkstra, 1997; Dijkstra & van Merriënboer, 1997). The problems and their relations are shown in Figure 1.

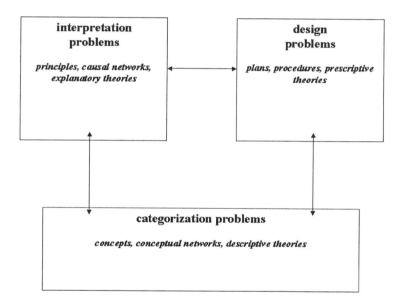

Figure 1. Three types of problems and their relationships

The result of solving a new problem is both knowledge and a problem-solving method. Different labels have been and are used for this result. The label knowledge is general. For the reflection on the reality and the construction of the cognitive content of this reflection the labels cognitive construct or declarative knowledge are used. For the problem-solving method the labels procedural knowledge or procedure are used. The latter can be either an algorithm or a heuristic dependent on the well- or ill-structuredness of the problem (Dijkstra, 1999).

Categorization Problems

In case of categorization or description problems, instances must be assigned to categories or relationships between entities have to be found. The knowledge resulting from this activity is labeled concepts, relationships, conceptual networks and descriptive systems. It is supposed that the content of the formal sciences (e.g., mathematics and programming languages) is included as descriptive knowledge and problem-solving methods.

Interpretation Problems

In case of solving an interpretation problem, the cognitive constructs are principles, causal networks and explanatory theories. The general method to solve such problems is to formulate an hypothesis about a supposed relationship between an independent and a dependent variable; make a prediction concerning what will happen in a specified situation after a certain time lapse; test the prediction, indicating whether it is confirmed or falsified, and, if relevant, specify the range of the probability of occurrence of a certain event. Explanatory theories predict changes of objects and relationships and lead to an understanding of the causal mechanisms involved. The content belongs to the empirical sciences (e.g., physics, neurology, psychology, etc.).

Design Problems

For solving design problems, an artifact must be imagined and a first sketch, outline or plan has to be created and made. Concepts and interpretations form the knowledge that is used to solve design problems. The cognitive constructs are the images of the artifact and the rules and criteria that have to be met in order to achieve a "good" design. If the design is accepted by those who requested it, then it can be realized. This means that it can be produced (a car), constructed (a house, a bridge), interpreted (a composition by an orchestra), developed (an instructional program) or implemented (an organizational structure). A design problem has different sub-problems which are dependent on the "life cycle" of the artifact: (1) the design; (2) the realization; (3) the use and maintenance; and, (4) archiving, restoring, discarding or recycling. Objects to be designed and realized should meet four different sets of conditions and criteria: (1) principles and rules of a "good" design, which means that pertinent laws and principles are adequately applied (e.g., a house should not come down, a car should be stable on the road, an instructional program should satisfy recognized principles of learning); (2) functional requirements - designs should be functional and objects should fulfill human needs; (3) esthetic concerns - the artistic value of a design should satisfy the tastes and preferences of a group of people that often will vary over time; and, (4) financial constraints - the financial means that are available should be used efficiently.

Subcategories

The problems of the three main categories can be further distinguished into subcategories, based on the degree of well- and ill-structuredness, complexity, generality and abstractness. A well-structured problem is a problem the solution of which can only be right or wrong, whereas the solution of an ill-structured problem can only be better or worse. The degree of complexity of a problem is related to the amount of knowledge involved and to the number of operations required for the solution. The degree of generality is related to all objects of a category or taxonomy of categories, whereas the degree of abstractness means considering objects and their relationships looking away from their empirical existence (see Dijkstra & van Merriënboer, 1997, and the chapters by Jonassen et al. and Spector in this volume for additional details on these subcategories).

What should instructional designers do with this knowledge about problem solving and types of problems? All this knowledge is supposed to be basic for an instructional design theory and for a problem-based instructional design model. As already argued, theories of knowledge and relevant methods and principles specific to particular subject domains are of general importance for the design of instruction, but they are not specific enough for that job. It is necessary to adapt instruction to the way human beings solve problems if we are to expect instruction to lead efficiently to new knowledge and to the development and refinement of skills. Thus, the psychology of problem solving and learning has to be brought to bear in the design of instruction. In the following three sections this will be elaborated.

INSTRUCTIONAL COMMUNICATION

Instruction is one part of a communication between a teacher (tutor, mentor, instructional program, etc.) and a learner about objects in a reality and conceptions about those objects, such as how to categorize them, how they change and how to design them. The other part of the communication is the learner's reaction to the instruction such as giving answers, asking questions or performing a task. For education, the concept of "object" or "entity" is important and includes the following: (a) real objects such as pebbles, plants, houses, the moon; (b) "inferred" objects, such as atoms and molecules; and, (c) systems of objects, such as the solar system.

The goals of education formulated and accepted by governments and communities mostly determine which objects and which conceptions will become the focus of education. The executive boards and human resource divisions of industrial and other organizations formulate training goals for their personnel. In short, many educational goals are not determined by learners. Of course it is possible and even likely that students will formulate their own goals which may or may not align well with those of others. Nevertheless, students will ask for and require instructional communication. The goal of instructional communication is to help students acquire knowledge and learn skills for performing tasks. Instruction is an activity that is intended to support the development of knowledge and skills and this activity can be structured from very general to very specific guidance. The instructional part of a communication is an activity expressed in language, gestures, and opportunities for practice in environments and with objects that are designed for learning. In typical circumstances, the communication takes the form of an interaction between a teacher and a learner about the objects involved. In cooperative learning, the communication can be an interaction among members of a group of students about the objects involved. Instruction implies that students need to be coached to find the relevant features of objects and to learn how to operate on those features to produce a desired outcome.

In a problem-solving instructional sequence, students often need to find regularities in the change of objects in order to learn how to describe and understand those changes. Students require encouragement to continue a problem-solving process, especially when it is experienced as difficult. A well-established instructional principle is that students require feedback after they come up with a solution to a problem or with an object they have designed and produced. All students, regardless in which level of education – elementary, secondary or academic, are confronted with a huge amount of subject matter that has to be mastered as knowledge and skills. A teacher requires an answer to the question of how to design relevant instructional communications. Students require assistance in structuring problems and in understanding the content of the subject matter as knowledge and skills. Because instructional communication concerns objects in and ideas about reality, it is necessary for an instructional designer to have knowledge of how to represent this reality. For the representation of reality, media are necessary.

REALITY AND REPRESENTATIONS OF REALITY

Because the content of instruction is about objects in a reality, the teacher has to solve the problem whether to use real objects or a representation of those objects or both. The argument in favor of using the real objects is that students can perceive these with their senses, experience them directly, operate on them to learn how they behave and how they are used, and therefore more easily transfer learning outcomes outside the instructional context. It is clear, however, that real objects are not always available or appropriate. The reasons to use a representation of a reality include the following: (a) the objects are not (easily) perceivable or not available (e.g., bacteria, planets, historic monuments in a foreign country); (b) Necessary experiments to determine the structure of reality are inappropriate in an instructional setting (e.g., not every school has a particle accelerator at its disposal, so synthetic experiments in virtual environments can be constructed); (c) the duration of a process makes it inappropriate for an instructional context (e.g., an evolutionary process might be accelerated using a simulation); and, (d) using real objects involves a risk for damage and personal safety. When a representation of real objects is used, the teacher has to answer two questions. The first question is whether and how an object should be represented (picture, drawing, photograph, slide, transparency) or whether the change of an object or change of its position has to be shown (movie, time-lapse photography, animation, simulation). The second question is whether a demonstration model or a simulator has to be used. In the last case, the objects may be used in such a way that the risk of damage is minimized and/or experiments can be conducted artificially that would not otherwise be possible.

Medium and Multimedia

The development from pictograms and pictographic languages to script has changed the nature of instructional communications. Now objects (entities, things, events and situations) can be and are represented by signs; conceptions about objects and relationships are described using signs. Signs have become the basic medium to represent objects and ideas (Seel & Winn, 1997). Besides the development of signs, the technical development of information carriers is an important milestone in the use of media. The use of clay tablets, parchment and paper made instruction independent of time and place; many persons could use instructional messages. Industrial production of paper and the invention of the printing press made mass production of pictures and text possible. In the 19th and 20th century, other information carriers were developed, such as celluloid and silicon chips, making it possible to mass produce and distribute widely larger chunks and different kinds of information. In instructional programs, communications with students are anticipated and planned. However, no information carrier reaches the qualities of a conversation between a learner and a tutor or coach. Individual conversational styles and approaches have been tried in books, programmed instruction and computer-based instruction. Probably a conversational level of communication is best approximated in computer-based tele-coaching, but person-to-person modeling of problem solving and learning is likely to be required and useful in many instructional settings.

The label 'medium' is utilized in those cases in which the use of signs and the information carrier for the development of knowledge and skills involves only one human sense, for example vision. The most widely known example is the use of pictures (to represent objects) and text (to describe the conceptions about objects). The label 'multimedia' is used to describe teaching methods and learning materials that utilize different senses of a learner and not just one (Romiszowski, 1997). One might also distinguish the use of multiple media and multimedia, with the latter being the integration of multiple media in support of a specific goal.

Today, the use of multimedia is especially applied to the use of computers in education, because it is possible to digitally store all kinds of information, including auditory, textual, and visual - still and motion pictures. The digital revolution also made it possible to mix these representations for educational purposes. Moreover, because of the increased processing power of digital computers, the interactive use of multimedia presentations opens new possibilities for education. This fact combined with the connection of computers in global networks (the Internet) makes it possible to get fast access to different sources of information. As already suggested, this wealth of resources complicates the task of selecting and sequencing materials to support improvements in problem-solving capabilities.

A PROBLEM-BASED INSTRUCTIONAL DESIGN MODEL

The aforementioned studies of concept learning do show that the most rich knowledge human beings have is the knowledge of basic-level objects. This knowledge is a result of direct interactions with the world through perception with all the senses and through manipulation involving objects. These interactions provide learners answers to questions about the nature of objects, parts, and relationships. Humans rely on experiential image schemas and try to apply and use them when appropriate. Lakoff (1987) noted that observation technologies, such as microscopes and telescopes, are used to expand basic-level experience. When it is not possible to use direct or extended observation, photographs and then graphs and diagrams are useful. "The technological extension of basic-level perception and manipulation make us confident that science provides us with real knowledge" (p. 298). For the design of instruction, the availability and use of basic-level objects should be the point of departure upon which including other representation and media is founded. It is fundamental to instructional design to include perception and manipulation of real and represented objects in order to develop appropriate experiential schemas.

To design instruction that is directed to experiential learning, intended for the acquisition of usable knowledge and transferable skills, the following problem-based instructional design model, which has five general components, is proposed. The content of the components may differ from subject to subject. They have to be analyzed in further detail in such a way that sequences of design steps can be developed. Often special instructional-design knowledge for the subject involved is needed. The fourth component is elaborated in more detail consistent with the emphasis in this chapter and because it is generally the least well elaborated in the literature.

1. The designer should recognize the original problem situation, identifying which objects were used and how this situation was described to find a solution. If the problem situation contains several sub-problems, it should be analyzed to find the categories of problems involved. A plan (design) has to be made with regard to how instructional communications and activities will be made. A decision has to be made concerning how objects will be represented and manipulated.

2. For each type of problem, the designer should develop situations for experiential learning. That means the designer will describe problems that can be solved by the learners or a group of learners in order to develop the general knowledge and learn the problem-solving methods for that unit of instruction.

3. The designer should try to find a balance between tutorial and experiential activities. Key concerns and questions include the following: Which information should be given before questions are asked? Which examples should be given of a sequence of operations necessary to solve a category of problems? Is embedded refreshment of prerequisite knowledge useful? Will it be helpful to present supportive knowledge for making an analogy? Is collaboration with others a detractor or an accelerator for a particular learning situation?

4. For each category of problems, the experiential learning situation should be imagined and described, and a decision made whether to operate on reality or on a representation of reality. Considerations for each category are:

Categorization. For categorization problems, the objects to be categorized should be given to students or a portrayal of the objects or situations should be made available. Students have to find defining and characteristic features of objects and then categorize the objects. This form of learning is labeled concept learning where a concept is the knowledge used to categorize objects. The procedure to categorize is labeled the identification algorithm.

Interpretation. For interpretation problems, the learners should be stimulated to find regularities in a dependent variable after a hypothesis suggests how to manipulate an independent variable. The data will be analyzed by solving an equation to find the functional relationship or by finding a correlation between variables. Learners will discover dependencies and understand mechanisms that cause changes in objects. This type of learning is often labeled discovery learning.

Design. Helping learners solve design problems is probably the most challenging and complex task for instructional designers. In the first phase of the life cycle of an artifact, a plan or sketch of the object should be made. Learners are informed about the rules for a "good" design, and about functionality and esthetics. Students will imagine an artifact and make plans and sketches. Feedback from tutors is a necessary condition. For learning to construct an object – the second phase of the life cycle of an artifact, students create an object, for example, by making a painting, constructing a simple apparatus, writing a computer program, and so on. The realization of complex construction problems often involves several persons who have to cooperate. In some cases, the objects are realized by a group of persons that is composed of many skilled craftsmen who learn their skills in special team training programs (Van Berlo, 1999). For learning to use and maintain objects – the third phase in the life cycle of artifacts, it is also necessary to differentiate simple from complex situations. Complex problems include trouble shooting, air traffic control, navigating at sea, and leading an organization (Gott, Lesgold & Kane, 1997; van Merriënboer & Dijkstra, 1997). For learning about the final phase of a design problem, different questions have to be addressed in order to decide whether an object will be saved for a long period or should be discarded or recycled. To support learning how to make decisions about archiving and reuse, students can explore and critique relevant aspects of decisions and arguments (e.g., cost-benefit tradeoffs, volatility of information, etc.). The designer of instruction for design problem-solving tasks should analyze the problem into the four phases, each of which has subcategories of problems. Then, at the subcategory and sub-problem level, the designer should describe the knowledge and skills involved. The problem-solving method or task should be developed using an appropriate task analysis method (see Jonassen, Tessmer & Hannum, 1999, for example). Instructional methods for the acquisition of knowledge and practicing the skills have to be selected. These may involve practice in simulations, role playing, working with models of machines, and so on. Of course there will be a moment in which the real problem has to be solved, first during an internship, and later independently, in an ideal learning and development situation.

5.   After solving a number of problems from a certain category, the desired knowledge and skills should develop and new problems should then be attempted. If this activity meets the criteria that are defined in advance, the designer will make a decision that the knowledge and skills are developed and learned in such a way that a desired level of expertise is reached (e.g., as part of a confirmative evaluation).

CONCLUDING REMARKS

This chapter described how epistemological and psychological theories are applied for the design of instruction. However there is no direct "translation" from epistemological assumptions to the conception of problems that increase our knowledge and methods, and from there to application rules for the design and development of a "constructivist" learning environment. If the assumption that the growing human intelligence constructs the external world is true, then this is true in all situations into which human beings are brought and in which they bring themselves, such as their homes and home environment, their schools and classrooms, and the towns and museums they visit. These situations include those in which people are talking, listening and reading, wherever they happen to be. In all these situations, human beings are able to actively construct knowledge. In all situations knowledge construction is possible, regardless of whether that situation occurs in a room in which a lecture is given, in a library in which a book is read, or in a classroom in which students participate in a discussion, solve a math problem or work through a multimedia simulation. Of importance is what the students have to do in all these situations and whether these activities contribute to imagining the real objects, answering questions about their change and developing methods in such a way that new knowledge and skills can be developed and new objects designed. All environments can function as learning environments. When a learning environment is designed, it has to be evaluated with regard to whether it has the features that are valuable for the construction of desired knowledge and skills.

The choice for a problem-based instructional design model is made in order to provide optimal means to support the imagining, perception and manipulation of objects as well as the invention and production of objects. The choice is founded on assumptions about how human beings develop knowledge and skills, and it is based on the results of psychological studies of problem solving, thinking and learning. Problem solving situations make students work toward a new solution. This necessitates the development of new knowledge and methods. After sufficient practice, the use of a method develops into a skill. Generally speaking, instruction is an activity to support the development of knowledge and skills. For instructional designers and for teachers, this activity includes inventing and constructing objects and situations (or representations of these), questioning students, and giving tasks to students in such a way that students can find relevant features and see what happens when they manipulate "things" and when they have to make "things" themselves. For teachers, the task includes providing guidance and feedback, if this is judged as necessary by both the teacher and the student. The design of instruction is not the analysis and sequencing of information that should be converted into knowledge by the students. The design of instruction is making the plan for and the construction of situations and objects that can be used for the formulation of problems. These problems guide the perception and manipulation of objects, require the students to make predictions and to design and construct objects themselves.

For young children, the process of constructing the world is a natural process. It is realized in interaction with "the world" and with coaching from parents. This means that the perception and manipulation of basic-level objects is fostered by guidance and then leads to kinesthetic image schemas and to categorization. This basic-level activity remains important throughout a human life, and those who design instruction should realize opportunities for this at all levels of education. For children in elementary school, the use of kinesthetic image schemas and the knowledge of categories create new possibilities for exploration and development of new knowledge. Children can imagine a situation and understand a problem.

The interpretation Piaget has given to the process of how the young child constructs the world is still valid. However, it should now be clear that for children and students in elementary and secondary education, for students in higher education, and for adult learners the situations are different. Situations are extended, modified and systematically structured, but they still have the features of supporting the perception, manipulation and conception of a "certain part of the reality." This process can be repeated again and again for new "realities" and learning situations.

Because the amount of information and problem-solving methods are so extensive, it is impossible to have learners repeat all the actions that resulted in developing that knowledge base; that is to say that it is unreasonable to expect learners to re-construct entire knowledge bases; instead, they need to learn how to make effective use of existing knowledge bases, including their own. Instruction is then a mixture of experience with objects and guidance of actions with and to those objects for some realistic and meaningful purpose. The type of problem provides essential clues for the instructional designer with regard to deciding how to develop actual instruction (i.e., what objects and activities to represent, how to represent objects and structure activities, etc.). Students should be able to construct knowledge and practice skills in every learning environment - this is the real meaning of constructivism.

For an evaluation of what is learned, the traditional criteria of generalization and transfer of knowledge remain important. The same is true for automation of a procedure (skill). But the goal of education exceeds the acquisition of knowledge and skills. The integration of knowledge and skills in the whole personality and the adequate use of these in social situations is necessary. The result of education, then, is the development of competent human beings, wherein competence is understood to include an integration of knowledge, skills, and attitudes.

REFERENCES

Anderson, J. R. (1982). Acquisition of cognitive skill. *Psychological Review, 89*, 369 - 406.

Bereiter, C. (1999). *Education and mind in the knowledge age.* [Published and available on the Internet at http://csile.oise.utoronto.ca/edmind/main.html.]

Berlo, M. P. W. van (1999). *Guidelines supporting the analysis of team tasks and the design of team training scenarios: TNO-report TM-99-B002.* Soesterberg, The Netherlands: TNO Human Factors Research Institute.

Duncker, K. (1945). On problem-solving. *Psychological Monographs, 58*, Whole No. 270.

Duffy, T. M., & Jonassen, D. H. (Eds.) (1992). *Constructivism and the technology of instruction: A conversation.* Hillsdale, NJ: Lawrence Erlbaum.

Dijkstra, S. (1997). The integration of instructional systems design models and constructivistic design principles. *Instructional Science, 25*, 1-13.

Dijkstra, S. (1999). Instructional design for the development of knowledge and the learning of skills. In Schulz, W. K. *Aspekte und Probleme der didaktischen Wissensstrukturierung.* [How to structure knowledge for the purpose of instructional design]. Frankfurt am Main: Peter Lang.

Dijkstra, S. & van Merriënboer, J. J. G. (1997). Plans, procedures, and theories to solve instructional design problems. In S. Dijkstra, N. Seel, F. Schott & R. D. Tennyson (Eds), *Instructional design: international perspectives, Volume 2* (pp. 23-43). Mahwah, NJ: Lawrence Erlbaum.

Gagné, R. M. & Merrill, M. D. (1990). Integrative goals for instructional design. *Educational Technology Research and Development, 38*(1), 23-30.

Glaserfeld, E. von (1996). *Radical constructivism.* London: The Falmer Press.

Gott, S. P., Lesgold, A., & Kane, R. S. (1997). *Tutoring of transfer for technical competence.* In S. Dijkstra, N. Seel, F. Schott & R. D. Tennyson (Eds*), Instructional design: International perspectives, Volume 2* (pp. 221-250). Mahwah, NJ: Lawrence Erlbaum Associates, Publishers.

Jonassen, D. H. (1992). Objectivism versus Constructivism: Do We Need a New Philosophical Paradigm. *Educational Technology: Research and Development,* 39, 5 -14.

Jonassen, D. H., Tessmer, M, & Hannum, W. H. (1999) *Task analysis methods for instructional design.* Mahwah, NJ: Lawrence Erlbaum.

Lakoff, G. (1987). *Women, fire and dangerous things.* Chicago: The University of Chicago Press.

Merriënboer, J. J. G. van & Dijkstra, S. (1997). The four-component instructional-design model for training complex cognitive skills. In Tennyson, R. D., Schott, F., Seel, N. & Dijkstra, S. (Eds). *Instructional design: international perspectives, Volume 1* (pp. 427-446). Mahwah, NJ: Lawrence Erlbaum.

Piaget, J. (1937). *La construction du réel chez l'enfant.* [The child's construction of the reality]. Neuchâtel: Delachaux et Niestlé.

Piaget, J. (1970). *Epistémologie génétique.* [Genetic epistemology]. Paris: Presses Universitaires de France.

Polya, G. (1954). *How to solve it.* Princeton, NJ: Princeton University Press.

Rosch, E. (1978). Principles of categorization. In E. Rosch & B. B. Lloyd (Eds.), *Cognition and Categorization* (pp. 28-46). Hillsdale, NJ: Lawrence Erlbaum Associates.

Romiszowski, A. (1997). The use of telecommunication in education. In S. Dijkstra, N. Seel, F. Schott & R. D. Tennyson. (Eds.), *Instructional design: international perspectives, Volume 2* (pp. 183-220). Mahwah, NJ: Lawrence Erlbaum.

Rüttgers, J. (1999). *Hochschulen für das 21. Jahrhundert.* [Higher education for the 21st century]. (see http://www.bmbf.de/deutsch/veroeff/dokus/hochschul.htm)

Seel, N. M. & Winn, W. D. (1997). Research on media and learning: distributed cognition and semiotics. In Tennyson, R. D., Schott, F., Seel, N. & Dijkstra, S. (Eds), *Instructional design: international perspectives, Volume 1* (pp. 293-326). Mahwah, NJ: Lawrence Erlbaum.

THERESA M. ANDERSON

CONCLUSION

Keywords: constructivism, instructional technology, *ibstpi* competencies

Abstract: This conclusion summarizes and discusses the preceeding chapters of this book providing three organizing frameworks to facilitate reader assimilation of the scope and depth of the contributors' ideas, theories and constructs. Conceptual frameworks, including the AECT definiton of instructional teachnology, instructional scaffolding of contents and the *ibstpi* professional competencies for instructional designers, are used as a starting point for review of the chapters. It is hoped that this summary will provide the impetus for further dialogue and debate on the material presented in this book.

One of the editorial challenges of this book has been to integrate the diverse content, contexts and thinking generated from an international conference on *Integrated and Holistic Perspectives on Learning, Instructional and Technology*. This was the second conference offering on this general topic (additional conferences are planned) and the subject matter had moved beyond general introductory issues in educational technology to more advanced application guidelines and theoretical frameworks pertaining to the role and integration of technology in learning and instruction. In terms of understanding concepts and issues, conference participants had the luxury of general question and answer sessions in addition to informal and lengthy discussions with both presenters and fellow attendees. This additional context is, of course, not available to the reader of this book. So a significant editorial challenge has been to provide a framework to help readers understand key concepts and issues without the benefit of those additional collaborative contacts with colleagues. This conclusion is one attempt to try to fulfill the collaborative role of an after-hours session in addition to providing a general recap and follow up to the discussions by the various contributors.

My goal for this conclusion is to provide a brief summary of the proceeding chapters and perhaps also a roadmap to the reader seeking further direction in how to use this book for both personal and professional benefit. Consequently, I will provide here three different kinds of organizing frameworks as an initial staring point for individual reader assimilation. The first relates the various chapters to evolving conceptions of the discipline of instructional technology. The second relates the various chapters via

J.M. Spector and T.M. Anderson (eds.),
Integrated and Holistic Perspectives on Learning, Instruction and Technology, 233–242.
© 2000 *Kluwer Academic Publishers. Printed in the Netherlands.*

instructional scaffolding or sequencing broadly conceived. The third relates the chapters to the professional practice of instructional design detailed through the professional practice competencies of the International Board of Standards for Training, Performance and Instruction (*ibstpi*).

CHAPTER CONTENTS RELATED TO THE AECT DEFINITION OF INSTRUCTIONAL TECHNOLOGY

There are many different ways of trying to synthesize and assimilate the diverse concepts and findings of these chapters. One way is to look at how the authors' ideas align with or contribute to the precepts put forth by a relevant professional association, such as the Association for Educational Communications and Technology (AECT). AECT defines instructional technology as "the theory and practice of design, development, utilization, management and evaluation of processes and resources for learning" (Seels & Richey, 1994, p.9). This definition of instructional technology reflects significant evolution from the 1963 National Educational Association (NEA) definition of educational technology, which started with "audiovisual communications" and defined educational technology in terms of "messages which control the learning process" (Seels & Richey, 1994, pg. 15).

A quick review of an initial definition of educational technology is helpful to demonstrate how this book contributes to the evolution of the field. The Technological Development Project of the NEA provided the first definition of educational technology which stated :

> "Audiovisual communications is that branch of educational theory and practice primarily concerned with the design and use of messages which control the learning process. It undertakes (a) the study of the unique and relative strengths and weaknesses of both pictorial and nonrepresentational messages which may be employed in the learning process for any purpose and (b) the structuring and systematizing of messages by men and instruments in an educational environment. These undertakings include the planning, production, selection, management and utilization of both components and entire instructional systems. It's practical goal is the efficient utilization of every method and medium of communication which can contribute to the development of the learners full potential" (according to Ely, 1963, as reported in Seels & Richey, 1994, pg. 15)

The purpose of the original definition was "to provide a working definition for the field which will serve as a framework for future developments and lead to improvement in instruction" (Ely, 1963, p. 8, as reported in Seels & Richey, 1994). The definition has indeed undergone subsequent revisions from numerous sources since its inception. Consider our contributing authors. They represent a cross-section of the instructional design profession. The diversity among them in terms of context, viewpoint, geographical location, practice and expertise underscores the increasing diversity of all aspects of the instructional design field. As a consequence, any adequate definition must be broader in scope now than in the past. In addition, we no longer view instructional technology from a strictly "message control approach." We increasingly discuss a constructivist approach to complex learning, and this is especially noteworthy in the discussions of both theory and practice in this volume.

Chapters by Jonassen, Al-Diban and Blumschein, Dijkstra, Spector, Achtenhagen, and Goodyear provide a historical and present day overview of the instructional technology field and the evolution from a behaviorist to a constructivist viewpoint (see also, Gagné, 1985; Romiszowski, 1993; Skinner, 1954). Dijkstra discusses the creation of schema through external environmental interactions. Seel, Al-Diban and Blumschein, and Achtenhagen illustrate this concept by providing specific schema and learning tasks for particular contexts. From specific learning tasks to lifelong learning concepts (discussed at length by Goodyear, Marshall and Rossett, and Wagner), these chapters reflect growing agreement that learners construct internal schema that facilitate the acquisition of new knowledge. This notion parallels the evolution of the instructional technology field from a focus on message control and transmission (see Jonassen, Hernandez-Serrano and Choi) to more learner-centered activities in more complex, technology-supported learning environments. In addition, the contributors to this volume incorporate increasingly complex technological systems moving significantly beyond the mere hardware of "audiovisual communications" to integrated multimedia, simulation-based learning, web-based collaborative environments, virtual worlds, and so on.

The authors further reflect the dynamic merger of theory and practice in instructional design in this book by discussing all aspects of the 1994 AECT definition including the *design* (Alessi, Dijkstra, Jonassen, Hernandez-Serrano and Choi, Spector, Park and Etgen), *development* (Achtenhagen, Dunnagan and Christensen), *utilization* (Marshall and Rossett, Goodyear, Wagner, Savenye) and *evaluation* (Park and Etgen, Savenye, Seel, Al-Diban and Blumschein) of processes and resources for learning. The content of all of the chapters addresses more than a single component of the AECT definition, and the diversity and representation across multiple domains is evident throughout.

I would be remiss in reviewing these definitions to not comment on how visionary the original creators of the NEA definition were. Instructional designers of the past and present (as evident in the contributions to this volume) have been and are still primarily concerned with learning effectiveness or the development of the learner's full potential. We owe that much to the original definition, which has initiated and provoked ongoing debate, dialogue and investigation. Currently, the 1994 AECT definition does not include any mention of a specific technology but instead refers to the processes and resources for learning, which reflects the holistic approach to learning advocated by this book.

INSTRUCTIONAL SCAFFOLDING

Another way to look at these chapters is to look at common themes or ways to scaffold or sequence the content achieving higher levels of complexity or specificity as desired. A few examples will serve as an initial starting point in helping readers to integrate these chapters. From a theoretical viewpoint Dijkstra and Jonassen, Hernandez-Serrano and Choi discuss the constructivist viewpoint of instruction and learning. However, Jonassen, Hernandez-Serrano and Choi elaborate on the technology systems that support constructivist learning while Dijkstra discusses the implications and psychology of a constructivist viewpoint for instructional design. Specific application examples from a variety of contexts are provided by Savenye, Dunnagan and Christensen, Seel, Al-Diban and Blumschein, Spector and Achtenhagen. Savenye's chapter demonstrates program revisions based on learner input. The merger of learner needs and instructional design is one component of the chapter by Park and Etgen. From a hierarchical standpoint, these chapters progress along the theory to practice continuum (discussed both by Goodyear and by Dunnagan and Christensen) with specific methodologies provided to facilitate that process.

The design and application of instructional models is another area where this book provides opportunities for scaffolding of contents. Alessi, Achtenhagen, and Seel, Al-Diban and Blumschein discuss mental models and their role in knowledge construction and problem solving. Alessi discusses the instructional design issues associated with building versus using simulations. The latter is illustrated by Seel, Al-Diban and Blumschein's watershed and global economic model and by Achtenhagen's vocational model to demonstrate and transfer learning to complex domains. Seel, Al-Diban and Blumschein's research incorporates using an established model and creating a new model to acquire knowledge in a complex domain. Park and Etgen discuss the empirical and theoretical implication of object representation and presentation, which is further supported by Seel, Al-Diban and Blumschein's research that reports that in the absence of pre-existing knowledge learners commonly adopt the whatever model is presented to them. Readers exploring the concept of mental models will find both theory and related applications in these chapters. In this fashion, a comprehensive understanding of both the theory behind mental models and the practice of designing instruction to facilitate learner construction of appropriate mental models is available in this volume. A review of Dijsktra's chapter will provide additional information on object representation and initial sequencing of instruction for technology applications.

For a review of instructional technology in the business and industry context, the reader is referred to chapters by Achtenhagen, Wagner and Dunnagan and Christensen. Wagner's competency-based approach to training in business and industry links individual competencies with organizational mission. This can be viewed as a later-term exploration of Achtenhagen's initial vocational training of apprentices. Goodyear also discusses the need to target and design instruction to meet learner needs and situate instruction in the learner's context, whether that be in business, in academia or even at home. Dunnagan and Christensen provide an instructional design model that incorporates the complexity of dynamic environments, and they reflect on the mistake of using static models for dynamic situations. These chapters again progress along the continuum of instructional design competence (Dunnagan and Christensen, Wagner) from theory (Dijkstra, Goodyear) to practice for specific contexts (Achtenhagen, Seel, Al-Diban and Blumschein).

In the academic sector, Marshall and Rossett, and Savenye discuss learning strategies and practices in the context of K-12 and higher education. Marshall and Rossett discuss communities of practice for teaching professionals, and Savenye discusses pre-service teacher education for technology training. From a lifelong learning perspective, Savenye's online discussion group can be a viewed as a community of practice. In this fashion, pre-service teachers are not only "learning" the instructional content of the distance education classes but are "learning" how to continue to incorporate technology into their professional practices through their involvement in on-line communities of practice. Goodyear's chapter further elaborates the need for communities of practice to provide "local" havens for individual learners or learning communities. Highlighting a common theme of this book, lifelong learning strategies need to be designed into the instruction from both a design and application approach. These chapters suggest one method to accomplish this in the higher education setting.

Another example of the scaffolding of instructional design concepts can be found in chapters by Goodyear, Park and Etgen, Wagner and Dunnagan and Christensen. With regard to the design of instruction, both Goodyear and Park and Etgen discuss the benefits of multimedia in instruction, while Wagner and Dunnagan and Christensen review the initial needs assessment to support instructional design. Goodyear provides a general overview of multimedia benefits, and Park and Etgen explain the basic principles of constructing multimedia instruction. In addition, Jonassen, Hernandez-Serrano and Al-Diban provide an overview of technology tools to support learning. As previously stated, specific examples of technology learning applications can be reviewed in the chapters by Achtenhagen, Marshall and

Rossett, Saveyne and Wagner. These examples cover a range of contexts, so the reader may choose to review all contexts or focus on specific chapters based on interest.

Although not an exhaustive review of the contexts, theories or applications of this book, these examples provide a few of the ways the chapters may be integrated and sequenced based on reader interest in particular aspects of instructional design.

THE *IBSTPI* STANDARDS

The instructional design profession has borrowed from and elaborated the findings of many other fields (see for example Gustafson and Branch, 1997, and the discussion in Goodyear's and Spector's chapters for additional information on this issue). Schön (1983) advocates having an established body of knowledge and specific educational and practice guidelines as one of the distinguishing characteristics of a "true profession". One organization attempting to provide such guidelines for the professional practice of instructional design is the International Board of Standards for Training, Performance and Instruction (*ibstpi*). *ibstpi* has recently updated its instructional design standards and created 23 design competencies in four domains including (Richey and Fields, 2000):

- Professional Foundations
- Planning and Analysis
- Design and Development
- Implementation and Management

Within the four domains, *ibstpi* identifies 122 performance standards, some of what are regarded as essential (specific skills and knowledge which every instructional designer should know), and some of which are regarded as advanced (skills and knowledge which only the most advanced instructional designer is expected to master). A complete list of the *ibstpi* competencies and associated performance statements is available in Richey and Fields (2000). The standards upon which that book is based are available at the *ibstpi* website (http://www.ibstpi.org/98comp.html). For the purpose of this conclusion, a third way to integrate the chapters of this book is to look at how the chapters can be used by practitioners to develop various foundational and advanced *ibstpi* instructional designer competencies.

ibstpi Standard: Apply current research and practice to the field of instructional design (advanced competency). Each of the chapters of this book contributes to this competency in that they focus on the integration of new technologies or provide theoretical or practical examples of the integration of technology into the instructional design field. In addition, chapters by Dunnagan and Christensen and Spector specifically address the integration of theory and practice along a continuum of competence for instructional designers. Spector provides both discussion of and examples of success indicators to transform theory into practice as a model for instructional designer who wish to develop this competency.

ibstpi Standard: Apply concepts, techniques and theory of other disciplines to problems of learning, instruction and instructional design (advanced competency). Chapters by Dijkstra and Goodyear especially explore related disciplines and their evolution and impact on current instructional design practices. Jonassen, Hernandez-Serrano and Choi also contribute to the development of this competency by discussing the constructivist viewpoint of instructional design. The chapter by Spector discusses the need for a more directed approach to incorporating theory into practice regardless of the initial discipline involved.

ibstpi Standard: Conduct a needs assessment (essential competency). Dunnagan and Christensen provide an overview of the process and pitfalls of a situational evaluation as a precursor to instructional design decisions in addition to providing a model to complete this process. Their chapter provides a framework for instructional designers seeking to develop this essential skill.

ibstpi Standard: Develop a curriculum or program (essential competency). Chapters by Achtenhagen and Savenye provide examples in addition to discussion regarding both the development and implementation of specific programs. They also provide different contextual setting and instructional problems to provide a richer instructional base for designers striving to develop this competency.

ibstpi Standard: Determine the extent to which organizational mission, philosophy and values influence the design and success of a project (advanced competency); and, link design efforts to strategic plans of the organization (advanced competency). Wagner provides a practical approach to the development of lifelong learning opportunities which both reflect and support organizational mission and strategy. In addition, Dunnagan and Christensen discuss organizational influences on instructional design and implementation strategies and Achtenhagen discusses the specific integration of instruction into a vocational education program situated in part in an actual work setting.

ibstpi Standard: Analyze the characteristics and benefits of existing and emerging technologies and their use in the instructional context (essential competency). Jonassen, Hernandez-Serrano and Choi, and Goodyear focus specifically on technology based instructional systems while Alessi's discussion of instructional modeling and Park and Etgen's review of object representation may provide the impetus for designers to incorporate these practices into their design strategies. In addition, the introductory comments by Spector and the entire theme of this book is the integration of technology into instructional contexts.

ibstpi Standard: Accommodate cultural factors that may influence learning in the design (essential competency). International diversity in instructional design and applications is represented in chapters by Achtenhagen, and Seel, Al-Diban and Blumschein. In addition Park and Etgen discusses learning style differences in low and high spatial ability learners, which is a specific component of *ibstpi* standard #17, an essential competency. What is especially noteworthy is that *ibstpi* regards an awareness of cultural issues in designing instruction as an essential competency for all designers.

By contributing to the development of essential and advanced instructional designer competencies, this book contributes to the advancement and continued development of the discipline and enables designers to fulfill their role on the design team.

FINAL COMMENTS

This conclusion has proposed three frameworks to assimilate the diverse concepts and ideas presented in this book. Are there other frameworks to integrate this information? Absolutely, for at the very least this volume has advocated and highlighted the individual "meaning making" which is a foundation of personalized learning. Can content be sequenced in additional ways? Do additional *ibstpi* standards apply? Do the chapters reflect increasing complexity of the AECT definition of instructional technology than those highlighted? Of course. Constructive debate has been a part of this volume and was certainly a component of many after-hours sessions at the original conference. It is hoped that this conclusion provides an initial point of reference for readers to continue to question and refine both the theoretical and practical framework of the instructional design discipline.

This book has focused on the big issues with regard to instructional design and has demonstrated that theory can no longer be separate and distinct from practice, as the boundaries become increasing blurred between the two, and as technology enables us to design and deliver instruction at any time, at any place, to facilitate "just-in-need" instructional solutions. However, as we strive to better understand complex learning and the design of dynamic systems to support such learning, technology is but one component of that holistic process. It is incumbent upon practitioners and researchers alike to continue to strive to facilitate and support that dynamic process we call learning through greater understanding of the complexities of the learning process.

Concept	Highlights	Chapters
AECT Definition of Instructional Technology	The authors address the dynamic merger of theory and practice in instructional design by discussing all aspects of the 1994 AECT definition including design (Alessi, Dijkstra, Jonassen et al., Spector, Park & Etgen), development (Achtenhagen, Dunnagan & Christensen), utilization (Seel et al., Wagner, Savenye) and evaluation (Park & Etgen).	3, 4, 5, 7, 8, 9, 10, 11, 12
Business and Industry Context	Dunnagan & Christensen discuss organizational influences on instructional design and implementation. Achtenhagen discusses the integration of instruction into a vocational education program. Wagner presents a competency model for the business and industry context.	4, 6, 9
Communities of Practice	Marshall and Rossett discuss communities of practice for teaching professionals. Goodyear elaborates on the need for communities of practice as "local" havens for individual learners or learning communities.	1, 2
Competency Models	Wagner's competency-based approach to training in business and industry links individual competencies with organizational mission. Achtenhagen addresses vocational competencies through a German apprenticeship-training program.	6, 9
Constructivism	Chapters by Jonassen et al., Seel et al., Dijkstra, Spector, Achtenhagen, and Goodyear provide a historical overview of the instructional technology field and the evolution from a behaviorist to a constructivist viewpoint. Jonassen et al. elaborate on the technology systems that support constructivist learning while Dijkstra discusses the implication and psychology of a constructivist viewpoint for instructional design.	1, 5, 7, 8 12
Higher Education Context	Marshall & Rossett and Savenye discuss learning strategies and practices in the educational context. Marshall & Rossett discuss communities of practice for teaching professionals; Savenye discusses pre-service teacher education for technology training.	2, 3
Lifelong Learning	Wagner provides a practical organizational approach to the development of lifelong learning opportunities. Marshall & Rossett discuss lifelong learning for teacher. Goodyear discusses lifelong learning from a historical and practical approach.	1, 2, 6
Mental Models	Alessi, Achtenhagen, and Seel et al. discuss mental models and their role in knowledge construction and problem solving.	8, 9, 10
Multimedia Applications	Goodyear provides a general overview of multimedia benefits. Park & Etgen explain the basic principles of constructing multimedia instruction. Jonassen et al. provide an overview of technology tools to support learning. Achtenhagen, Marshall & Rossett, Saveyne, and Wagner provide specific examples of technology learning applications.	1, 2, 3, 6, 7, 9, 11
Object Representation in Instructional Technology	Park & Etgen discuss the empirical and theoretical implication of object representation and presentation which is further supported by Seel et al. who find that without preexisting knowledge learners adopt the instructional model presented to them. A review of Dijsktra's chapter will provide additional information on object representation and initial sequencing of instruction for technology applications.	8, 11, 12
Situational Evaluation	Dunnagan & Christensen provide an overview of the process and pitfalls of a situational evaluation. Achtenhagen discusses the specific integration of instruction into a vocational education program.	4, 8
Technology Applications	Specific examples can be found in chapters by Achtenhagen, Marshall & Rossett, Saveyne and Wagner. These examples cover: vocational education (Achtenhagen), higher education (Marshall and Rossett) and Business and Industry (Wagner). Jonassen et al. and Goodyear focus specifically on technology-based instructional systems. Alessi discusses instructional modeling, and Park & Etgen review object representation. In addition, the introductory comments by Spector and the entire theme of this book is the integration of technology into instructional contexts.	1, 2, 3, 5, 6, 7, 9, 10, 11

Table 1. Summary of key concepts by book chapter.

REFERENCES

Ely, D. P. (1963). The changing role of the audiovisual process in education: A definition and glossary of related terms. TCP Monograph No. 1. *AV Communication Review, 11*(1) Supplement no. 6.

Gagné, R. M. (1985). *The Conditions of Learning (4th Ed)*. New York: Holt, Reinhart and Winston.

Gustafson, K .L., & Branch, R. M. (1997). *Survey of instructional development models* (3rd edition). Syracuse, NY: ERIC Clearinghouse on Information and Technology.

Schön, D. (1983). *The reflective practitioner: How professionals think in action*. New York: Basic Books.

Seels, B. R. & Richey, R. C. (1994) *Instructional technology: The definition and domains of the field*. Washington, DC: Association for Educational Communications and Technology.

Richey, R. C., & Fields, D. F. (Eds.) (2000). *Instructional design competencies: The standards* (3rd Ed.). Syracuse, NY: ERIC Clearinghouse on Information and Technology & The International Board of Standards for Training, Performance & Instruction.

Romiszowski, A. J. (1993). *Designing instructional systems*. London: Kogan Page Ltd.

BIBLIOGRAPHY

Achtenhagen, F. (1992). The relevance of content for teaching-learning processes. In F. K. Oser, A. Dick & J. L. Patry (Eds.), *Effective and responsible teaching – the new synthesis* (pp. 315-328). San Francisco: Jossey-Bass.

Achtenhagen, F. (1994). How should research on vocational and professional education react to new challenges in life and in the workplace? In W. J. Nijhof & J. N. Streumer (Eds.), *Flexibility in training and vocational education* (pp. 201-247). Utrecht: Lemma.

Achtenhagen, F. (in press). Criteria for the Development of Complex Teaching-Learning Environments. *Instructional Science*.

Achtenhagen, F., & Grubb, W. N. (in press). Vocational and occupational education: Pedagogical complexity – institutional diversity. In V. Richardson (Ed.), *Fourth Handbook of Research on Teaching*. Washington: AERA.

Achtenhagen, F., Nijhof, W. J., & Raffe, D. (1995). *Feasibility Study: Research scope for vocational education in the framework of COST social sciences*. European Commission, Directorate General: Science, Research and Development. Social Sciences, COST Technical committee, Vol 3. Brussels, Luxembourg: ECSC-EC-EAEC.

Ahn, W. K., Brewer, W. F., & Mooney, R. J. (1992). Schema acquisition from a single example. *Journal of Experimental Psychology: Learning, Memory, and Cognition, 18* (2), 391-412.

Al-Diban, S., & Seel, N. M. (1999). Evaluation als Forschungsaufgabe von Instruktionsdesign. Dargestellt am Beispiel einer multimedialen Lernumgebung. *Unterrichtswissenschaft, 27* (1), 29-60. [Evaluation as a research problem of instructional design.]

Alessi, S. M. (1988). Fidelity in the design of instructional simulations. *Journal of Computer-based Instruction, 15*(2), 40-47.

Alessi, S. M. (2000). Simulation design for training and assessment. In H. F. O'Neil, Jr., & D. Andrews (Eds.), *Aircrew training: Methods, technologies, and assessments*. Mahwah, NJ: Lawrence Erlbaum.

Alessi, S. M. (2000). Designing educational support in System Dynamics based interactive learning environments. *Simulation & Gaming, 31*(2), 178-196.

Alessi, S. M., & Trollip, S. R. (1991). *Computer-based instruction: Methods & development (2nd Ed.).* Englewood Cliffs, NJ: Prentice Hall.

Anders, P. (1999). *Envisioning cyberspace: Designing 3D electronic spaces*. New York: McGraw Hill.

Anderson, J. R. (1982). Acquisition of cognitive skill. *Psychological Review, 89,* 369 - 406.

Anderson, J. R., Reder, L. M., & Simon, H. A. (1996). Situated learning and education. *Educational Researcher, 25*(4), 5-11.

Anderson, S. E., & Harris, J. B. (1995, April). *Educators' use of electronic networks: An e-mail survey of account-holders on a statewide telecomputing system*. Paper presented at the meeting of the American Educational Research Association, San Francisco, CA.

Andrews, D. H., Carroll, L. A., & Bell, H. H. (1995). The future of selective fidelity in training devices. *Educational Technology, 35*(6), 32-36.

Andrews, D. H., Dineen, T., & Bell, H. H. (1999). The use of constructive modeling and virtual simulation in large-scale team training: A military case study. *Educational Technology, 39*(1), 24-28.

Andrews, D., Waag, W., & Bell, H. (1992). Training technologies applied to team training: military examples. In R. Swezey & E. Salas (Eds.), *Teams: Their training and performance* (pp. 283-328). Norwood New Jersey: Ablex Publishing Corporation.

Anzai, Y., & Yokoyama, T. (1984). Internal models in physics problem solving. *Cognition and Instruction, 1*, 397-450.

Asp, S. (1979, April). *How does the mode of presentation affect story comprehension?* Paper presented at the Annual Meeting of the American Educational Research Association, San Francisco, CA.

Ausubel, D. P. (1968). *Educational psychology: A cognitive view.* New York: Holt, Rinehart Winston.

Baddeley, A. D. (1992). Working memory. *Science, 255,* 556-559

Bagget, P. (1984). Role of temporal overlap of visual and auditory material in forming dual media associations. *Journal of Educational Psychology, 7-6*, 408-417.

Bassi, L. J. (1997, December). Harnessing the power of intellectual capital. *Training & Development, 51,* 25-30.

Bates, J. (Ed.) (1995). *Telematics for flexible and distance learning (DELTA).* Final report. Brussels: European Commission DG XIII_C.

Beaudoin, M. (1990). The instructor's changing role in distance education. *The American Journal of Distance Education 4*(2), 21-9.

Beck, K. (1993). *Dimensionen der ökonomischen Bildung. Meßinstrumente und Befunde.* Nürnberg: Universität (Abschlußbericht zum DFG-Projekt 'Wirtschaftskundlicher Bildungs-Test [WBT]. Normierung und internationaler Vergleich).

Bereiter, C. (1999). *Education and mind in the knowledge age.* [Published and available on the internet at http://csile.oise.utoronto.ca/edmind/main.html.]

Berlo, M. P. W. van (1999). *Guidelines supporting the analysis of team tasks and the design of team training scenarios: TNO-report TM-99-B002.* Soesterberg, The Netherlands: TNO Human Factors Research Institute.

Bertol, D. (1997). *Designing digital space: An architect's guide to virtual reality.* New York: John Wiley.

Biggs, J. (1999). *Teaching for quality learning at university: What the student does.* Buckingham: Open University Press.

Blackboard, Inc. (1998). *Courseinfo 2.0 Instructor's Manual.* Washington, D.C.

Block, J. H. (1972). *Mastery Learning.* New York: Holt, Rinehart & Winston.

Bloom, B. S. (1971). Mastery learning. In J. H. Block (Ed.), *Mastery Learning* (pp. 47-53). New York: Holt, Rinehart & Winston.

Bloom, B. S. (Hrsg.) (1972). Taxonomie von Lernzielen im kognitiven Bereich. Weinheim: Beltz. [Taxonomy of educational objectives. Handbook I: Cognitive domain.]

Brett, C. (1997, March). *Communities of inquiry among pre-service teachers investigating mathematics.* Paper presented at the meeting of the American Educational Research Association, Chicago, IL.

Breuleux, A., Laferriere, T., & Bracewell, R. (1998). Networked learning communities in teacher education. In McNeil, S. (Ed.), *SITE 98: Society for Information Technology & Teacher Education International Conference* (pp.1170-75). Charlottesville, VA: Association for the Advancement of Computing in Education (AACE).

Briggs, P. (1990). The role of the user model in learning as an internally and externally directed activity. In D. Ackermann & M. J. Tauber (Eds.), *Mental models and human-computer interaction 1* (pp. 195-208). Amsterdam: Elsevier.

Bronack, S. C., & Kilbane, C. R. (1998). CaseNET: Teaching decisions via a web-based learning environment. In McNeil, S. (Ed.), *SITE 98: Society for Information Technology & Teacher Education International Conference.* Charlottesville, VA: Association for the Advancement of Computing in Education (AACE).

Brown, J. C. A., & Duguid, P. (1989). Situated cognition and the culture of learning. *Educational Researcher, 18,* 32-42.

Bruner, J. S. (1966). *Toward a theory of instruction.* Cambridge, MA: Harvard University Press.

Bull, B. (1994). *Professional development and teacher time: Principles, guidelines, and policy options for Indiana.* Bloomington, IN: Indiana University Education Policy Center.

Bull, G., Bull, G., & Sigmon, T. (1997, September). Common protocols for shared communities. *Learning and Leading with Technology,* 25(1), 50-53.

Bull, G., Harris, J., Lloyd, J., & Short, J. (1989). The electronic academic village. *Journal of Teacher Education, July-August,* 27-31.

Buttler, F. (1992). Tätigkeitslandschaft bis 2010 [Structure of jobs until 2010]. In F. Achtenhagen & E. G. John (Eds.). *Mehrdimensionale Lehr-Lern-Arrangements* (pp. 162-182) [Multidimensional teaching-learning arrangements]. Wiesbaden: Gabler.

Carmel, E., Crawford, S., & and Chen, H. (1992). Browsing in hypertext: A cognitive study. *IEEE Transactions on Systems, Man & Cybernetics, 22(5),* 865-884.

Carroll, J. B. (1963). A model of school learning. *Teachers College Record, 64,* pp. 723-733.

Carswell, C. M., & Wickens, C. D. (1987). Information integration and the object display: An interaction of task demands and display superiority. *Ergonomics, 30,* 511-527.

Casey, C. (1996). Incorporating cognitive apprenticeship in multi-media. *Educational Technology Research and Development, 44* (1), 71-84.

Center for Working Life, the Royal Institute of Technology, Stockholm, Sweden and the University of Aarhus, Denmark.

Chandler, P., & Sweller, J. (1992). The split-attention effect as a factor in the design of instruction. *British Journal of Educational Psychology, 62,* 233-246.

Chinn, C. A., Brewer, W. F. (1993). The role of anomalous data in knowledge acquisition: A theoretical framework and implications for science instruction. *Review of Educational Research, 63* (1), 1-49.

Christensen, D. L., Dunnagan, C. B., & Tennyson, R. D. (1998). The future of instructional theory: Lessons learned. *Journal of Structural Leaning & Intelligent Systems, 13(2),* 103-113.

Cicognani, A. (2000). Architectural Design for Online Environments. In B. Kolko (Ed.), *Virtual Commons: Policy and Community in an Electronic Age.* New York: Columbia University Press.

Coburn, P., Kelman, P., Roberts, N., Snyder, T. F. F., Watt, D. H., & Weiner, C. (1985). *Practical guide to computers in education* (2nd Ed.). Reading, MA: Addison-Wesley.

Cognition and Technology Group at Vanderbilt (CTGV) (1997). *The Jasper project. Lessons in curriculum, instruction, assessment, and professional development.* Hillsdale, NJ: Lawrence Erlbaum.

Collins, A. (1994). Goal-based scenarios and the problem of situated learning: A commentary on Andersen Consulting's design of goal-based scenarios. *Educational Technology, 34(9),* 30-32.

Collins, A., Brown, J. S. & Newman, S. E. (1989). Cognitive apprenticeship: Teaching the crafts of reading, writing, and mathematics. In L. B. Resnick (Ed.) (1989), *Knowing, learning, and instruction* (pp. 453-494). Hillsdale, NJ: Erlbaum.

Collins, A., Brown, J. S., & Holum, A. (1993). Cognitive apprenticeship: Making thinking visible. *American Educator, 15* (3), 6-11, 38-46.

Collis, B. (1996). *Tele-learning in a digital world - the future of distance learning.* Boston, MA: International Thompson Computer Press.

Craik, K. J. W. (1943). *The nature of explanation.* Cambridge: Cambridge University Press.

Cronbach, L. J., & Snow, R. E. (1977). *Aptitudes and Instructional Methods: A handbook for research on interactions.* New York: Irvington.

Crook, C., & Light, P. (1999). Information technology and the culture of student learning. In J. Bliss, R. Saljo, & P. Light (Eds.), *Learning sites: Social and technological resources for learning* (pp. 183-193). Oxford: Pergamon.

Cuban, L. (2000). High-tech schools and low-tech teaching. In Hirschbuhl, J. J., & Bishop, D. (Eds.), *Computers in education: Annual editions, 00/01* (pp. 15-16). Guilford, CN: Dushkin/McGraw-Hill.

Cunningham, C. (Ed.) (1997). *Perspectives: Instructional technology for teachers.* Boulder, CO: Coursewise Publishing.

Davenport, T. H., & Prusak, L. (1998). *Working knowledge: How organizations manage what they know.* Boston: Harvard Business School Press.

Davidsen, P., Gonzalez, J. J., Muraida, D. J., Spector, J. M., & Tennyson, R. D. (1995). Applying system dynamics to courseware development. *Computers in Human Behavior, 11*(2), 325-339.

Davis, N. (1999, Autumn/Winter). The globalization of education through teacher education with new technologies: a view informed by research. *Educational Technology Review, 12,* 8-12.

De Jong, T., & van Joolingen, W. R. (1998). Scientific discovery learning with computer simulations of conceptual domains. *Review of Educational Research, 68*(2), 179-201.

Dean, R. S., Garabedian, A. A., & Yekovich, F. R. (1983). The effect of modality shifts on proactive interference in long-term memory. *Contemporary Educational Psychology, 8,* 28-45.

Dede, C. J. (1991). Emerging technologies: Impacts on distance learning. *Annals of the American Academy of Political and Social Science* (514), 146-58.

Dede, C. J. (1996). The evolution of constructivist learning environments: Immersion in distributed, virtual worlds. In B. G. Wilson (Ed.), *Constructivist learning environments: Case studies in instructional design* (pp. 165-175). Englewood Cliffs, NJ: Educational Technology Publications.

Dede, C. J. (2000). Evaluating the effectiveness of technology initiatives. In Hirschbuhl, J. J., & Bishop, D. (Eds.), *Computers in education: Annual editions, 00/01* (pp. 43-46). Guilford, CN: Dushkin/McGraw-Hill.

Descy, D. E. (1997, November, December). Accessible web page design. *TechTrends,* 3-6.

Dewar, J. A., Hodges, J. S., Bankes, S. C., Lucas, T., Vye, P., & Saunders-Newton, D. K. (1996). *Credible uses of the distributed interactive simulation (DIS) system.* Santa Monica, CA: The Rand Corporation.

Dick, W. & Carey, L. (1996). The systematic design of instruction (4th Ed.). New York: HarperCollins.

Dijkstra, S. (1997). The integration of instructional systems design models and constructivistic design principles. *Instructional Science, 25,* 1-13.

Dijkstra, S. (1999). Instructional design for the development of knowledge and the learning of skills. In Schulz, W. K. *Aspekte und Probleme der didaktischen Wissensstrukturierung.* [How to structure knowledge for the purpose of instructional design]. Frankfurt am Main: Peter Lang.

Dijkstra, S., Seel, N. M., Schott, F. & Tennyson, R. D. (Eds.) (1997). *Instructional Design: International Perspectives, Vol. 2.* Mahwah, NJ: Lawrence Erlbaum.

Dijkstra, S. & van Merriënboer, J. J. G. (1997). Plans, procedures, and theories to solve instructional design problems. In S. Dijkstra, N. Seel, F. Schott & R. D. Tennyson (Eds), *Instructional design: international perspectives, Volume 2* (pp. 23-43). Mahwah, NJ: Lawrence Erlbaum.

Dillon, J. T. (1986). Student questions and individual learning. *Educational Theory, 36,* 333-341.

Dinter, F. (1998). Zur Diskussion des Konstruktivismus im Instruktionsdesign. *Unterrichtswissenschaft, 26* (3), 254-287.

Dinter, F. R., & Seel, N. M. (1994). What does it mean to be a constructivist in I.D.? An epistemological reconsideration. In J. Lowyck & J. Elen (Eds.), *Modelling I.D.-research* (pp. 49-66). Leuven: Proceedings of the first workshop of the SIG on instructional design of EARLI.

Dole, J. A., & Sinatra, G. M. (1998). Reconceptualizing change in the cognitive construction of knowledge. *Educational Psychologist, 33* (2/3), 109-128.

Dörner, D. (1996) (Translated by Rita and Robert Kimber). *The logic of failure: Why things go wrong and what we can do to make them right.* New York: Holt.

Dreyfus, H. L. & Dreyfus, S. E. (1986). *Mind over machine: The power of human intuition and expertise in the era of the computer.* New York: Free Press.

Drucker, P. F. (1994, November). The age of social transformation. *The Atlantic Monthly, 275* (5), 53-80.

Duffy, T. M., & Jonassen, D. H. (Eds.) (1992). *Constructivism and the technology of instruction: A conversation.* Hillsdale, NJ: Lawrence Erlbaum.

Duncker, K. (1945). On problem-solving. *Psychological Monographs, 58,* Whole No. 270.

Eastmond, D., & Ziegahn, L. (1995). Instructional design for the online classroom. In Berge, Z., & Collins, M. (Eds.), *Computer mediated communication and the online classroom,* Vol. 3, pp. 59-80. New Jersey: Hampton Press, Inc.

Eckblad, G. (1981). *Scheme theory. A conceptual framework for cognitive-motivational processes.* London: Academic Press.

Edelson, D. C., Pea, R. D., & Gomez, L. (1996). Constructivism in the collaboratory. In B.G. Wilson (Ed.), *Constructivist learning environments: Case studies in instructional design.* Englewood Cliffs, NJ: Educational Technology Publications.

Eggers, R. M., & McGonigle, D. (1996). Internet-distributed college courses: Instructional design issues. In *Proceedings of Selected Research and Development Presentations at the 1996 National Convention of the Association for Educational Communications and Technology,* 18th, Indianapolis, IN. ERIC Document ED 397 790.

Ellis, A. L, Wagner, E. D., & Longmire, W. (1999). *Managing web-based training.* Alexandria, VA: American Society for Training and Development.

Ely, D. P, Foley, A., Freeman, W., & Scheel, N. (1995). Trends in educational technology 1991. In *Instructional technology: Past, present and future* (2nd Ed.). Englewood, CO: Libraries Unlimited, pp. 34-60.

Ely, D. P. (1963). The changing role of the audiovisual process in education: A definition and glossary of related terms. TCP Monograph No. 1. *AV Communication Review, 11*(1) Supplement no. 6.

EME Corporation. (1999). *Burette.* [Computer program]. Stuart, FL: EME Corporation.

Engeström, Y. (1999). Activity theory an individual and social transformation. In Y. Engeström, R. Miettinen, & R.L. Punamäki (Eds.), *Perspectives on activity theory* (pp. 19-38). Cambridge: Cambridge University Press.

Entwistle, N. (1996). Recent research on student learning and the learning environment. In J. Tait & P. Knight (Eds.), *The management of independent learning* (pp. 97-112). London: Kogan Page.

Ericsson, K. A., & Smith, J. (Eds.) (1991). *Toward a general theory of expertise: Prospects and limits.* New York: Cambridge University Press.

Faria, A. J. (1998). Business simulation games: Current usage levels - An update. *Simulation & Gaming, 29*(3), 295-308.

Farmer, J. A., Buckmaster, A., & Legrand, A. (1992). Cognitive apprenticeship: Implications for continuing professional education. *New Directions for Adult and Continuing Education, 55,* 41-49.

Flake, J. L., McClintock, C. E., & Turner, S. (1990). *Fundamentals of computer education* (2nd Ed.). Belmont, CA: Wadsworth.

Fletcher, J. D. (1996). Does this stuff work? Some findings from applications of technology to education and training. *Proceedings of Conference on Teacher Education and the Use of Technology Based Learning Systems.* Warrenton, VA: Society for Applied Learning Technology, 1996.

Flowers, S. (1996). *Software failure.* London: Wiley.

Floyd, C., Mehl, W. M., Reisin, F. M., Schmidt, G., & Wolf, G. (1989). Out of Scandinavia: Alternative approaches to software design and system development. *Human-Computer Interaction,* 4(4), 253-350.

Ford, P., Goodyear, P., Heseltine, R., Lewis, R., Darby, J., Graves, J., Sartorius, P., Harwood, D., & King, T. (1996). *Managing change in higher education: A learning environment architecture*. Buckingham: Open University Press.

Forrester, J. W. (1961). *Industrial dynamics*. New York: John Wiley & Sons, Inc.

Forrester, J. W. (1968). *Principles of systems (Second preliminary edition)*. Cambridge, MA: Wright-Allen Press, Inc.

Forrester, J. W. (1969). *Urban dynamics*. Cambridge, MA: The M.I.T. Press.

Forrester, J. W. (1971). *World dynamics*. Cambridge, MA: Wright-Allen Press, Inc.

Forrester, J. W. (1971, January). *Counterintuitive behavior of social systems*. Cambridge, MA: *Technology Review*, Massachusetts Institute of Technology Alumni Association.

Funke, J. (1991). Solving complex problems: Exploration and control of complex systems. In R. J. Sternberg & P. A. Frensch (Eds.), *Complex problems solving: Principles and mechanisms*. Hillsdale, NJ: Erlbaum.

Gaddy, C., & Wachtel, J. (1992). Team skills training in nuclear power plant operations. In R. Swezey & E. Salas (Eds.), *Teams: Their training and performance* (pp. 379-396). Norwood New Jersey: Ablex Publishing Corporation.

Gagné, R. M. (1967). *Learning and Individual differnences*. Columbus, OH: Merrill.

Gagné, R. M. (1985). *The Conditions of Learning (4th Ed)*. New York: Holt, Reinhart and Winston.

Gagné, R. M. (1995). Learning processes and instruction. *Training Research Journal, 1*, 17-28.

Gagné, R. M., & Merrill, M. D. (1990). *Integrative goals for instructional design*. *Educational Technology Research and Development, 38*(1), 23-30.

Gagné, R. M., Briggs, L J., & Wager, W. W. (1992). *Principles of instructional design* (4th Ed.). Fort Worth, TX: Harcourt, Brace.

Galili, I., Bendall, S., & Goldberg, F. (1993). The effects of prior knowledge and instruction on understanding image formation. *Journal of Research in Science Teaching, 30* (3), 271-301.

Geisert, P. G., & Futrell, M. K. (1995). *Teachers, computers, and curriculum: microcomputers in the curriculum* (2nd Ed.). Needham Heights, MA: Simon and Schuster.

Gentry, C. G., & Csete, J. (1995). Educational technology in the 1990s. *In Instructional technology: past, present and future* (2nd Ed.), pp. 20-33. Englewood, CO: Libraries Unlimited.

Gery, G. J. (1991). *Electronic performance support systems*. Tolland, MA: Gery Performance Press.

Gibson, J. J. (1979). An ecological approach to visual perception. Hillsdale, NJ: Lawrence Erlbaum Associates.

Gilbert, S. W. (2000). Making the most of a slow revolution. In Hirschbuhl, J. J., & Bishop, D. (Eds). *Computers in education: Annual editions, 00/01* (pp. 125-139). Guilford, CN: Dushkin/McGraw-Hill.

Glaser, R. (1990). The reemergence of learning theory within instructional research. *American Psychologist, 45* (1), 29-39.

Glaserfeld, E. von (1996). *Radical constructivism*. London: The Falmer Press.

Glenburg, A. M., & Kruley, P. (1992). Pictures and anaphora: Evidence for independent processes. *Memory & Cognition, 20*, 461-471.

Goodyear, P. (1995). Situated action and distributed knowledge: A JITOL perspective on electronic performance support systems. *Educational and Training Technology International, 32*(1), 45-55.

Goodyear, P. (1996). Asynchronous peer interaction in distance education: the evolution of goals practices and technology. *Training Research Journal, 1*, 71-102.

Goodyear, P. (1999). Educational technology, virtual learning environments and architectural practice. In D. Ely, L. Odenthal, & T. Plomp (Eds.), *Educational science and technology: Perspectives for the future* (pp. 74-91). Enschede: Twente University Press.

Goodyear, P., & Steeples, C. (1993). Computer-mediated communication in the professional development of workers in the advanced learning technologies industry. In J. Eccleston, B. Barta, & R. Hambusch (Eds.), *The computer-mediated education of information technology professionals and advanced end-users* (pp. 239-247). Amsterdam: Elsevier.

Goodyear, P., & Steeples, C. (1998). Creating shareable representations of practice. *Association for Learning Technology Journal, 6*(3), 16-23.

Goodyear, P., & Steeples, C. (1999). Asynchronous multimedia conferencing in continuing professional development: issues in the representation of practice through user-created videoclips. *Distance Education.*

Gott, S. P., Lesgold, A., & Kane, R. S. (1997). *Tutoring of transfer for technical competence.* In S. Dijkstra, N. Seel, F. Schott & R. D. Tennyson (Eds*), Instructional design: International perspectives, Volume 2* (pp. 221-250). Mahwah, NJ: Lawrence Erlbaum Associates, Publishers.

Grabinger, R. S. (1989). Screen layout design: Research into the overall appearance on the screen. *Computers in Human Behavior, 3,* 173-183.

Greeno, J. (1997). On claims that answer the wrong question. *Educational Researcher, 26*(1), 5-17.

Greeno, J. G. (1989). Situations, mental models, and generative knowledge. In D. Klahr & K. Kotovsky (Eds.), *Complex information processing* (pp. 285-318). Hillsdale, NJ: Lawrence Erlbaum.

Greeno, J. G., Smith, D. R., & Moore, J. L. (1993). Transfer of situated learning. In D. K. Detterman & R. J. Sternberg (Eds.), *Transfer on trial: Intelligence, cognition, and instruction* (pp. 99-167). Norwood, NJ: Ablex.

Greer, B. (1997). Modelling reality in mathematics classrooms: The case of word problems. *Learning and Instruction, 7* (4), 293-307.

Gunawardena, C. N. (1992). Changing faculty roles for audiographics and online teaching. *The American Journal of Distance Education 6*(3), 58-71.

Gustafson, K .L., & Branch, R. M. (1997). *Survey of instructional development models* (3<rd edition). Syracuse, NY: ERIC Clearinghouse on Information and Technology.

Hanna, J. (1986). Learning environments criteria. In R. Ennals, R. Gwyn, & L. Zdravchev (Eds.), *Information technology and education: The changing school.* Chichester, UK: Ellis Horwood.

Hannafin, M. J., & Land, S. M. (1997). The foundations and assumptions of technology-enhanced student-centered learning environments. *Instructional Science 25,* 167-202.

Hannafin, M. J., Hannafin, K. M., Land, S. M., & Oliver, K. (1997). Grounded practice and the design of constructivist learning environments. *Educational Technology Research and Development 45(*3), 101-17.

Hannafin, R. D., & Savenye, W. C. (1993, June). Technology in the classroom: the teacher's new role and resistance to it. *Educational Technology,* 26-31.

Hegarty, M., & Just, M. A. (1993). Constructing mental models of machines from text and diagrams. *Journal of Memory and Language, 32,* 717-742.

Heinich, R., Molenda, M., Russell, J. D., & Smaldino, S. E., (1999). *Instructional media and technologies for learning.* Upper Saddle River, NJ: Merrill, an imprint of Prentice Hall.

Herbert, J. M., & McNergney, R. F. (Eds.) (1995). *Guide to foundations in action videocases: teaching and learning in multicultural settings.* Boston: Allyn & Bacon.

Hicks, W. B., & Tillin, A. M. (1970). *Developing multi-media libraries.* New York: Bowker.

High Performance Systems. (1987). *Stella.* [Computer program]. Lyme, NH: High Performance Systems.

Hill, J. R., & Hannafin, M. J. (1997). Cognitive strategies and learning from the world wide web. *Educational Technology Research and Development 45*(4), 37-64.

Hillier, B. (1999). *Space is the machine: A configurational theory of architecture.* Cambridge: Cambridge University Press.

Hillier, B., & Hanson, J. (1989). *The social logic of space*. Cambridge: Cambridge University Press.

Hirumi, A., & Bermudez, A. (1996). Interactivity, distance education and instructional systems design converge on the information superhighway. *Journal of Research on Computing in Education, 29*(1), 1-16.

Holtzman, S. (1994). *Digital mantras: The languages of abstract and virtual worlds*. Cambridge Mass: MIT Press.

Honey, M., & Henriquez, A. (1993). *Telecommunications and K-12 educators: Findings from a national survey*. Center for Technology in Education: New York, NY.

Honey, M., Culp, K. M., & Carrigg, F. (1999, July). *Perspectives on technology and education research: Lessons from the past and present*. Paper presented at the Secretary's Conference on Educational Technology, Washington, DC, 12-13 July 1999.

Hopkins, D. (1993). *A teacher's guide to classroom research* (2nd ed.). Bristol, PA: Open University Press.

Hopper, M. E. (1993). *Courseware projects in advanced educational computing environments*. Unpublished doctoral dissertation. West Lafayette, IN: Purdue University.

Horton, W. (1999, April). *WBT and knowledge management, allies or arch-enemies*. Paper presented at the WBT Conference, San Diego, CA.

Hübner, R. (1989). Methoden zur Analyse und Konstruktion von Aufgaben zur kognitiven Steuerung dynamischer Systeme. *Zeitschrift für Experimentelle und Angewandte Psychologie, 36* (2), 211-238.

Imagine That, Inc. (2000). *Extend*. [Computer program]. San Jose, CA: Imagine That, Inc.

Interactive Magic. (1996). *Capitalism*. [Computer program]. Research Triangle Park, NC: Interactive Magic.

Interactive Magic. (1997). *Capitalism Plus*. [Computer program]. Research Triangle Park, NC: Interactive Magic.

International Society for Technology in Education (ISTE). (1998). *National standards for technology in teacher preparation*. (http://www.iste.org/Standards/NCATE/intro.html)

International Society for Technology in Education (ISTE). (June, 1998). *National educational technology standards for students*. Eugene, Oregon.

Ishi, H., & Yamauchi, H. (1994). A study of cognitive loading in dual-coding theory. *Perceptual and Motor Skills*, 79, 458.

Jackson, S., Stratford, S. J., Krajcik, J., & Soloway, E. (1995, March). *Model-It: a case study of learner-centered software for supporting model building*. Proceedings of the Working Conference on Technology Applications in the Science Classroom, The National Center for Science Teaching and Learning, Columbus, OH.

Jackson, S., Stratford, S. J., Krajcik, J., & Soloway, E. (1996). Making dynamic modeling accessible to pre-college science students. *Interactive Learning Environments*, 4(3), 233-257.

Jih, H. J, & Reeves, T. C. (1992). Mental models: A research focus for interactive learning systems. *Educational Technology Research and Development, 40* (3), 39-53.

Johnson, W. B., & Norton, J. E. (1992). Modeling student performance in diagnostic tasks: A decade of evolution. In J. W. Regian & V. J. Shute (Eds.), *Cognitive approaches to automated instruction*. Hillsdale, NJ: Lawrence Erlbaum.

Johnson-Laird, P. N. (1983). *Mental models. Towards a cognitive science of language, inference, and consciousness*. Cambridge: Cambridge University Press.

Johnson-Laird, P. N. (1989). Mental models. In M. I. Posner (Ed.), *Foundations of cognitive science* (pp. 469-499). Cambridge, MA:The MIT Press.

Jonassen, D. H. (1992). Objectivism versus Constructivism: Do We Need a New Philosophical Paradigm. *Educational Technology: Research and Development*, 39, 5 -14.

Jonassen, D. H. (2000). *Computers as mindtools for schools: Engaging critical thinking*. Columbus, OH: Prentice Hall.

Jonassen, D. H., Beissner, K., & Yacci, M. A. (1993). *Structural knowledge: Techniques for representing, conveying, and acquiring structural knowledge*. Hillsdale, NJ: Lawrence Erlbaum Associates.

Jonassen, D. H., & Grabowski, B. L. (1993). *Handbook of individual differences, learning and instruction*. Hillsdale, NJ: Lawrence Erlbaum Associates

Jonassen, D. H., Peck, K. L., & Wilson, B. G. (1999). *Learning with technology: A constructivist perspective*. New Jersey: Prentice Hall, Inc.

Jonassen, D., & Reeves, T. (1996). Learning with technology: using computers as cognitive tools. In D. Jonassen (Ed.), *Handbook of research for educational communications and technology* (pp. 693-719). New York: Macmillan.

Jonassen, D. H., Tessmer, M, & Hannum, W. H. (1999) *Task analysis methods for instructional design*. Mahwah, NJ: Lawrence Erlbaum.

Jonassen, D., Prevish, T., Christy, D., & Stavurlaki, E. (1999). Learning to solve problems on the Web: Aggregate planning in a business management course. *Distance Education: An International Journal, 20*(1), 49-63.

Jonassen, D. H. & Land S. M. (2000). *Theoretical foundations of learning environments*. Mahwah, NJ: Lawrence Erlbaum Associates

Jonassen, D. H. (1999). Designing constructivist learning environments. In C. M. Reigeluth (Ed.), *Instructional design theories and models: A new paradigm of instructional theory* (Vol II.) (pp. 215-240). Mahwah, NJ: Lawrence Erlbaum Associates.

Jonassen, D. H. (2000). Revisiting activity theory as a framework for designing student-centered learning environments. In D. H. Jonassen & S. M. Land (Eds.), *Theoretical foundations of learning environments* (pp. 89-121). Mahwah, NJ: Lawrence Erlbaum Associates

Jones, C. (1998). *Context, content and cooperation: an ethnographic study of collaborative learning online*. Unpublished PhD, Manchester Metropolitan University, Manchester.

Kapor, M. (1996). A software design manifesto. In T. Winograd (Ed.), *Bringing design to software* (pp. 1-9). New York: Addison Wesley.

Kaufman, R., Thiagarajan, S., & MacGillis, P. (Eds.) (1996). *Guidebook for performance improvement : Working with individuals & organizations*. San Francisco: Jossey-Bass.

Keller, F. S. (1968). Good-bye teacher! *Journal of Applied Behavioral Analysis, 1*, pp. 79-84.

Kemp, J. E., & Dayton, D. K. (1985). *Planning and producing instructional media* (5th Ed.). Cambridge, MA: Harper & Row.

Khan, B. H. (Ed.). (1997). *Web-based instruction*. Englewood Cliffs, NJ: Educational Technology Publications.

Kieras, D. E., & Bovair, S. (1984). The role of a mental model in learning to operate a device. *Cognitive Science, 8*, 255-273.

Kindfield, A. C. H. (1993). Biology diagrams: Tools to think with. *Journal of the Learning Sciences, 3* (1), 1-36.

King, A. (1989). Effects of self-questioning training on college students' comprehension of lectures. *Contemporary Educational Psychology, 14*, 366-381.

King, A. (1992). Facilitating elaborative learning through guided student-generated questioning. *Educational Psychologist, 27*, 111-126.

Kinnear, J. (1998). *Catlab*. [Computer program]. Stuart, FL: EME Corporation.

Kirshner, D., & Whitson, J. (1998). Obstacles to understanding cognition as situated. *Educational Researcher, 27*(8), 22-8.

Klemp, G. O. (Ed.) (1980). *The assessment of cccupational competence*. Washington, DC: Report to the National Institute of Education.

Kobus, D. A., Moses, J. D., & Bloom, F. A. (1994). Effect of multi-modal stimulus presentation on recall. *Perceptual and Motor Skills, 78*, 320-322.

Kollock, P. (1999). The economies of online cooperation: Gifts and public goods in cyberspace. In M. A. Smith & P. Kollock (Eds.) *Communities in cyberspace*. London: Routledge.

Kolodner, J., & Guzdial, M. (1996). Effects *with* and *of* CSCL: Tracking learning in a new paradigm. In T. Koschmann (Ed.), *CSCL: Theory and practice* (pp. 307-320). Mahwah, NJ: Erlbaum.

Koschmann, T., Kelson, A. C., Feltovich, P. J., & Barrows, H. S. (1996). Computer-Supported problem-based learning: A principled approach to the use of computers in collaborative learning. In T. Koschmann (Ed.), *CSCL: Theory and practice* (pp. 83-124). New Jersey: Mahwah.

Kourilsky, M., & Wittrock, M. C. (1992). Generative teaching: An enhancement strategy for the learning of economics in cooperative groups. *American Educational Research Journal, 29* (4), 861-876.

Kruley, P., Sciama, S. C., & Glenburg, A. M. (1994). On-line processing of textual illustrations in the visuospatial sketchpad: Evidence from dual-task studies. *Memory & Cognition, 22*, 261-272.

Lajoie, S. P., & Lesgold, A. (1989). Apprenticeship training in the workplace: Computer-coached practice environment as a new form of apprenticeship. *Machine-Mediated Learning, 3*, 7-28.

Lajoie, S. P., & Derry, S. (Eds.). (1993). *Computers as cognitive tools.* Hillsdale New Jersey: Lawrence Erlbaum Associates.

Lakewood Publications. (1998). Third world KM: The best place to start? *Online Learning News* [On-line serial], *1* (39).

Lakoff, G. (1987). *Women, fire and dangerous things.* Chicago: The University of Chicago Press.

Latour, B. (1995). Mixing humans and nonhumans together: the sociology of a door-closer. In S. L. Star (Ed.), *Ecologies of knowledge.* New York: State University of New York Press.

Lave, J. (1988). *Cognition in Practice: Mind, mathematics, and culture in everyday life.* Cambridge, UK: Cambridge University Press.

Lave, J., & Wenger, E. (1991). *Situated learning: Legitimate peripheral participation.* Cambridge: Cambridge University Press.

Lee, S. H., & Boling, E. (1996). Motivational screen design guidelines for effective computer-mediated instruction. In *Proceedings of Selected Research and Development Presentations at the 1996 National Convention of the Association for Educational Communications and Technology* (18th Ed.) (pp. 401-12). Indianapolis, IN: ERIC Document ED 397 811.

Leont'ev, A. (1974). The problem of activity in psychology. *Soviet Psychology, 13*(2), 4-33.

Lewandowski, L. J., & Kobus, D. A. (1993). The effects of redundancy in bimodal word processing. *Human Performance, 6*, 229-239.

Lewis, J., Whitaker, J., & Julian, J. (1995). Distance education for the 21st century: The future of national and international telecomputing networks in distance education. In Berge, Z., & Collins, M. (Eds.), *Computer mediated communication and the online classroom*, Vol. 3, pp. 13-30. New Jersey: Hampton Press, Inc.

Lockard, J., Abrams, P. D., Many, W. A. (1990). Microcomputers for_educators *(2nd Ed.).* New York: Harper Collins.

Lombard, M., & Ditton, T. (September, 1997). At the heart of it all: The concept of social presence. *Journal of Computer Mediated Communication 3*(2), 1-38.

Lowther, D. L., & Morrison, G. R. (1998, March). The NTeQ model: a framework for technology integration. *TechTrends*, 33-38.

Lucia, A. D., & Lepsinger, R. (1999). *The art and science of competency models: Pinpointing critical success factors in organizations.* San Francisco: Jossey-Bass/Pfeiffer.

Luck, D. D., & Hunter, J. M. (1997, January). Visual design principles applied to world wide web construction. In *VisionQuest: Journeys toward Visual Literacy. Selected Readings from the 28th Annual Conference of the Visual Literacy Association.* Cheyenne, Wyoming, October, 1996. ERIC document ED 408 985.

Macromedia. (1999). *Authorware 4.* [Computer program]. San Francisco, CA: Macromedia.

Makochieng, O. (1999). *Effects of information technology on the learning process: Formative evaluation of a technology based curriculum for postgraduate orthodontics education.* Unpublished *hovedfag* thesis. Bergen, Norway: Department of Information Science, University of Bergen.

Mandinach, E. B., & Cline, H. F. (1994). *Classroom dynamics: Implementing a technology-based learning environment.* Hillsdale, NJ: Lawrence Erlbaum.

Mandinach, E. B., & Cline, H. F. (1996). Classroom dynamics: The impact of a technology-based curriculum innovation on teaching and learning. *Journal of Educational Computing Research, 14*(1), 83-102.

Marton, F., Hounsell, D., & Entwistle, N. (Eds.). (1997). *The experience of learning* (2nd ed.). Edinburgh: Scottish Academic Press.

Masie, E. (1998, April). Emerging acronyms spell market change. *Computer Reseller News.* April 27, 1998, p. 59.

Maxis. (1996). *Sim City.* [Computer program]. Walnut Creek, CA: Maxis.

Maxis. (1996). *Sim Farm.* [Computer program]. Walnut Creek, CA: Maxis.

Maxis. (1998). *Sim Earth.* [Computer program]. Walnut Creek, CA: Maxis.

Mayer, R. E. (1989). Models for understanding. *Review of Educational Research, 59* (1), 43-64.

Mayer, R. E., Steinhoff, K., Bower, G., & Mars, R. (1995). A generative theory of textbook design: Using annotated illustrations to foster meaningful learning of science text. *Educational Technology Research and Development,* 43, 31-43.

Mayer, R., & Anderson, R. (1991). Animations need notations: An experimental test of a dual-coding hypothesis. *Journal of Educational Psychology,* 83, 484-490.

Mayer, R., & Anderson, R. (1992). The instructive animation: Helping students build connections between words and pictures in multimedia learning. *Journal of Educational Psychology,* 84, 444-452.

Mayer, R., & Gallini, J. (1990). When is an illustration worth ten thousand words. *Journal of Educational Psychology,* 82, 715-726.

Mayer, R., & Sims, V. K. (1994). For whom is a picture worth a thousand words? Extension of a dual-coding theory of multimedia learning. *Journal of Educational Psychology,* 86, 3 89-40 1.

Mayer, R., Bover, W., Bryman, A., Mars, R., & Tapangco, L. (1996). When less is more: Meaningful learning from visual and verbal summaries of science textbook lessons. *Journal of Educational Psychology,* 88, 64-73.

McCombs, B.L. (1992). *Learner centered psychological principles.* Washington, DC: American Psychological Association, in collaboration with the Mid-continent Regional Educational Laboratory.

McCullough, M. (1996). *Abstracting craft: The practiced digital hand.* Cambridge Mass: MIT Press.

McIsaac, M. S., & Gunawardena, C. N. (1996). Distance education. In Jonassen, D. H. (Ed.). *Handbook of Research for Educational Communications and Technology.* New York, NY: Simon and Schuster McMillan, 403-37.

McMahon, T. A. (1997, April). *From isolation to interaction? Network-based professional development and teacher professional communication.* Paper presented at the meeting of the American Educational Research Association, Chicago, IL.

McManus T. (1998). *Special considerations for designing internet based instruction.* (http://ccwf.cc.utexas.edu/~mcmanus/special.html).

Merriënboer, J. J. G. van & Dijkstra, S. (1997). The four-component instructional-design model for training complex cognitive skills. In Tennyson, R. D., Schott, F., Seel, N. & Dijkstra, S. (Eds). *Instructional design: international perspectives, Volume 1* (pp. 427-446). Mahwah, NJ: Lawrence Erlbaum.

Merrill, M. D., Drake, L., Lacy, M. J., Pratt J., & the ID2 Research Group (1996). Reclaiming instructional design. *Educational Technology,* 36(5), 5-7.

Merrill, M. D., Jones, M. K., & Li, Z. (1992). Second generation instructional design. *Educational Technology, 31*(6), 7-12.

Merry, U. (1995). *Coping with uncertainty: Insights from new sciences of chaos, self-organization, and complexity.* New York: Praeger.

Merseth, K. K. (1992, May). First aid for first-year teachers. *Phi Delta Kappan, 73* (9), p. 678-83.

Milheim, W. D. (1995). Virtual reality and its potential applications in education and training. *Machine-Mediated Learning, 5*(1), 43-55.

Miyake, N., & Norman, S. A. (1979). To ask a question, one must know enough to know what is not known. *Journal of Verbal Learning and Verbal Behavior, 18*, 357-364.

Moller, L., (1998). Designing communities of learners for asynchronous distance education. *Educational Technology Research and Development, 46*(4), 115-22.

Montague, W. E. (1988). *What works: Summary of research findings with implications for Navy instruction and learning* (NAVEDTRA 115-1). Pensacola, FL: Chief of Naval Education and Training.

Montague, W. E. (1988). *What works: Summary of research findings with implications for Navy instruction and learning* (NAVEDTRA 115-1). Pensacola, FL: Chief of Naval Education and Training.

Moore, M. G. (1989). Distance education: a learner's system. *Lifelong learning: an omnibus of practice and research, 12*(8), 8-11.

Moore, M. G., & Kearsley, G. (1996). *Distance education: a systems view.* Belmont, CA: Wadsworth.

Morecroft, J. D. W. & Sterman, J. D. (Eds.) (1994). *Modeling for learning organizations.* Portland: Productivity Press.

Morris, R .C. T. (1994). Toward a user-centered information service. *Journal of the American Society for Information Science, 45*(1). 20-30.

Morrow, D. G., Bower, G. H., & Greenspan, S. (1989). Updating situation models during narrative comprehension. *Journal of Memory and Language, 28*, 292-312.

Mousavi, S. Y., Low, R., & Sweller, J. (1995). Reducing cognitive load by mixing auditory and visual presentation modes. *Journal of Educational Psychology, 87*, 319-334.

Muffoletto, R. (1997, March). Reflections on designing and producing an internet-based course. *TechTrends,* 50-3.

Nardi, B., & O'Day, V. (1999). *Information ecologies: Using technology with heart.* Cambridge Mass: MIT Press.

Neyland, D. L. (1997). *Virtual combat.* Mechanicsburg, PA: Stackpole Books.

Niegemann, H. M. (1995). Zum Einfluß von "modelling" in einer computergestützten Lernumgebung: Quasi-experimentelle Untersuchung zur Instruktionsdesign-Theorie. *Unterrichtswissenschaft, 23* (1), 75-87.

Norman, D. A. (1983). Some observations on mental models. In D. Gentner & A. L. Stevens (Eds.), *Mental models* (pp. 7-14). Hillsdale, NJ: Erlbaum.

Nussbaum, J., & Novick, S. (1983). Alternative frameworks, conceptual conflict and accommodation: Toward a principled teaching strategy. *Instructional Science, 11*, 183-300.

O'Dell, C., & Grayson, C. J., Jr. (1998). *If only we knew what we know.* New York: The Free Press.

O'Neil, H. F. Jr., Allred, A., & Baker, E. L. (1992). *Measurement of workforce readiness competencies: Review of theoretical frameworks* (CSE Technical Report No. 343). Los Angeles: University of California, Center for Research on Evaluation Standards and Student Testing.

Oblinger, D. G. (2000). Technology and change: impossible to resist. In Hirschbuhl, J. J., & Bishop, D. (Eds). *Computers in Education: Annual Editions, 00/01.* Guilford, CN: Dushkin/McGraw-Hill, pp. 17-29.

Ormrod, J. E. (1998). *Educational Psychology: Developing Learners, 2nd Ed.* New York: Merrill Prentice Hall.

Paivio, A. (1986). *Mental representations: A dual-coding approach.* New York: Oxford University Press.

Papert, S. (1980). *Mindstorms: Children, computers, and powerful ideas.* New York: Basic Books.

Pappo, H. A. (1998). *Simulations for skills training.* Englewood Cliffs, NJ: Educational Technology Publications.

Park, I., & Hannafin, M. J. (1993). Empirically-based guidelines for the design of interactive multimedia. *Educational Technology Research and Development*, 41, 63-85.

Park, O. & Hopkins, R. (1993). Instructional conditions for using dynamic visual displays: A review. *Instructional Science*, 21, 427-449.

Park, O. (1997). Adaptive instructional systems. In D. H. Jonassen (Ed.), *Handbook of research on educational technology and communication.* Academic Press.

Perez, R. S., & Emery, C. D. (1995). Designer thinking: How novices and experts think about instructional design. *Performance Improvement Quarterly, 8(3)*, 80-89.

Perez, R. S., & Neiderman, E. C. (1992). Modeling the expert training developer. In R. J. Seidel & P. Chatelier (Eds.), *Advanced Training Technologies Applied to Training Design.* New York, NY: Plenum Press.

Piaget, J. (1937). *La construction du réel chez l'enfant.* [The child's construction of the reality]. Neuchâtel: Delachaux et Niestlé.

Piaget, J. (1970). *Epistémologie génétique.* [Genetic epistemology]. Paris: Presses Universitaires de France.

Pieters, J. M., & deBruijn, H. F. M. (1992). Learning environments for cognitive apprenticeship: From experience to expertise. In P. A. M. Kommers, D. H. Jonassen & T. Mayes (Eds.), *Cognitive tools for learning* (pp. 241-248). Berlin: Springer.

Pirolli, P. (1991). Computer-aided instructional design systems. In H. Burns, J. Parlett, & C. Redfield (Eds.), *Intelligent Tutoring Systems: Evolution in Design* (pp. 105-125). Hillsdale New Jersey: Lawrence Erlbaum Associates.

Polya, G. (1954). *How to solve it.* Princeton, NJ: Princeton University Press.

Porter, L. A. (1997). *Creating the virtual classroom - distance learning with the internet.* New York, NY: John Wiley and Sons.

PowerSim. (1999). *PowerSim.* [Computer program]. Bergen, Norway: PowerSim.

Practising Law Institute. (1996). *The Interactive Courtroom.* [Computer program]. New York: Practising Law Institute.

Prince, C., Chidester, T., Bowers, C., & Cannon-Bowers, J. (1992). Aircrew coordination - achieving teamwork in the cockpit. In R. Swezey & E. Salas (Eds.), *Teams: Their training and performance* (pp. 329-354). Norwood New Jersey: Ablex Publishing Corporation.

Psotka, J. (1995). Immersive training systems: Virtual reality and education and training. *Instructional Science*, 23(5-6), 405-431.

Pugh, A. L. (1983). *DYNAMO user's manual: including DYNAMO II/370, DYNAMO II/F, DYNAMO III/370, DYNAMO III/F, DYNAMO III/F+, DYNAMO IV/370, and Gaming DYNAMO. 6th ed.* Cambridge, MA: M.I.T. Press.

Pugh-Roberts Associates. (1982). *Micro-DYNAMO.* [Computer program]. Reading, MA: Addison-Wesley.

Ragan, T. J., & Smith, P. J. (1996). Conditions-based models for designing instruction. In Jonassen, D. H. (Ed.). *Handbook of Research for Educational Communications and Technology.* New York, NY: Simon and Schuster McMillan, 541-69.

Reigeluth, C. M. (Ed.) (1983). *Instructional design theories and models: An overview of their current status.* Hillsdale, NJ: Erlbaum.

Reigeluth, C. M. (Ed.) (1999). *Instructional design theories and models: A new paradigm of instructional theory, Vol II.* Mahwah, NJ: Erlbaum.

Reigeluth, C. M., & Curtis, R. V. (1987). Learning situations and instructional models. In R. M. Gagné (Ed.). *Instructional Technology Foundations,* 175-206. Hillsdale, NJ: Erlbaum.

Reiser, R. A. (1987). Instructional technology: a history. In R. M. Gagné (Ed.). *Instructional Technology: Foundations.* Hillsdale, NJ: Erlbaurm, pp. 11-48.

Reiser, R. A., & Ely, D. P. (1997). The field of educational technology as reflected through its definitions. *Educational Technology, Research and Development, 45*(3), 65-74.

Reiser, R. A., & Salisbury, D. R. (1995). Instructional technology and public education in the United States: the next decade. *In Instructional technology: past, present and future* (2nd Ed.) (pp. 254-262). Englewood, CO: Libraries Unlimited.

Renkl, A., Mandl, H., & Gruber, H. (1996). Inert knowledge: Analyses and remedies. *Educational Psychologist, 31*(2), 115-121.

Resnick, L. B. (Ed.) (1989). *Knowing, learning, and instruction.* Hillsdale, NJ: Lawrence Erlbaum.

Reynolds, R. E., Sinatra, G. M., & Jetton, T. L. (1996). Views of knowledge acquisition and representation: A continuum from experience centered to mind centered. *Educational Psychologist, 31* (2), 93-104.

Rheingold, H. (1993). *The virtual community: Homesteading on the electric frontier.* New York: Addison-Wesley.

Richards, T. (1998). *The Emergence of open standards for learning technology.* San Francisco, CA: Macromedia, Inc. (http://www.learnativity.com/standards.html)

Richey, R. C. & Fields, D. F. (Eds.) (2000). *Instructional design competencies: The standards* (3rd Ed.). Syracuse, NY: ERIC Clearinghouse on Information and Technology & The International Board of Standards for Training, Performance & Instruction.

Rieber, L. P. (1989). Computer-based microworlds: A bridge between constructivism and direct instruction. *Educational Technology Research and Development, 40* (1), 93-106.

Rieber, L. P. (1994, April). *An instructional design philosophy of interaction based on a blending of microworlds, simulations, and games.* Paper presented at the Annual Meeting of the American Educational Research Association, New Orleans, April 4-8.

Riel, M. M., & Levin, J. A. (1990). Building electronic communities: success and failure in computer networking. *Instructional Science, 19,* 145-169.

Rips, L. J. (1987). Mental muddles. In M. Brand, & R. M. Harnish (Eds.), *The representation of knowledge and belief* (pp. 259-286). Tucson: University of Arizona Press.

Ritchie, D. C., & Hoffman, B. (1997). *Using instructional design principles to amplify learning on the World Wide Web.* ERIC Document ED 415 835.

Roberts, N., Anderson, D., Deal, R., Garet, M., & Shaffer, W. (1983). *Computer Simulation: A System Dynamics Modeling Approach.* Reading, MA: Addison-Wesley.

Roblyer, M. D., & Edwards, J. (2000). *Integrating educational technology into teaching* (2nd Ed.). Upper Saddle River, NJ: Merrill, an imprint of Prentice Hall.

Romiszowski, A. (1997). The use of telecommunication in education. In S. Dijkstra, N. Seel, F. Schott & R. D. Tennyson. (Eds.), *Instructional design: international perspectives, Volume 2* (pp. 183-220). Mahwah, NJ: Lawrence Erlbaum.

Romiszowski, A. J. (1993). *Designing instructional systems.* London: Kogan Page Ltd.

Rosch, E. (1978). Principles of categorization. In E. Rosch & B. B. Lloyd (Eds.), *Cognition and Categorization* (pp. 28-46). Hillsdale, NJ: Lawrence Erlbaum Associates.

Rossett, A., & Marshall, J. (1999). Signposts on the road to knowledge management. In K. P. Kuchinke (Ed.), *Proceedings of the 1999 AHRD Conference: Vol. 1* (pp. 496-503). Baton Rouge, LA: Academy of Human Resource Development.

Rothwell, W. J. (1996). *Beyond training and development: State of the art strategies for enhancing human performance.* New York: American Management Association.

Rowland, G. (1992). What do instructional designers actually do? An initial investigation of expert practice. *Performance Improvement Quarterly,* 5(2), 65-86.

Royer, J. M., Cisero, C. A., & Carlo, M. S. (1993). Techniques and procedures for assessing cognitive skills. *Review of Educational Research,* 63 (2), 201-243.

Rüttgers, J. (1999). *Hochschulen für das 21. Jahrhundert*. [Higher education for the 21st century]. (see http://www.bmbf.de/deutsch/veroeff/dokus/hochschul.htm)

Salomon, G. (1993) (Ed.). *Distributed cognitions: Psychological and educational considerations*. New York: Cambridge University Press.

Sasse, M. A. (1991). How to t(r)ap users. In D. Ackermann & M. J. Tauber (Eds.), *Mental Models and Human-Computer Interaction 2*. Amsterdam: Elsvier.

Savenye, W. (1998, June). *Evaluating the impact of video and web-based distance learning courses*. Paper presented at the annual meeting of EDMEDIA/TELECOM, Freiburg, Germany, June 20-25, 1998.

Savenye, W. C., Davidson, G. V., & Smith, P. L. (1991). Teaching instructional design in a computer literacy course. *Educational Technology Research and Development, 39* (3), 49-58.

Savenye, W., & Smith, K. (1997). *Enhancing interaction in an outcomes-based distance learning environment*. Paper presented at the annual meeting of the Association for Communications and Technology, Albuquerque, New Mexico, February 12-16, 1997.

Savery, J. R., & Duffy, T. M. (1996). Problem based learning: An instructional model and its consructivist framework. In B. G. Wilson (Ed.), *Constructivist learning environments: Case studies in instructional design* (pp. 135-150). Englewood Cliffs, NJ: Educational Technology Publications.

Scandura, J. M. (1995). Theoretical foundations of instruction: Past, present, and future. *Journal of Structural Learning, 12*(3), 231-243.

Schank, R. C. (1995). *Engines for education*. Mahwah, NJ: Lawrence Erlbaum Associates.

Schank, R., & Cleary, C. (1995). *Engines for education*. Hillsdale, NJ: Lawrence Erlbaum.

Schank, R.C., Fano, A., Bell, B., & Jona, M. (1993/94). The design of goal-based scenarios. *Journal of the Learning Sciences, 3* (4), 305-345.

Schiffman, S. S. (1995). Instructional systems design: five views of the field. *In Instructional technology: past, present and future* (2nd Ed.) (pp. 131-144). Englewood, CO: Libraries Unlimited.

Schön, D. (1983). *The reflective practitioner: How professionals think in action*. New York: Basic Books.

Schon, D. (1984). The architectural studio as an example of education for reflection-in-action. *Journal of Architectural Education, 38*, 2-9.

Schon, D., & Bennett, J. (1996). Reflective conversation with materials. In T. Winograd (Ed.), *Bringing design to software* (pp. 171-184). New York: Addison Wesley.

Schott, F., & Driscoll, M. (1997). On the architectonics of instructional theory. In R. D. Tennyson, F. Schott, N. Seel, & S. Dijkstra (Eds.), *Instructional design: International perspectives, Volume 1: Theory, research, and models* (pp. 135-173). Mahwah, NJ: Erlbaum.

Seel, N. (1999). Instruktionsdesign: Modelle und Anwendungsgebiete [Instructional Design: Models and Applications]. *Unterrichtswissenschaft, 27*, p. 2-11.

Seel, N. M. & Winn, W. D. (1997). Research on media and learning: distributed cognition and semiotics. In Tennyson, R. D., Schott, F., Seel, N. & Dijkstra, S. (Eds), *Instructional design: international perspectives, Volume 1* (pp. 293-326). Mahwah, NJ: Lawrence Erlbaum.

Seel, N. M. (1991). *Weltwissen und mentale Modelle*. Göttingen: Hogrefe.

Seel, N. M. (1995). Mental models, knowledge transfer, and teaching strategies. *Journal of Structural Learning and Intelligent Systems, 12* (3), 197-213.

Seel, N. M. (1999). Educational diagnosis of mental models. Assessment problems and technology-based solutions. *Journal of Structural Learning and Intelligent Systems, 14* (1), 153-185.

Seel, N. M., & Dinter, F. R. (1995). Instruction and mental model progression: Learner-dependent effects of teaching strategies on knowledge acquisition and analogical transfer. *Educational Research and Evaluation, 1*(1), 4-35.

Seel, N. M., Al-Diban, S., Held, S., & Hess, C. (1998). Didaktisches Design multimedialer Lernumgebungen: Theoretische Positionen, Gestaltungsprinzipien, empirische Befunde. In G. Dörr & K.L. Jüngst (Hrsg.), *Lernen mit Medien. Ergebnisse und Perspektiven zu medial vermittelten Lehr- und Lernprozessen* (S. 87-119). Weinheim: Juventa.

Seels, B. R. & Richey, R. C. (1994) *Instructional technology: The definition and domains of the dield.* Washington, DC: Association for Educational Communications and Technology.

Seels, B. R. & Richey, R. C. (1994) *Instructional technology: The definition and domains of the field.* Washington, DC: Association for Educational Communications and Technology.

Seidel, R. J., & Perez, R S. (1994). An evaluation model for investigating the impact of innovative educational technology. In H. F. O'Niel & E. L. Baker (Eds.), *Technology assessment in software applications* (pp.177-212). Hillsdale, NJ: Erlbaum.

Senge, P.M. (1990). *The fifth discipline: The art and practice of the learning organization.* New York: Doubleday Books.

Sfard, A. (1998). On two metaphors for learning and the dangers of choosing just one. *Educational Researcher, 27*(2), 4-12.

Sharp, D. L. M., Bransford, J. D., Goldman, S. R., Risko, V. J., Kinzer, C. K., & Vye, N. J. (1995). Dynamic visual support for story comprehension and mental model building by young, at-risk children. *Educational Technology Research and Development, 43* (4), 25-42.

Shute, V. J. (1994). Learning processes and learning outcomes. In T. Husén & T. N. Postlethwaite (Eds.), *The international encyclopedia of education, Vol. 6* (pp. 3315-3325). Oxford: Pergamon & Elsevier Science Ltd.

Sieloff, C. (1999, September). *Why knowledge management projects fail.* Presentation made at the 1999 Meeting of Knowledge Management, September 17, 1999, San Francisco, CA.

Simonson, M., Smaldino, S., Albright, M., & Zvacek, S. (2000). *Teaching and learning at a distance: foundations of distance education.* Upper Saddle River, NJ: Merrill, an imprint of Prentice Hall.

Slotta, J. D., Chi, M. T. H., & Joram, E. (1995). Assessing students' misclassification of physics concepts: An ontological basis for conceptual change. *Cognition and Instruction, 13* (3), 373-400.

Smith, M., & Kollock, P. (Eds.). (1999). Communities in cyberspace. London: Routledge.

Smith, P. J., & Ragan, T. J. (1999). *Instructional design.* (2nd Ed.). Upper Saddle River, NJ: Merrill, an imprint of Prentice Hall.

Snodgrass, J. G., & Vanderwart, M. (1980). A standardized set of 260 pictures: norms for naming agreement, familiarity, and visual complexity. *Journal of Experimental Psychology: Learning, Memory and Cognition, 6,* 174-215.

Snow, R. E. (1990). New approaches to cognitive and conative assessment in education. *International Journal of Educational Research, 14* (5), 455-473.

Special Issue: Organizational Memory Systems (1999*). Journal of Organizational Computing and Electronic Commerce 9* (2 & 3).

Spector, J. M. (1998). President's corner. *Journal of Courseware Engineering,* 1, 1-4.

Spector, J. M. (1995). Integrating and humanizing the process of automating instructional design. In R. D. Tennyson & A. Barron (Eds.), *Automating instructional design: Computer-based development and delivery tools* (pp. 523-546). Brussels, Belgium: Springer-Verlag.

Spector, J. M. (1996). *Creativity and constructivity in learning environments. Educational Media International, 33*(2), 55-59.

Spector, J. M. (1998). The future of instructional theory: A synthesis of European & American perspectives. *Journal of Structural Learning, 13*(2), 115-128.

Spector, J. M. (on behalf of the Grimstad Group) (1995). Applying system dynamics to courseware development. *Computers in Human Behavior*, 11(2), 325-339.

Spector, J. M., & Davidsen, P. I. (1997). Creating engaging courseware using system dynamics. *Computers in Human Behavior*, 13(2), 127-155.

Spector, J. M., Arnold, E. M., & Wilson A. S. (1996). A Turing test for automatically generated instruction. *Journal of Structural Learning*, 12(4), 310-313.

Spiro, R. J., Feltovich, P. J., Jacobson, M. J., & Coulson, R. L. (1991). Cognitive flexibility, constructivism, and hypertext: Random access instruction for advanced knowledge acquisition in ill-structured domains. *Educational Technology, 31* (5), 24-33.

Starfield, A. M., Smith, K. A., & Bleloch, A. L. (1990). *How to model it: Problem solving for the computer age*. New York: McGraw-Hill.

Starr, R. M. (1997, May-June). Delivering instruction on the world wide web: Overview and basic design principles. *Educational Technology*, 7-15.

Sternberg, R. J. (1986). *Intelligence applied: Understanding and increasing your intellectual skills*. San Diego, CA: Harcourt Brace Jovanovich.

Stewart, T. A. (1997, June 23). Why dumb things happen to smart companies: Symptoms of bad brainpower management. *Fortune, 135,* 159-160.

Stewart, T. A. (1997). *Intellectual capital: The new wealth of organizations*. New York: Doubleday.

Stewart, T. A. (1998, October 12). Knowledge, the appreciating commodity. *Fortune, 138,* 199-200.

Stock, W. A., Kulhavy, R. W., Webb, J. M., Pridemore, D. R., & Verdi, M. P. (1993, April). *Map and text learning: The privilege of economical representation*. Paper presented at the Annual Meeting of the American Psychological Society, Arpil 19093, Chicago, IL.

Struck, S. J., & Fowler-Frey, J. (1996). *ESL online action research. Final report.* Lancaster, PN: Pennsylvania Association for Adult Continuing Education. (ERIC Document Reproduction Service No. ED 406 861)

Sullivan, H. J. & Higgins, N. (1983). *Teaching for Competence*. New York, NY: Teachers College Press.

Sullivan, H. J., Igoe, A. R., Klein, J. D., Jones, E. E., & Savenye, W. C. (1993). Perspectives on the future of educational technology. *Educational Technology Research and Development, 41* (2), 97-110.

Sweller, J. (1988). Cognitive load during problem solving: Effects on learning. *Cognitive Science*, 12, 257-285.

Sweller, J. (1989). Cognitive technology: Some procedures for facilitating learning and problem solving in mathematics and science. *Journal of Educational Psychology*, 81, 457-466.

Sweller, J. (1993). Some cognitive processes and their consequences for the organization and presentation of information. *Australian Journal of Psychology*, 45, 1-8.

Sweller, J. (1994). Cognitive load theory, learning difficulty and instructional design. *Learning and Instruction*, 4, 295-312.

Szulanski, G. (1996, Winter). Exploring internal stickiness: Impediments to the transfer of best practices within the firm. *Strategic Management Journal, 17,* 27-43.

Taylor, R. (1980). *The computer in the school: Tutor, tool, and tutee*. New York, NY: Teachers College Press.

Tennyson, R. D. (1995). Four generations of instructional system development. *Journal of Structural Learning, 12*, 149-164.

Tennyson, R. D., & Morrison, G. R. (2000). *Instructional development: Foundations, Process, and Methodology*. Columbus, OH: Merrill/Prentice-Hall.

Tennyson, R. D., Schott, F., Seel, N. M., & Dijkstra, S. (Eds.) (1997). *Instructional Design: International Perspectives, Vol. 1*. Mahwah, NJ: Lawrence Erlbaum.

The Institute for Higher Education Policy (2000). Quality on the line: Benchmarks for success in internet-based distance education. Washington, DC: The Institute for Higher Education Policy.

Tiffen, J., & Rajasingham, L. (1995). *In search of the virtual class: Education in an information society.* London & New York: Routledge.

Trondsen, E. (1999, September). *Learning on demand.* Presentation at the Stanford Research Institute: Learning On Demand Workshop, Palo Alto, CA. September 14, 1999.

Van Joolingen, W. R., King, S., & de Jong, T. (1997). The SimQuest authoring system for simulation-base discovery environments. In B. du Boulay & R. Mizoguchi (Eds.), *Knowledge and media in learning systems* (pp. 79-87). Amsterdam: IOS.

Veenman, M. V. J., & Elshout, J. J. (1995). Differential effects of instructional support on learning in simulation environments. *Instructional Science, 22*(5), 363-383.

Verdi, M. P., Peterson, S. E., Webb, J. M., Stock, W. A., & Kulhavy, R. W. (1993, April). *Creating maps from perceptual and verbal stimuli: Retrieving text and recreating maps.* Paper presented at the Annual Meeting of the American Educational Research Association, April, 1993, Atlanta, GA.

Volet, S. E. (1991). Modelling and coaching of relevant, metacognitive strategies for enhancing university students' learning. *Learning and Instruction, 1* (4), 319-336.

Vosniadou, S. & Brewer, W. F. (1994). Mental models of the day / night circle. *Cognitive Science, 18,* 123-183.

Waddill, P. J., McDaniel, M. A. (1992). Pictorial enhancement of text memory: Limitations imposed by picture type and comprehension skill. *Memory and Cognition, 20,* 472-482.

Waddill, P. J., McDaniel, M. A., & Einstein, G. O. (1988). Illustrations as adjuncts to prose: A test-appropriate processing approach. *Journal of Educational Psychology,* 80, 457-464.

Wagner, E. D. (1998). Are you ready for electronic learning? In *Learning without limits, 2nd Ed.,* pp 7 – 13. San Francisco: Informania

Wagner, E. D. (1999). Beyond Distance learning: Distributed learning systems, in H. Stolovich & E. Keeps (Eds.), *Handbook of Human Performance Technology (2nd Ed.)* (pp. 626-648). San Francisco: Jossey Bass.

Ward, G. (1988). *High-risk training: Managing training programs for high risk occupations.* London: Kogan Page.

Watts, G. D. & Castle, S. (1992, May). Electronic networking and the construction of professional knowledge. *Phi Delta Kappan, 73* (9), p. 684-89.

Weisher, P. (1998). *Digital space: Designing virtual environments.* New York: McGraw Hill.

Wenger, E. (1998). *Communities of practice.* Cambridge: Cambridge University Press.

Westbury, I., Hopmann, S., & Riquarts, H. (Eds.) (1999). *Teaching as a Reflective Practice – the German Didaktik Tradition.* Mahwah, NJ: Erlbaum.

Wertsch, J. (1998). *Mind as action.* Cambridge: Cambridge University Press.

White, B. Y. (1995). *Discrete models, computer microworlds, and scientific inquiry: An alternative approach to physics education.* San Francisco: American Educational Research Association

Wickens, C.D. (1992). *Engineering Psychology and Human Performance.* New York: Harper Collins Publishers, Inc.

Wilbur, S. (1998). Creating a community of learning using web-based tools. In R. Hazemi, S. Hailes, & S. Wilbur (Eds.), *The digital university: Reinventing the academy* (pp. 73-84). London: Springer.

Wilson, B. (Ed.). (1996). *Constructivist learning environments.* Englewood Cliffs NJ: Educational Technology Press.

Wilson, J. R., & Rutherford, A. (1989). Mental models: Theory and application in human factors. *Human Factors, 31,* 617-634.

Winograd, T., & Tabor, P. (1996). Software design and architecture. In T. Winograd (Ed.), *Bringing design to software* (pp. 10-16). New York: Addison Wesley.

Wisner, A. (1995). Situated cognition and action: implications for ergonomic work analysis and anthropotechnology. *Ergonomics, 38*(8), 1542-57.

Wisner, A. (1995). Understanding problem building: ergonomic work analysis. *Ergonomics, 38*(3), 595-605.

Withrow, F., Long, H, & Marx, G. (2000). Contemporary technology. In Hirschbuhl, J. J., & Bishop, D. (Eds.). *Computers in education: Annual editions, 00/01*, pp. 8-12. Guilford, CN: Dushkin/McGraw-Hill.

Wright, J. C., Huston, A. C., Ross, R. P., Calvert, S. L., Rolandelli, D., Weeks, L. A., Raeissi, P., & Potts (1984). Pace and continuity of television programs: Effects on children's attention and comprehension. *Developmental Psychology, 20*, 653-666.

Wyman, R. (1969). *Mediaware: selection, operation and maintenance.* Dubuque, IA: Wm. C. Brown.

Yee, P. L., Hunt, E. B., & Pellegrino, J. W. (1991). Coordinating cognitive information: task effects and individual differences in integrating information from several sources. *Cognitive Psychology, 23*, 615-680.

Young, M. F., Barab, S., & Garrett, S. (2000). Agent as detector: An ecological psychology perspective on learning by perceiving-acting systems. In D. H. Jonassen & S. M. Land (Eds.), *Theoretical foundations of learning environments* (pp. 147-171). Mahwah, NJ: Lawrence Erlbaum Associates.

Zaraza, R., & Fisher, D. (1997, August). *Introducing System Dynamics into the traditional secondary curriculum: The CC-STADUS project's search for leverage points.* Paper presented at the 15th International System Dynamics Conference, Istanbul, Turkey, August 19-22.

Zaraza, R., Joy, T., & Guthrie, S. (1998, July). *Modeling in the educational environment – Moving from simplicity to complexity.* Paper presented at the 16th International System Dynamics Conference, Quebec, Canada, July 20-23.

Zimmerman, S. O. & Greene, M. W. (1998). A five-year chronicle: Using technology in a teacher education program. In McNeil, S. (Ed.), *SITE 98: Society for Information Technology & Teacher Education International Conference* (p.1136-39). Charlottesville, VA: Association for the Advancement of Computing in Education (AACE).

INDEX

A

affordances
    integrating, 125–26
    in learning technologies, 114–25
    mindtools, 124–25
Arizona State University project, 40–41
    . *See also* Teaching with Technology
        course
articulation, 141
    . *See also* cognitive apprenticeship
asynchronous text-based, 10–11
autonomous learners, 5
    . *See also* lifelong learning

B

building simulations
    conditions for, 187–91
    and declarative learning, 182–84
    educational dilemma, 184–85
    environment, 192–93
    introduction, 177–79
    to *using* continuum, 179–81

C

CASENET, 30–31
categorization, 216–17
    problems, 220
CBL. *See* competency-based learning
CBT. *See* Computer-Based Training
CLE. *See* constructive Learning
        Environments
coaching, 140, 145
    . *See also* cognitive apprenticeship
cognitive apprenticeship
    components, 138–39
    MFS program, 142–46
    sequencing, 139–41
    teaching methods, 139–41
cognitive theories. *See* multimedia
        presentations
cognitive tools. *See* mindtools
communities of practice, 27–32
    introduction, 19–20
community building, 22–26
competency-based learning
    in practice, 98–101
    strategy, 96–97

competency models
    benefits, 96
    introduction, 95–96
complaint learner
    decline, 3, 5
    influence by, 2–3
complex learning, 159–61
Computer-Based Training
    areas of competence, 61–62
    decision makers, 72–74
    design decisions, 70–72
    dynamic process, 64–66
    evaluation process, 64–66
    strengths and weakness, 74–76
Computer-Supported Collaborative
        Learning, 122–23
Computer-Supported Collaborative
        Work, 114–15
computers in education, trends, 36–38
conceptual model, 134–35
    . *See also* mental models
Constructive Learning Environments,
        125–26
constructivism
    conceptions of learning, 107–11
    introduction, 104–8
    learning process, 111–12
    and learning technologies, 103,
        113–14
    perspective, 111–13
    and situated cognition, 129–30
CoVis project, 180
CSCL. *See* Computer-Supported
        Collaborative Learning
CSCW. *See* Computer-Supported
        Collaborative Work
culture of sharing, 23–25

D

Davenport & Prusak, 24–25
Dave's ESL Cafe, 29–30
decision-making process
    factors in, 70–72
    five steps in, 66–68
    framework, 63–66
    outcomes, 68–70
declarative learning, 182–84
design decisions, 70–72
design imagery, 2–3
design problems, 221

didactic level. *See* mastery learning
        approach
distance education
        in educational technology, 40–41
        implications, 55–57
        introduction, 35–40
        reflections on, 52–54
distributed cognition, 109–11
dynamic modeling tools, 123–24
        . *See also* mindtools

E

e-learning
        competency models, 95–96
        infrastructure, 92–93
        introduction, 91–92
        knowledge-management, 94–95
        performance improvement, 94–95
EdMAP, 31–32
educational simulations
        building, 177–79
        introduction, 175–76
        and model building, 176–79
        using, 176–77
        using to building continuum, 179–81
educational technologist, emerging role,
        3–4
electronic learning. *See* e-learning
Electronic Performance Support Systems,
        115–17
epistemology
        implications, 217–18
        instructional design, 213–14
        problem solving methods, 218–22
EPSS. *See* Electronic Performance
        Support Systems
ergonomics. *See* space and place
ESL Online Action Research Project, 28–
        29
exploration, 141, 146
        . *See also* cognitive apprenticeship

F

4M project
        assessment methods, 143–44
        design, 144–46
        introduction, 142–43
        methods, 146
        selected results, 146–53

G

German system of apprenticeship, 161–
        64
guided discovery learning, 136

H

holistic perspective. *See* lifelong learning
Hopper's criteria, 83–86, 88
hypermedia construction, 121–22

I

ibstpi model, 65
IDEELS, 87–88
image schemas, 215–16
instructional communication, 222–23
instructional design
        ambiguity, 76
        areas of competence, 61–63
        and epistemology, 217–18
        factors in, 70–72
        Hopper's criteria, 83–86, 88
        implications, 2
        issues, 3
        lessons learned, 63–64
        model, 224–27
        tasks and activities, 5
        theory, 79–83
        virtual enterprise, 168–69
instructional designer
        CBT, 74
        challenges, 63–64
        goal, 62–63
        role of, 72–74
instructional modeling, 165
intention-action-perception cycle, 111–13
intentional information searching, 118–19
International Society for Technology
        Education. *See* ISTE standards
internet based delivery. *See* web-based
        course
ISTE standards, 39–41

K

knowledge
    recurring distinctions, 9–10
    sharing, 20
    symbolic vs. situated, 9–10
knowledge-building communities, 122–23
knowledge management
    challenges, 21–22
    communities of practice, 27–32
    computer-based learning, 96–97
    culture of sharing, 23–25
    Davenport & Prusak, 24–25
    dynamics, 21–22
    and e-learning, 94–95
    and enabling technologies, 25
    introduction, 19–21
    and knowledge limiting occurrences, 24
    kompetansenettet, 98–101
    priority in, 25–26
    reasons for excitement, 20–21
    for schools, 21
    social aspects, 26–27
    and teachers, 26–32
    technical aspects, 26
    Toronto KM system, 22–23, 26–27

L

learning by constructing. *See* hypermedia construction; multimedia construction
learning by conversing. *See* Computer-Supported Collaborative Learning; knowledge-building communities
learning by experimenting. *See* microworlds; virtual reality
learning by exploring. *See* intentional information searching
learning by performance. *See* Electronic Performance Support Systems
learning by visualizing. *See* videography
learning by working. *See* Computer-Supported Collaborative Work
learning communities, 8–9

learning environment
    architectural analogy, 13–15
    designing, 6–7
    dynamic, 61–64
    physical, 8–9
    social aspects, 109
    static, 61–64
    tasks and activities, 6–7
    virtual, 12–13
learning spaces, 7–8
learning technologies
    affordances, 114–26
    introduction, 113–14
lifelong learning
    compliant learner, 3–5
    design implications, 2
    introduction, 1–4
    task design, 6
    . *See also* e-learning

M

mastery learning approach, 166–69
    evaluation, 172–73
    . *See also* German system of apprenticeship
meaning making, 108–9
megatrends, 155–57
mental models
    4M project, 142
    and cognitive apprenticeships, 138–39
    construction prerequisites, 133–35
    criticism, 131–32
    discussion, 153–55
    introduction, 129–31
    and teaching, 135–38
methodologists. *See* instructional designer
methodology. *See* instructional design
MFS program, 142–46
    methods, 146
    results, 146–51
microworlds, 117–18
mindtools
    affordances, 124–25
    types of, 123–25
modeling, 139, 144
modeling tools, 178
multimedia, and medium, 223–24

multimedia communication, 11
multimedia construction, 121–22
multimedia presentation
     introduction, 197–99
     principle I, 199–203
     principle II, 203–6
     principle III, 206–8
     principle IV, 208–10

O

occupational education and training, 161–
     64
online learning management system. *See*
     kompetansenettet
organization and community, 8–9
OrthODL, 84–87

P

Paivio's dual coding theory, 202, 204,
     209–10
performance improvement, in workplace,
     93–94
problem-solving methods, 218–20
procedural learning, 182

R

R & D. *See* research and development
reality, representations, 223–24
receptive meaningful learning, 136–37
reciprocity, anticipated, 23
research and development, 10–11

S

scaffolding, 140–41, 144–45
self-organized discovery learning, 136
semantic organization tools. *See also*
     mindtools
Shareable Representations of Practice.
     See SHARP
SHARP project, 11–12
simulation fidelity, 191–92
simulations, building, 177–79, 182
     benefits, 187–89
simulations, using, 176–77
     benefits, 185–87
situated cognition, 129–30
situational evaluation process, 66–68

. *See also* decision-making process
space and place, 7–8
STACI project, 181
static and dynamic environments, 61–64
STELLA project, 180–81, 184
subcategories, 221–22
submissive learners, 105–7
synchronous multimedia, 10–11

T

task design, reflexive, 6–7
tasks and activities, 5–7
teachers and technologies, review of, 35–
     40
teaching-learning environment, 173
     construction, 165–69
     evaluation, 172–73
     implementation, 169–71
Teaching with Technology course
     background, 41
     content, 42–43
     development, 41
     findings, 50–52
     formative evaluation, 48–50
     pilot course, 43–44
     revised, 45–48
technological infrastructure. *See* learning
     environment
technological innovations, history of, 33–
     35
TENET, 27–28
Theory into Practice
     framework, 80–82
     introduction, 79–80
     motivation, 82–84
Toronto KM system, 22–23, 26–27
TP. *See* Theory into Practice
transmissive teaching, 104–7

U

University of Toronto. *See* Toronto KM
     system
     . *See also* knowledge management
user-centered technologies, 5–6

using simulations
    to *building* continuum, 179–81
    conditions for, 185–87, 189–91
    educational dilemma, 184–85
    environment, 191–92
    introduction, 176–77
    and procedural learning, 182–84

V

videography, 119–20
virtual learning environment, 12–13
    architectural analogy, 13–16
virtual reality, 117–18
visualization tools. *See* mindtools
vocational education and training. *See*
    German system of apprenticeship

W

web-based course
    design, 41–43
    evaluation, 48–52
    implementation, 43–48
    reflections on, 52–54